8

Story and Art by
Rumiko Takahashi

Characters

TAISHO ERA

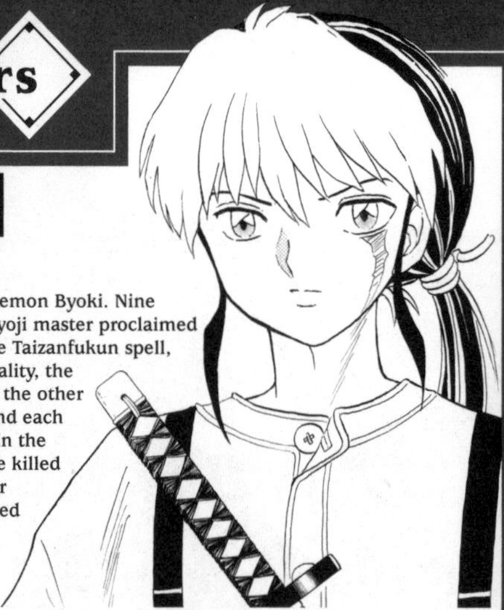

MAO

An exorcist cursed by the cat demon Byoki. Nine hundred years ago, Mao's onmyoji master proclaimed Mao his successor to inherit the Taizanfukun spell, which controls life spans. In reality, the master's intention was to goad the other five trainees into killing Mao and each other until only one survived. In the ensuing melee, Mao might have killed his master's daughter, Sana. For nine centuries, Mao has searched for Byoki to uncover the truth and purge his curse.

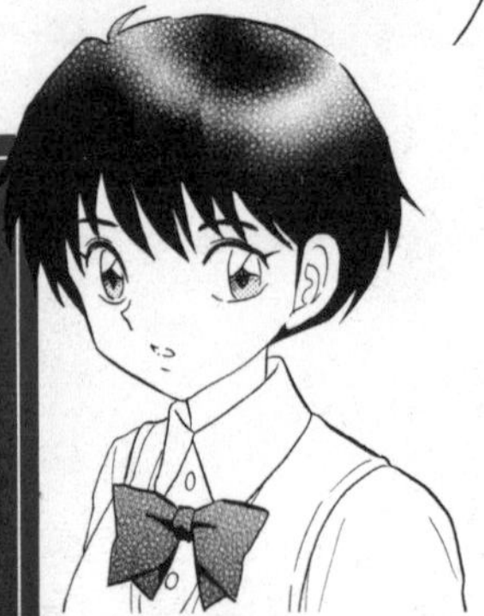

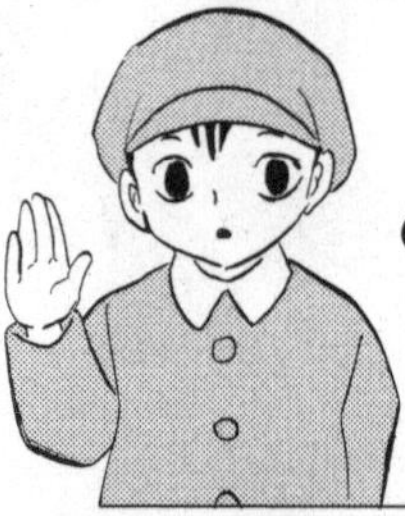

OTOYA

Mao's hard-working shikigami.

NANOKA KIBA

A third-year middle school student living in the present day. As a child, she was involved in a car accident that killed her parents and temporarily thrust her into the Taisho era. There, her body was cursed by Byoki. Nanoka's body, like Mao's, is a potential vessel that Byoki seeks to inhabit.

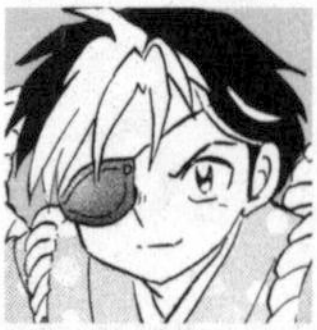

HYAKKA

Mao's senior apprentice. Wields fire spells.

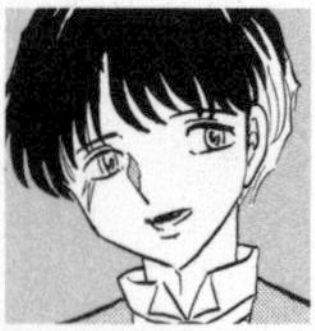

KAMON (KUCHINAWA)

Mao's senior apprentice. Wields tree spells.

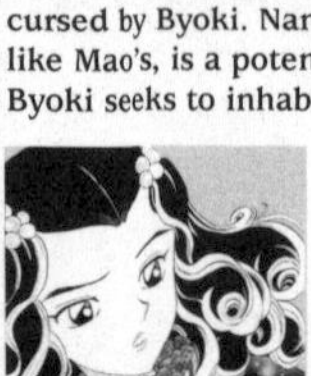

YURAKO

Her true identity might be Sana, the master's daughter. Works for Shiranui.

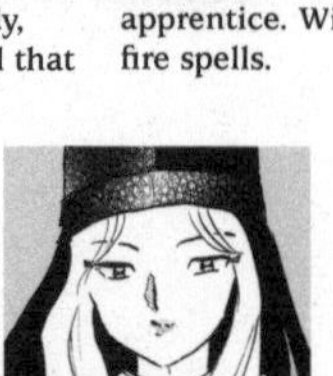

SHIRANUI

Mao's senior apprentice. Wields water spells. Seeks vengeance from Mao.

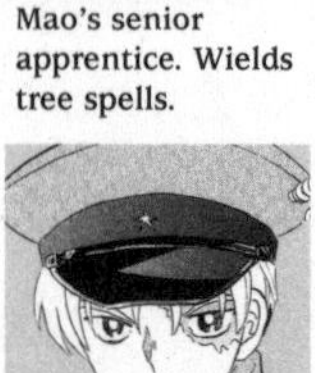

HAKUBI

Mao's senior apprentice. Wields metal spells. Works for Shiranui.

HEIAN PERIOD

HOUSE OF GOKO

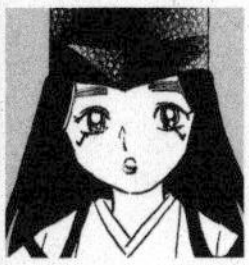

MASAGO
A Goko clan onymoji. The most powerful wielder of water spells.

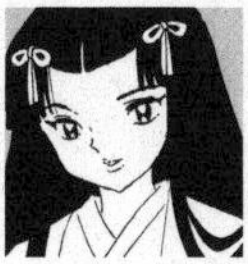

SANA
The master's daughter. Betrothed to Mao by her father. Murdered, possibly by Mao.

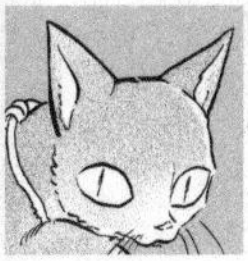

HAIMARU
Sana's beloved cat. Only liked her and Mao.

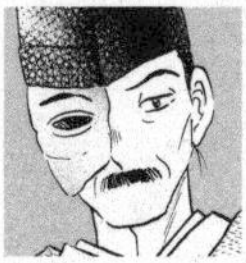

MASTER
The head of the Goko clan and Mao's former master. Wields forbidden spells and attempted to sacrifice Mao for his own ends.

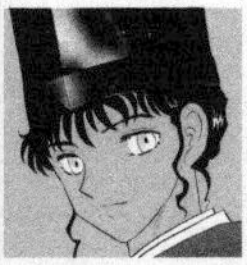

DAIGO
Mao's senior apprentice. He invited Mao to join the Goko clan. An experienced onmyoji, he was slain during the battle of succession.

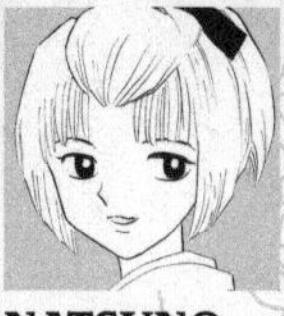

NATSUNO
Mao's senior apprentice. Wields earth spells.

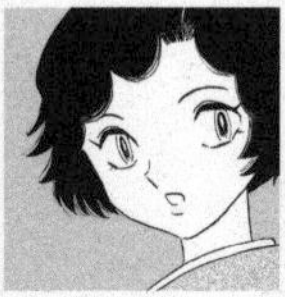

TENKO
Mao's ayakashi informant.

PRESENT DAY

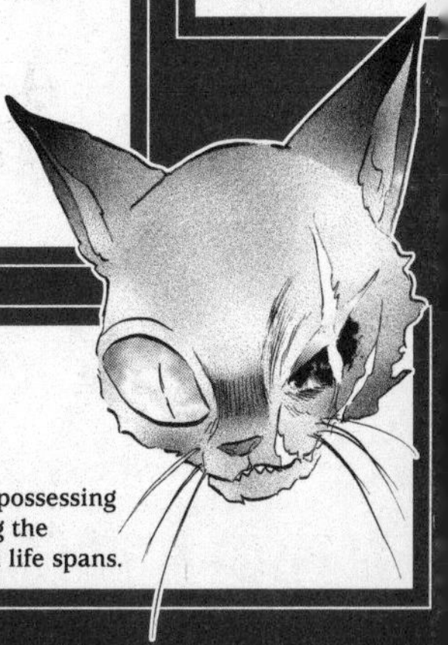

BYOKI
The kodoku cat who cursed Mao and Nanoka. Survives by possessing human bodies. After eating the forbidden scroll containing the Taizanfukun spell, he gained the ability to use it to control life spans.

Story thus far...

When Nanoka Kiba was seven years old, she was orphaned in a violent accident. Now fifteen, she passes by the spot where the accident occurred and is transported to the Taisho era. There she meets an exorcist named Mao. When they realize they have both been cursed by Byoki, a cat demon, they join forces to find him and free themselves.

Centuries ago, Mao's master told five of Mao's senior apprentices that he had chosen Mao as his successor. However, they could win the honor for themselves if they killed Mao. Now Mao and Nanoka are on a quest to reconcile with these apprentices and to find Sana, the woman Mao once loved.

While battling Shiranui, they discover the remains of Masago, Kamon's beloved. While Kamon and Mao are unsettled by memories of their past loves, Natsuno begins to tell them what she saw of Sana's fate centuries ago.

CONTENTS

Chapter 1:
Sana's Heart

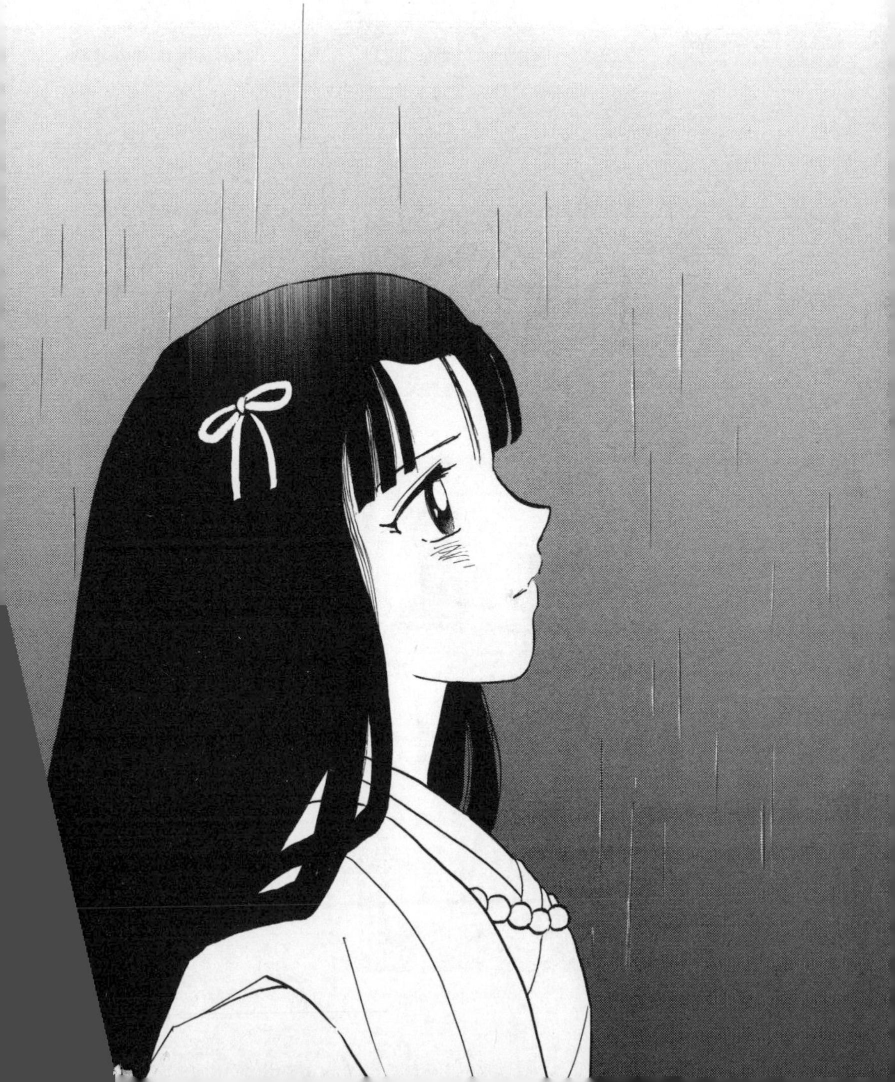

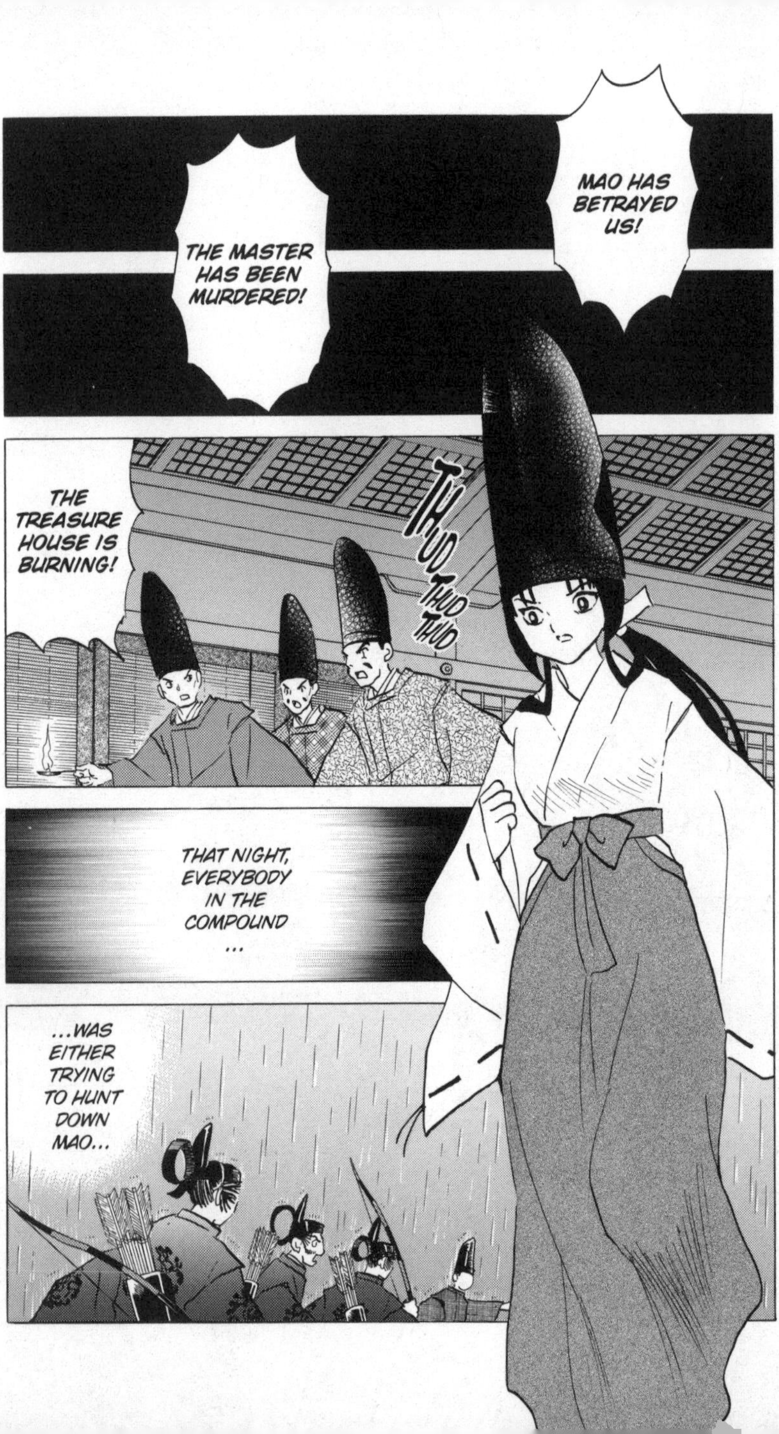
MAO HAS BETRAYED US!
THE MASTER HAS BEEN MURDERED!
THUD THUD THUD
THE TREASURE HOUSE IS BURNING!
THAT NIGHT, EVERYBODY IN THE COMPOUND ...
...WAS EITHER TRYING TO HUNT DOWN MAO...

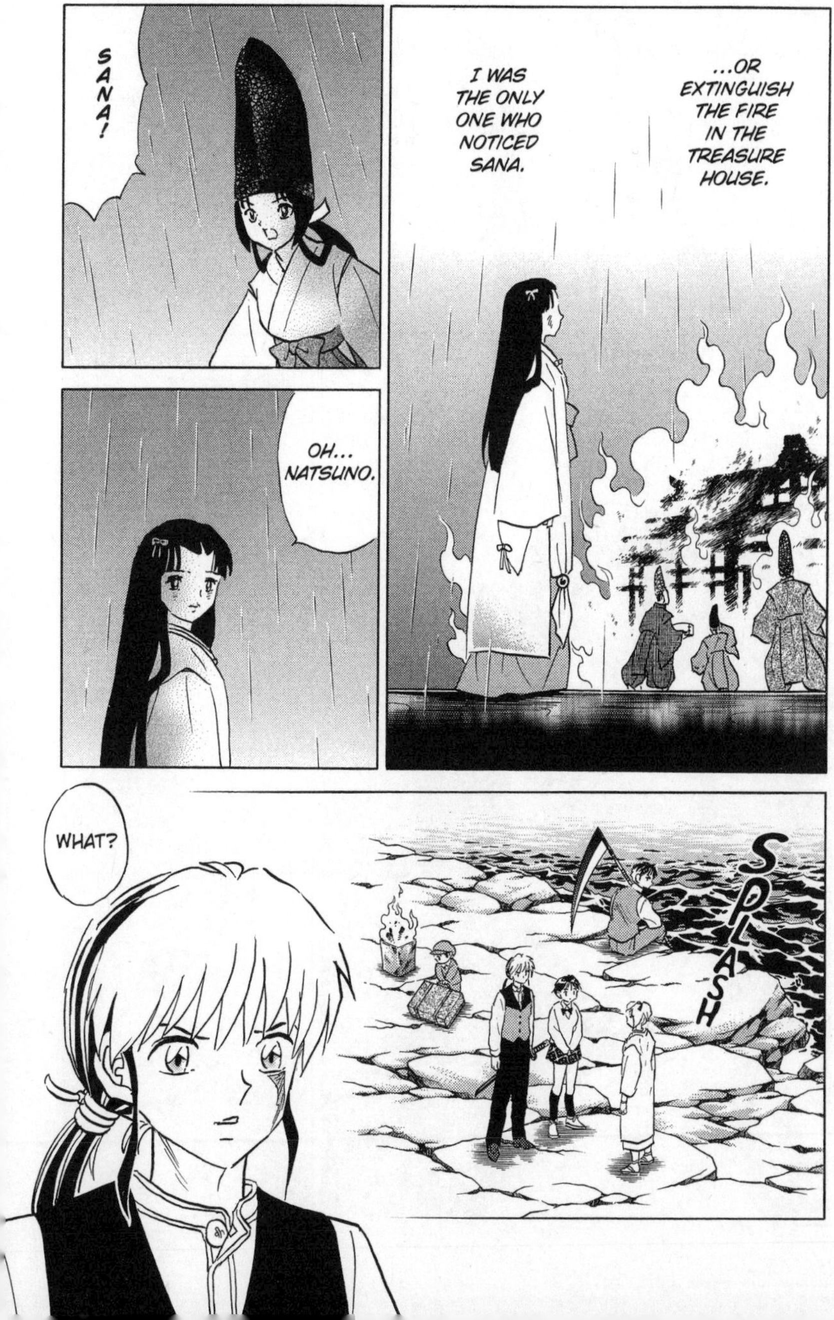
...OR EXTINGUISH THE FIRE IN THE TREASURE HOUSE.
I WAS THE ONLY ONE WHO NOTICED SANA.
SANA!
OH... NATSUNO.
SPLASH
WHAT?

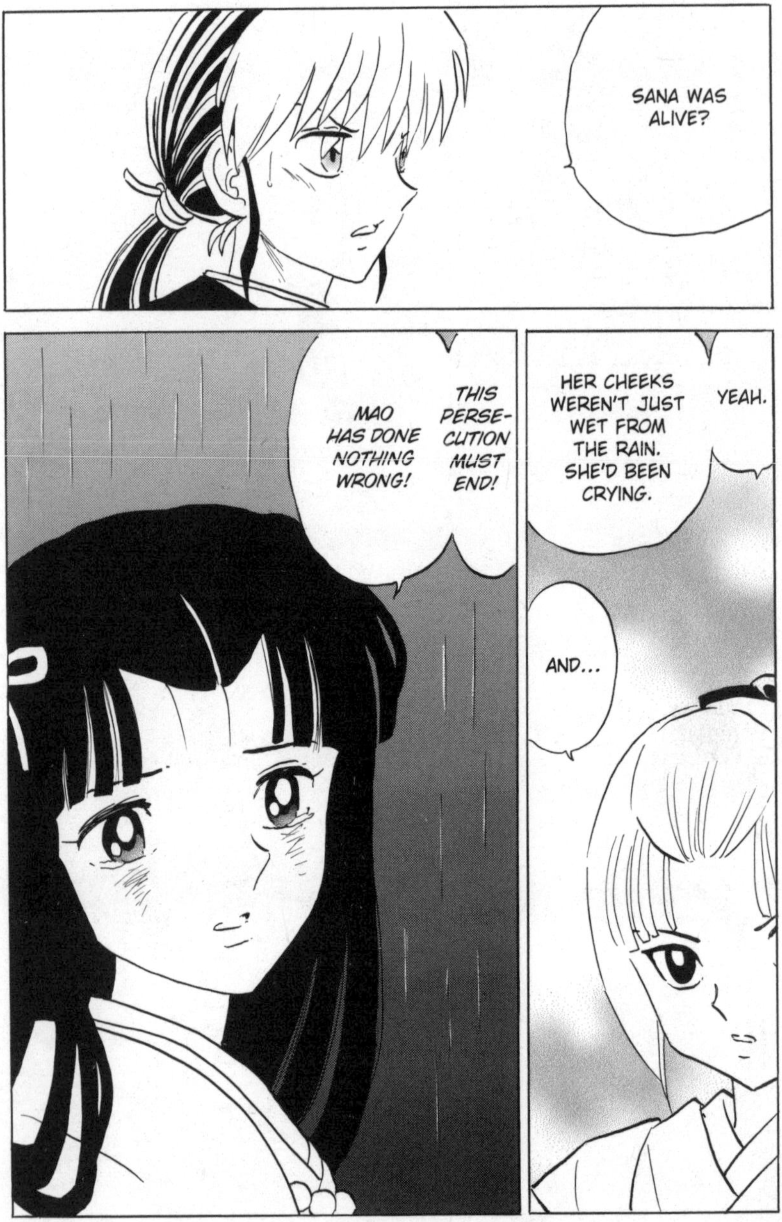
SANA WAS ALIVE?
YEAH.
HER CHEEKS WEREN'T JUST WET FROM THE RAIN. SHE'D BEEN CRYING.
AND...
THIS PERSE-CUTION MUST END!
MAO HAS DONE NOTHING WRONG!

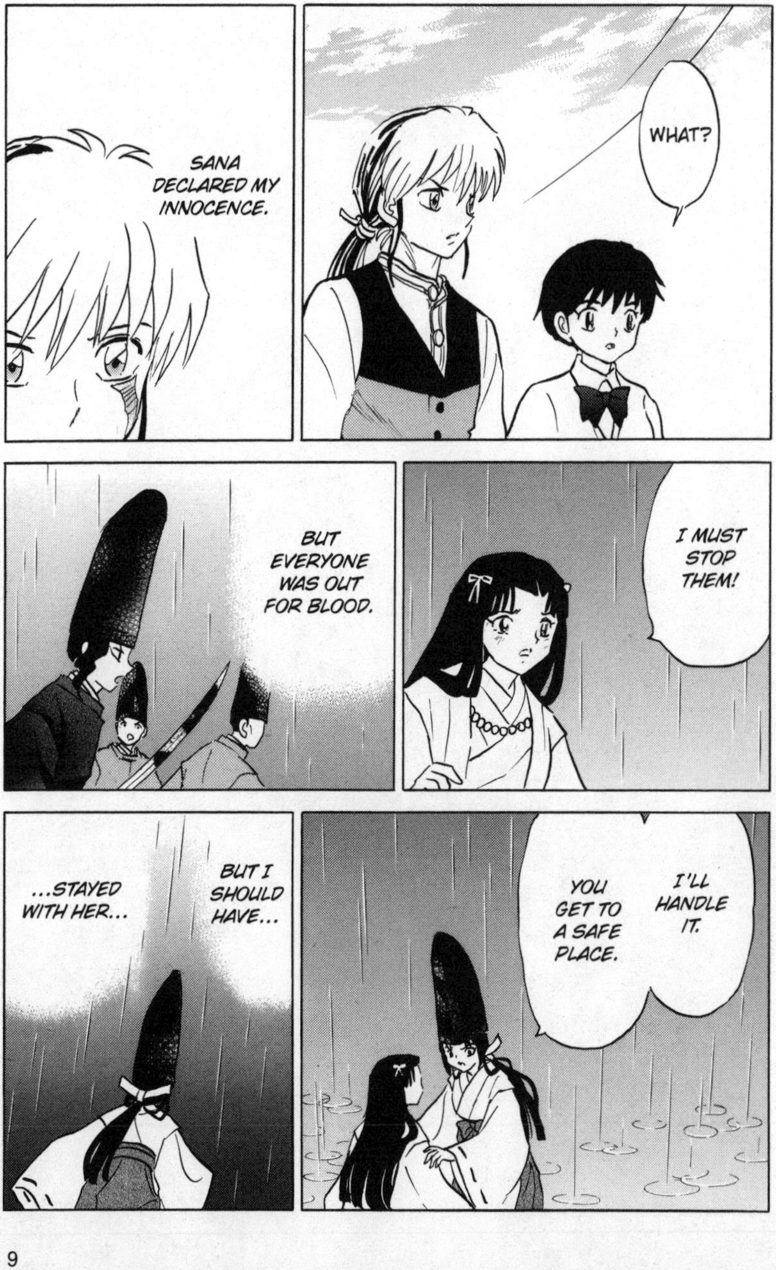
WHAT?
SANA DECLARED MY INNOCENCE.
I MUST STOP THEM!
BUT EVERYONE WAS OUT FOR BLOOD.
I'LL HANDLE IT.
YOU GET TO A SAFE PLACE.
BUT I SHOULD HAVE...
...STAYED WITH HER...

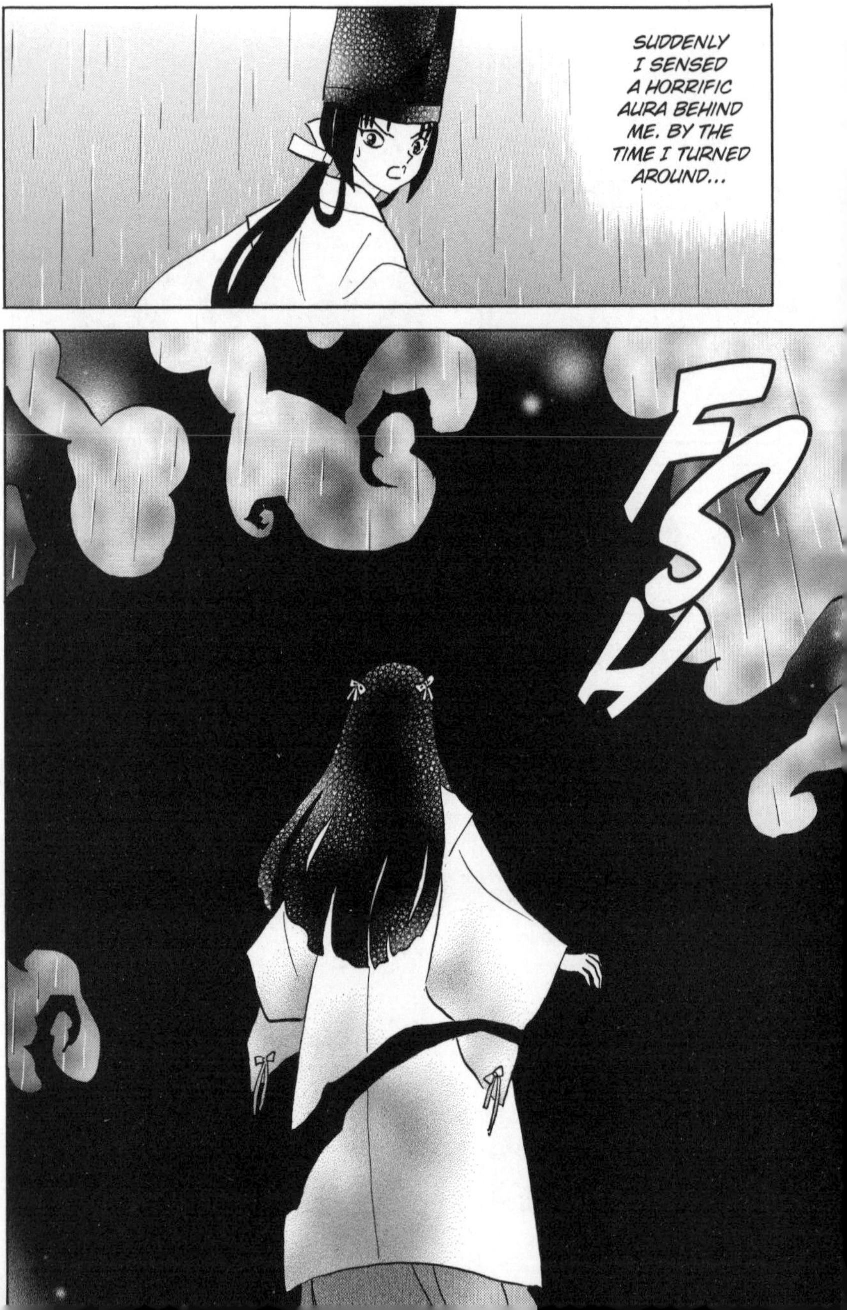
SUDDENLY I SENSED A HORRIFIC AURA BEHIND ME. BY THE TIME I TURNED AROUND...
FSSH

IT HAPPENED IN AN INSTANT.

S A N A !

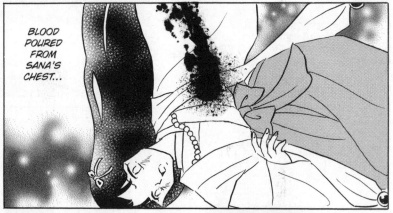

BLOOD POURED FROM SANA'S CHEST...

!

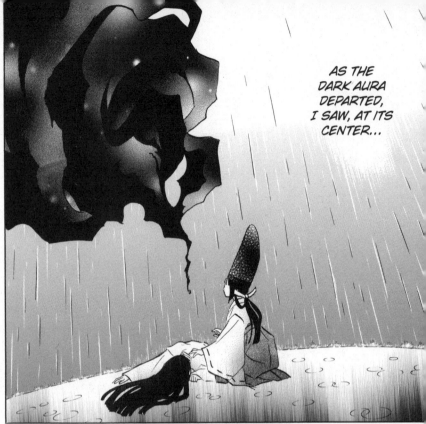

AS THE DARK AURA DEPARTED, I SAW, AT ITS CENTER...
...SOME-THING... RED.
IT HAD STOLEN SANA'S HEART!
SPLASH
WAS THAT EVIL AURA...

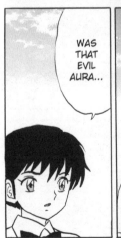

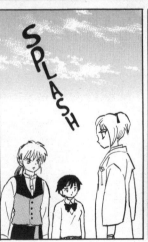

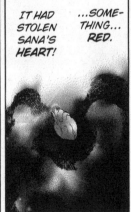

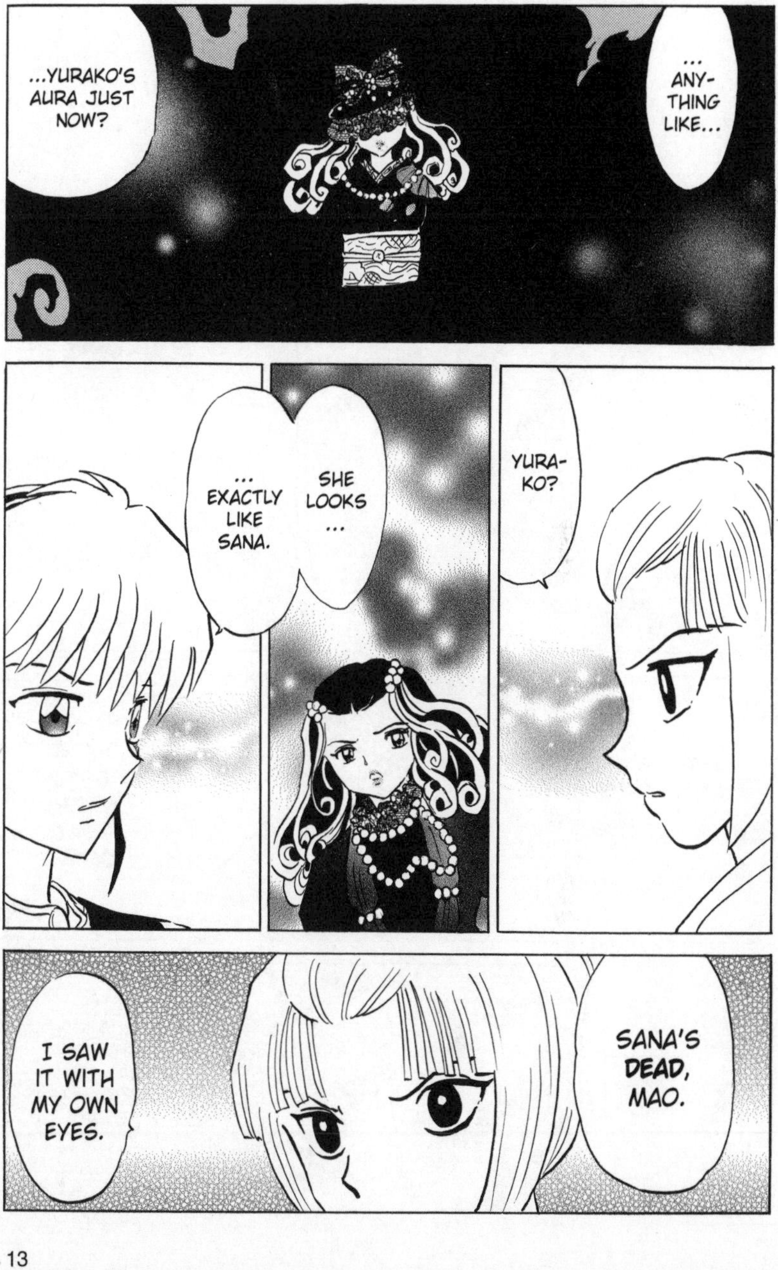
... ANY-THING LIKE...
...YURAKO'S AURA JUST NOW?
YURA-KO?
SHE LOOKS ...
... EXACTLY LIKE SANA.
SANA'S **DEAD,** MAO.
I SAW IT WITH MY OWN EYES.

NATSUNO...

WHY DIDN'T YOU TELL US THIS BEFORE?

AFTER THAT FATEFUL NIGHT, EVERYONE WAS CERTAIN THAT MAO HAD KILLED SANA.

I SAW IT TOO!

MAO IS A TRAITOR TO THE GOKO CLAN!

OUR SWORN ENEMY!

THAT'S RIGHT. HAKUBI RAN AROUND TELLING EVERYONE THAT STORY.

I WONDER WHY...

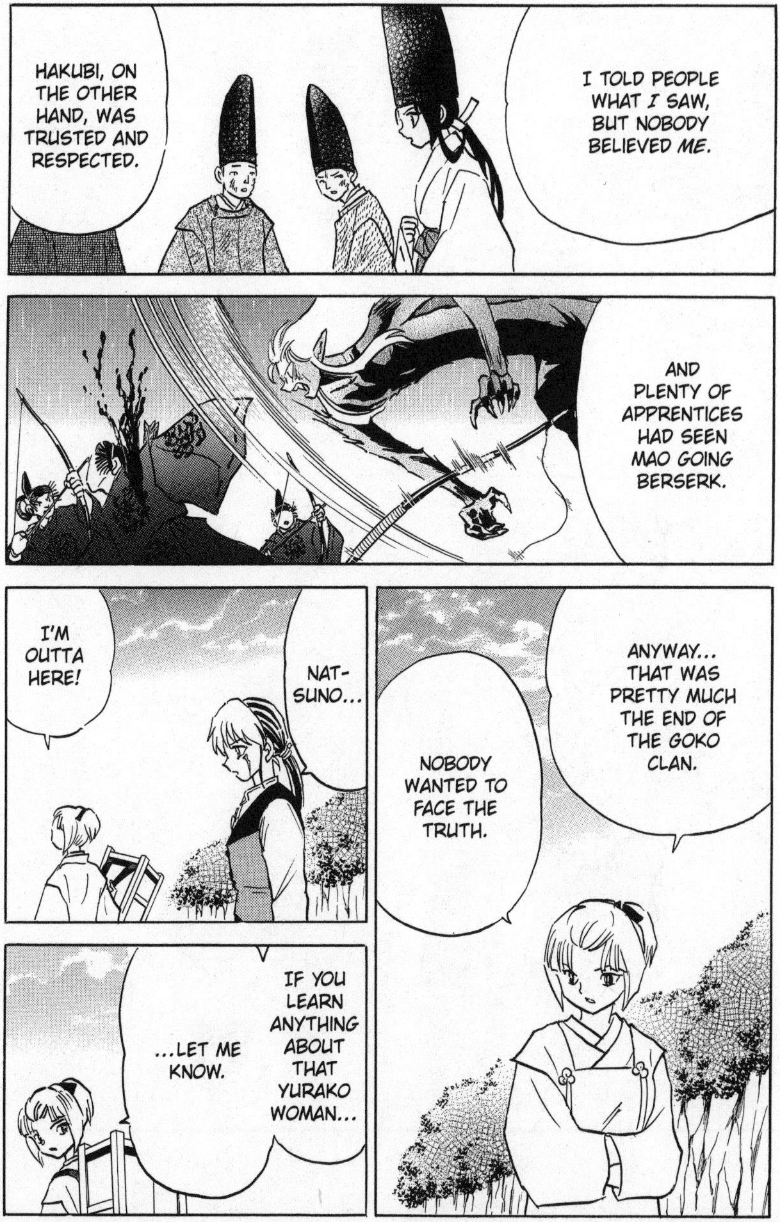
I TOLD PEOPLE WHAT *I* SAW, BUT NOBODY BELIEVED *ME*.
HAKUBI, ON THE OTHER HAND, WAS TRUSTED AND RESPECTED.
AND PLENTY OF APPRENTICES HAD SEEN MAO GOING BERSERK.
ANYWAY... THAT WAS PRETTY MUCH THE END OF THE GOKO CLAN.
NOBODY WANTED TO FACE THE TRUTH.
NAT-SUNO...
I'M OUTTA HERE!
IF YOU LEARN ANYTHING ABOUT THAT YURAKO WOMAN...
...LET ME KNOW.

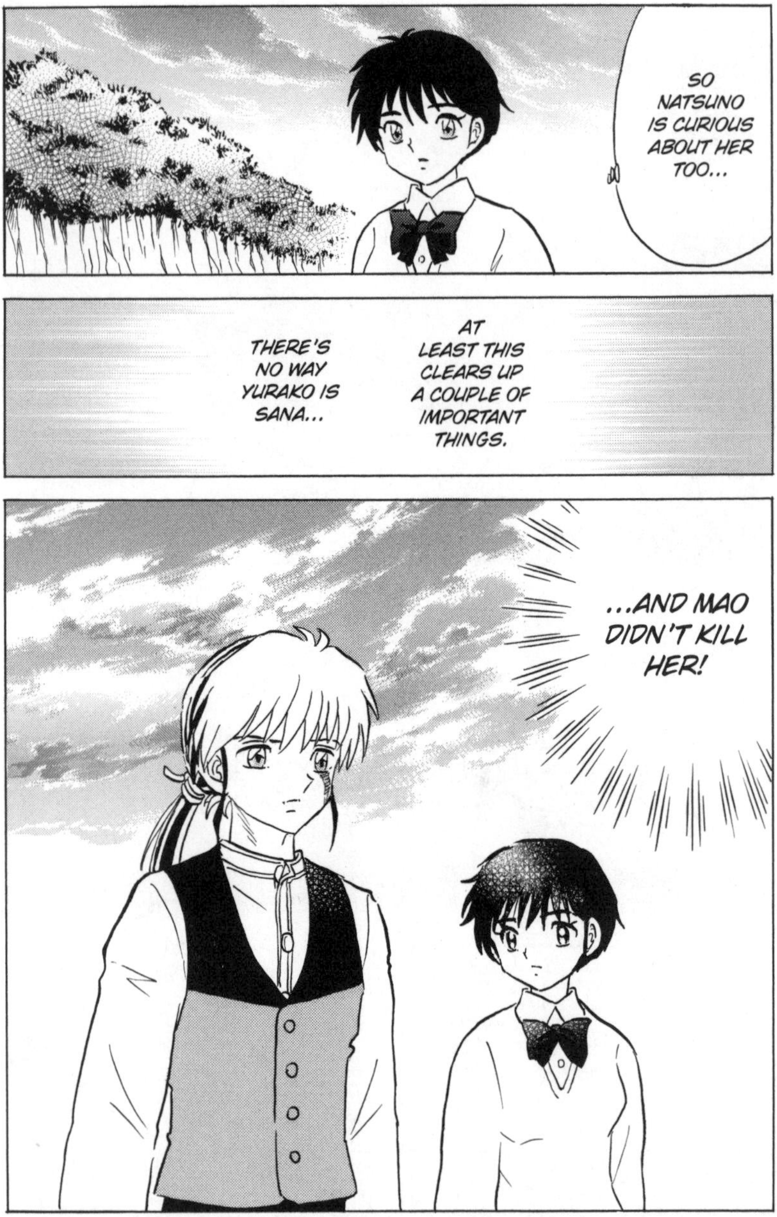
SO NATSUNO IS CURIOUS ABOUT HER TOO...
AT LEAST THIS CLEARS UP A COUPLE OF IMPORTANT THINGS.
THERE'S NO WAY YURAKO IS SANA...
...AND MAO DIDN'T KILL HER!

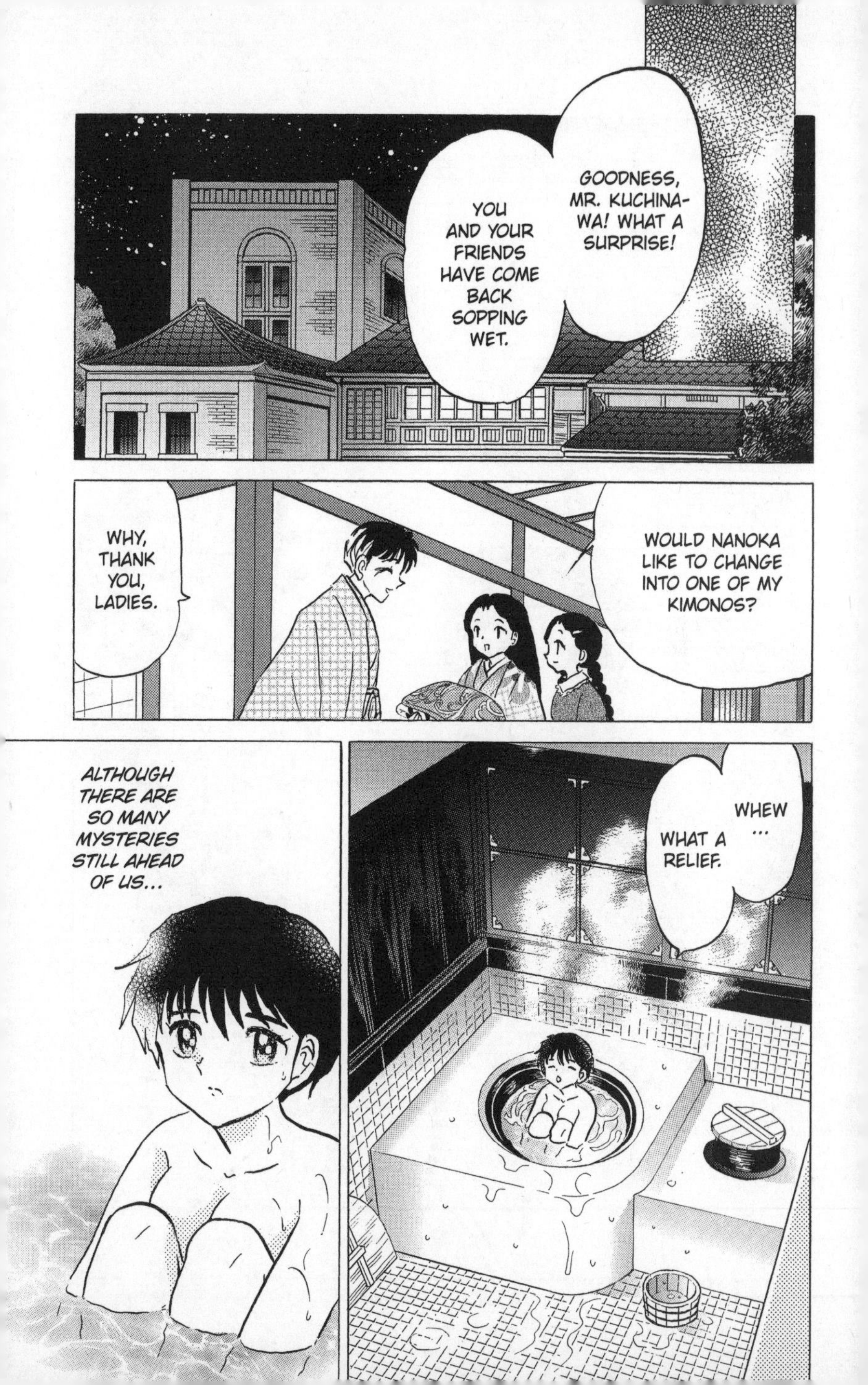
GOODNESS, MR. KUCHINAWA! WHAT A SURPRISE!
YOU AND YOUR FRIENDS HAVE COME BACK SOPPING WET.
WOULD NANOKA LIKE TO CHANGE INTO ONE OF MY KIMONOS?
WHY, THANK YOU, LADIES.
WHEW ...
WHAT A RELIEF.
ALTHOUGH THERE ARE SO MANY MYSTERIES STILL AHEAD OF US...

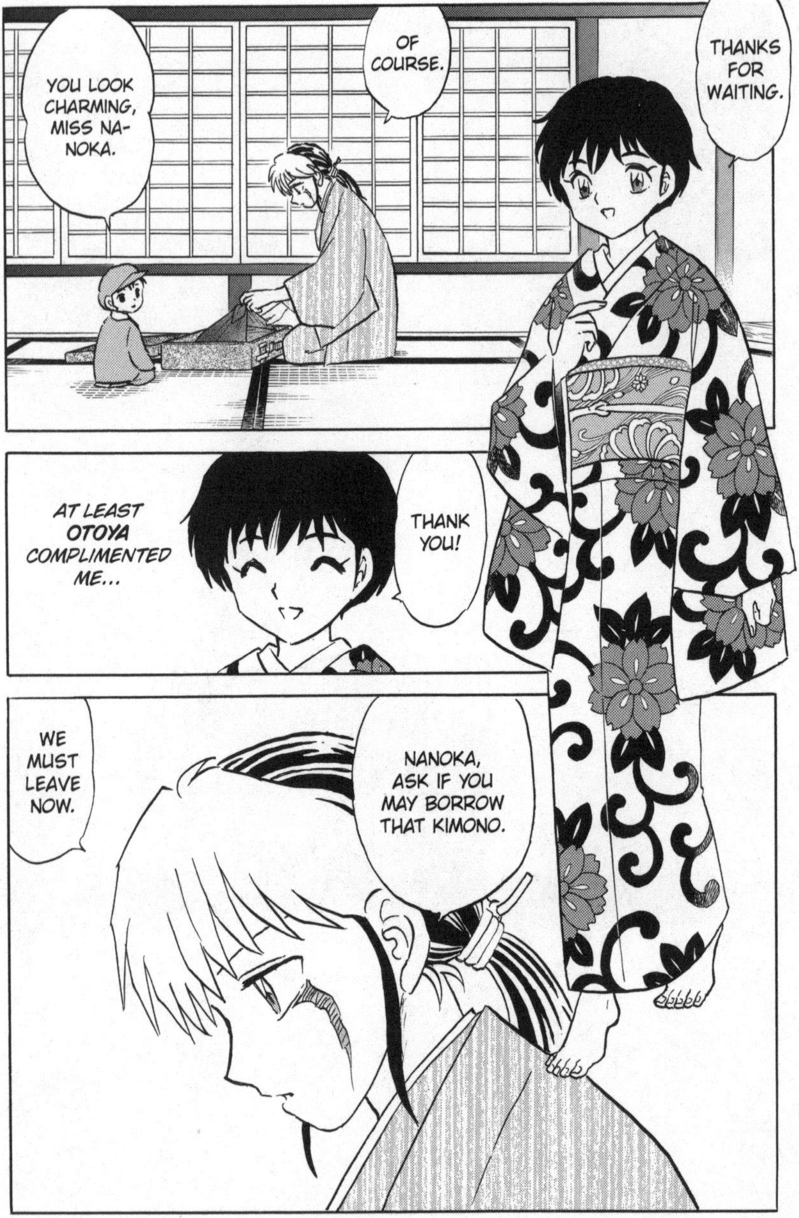
THANKS FOR WAITING.
OF COURSE.
YOU LOOK CHARMING, MISS NA-NOKA.
THANK YOU!
AT LEAST OTOYA COMPLIMENTED ME...
NANOKA, ASK IF YOU MAY BORROW THAT KIMONO.
WE MUST LEAVE NOW.

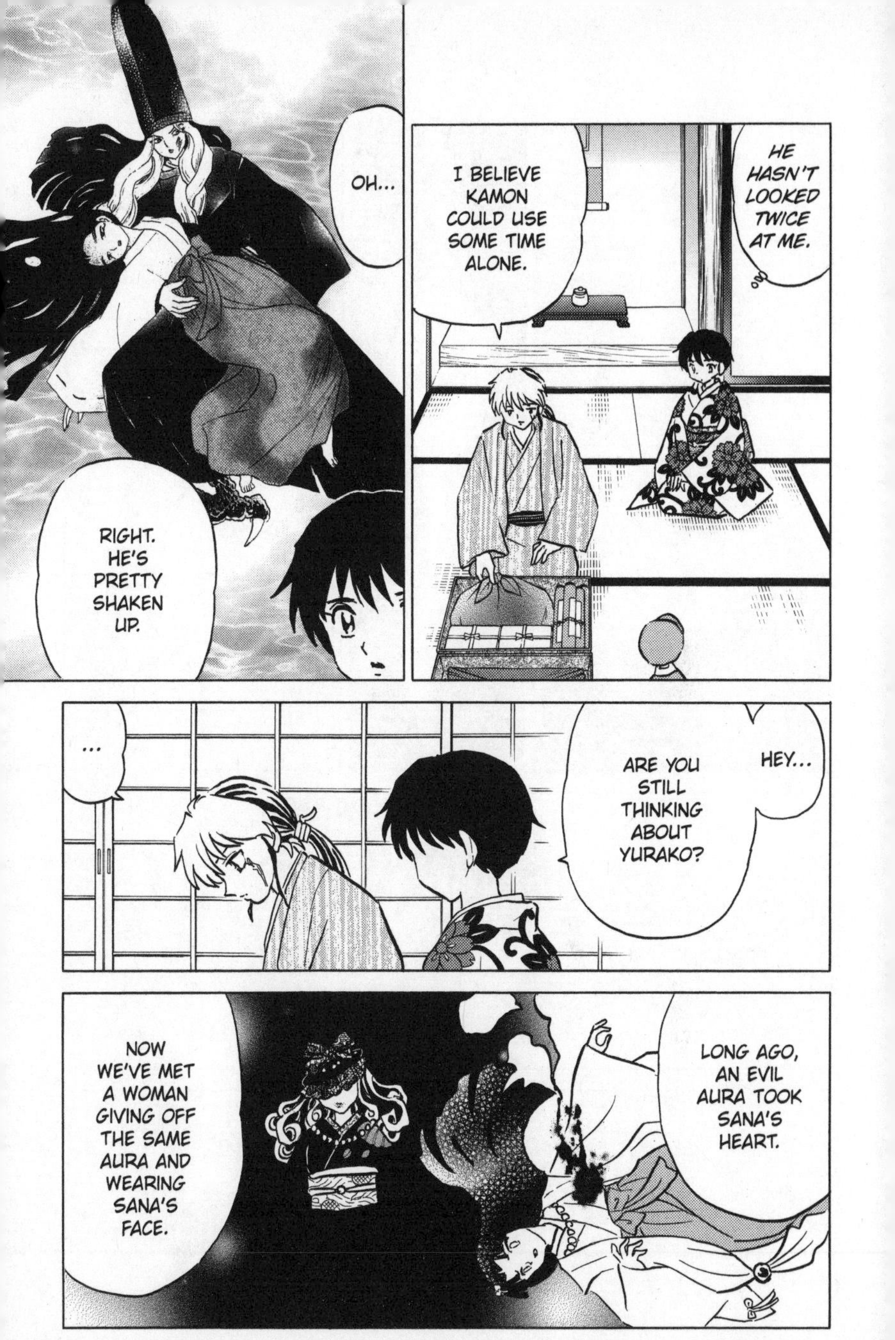
HE HASN'T LOOKED TWICE AT ME.
I BELIEVE KAMON COULD USE SOME TIME ALONE.
OH...
RIGHT. HE'S PRETTY SHAKEN UP.
HEY...
ARE YOU STILL THINKING ABOUT YURAKO?
...
LONG AGO, AN EVIL AURA TOOK SANA'S HEART.
NOW WE'VE MET A WOMAN GIVING OFF THE SAME AURA AND WEARING SANA'S FACE.

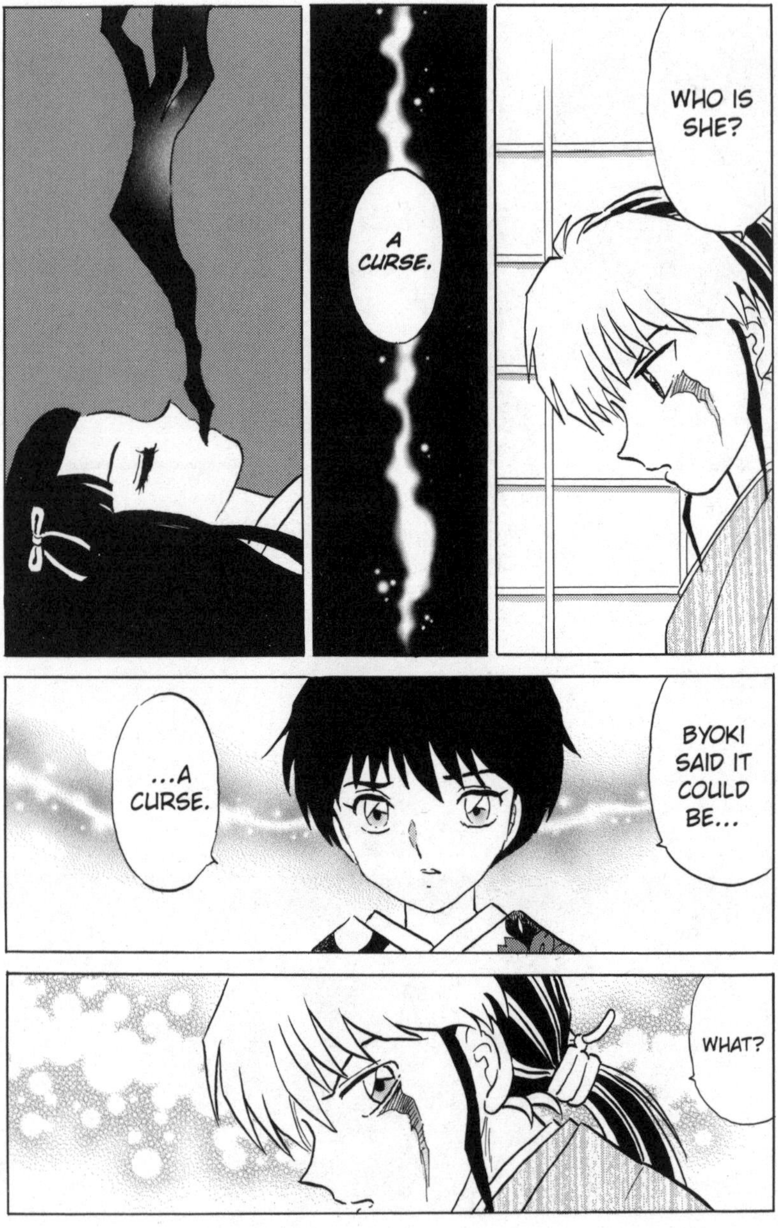
WHO IS SHE?
A CURSE.
BYOKI SAID IT COULD BE...
...A CURSE.
WHAT?

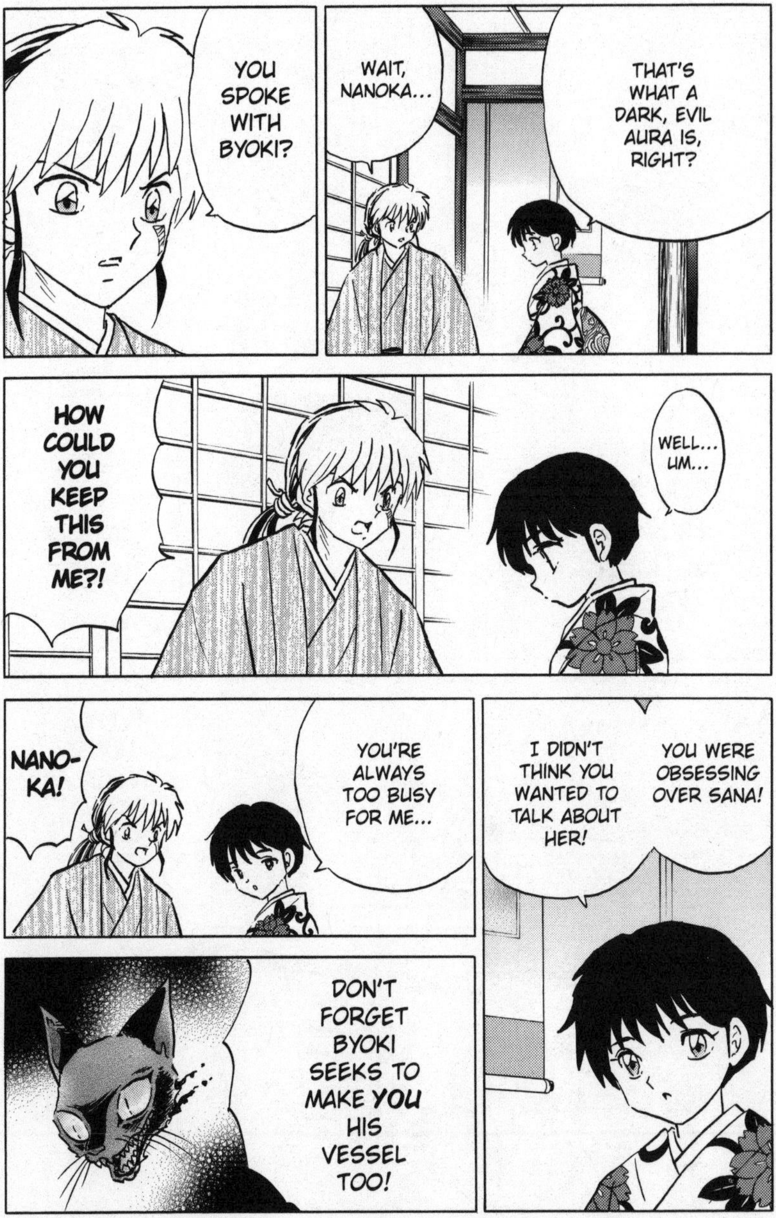
THAT'S WHAT A DARK, EVIL AURA IS, RIGHT?
WAIT, NANOKA...
YOU SPOKE WITH BYOKI?
WELL... UM...
HOW COULD YOU KEEP THIS FROM ME?!
YOU WERE OBSESSING OVER SANA!
I DIDN'T THINK YOU WANTED TO TALK ABOUT HER!
YOU'RE ALWAYS TOO BUSY FOR ME...
NANO-KA!
DON'T FORGET BYOKI SEEKS TO MAKE YOU HIS VESSEL TOO!

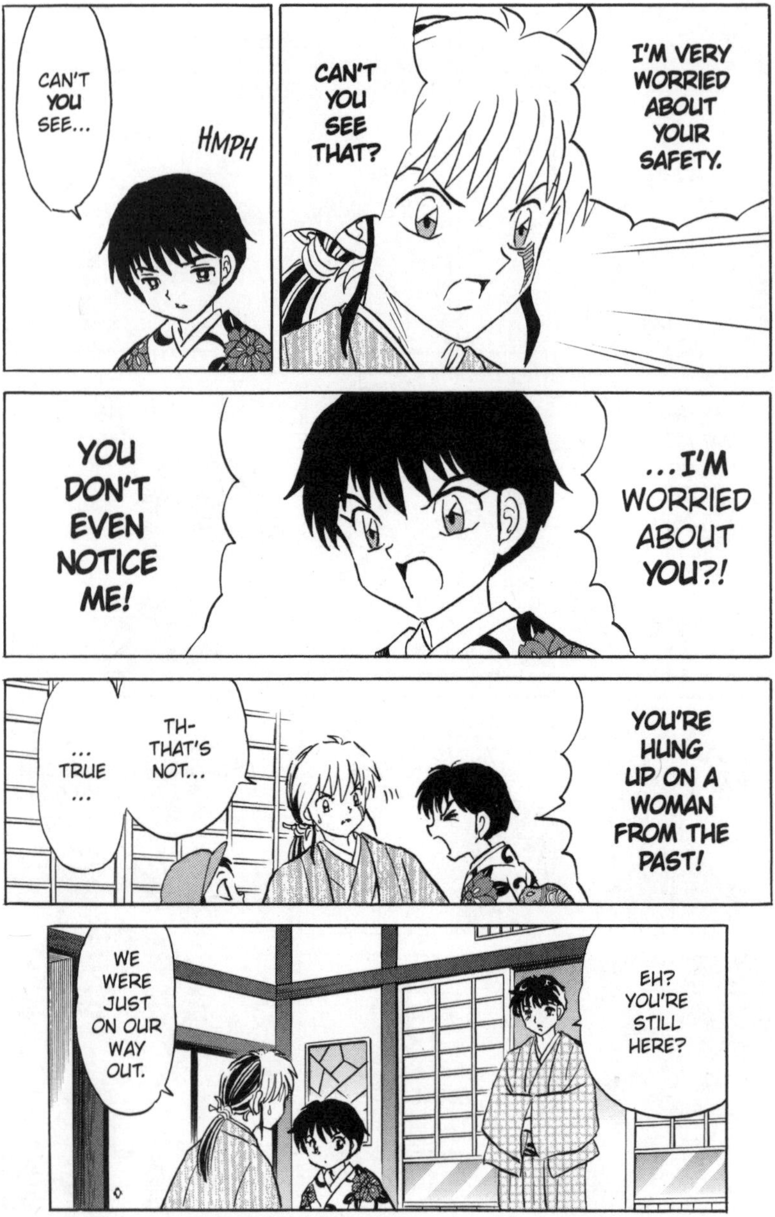
I'M VERY WORRIED ABOUT YOUR SAFETY.
CAN'T YOU SEE THAT?
HMPH
CAN'T YOU SEE...
...I'M WORRIED ABOUT YOU?!
YOU DON'T EVEN NOTICE ME!
YOU'RE HUNG UP ON A WOMAN FROM THE PAST!
TH- THAT'S NOT...
... TRUE ...
EH? YOU'RE STILL HERE?
WE WERE JUST ON OUR WAY OUT.

Chapter 2:
Exorcism

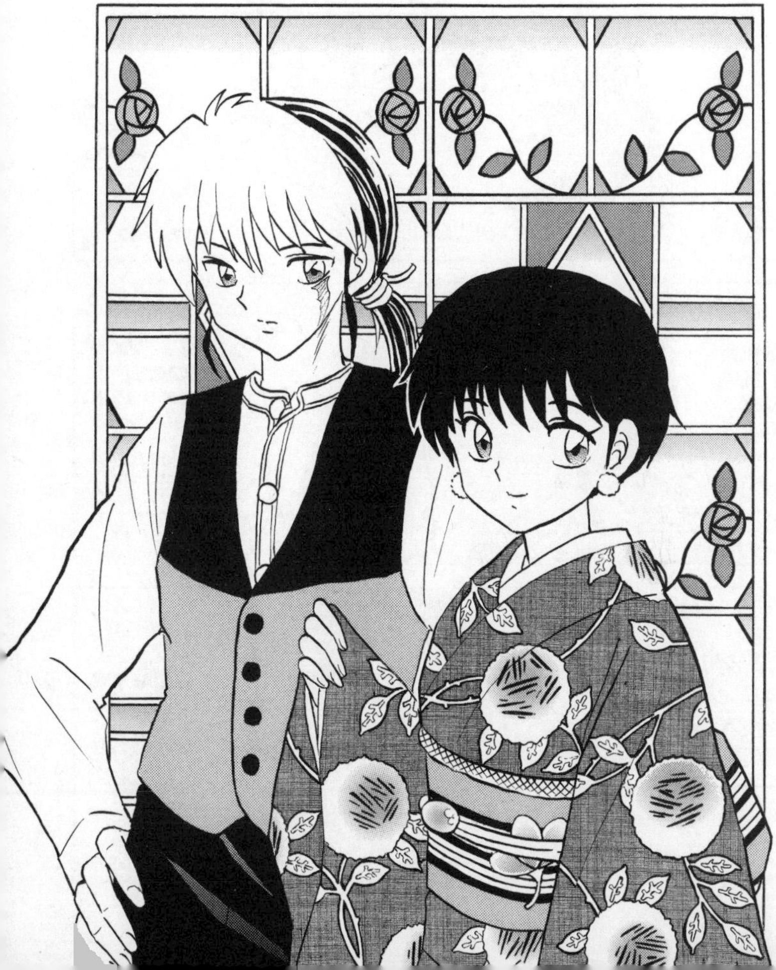

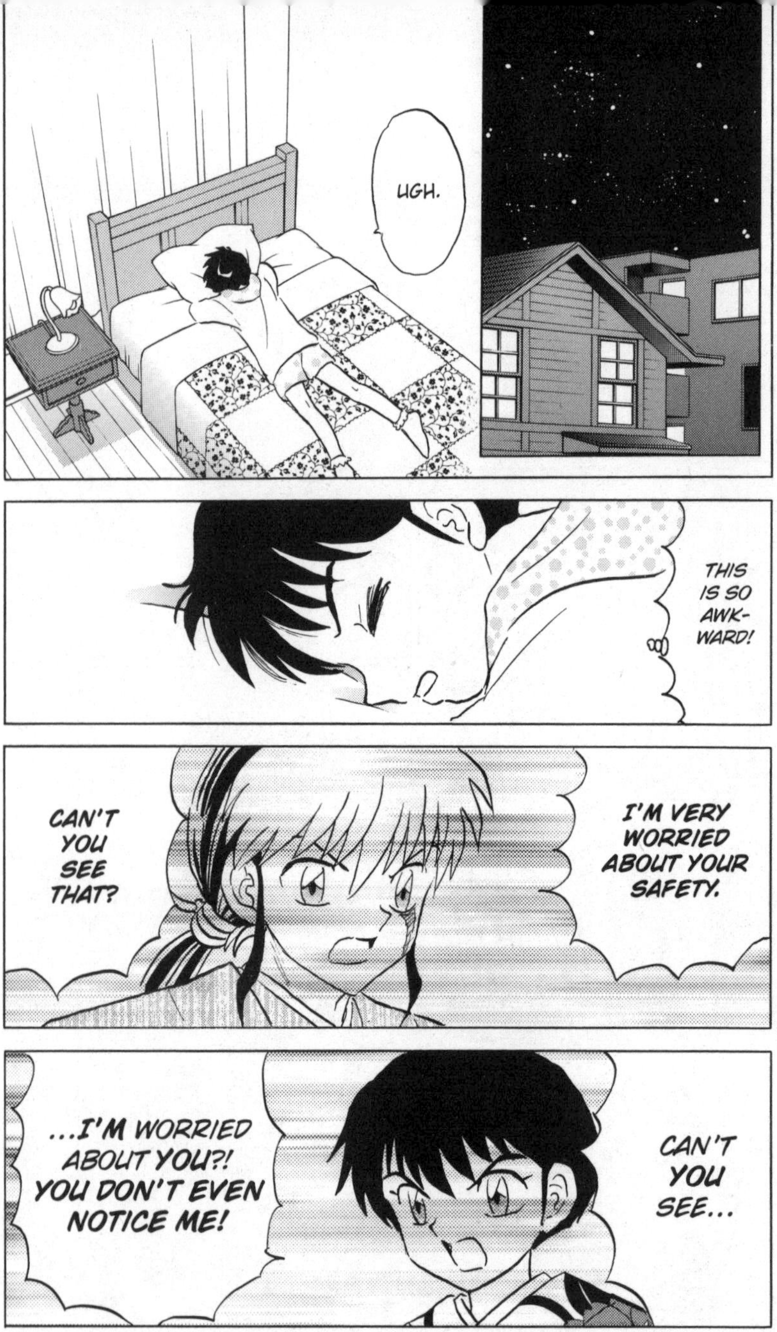
UGH.
THIS IS SO AWK-WARD!
I'M VERY WORRIED ABOUT YOUR SAFETY.
CAN'T YOU SEE THAT?
CAN'T YOU SEE...
...I'M WORRIED ABOUT YOU?! YOU DON'T EVEN NOTICE ME!

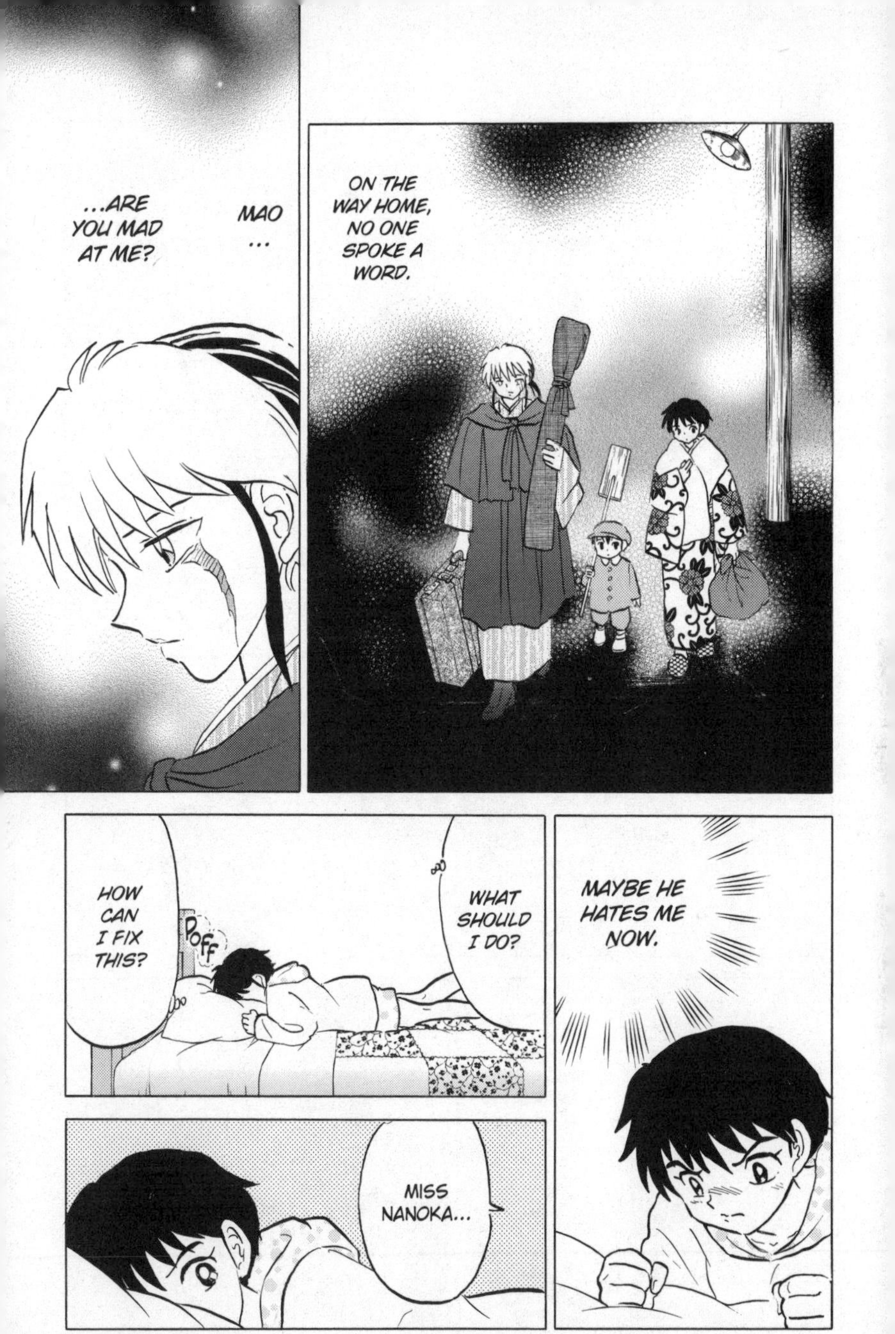
ON THE WAY HOME, NO ONE SPOKE A WORD.
MAO ...
...ARE YOU MAD AT ME?
MAYBE HE HATES ME NOW.
WHAT SHOULD I DO?
POFF
HOW CAN I FIX THIS?
MISS NANOKA...

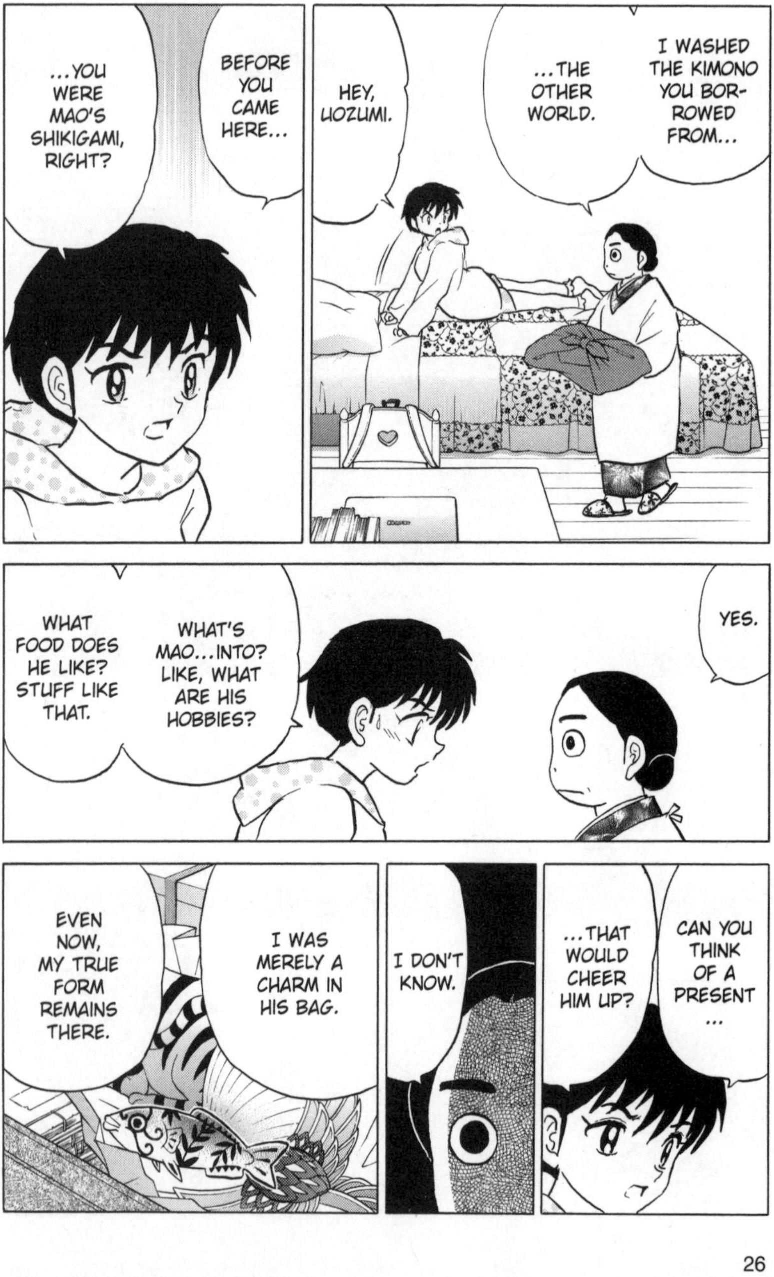
I WASHED THE KIMONO YOU BORROWED FROM...
...THE OTHER WORLD.
HEY, UOZUMI.
BEFORE YOU CAME HERE...
...YOU WERE MAO'S SHIKIGAMI, RIGHT?
YES.
WHAT'S MAO...INTO? LIKE, WHAT ARE HIS HOBBIES?
WHAT FOOD DOES HE LIKE? STUFF LIKE THAT.
CAN YOU THINK OF A PRESENT ...
...THAT WOULD CHEER HIM UP?
I DON'T KNOW.
I WAS MERELY A CHARM IN HIS BAG.
EVEN NOW, MY TRUE FORM REMAINS THERE.

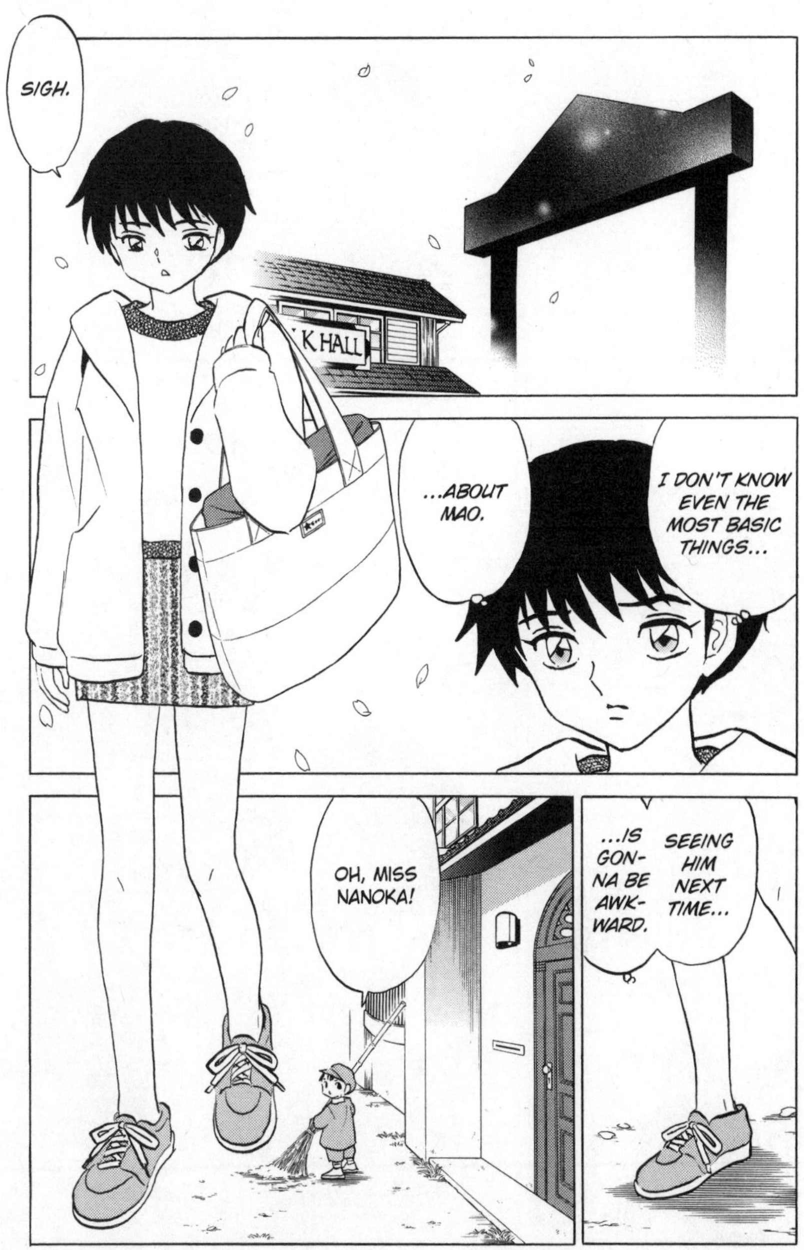
SIGH.
K HALL
I DON'T KNOW EVEN THE MOST BASIC THINGS...
...ABOUT MAO.
SEEING HIM NEXT TIME...
...IS GONNA BE AWKWARD.
OH, MISS NANOKA!

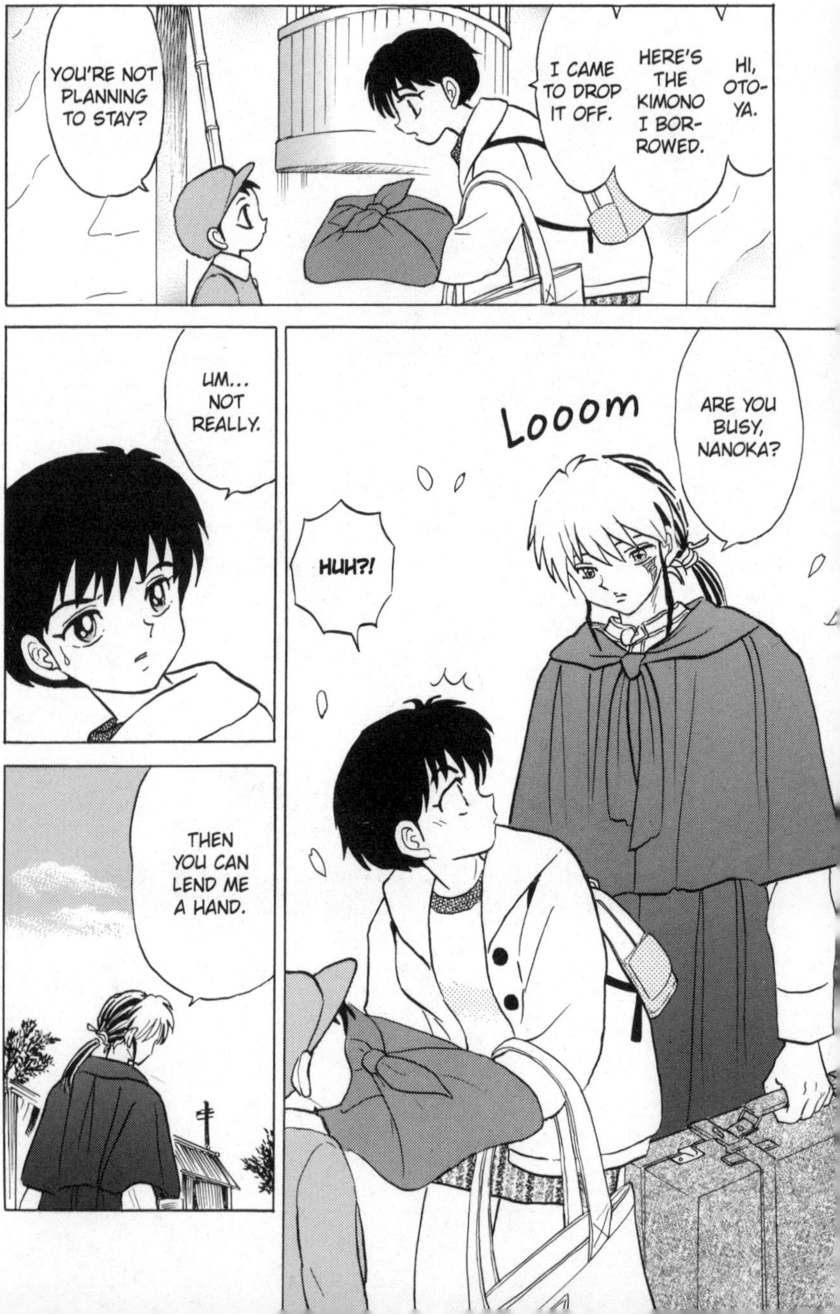
HI, OTO-YA.
HERE'S THE KIMONO I BORROWED.
I CAME TO DROP IT OFF.
YOU'RE NOT PLANNING TO STAY?
ARE YOU BUSY, NANOKA?
Looom
HUH?!
UM... NOT REALLY.
THEN YOU CAN LEND ME A HAND.

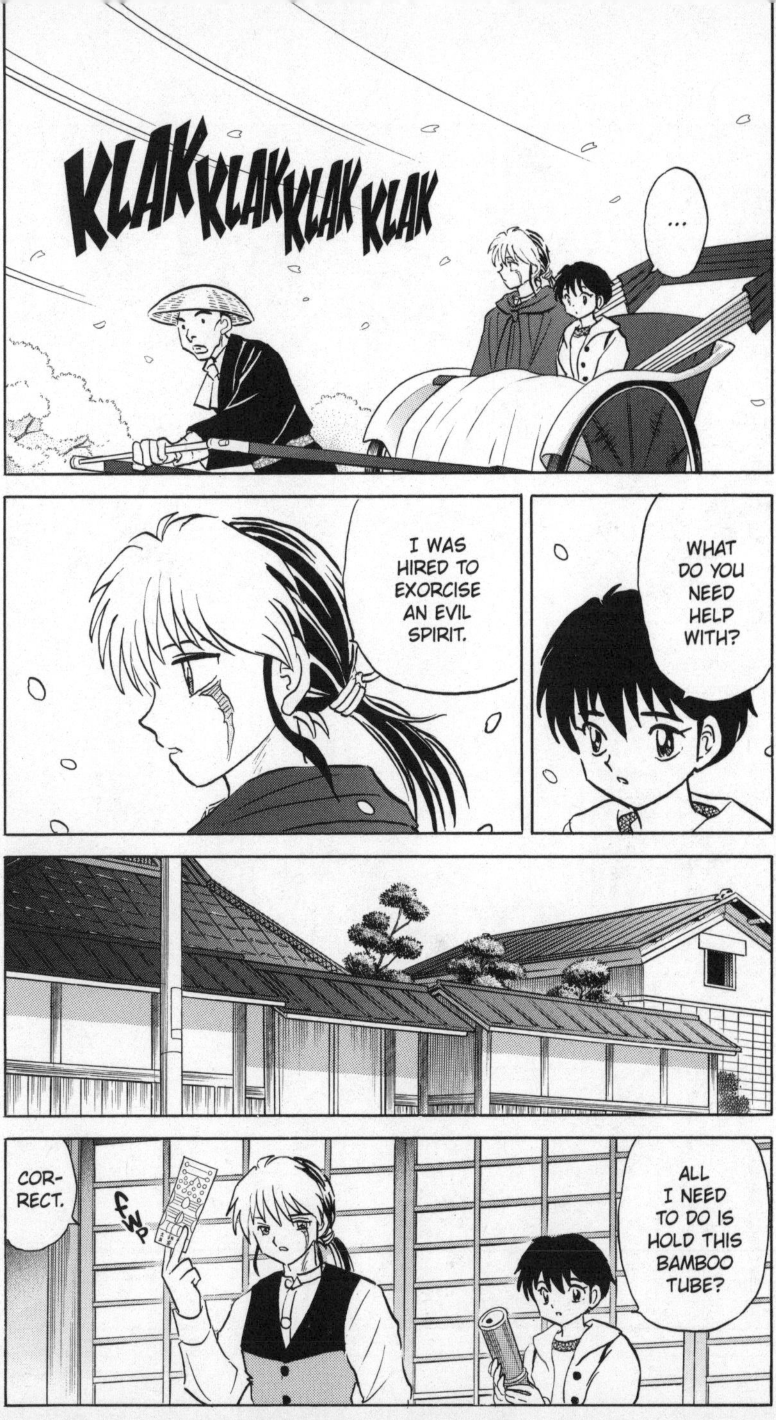
...
KLAK KLAK KLAK KLAK
WHAT DO YOU NEED HELP WITH?
I WAS HIRED TO EXORCISE AN EVIL SPIRIT.
ALL I NEED TO DO IS HOLD THIS BAMBOO TUBE?
FWP
COR-RECT.

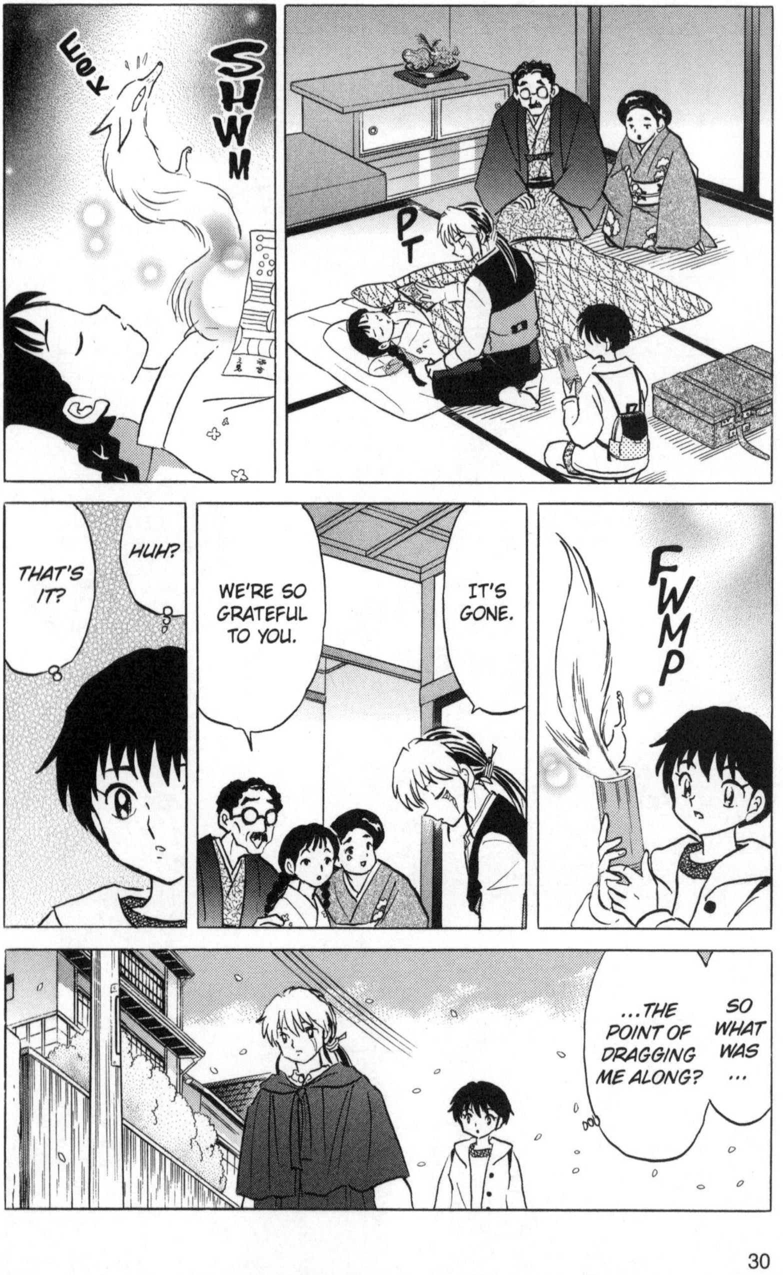
PT
SHWM
Eek
FWMP
IT'S GONE.
WE'RE SO GRATEFUL TO YOU.
HUH?
THAT'S IT?
SO WHAT WAS ...
...THE POINT OF DRAGGING ME ALONG?

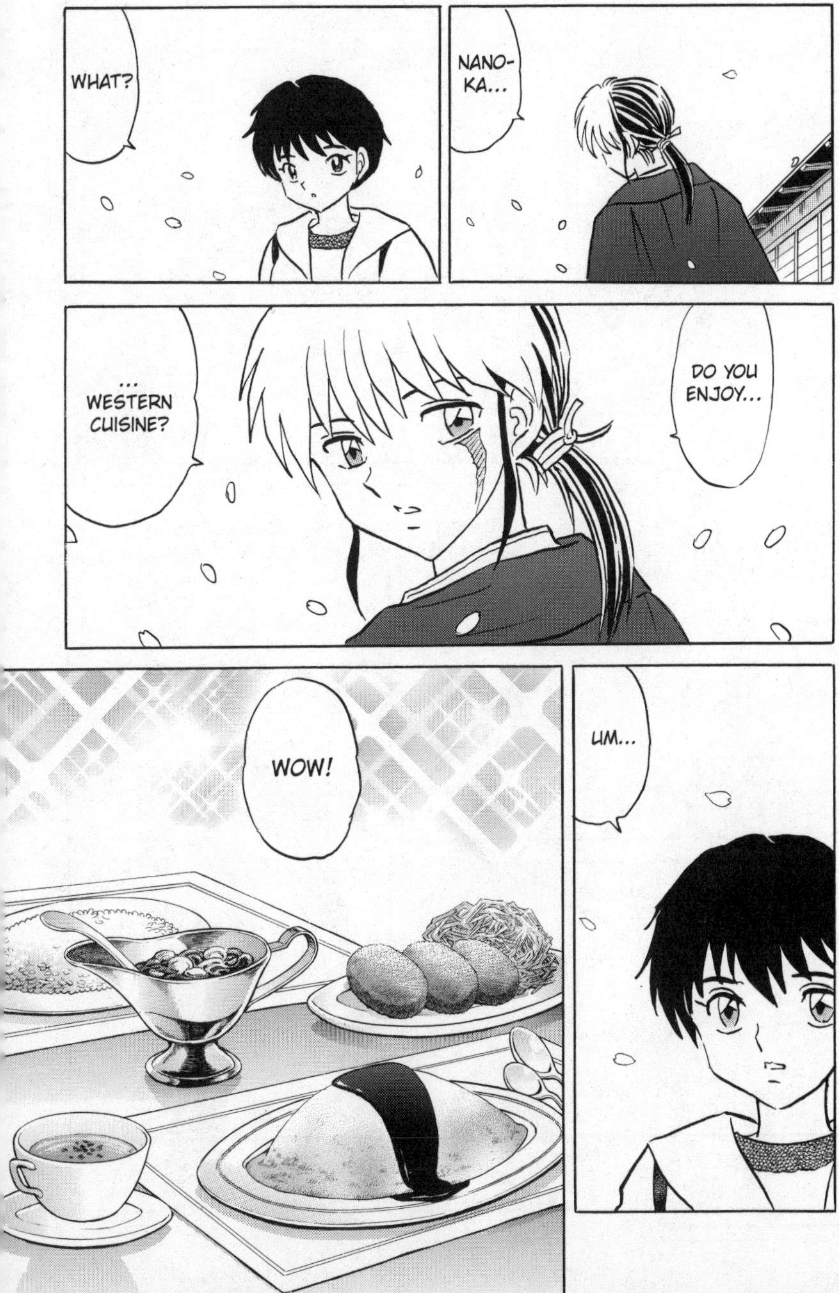
NANO-KA...
WHAT?
DO YOU ENJOY...
... WESTERN CUISINE?
UM...
WOW!

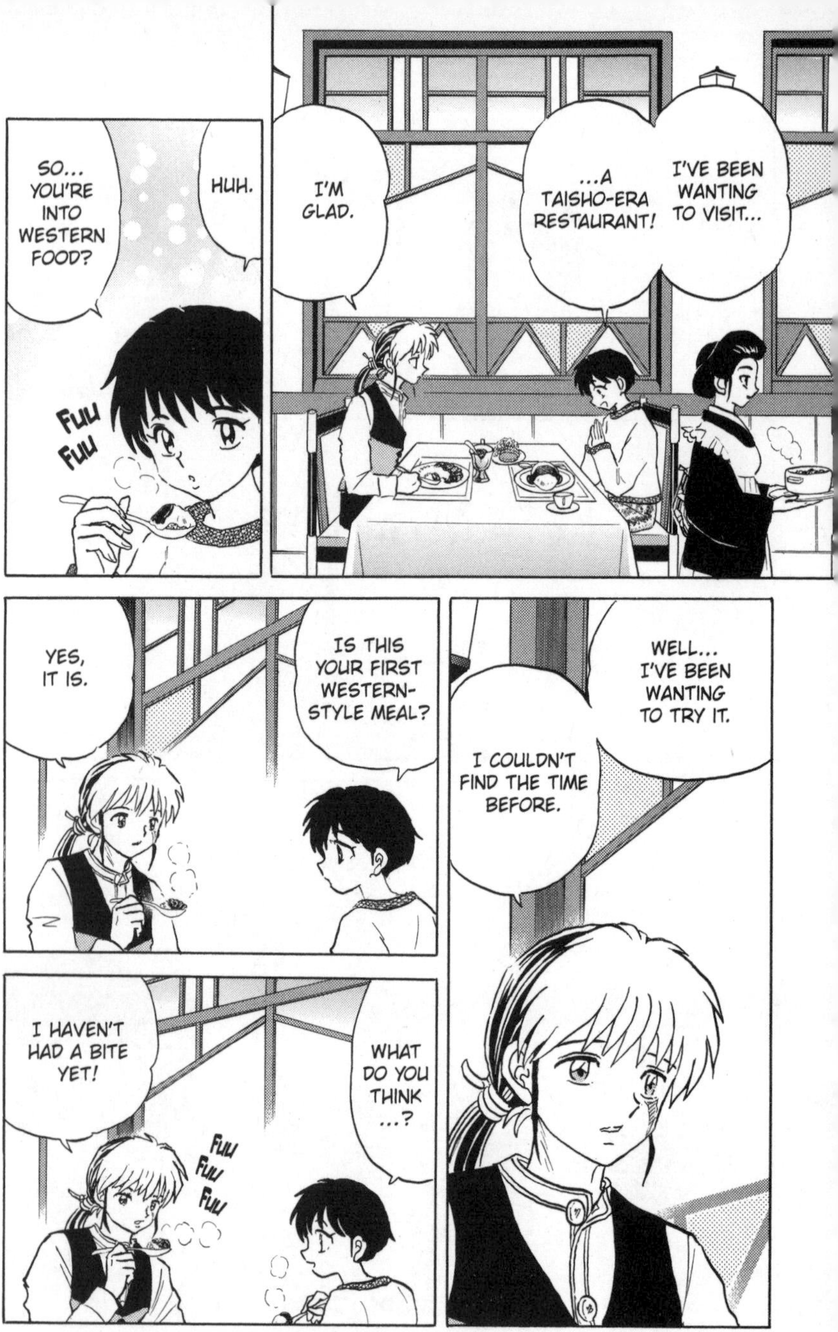
I'VE BEEN WANTING TO VISIT...
...A TAISHO-ERA RESTAURANT!
I'M GLAD.
HUH.
SO... YOU'RE INTO WESTERN FOOD?
FUU FUU
WELL... I'VE BEEN WANTING TO TRY IT.
I COULDN'T FIND THE TIME BEFORE.
IS THIS YOUR FIRST WESTERN-STYLE MEAL?
YES, IT IS.
WHAT DO YOU THINK ...?
FUU FUU FUU
I HAVEN'T HAD A BITE YET!

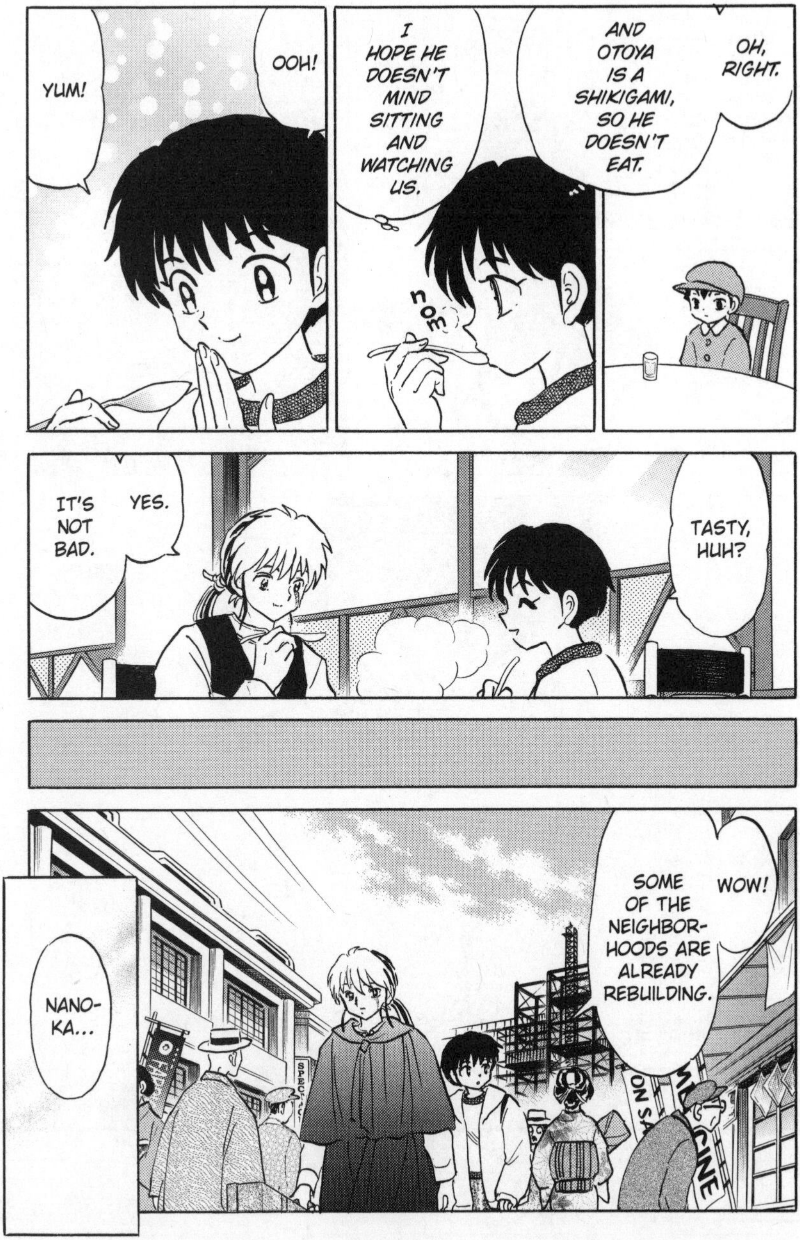
OH, RIGHT.
AND OTOYA IS A SHIKIGAMI, SO HE DOESN'T EAT.
I HOPE HE DOESN'T MIND SITTING AND WATCHING US.
nom
OOH!
YUM!
TASTY, HUH?
YES.
IT'S NOT BAD.
WOW!
SOME OF THE NEIGHBOR-HOODS ARE ALREADY REBUILDING.
NANO-KA...

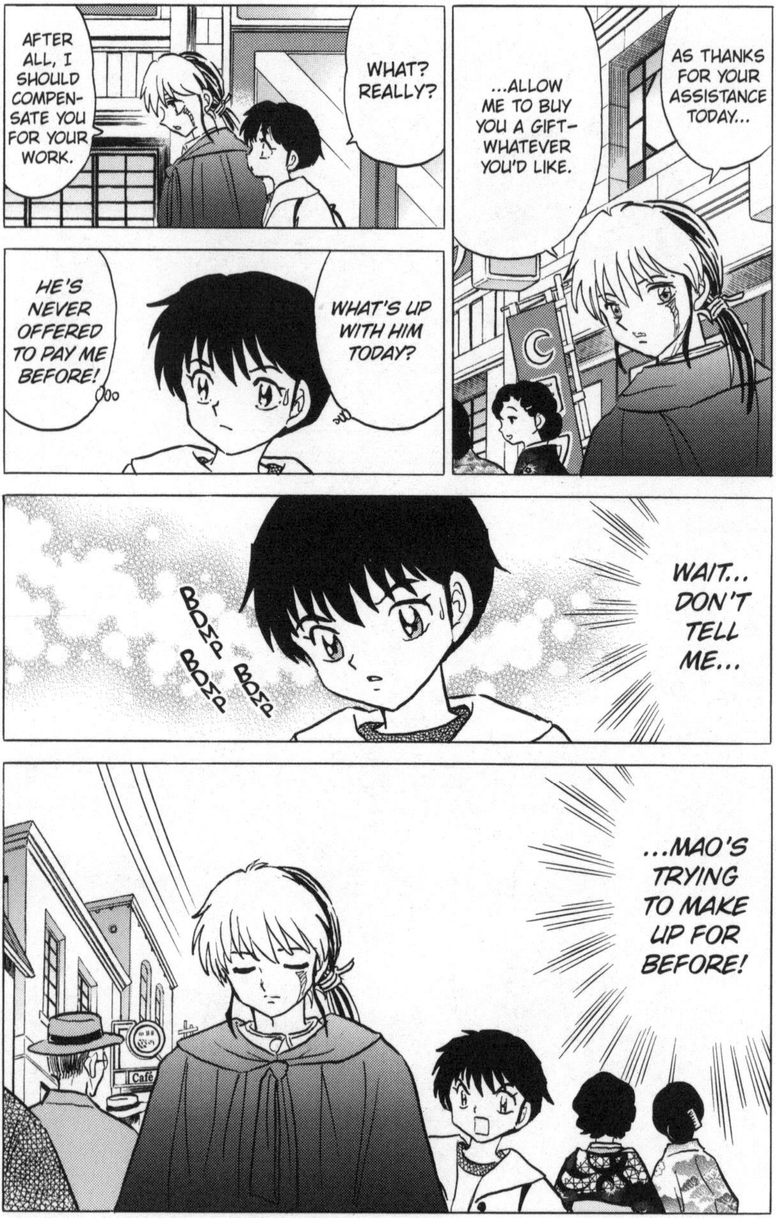
AS THANKS FOR YOUR ASSISTANCE TODAY...
...ALLOW ME TO BUY YOU A GIFT—WHATEVER YOU'D LIKE.
WHAT? REALLY?
AFTER ALL, I SHOULD COMPENSATE YOU FOR YOUR WORK.
WHAT'S UP WITH HIM TODAY?
HE'S NEVER OFFERED TO PAY ME BEFORE!
WAIT... DON'T TELL ME...
BDMP
BDMP
BDMP
...MAO'S TRYING TO MAKE UP FOR BEFORE!
Café

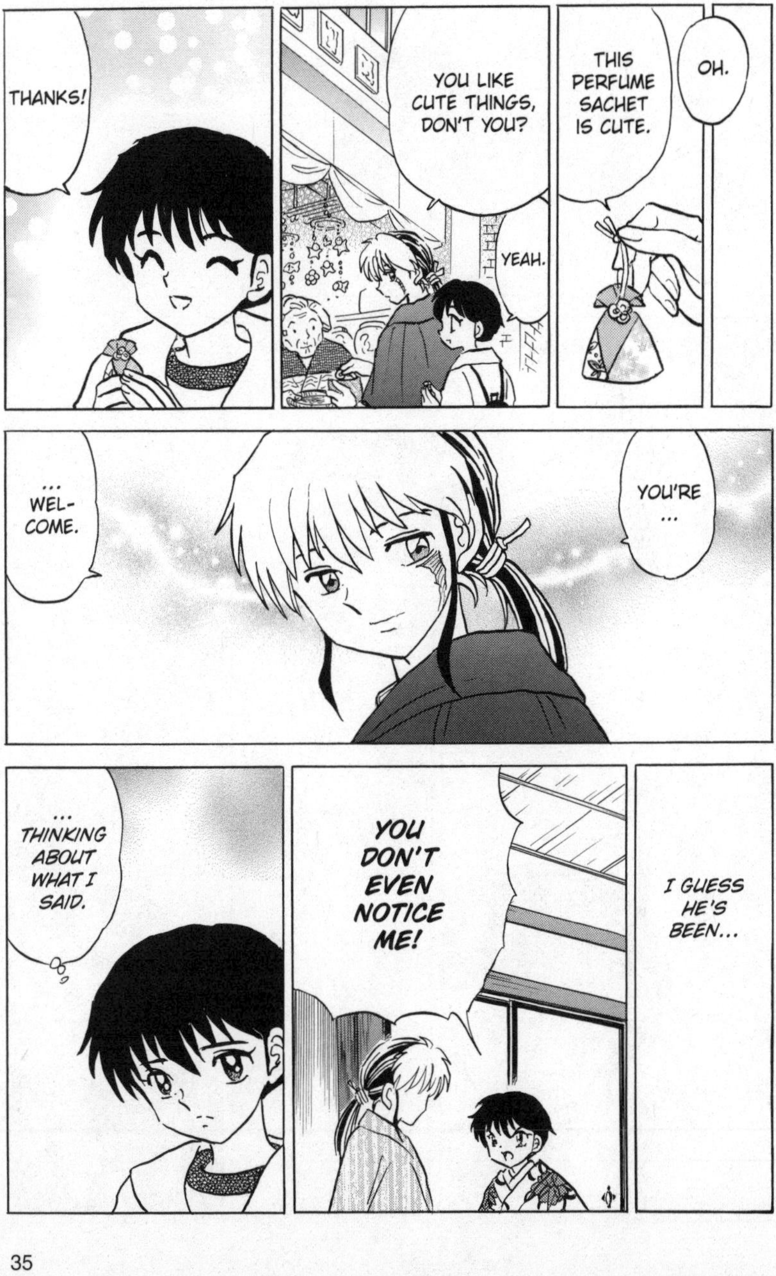
OH.
THIS PERFUME SACHET IS CUTE.
YOU LIKE CUTE THINGS, DON'T YOU?
YEAH.
THANKS!
YOU'RE ...
... WEL-COME.
I GUESS HE'S BEEN...
YOU DON'T EVEN NOTICE ME!
... THINKING ABOUT WHAT I SAID.

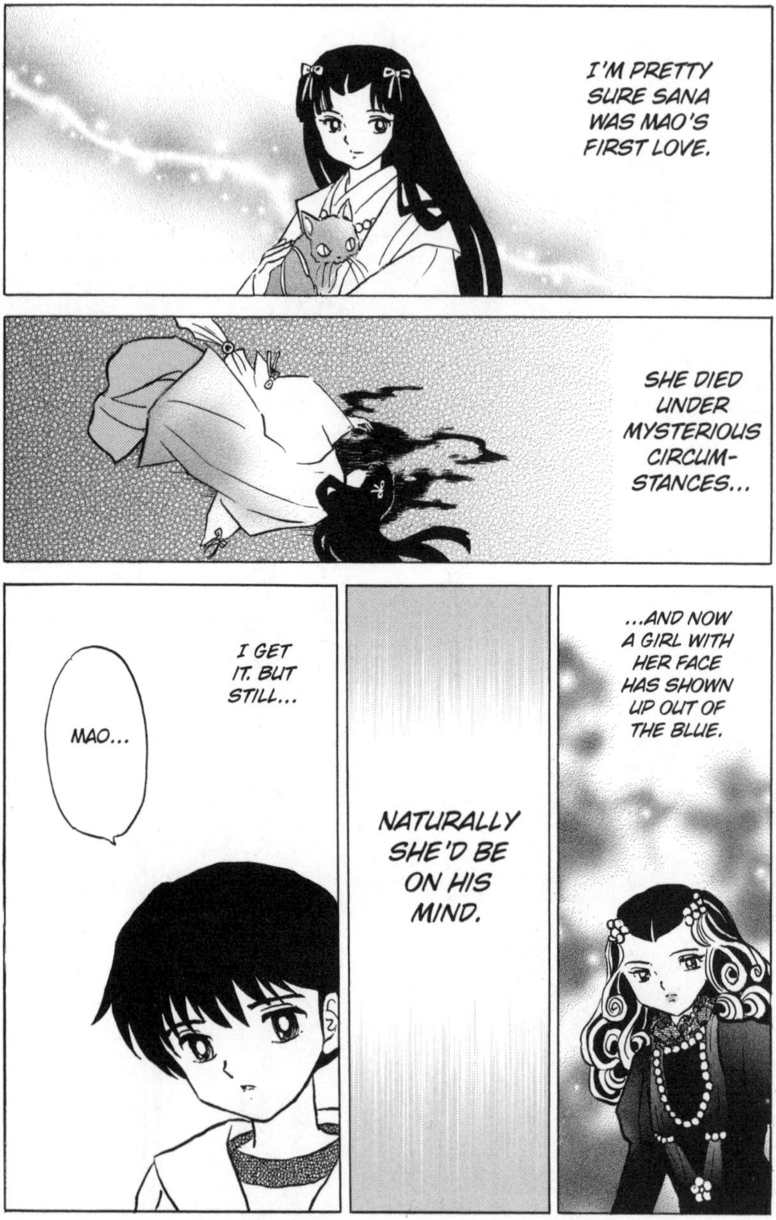
I'M PRETTY SURE SANA WAS MAO'S FIRST LOVE.
SHE DIED UNDER MYSTERIOUS CIRCUM-STANCES...
...AND NOW A GIRL WITH HER FACE HAS SHOWN UP OUT OF THE BLUE.
NATURALLY SHE'D BE ON HIS MIND.
I GET IT. BUT STILL...
MAO...

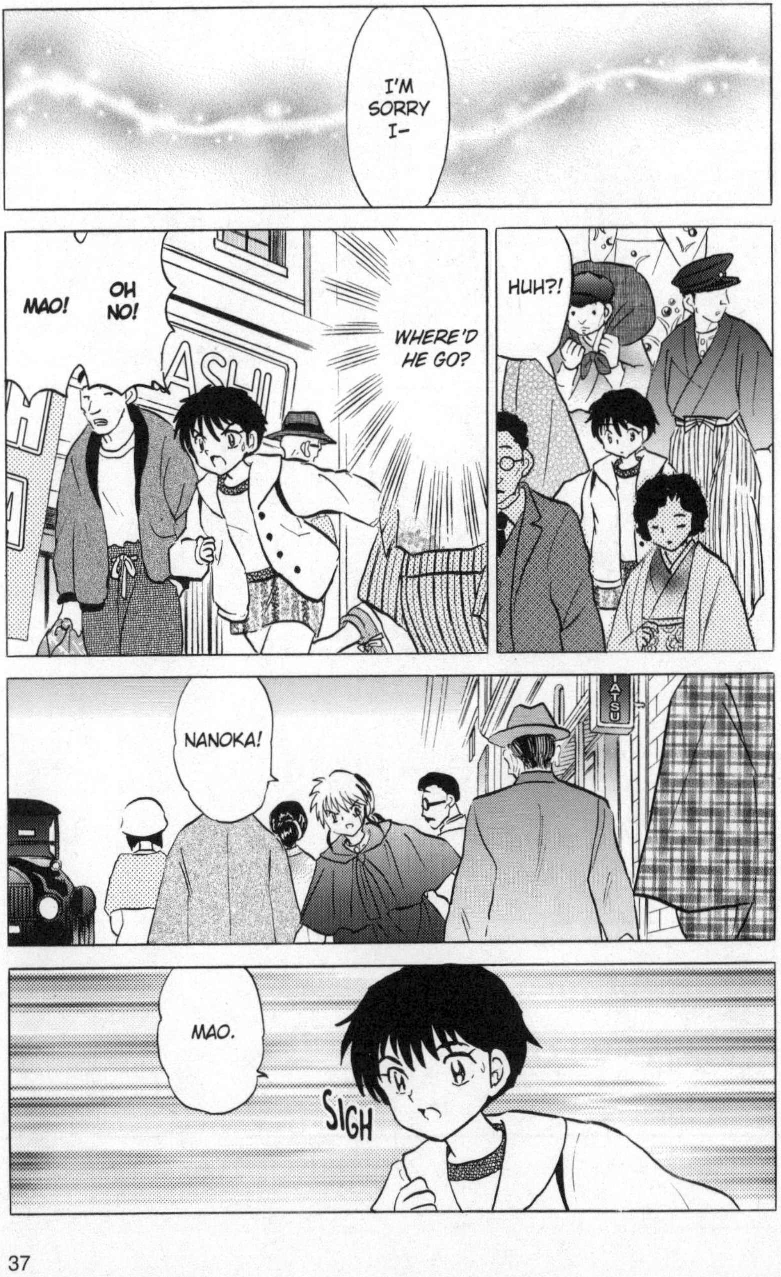
I'M SORRY I–
HUH?!
WHERE'D HE GO?
OH NO!
MAO!
NANOKA!
MAO.
SIGH

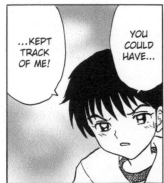

I TOTALLY FREAKED OUT!
huf huf huf
I WAS ALARMED WHEN I LOST YOU.
YOU COULD HAVE...
...KEPT TRACK OF ME!
THIS IS EXACTLY WHAT I'M TALKING ABOUT!
...
I... SEE.
I APOLOGIZE.
!
GRIP
LET'S GO.

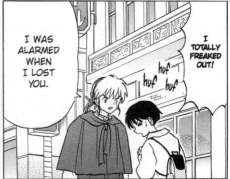

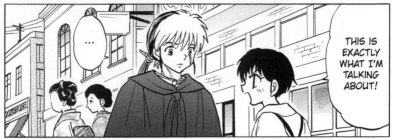

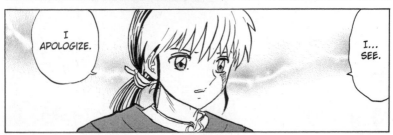

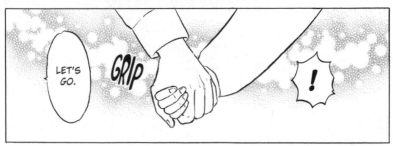

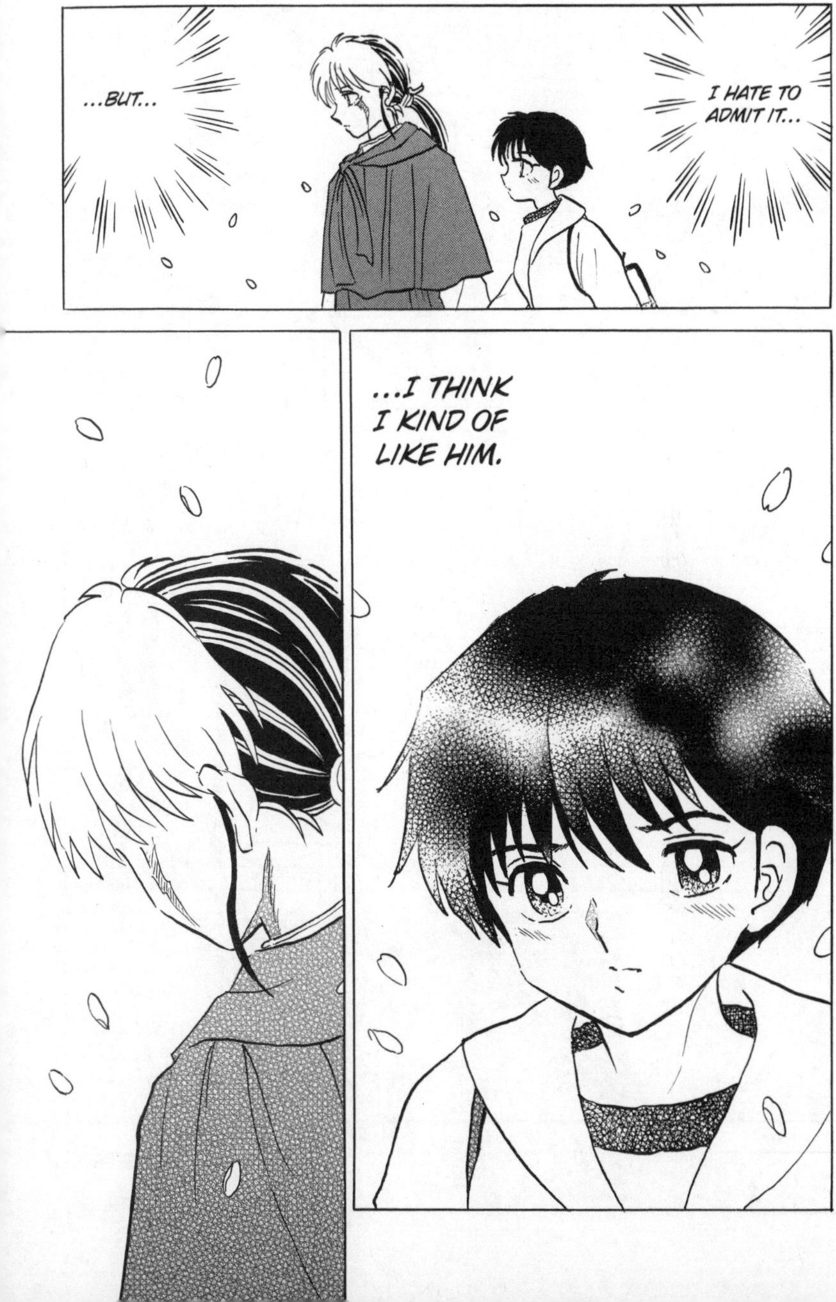
I HATE TO ADMIT IT...
...BUT...
...I THINK I KIND OF LIKE HIM.

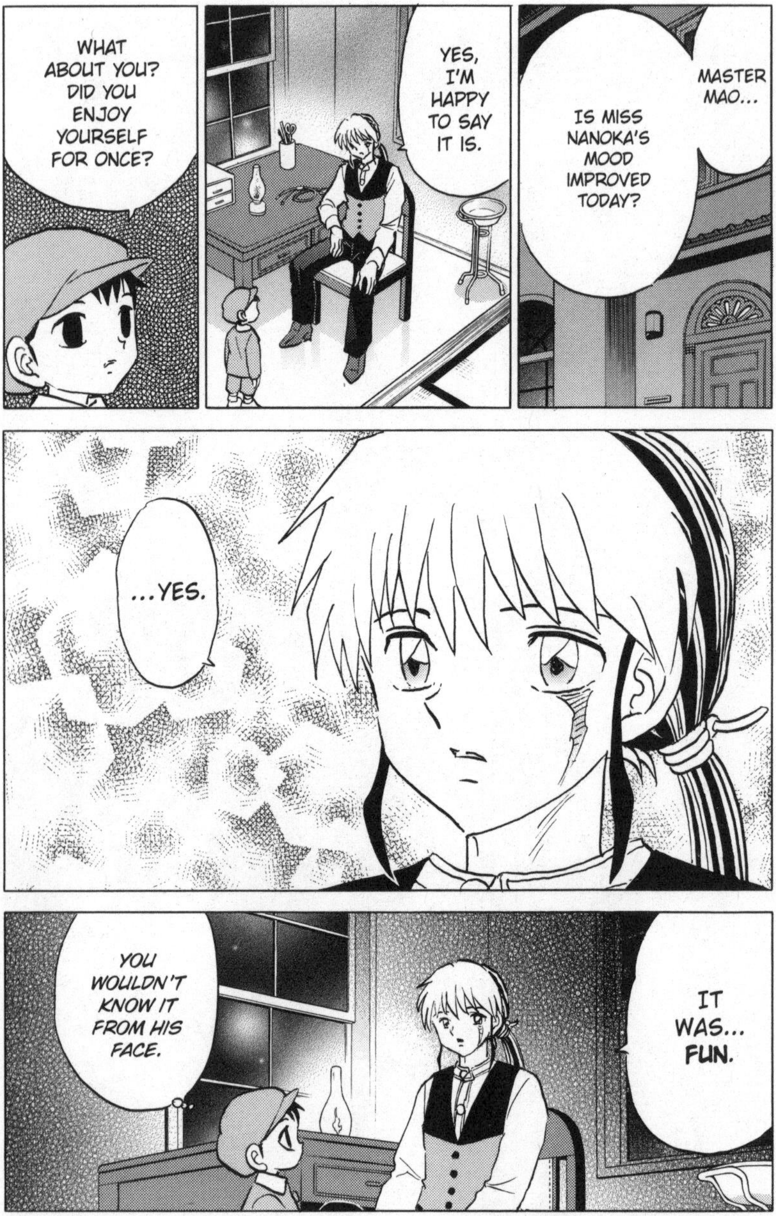
MASTER MAO...
IS MISS NANOKA'S MOOD IMPROVED TODAY?
YES, I'M HAPPY TO SAY IT IS.
WHAT ABOUT YOU? DID YOU ENJOY YOURSELF FOR ONCE?
...YES.
IT WAS... FUN.
YOU WOULDN'T KNOW IT FROM HIS FACE.

Chapter 3:
Phantom Slasher

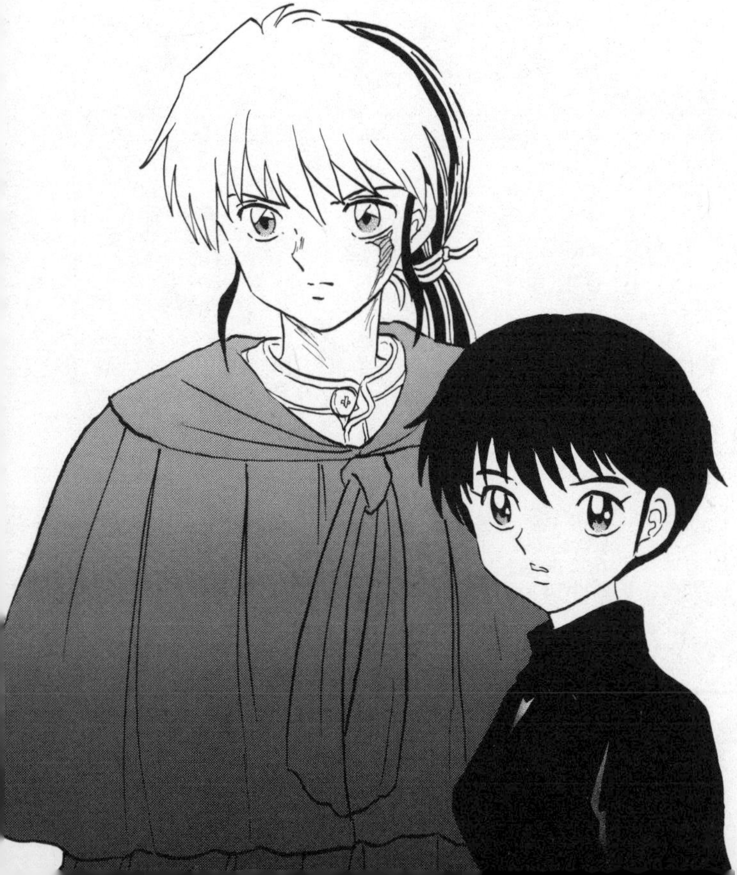

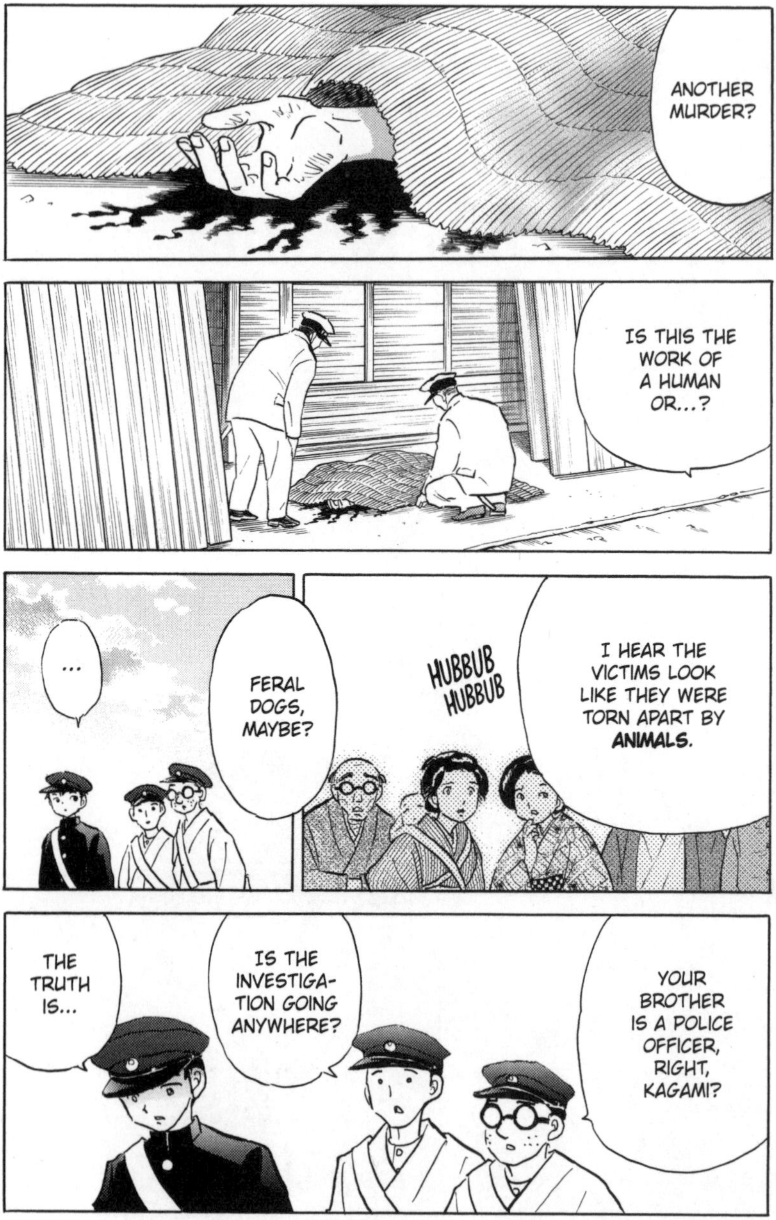

ANOTHER MURDER?
IS THIS THE WORK OF A HUMAN OR...?
I HEAR THE VICTIMS LOOK LIKE THEY WERE TORN APART BY **ANIMALS.**
HUBBUB HUBBUB
FERAL DOGS, MAYBE?
...
YOUR BROTHER IS A POLICE OFFICER, RIGHT, KAGAMI?
IS THE INVESTIGATION GOING ANYWHERE?
THE TRUTH IS...

...MY BROTHER...

...HAS BEEN SICK.

HE MIGHT HAVE TO RESIGN FROM THE FORCE.

HE'S CONVALESCING AT HOME NOW.

THAT'S A SHAME.

WHAT?

HELLO.

WELCOME HOME, BIG BROTHER.

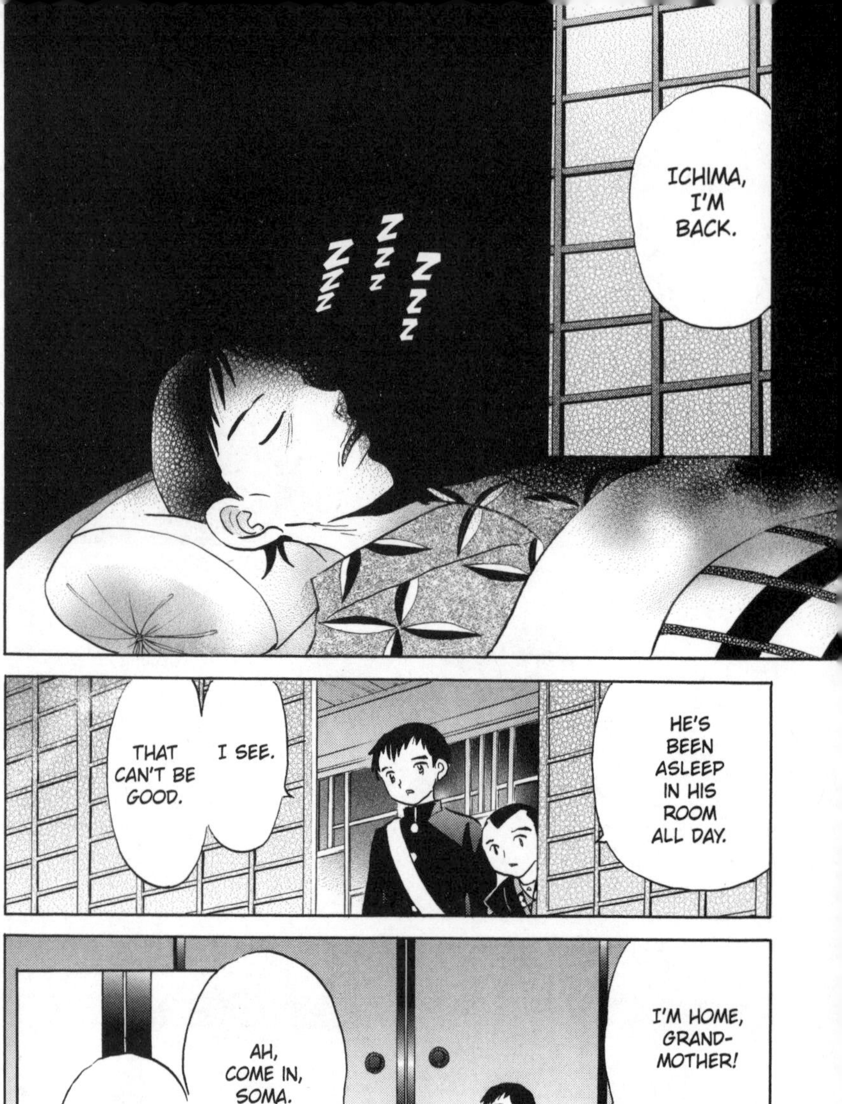
ICHIMA, I'M BACK.
ZZZ
ZZZ
ZZZ
HE'S BEEN ASLEEP IN HIS ROOM ALL DAY.
I SEE.
THAT CAN'T BE GOOD.
I'M HOME, GRAND-MOTHER!
AH, COME IN, SOMA.
I HAVE SOMETHING IMPORTANT TO TELL YOU.

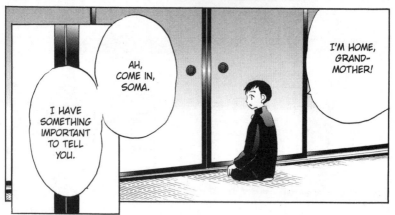

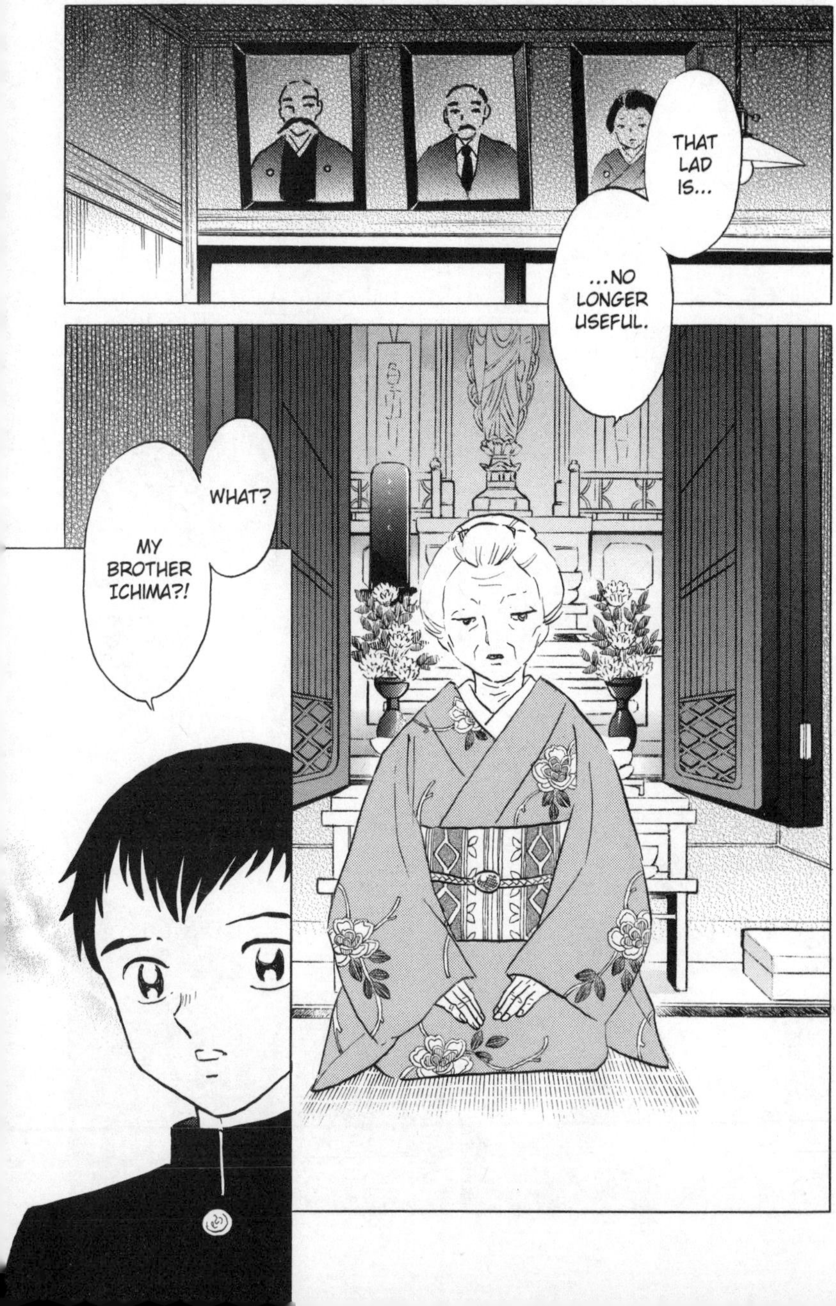
THAT LAD IS...
...NO LONGER USEFUL.
WHAT?
MY BROTHER ICHIMA?!

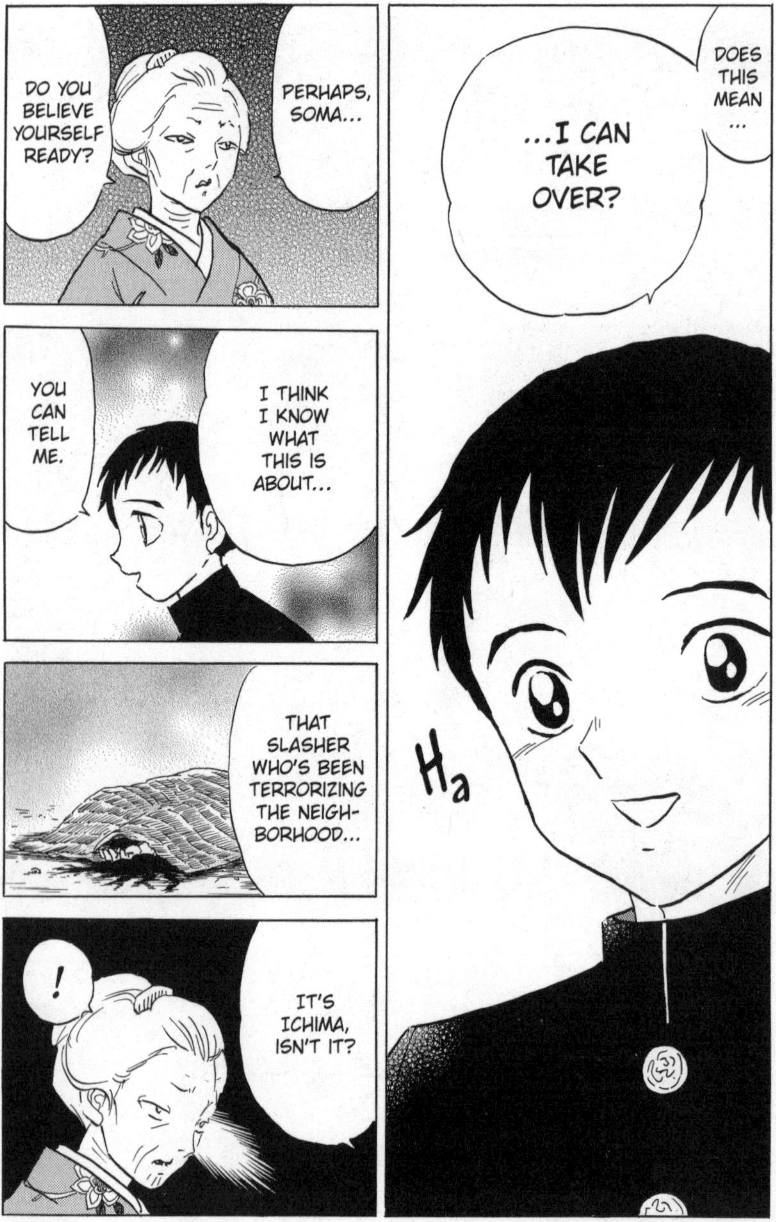
DOES THIS MEAN ...
...I CAN TAKE OVER?
Ha
PERHAPS, SOMA...
DO YOU BELIEVE YOURSELF READY?
I THINK I KNOW WHAT THIS IS ABOUT...
YOU CAN TELL ME.
THAT SLASHER WHO'S BEEN TERRORIZING THE NEIGH-BORHOOD...
IT'S ICHIMA, ISN'T IT?
!

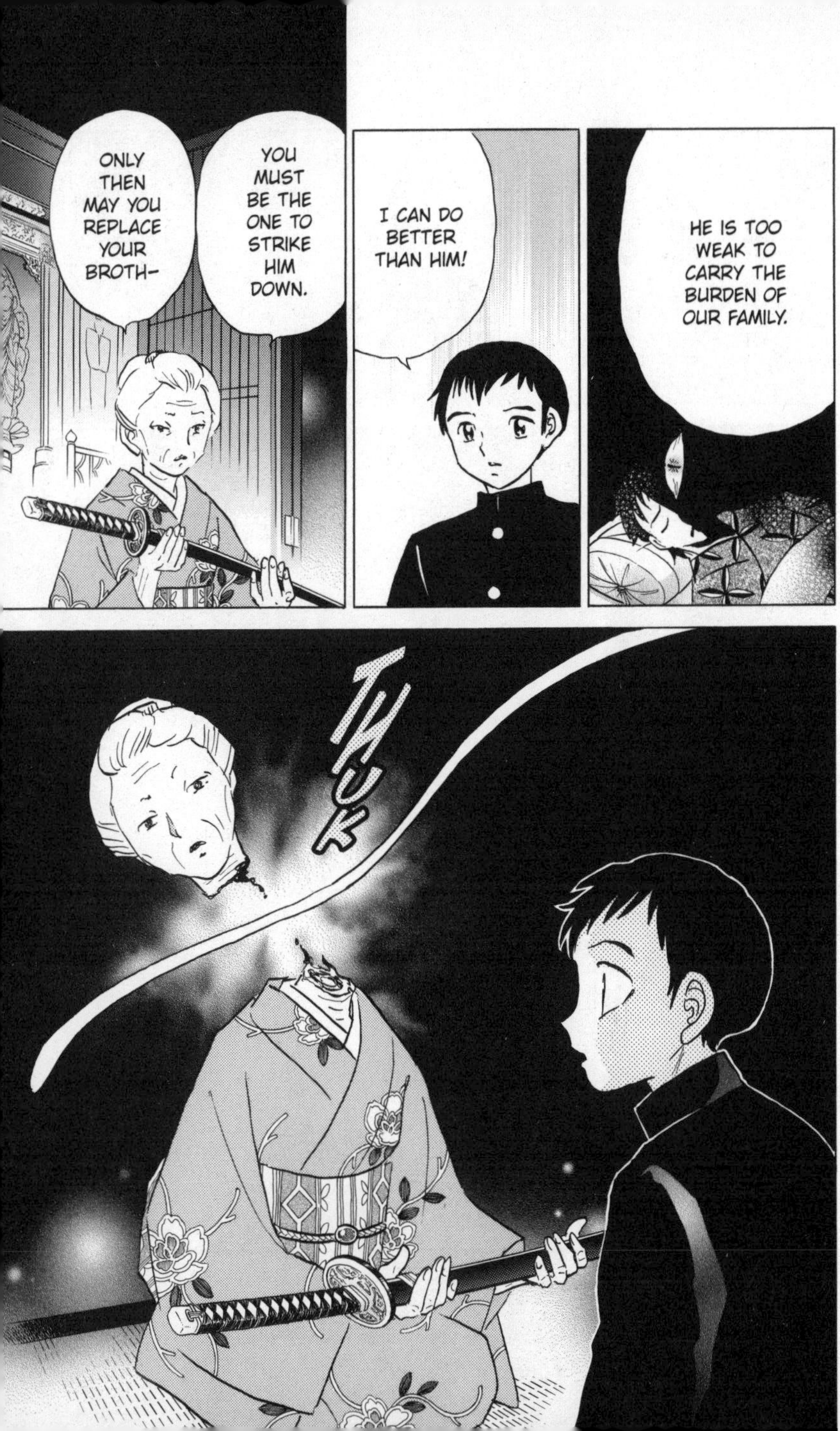
HE IS TOO WEAK TO CARRY THE BURDEN OF OUR FAMILY.
I CAN DO BETTER THAN HIM!
YOU MUST BE THE ONE TO STRIKE HIM DOWN.
ONLY THEN MAY YOU REPLACE YOUR BROTH-
THUNK

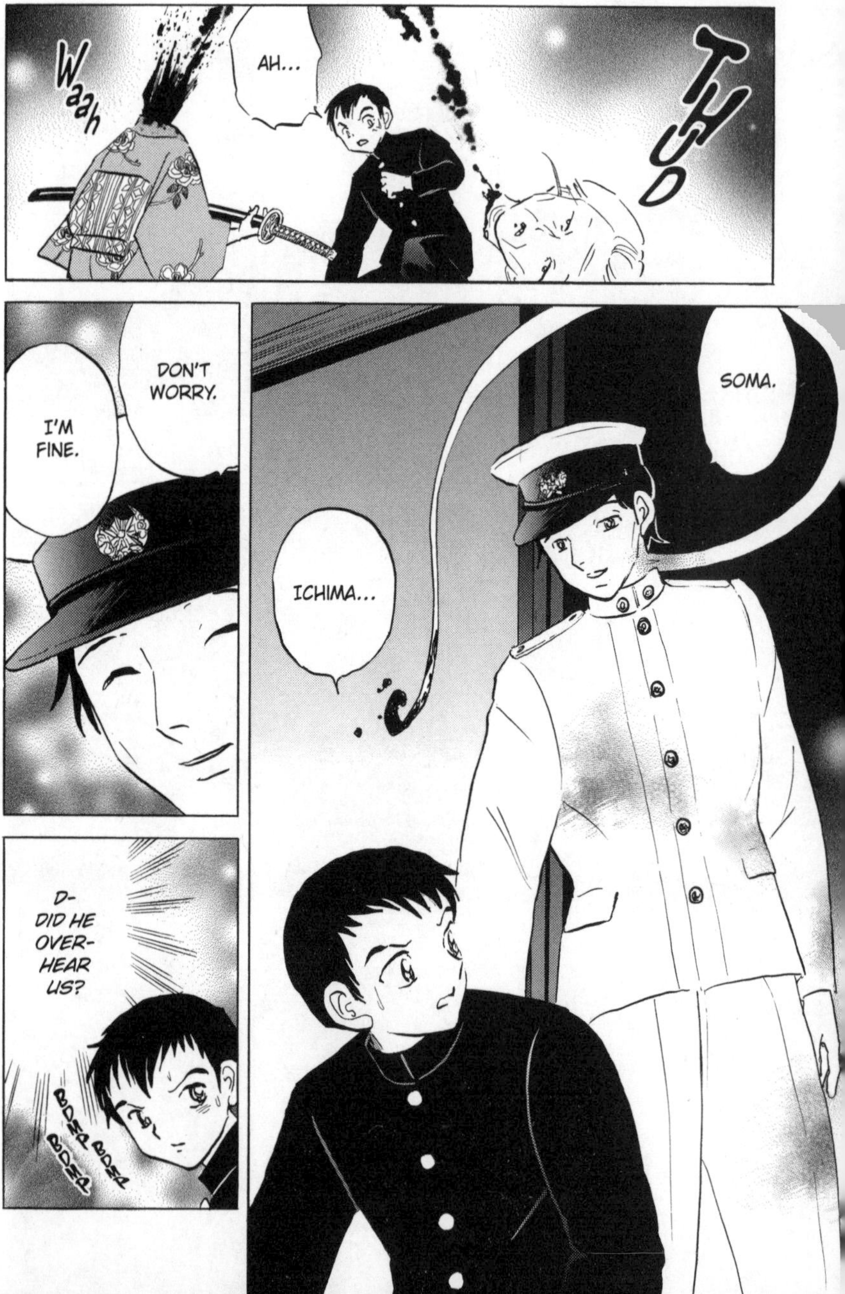
THUD
AH...
Waah
SOMA.
ICHIMA...
DON'T WORRY.
I'M FINE.
D- DID HE OVER-HEAR US?
BOMP BOMP
BOMP

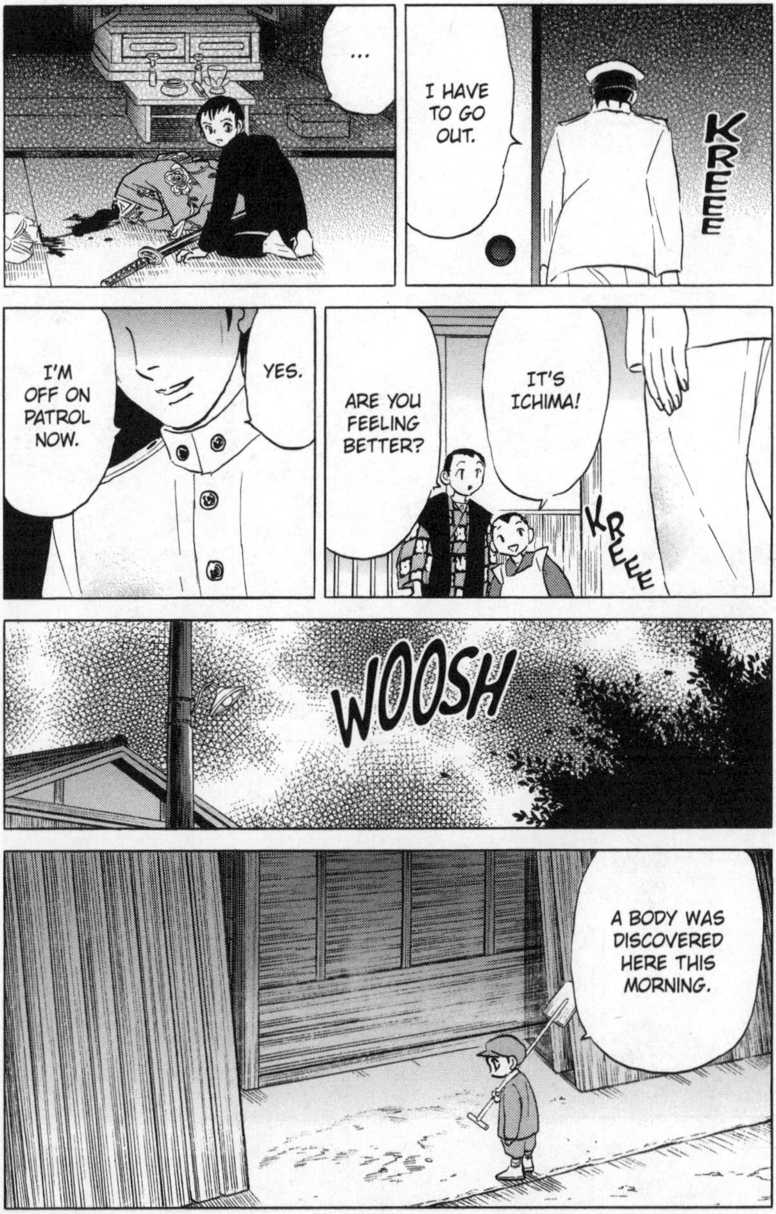
KREEE
I HAVE TO GO OUT.
...
IT'S ICHIMA!
ARE YOU FEELING BETTER?
KREEE
YES.
I'M OFF ON PATROL NOW.
WOOSH
A BODY WAS DISCOVERED HERE THIS MORNING.

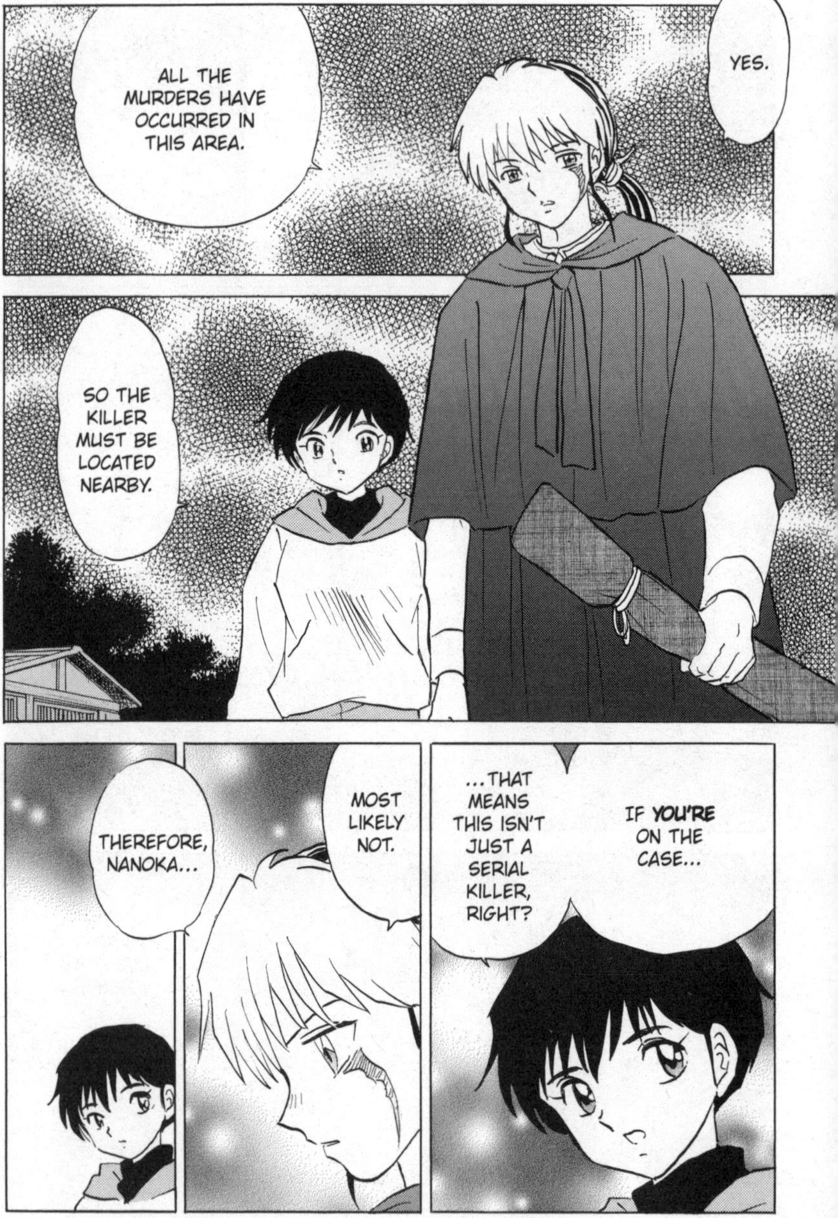
YES.
ALL THE MURDERS HAVE OCCURRED IN THIS AREA.
SO THE KILLER MUST BE LOCATED NEARBY.
IF **YOU'RE** ON THE CASE...
...THAT MEANS THIS ISN'T JUST A SERIAL KILLER, RIGHT?
MOST LIKELY NOT.
THEREFORE, NANOKA...

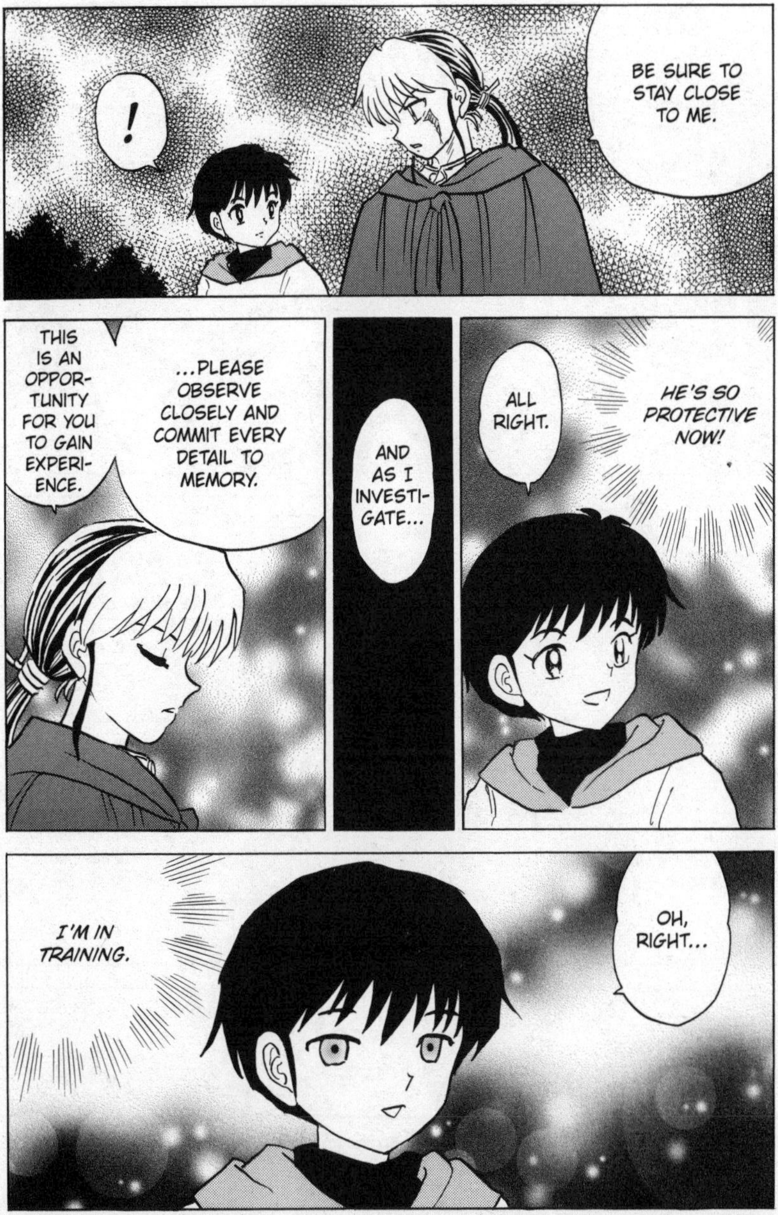
BE SURE TO STAY CLOSE TO ME.
!
HE'S SO PROTECTIVE NOW!
ALL RIGHT.
AND AS I INVESTI-GATE...
...PLEASE OBSERVE CLOSELY AND COMMIT EVERY DETAIL TO MEMORY.
THIS IS AN OPPOR-TUNITY FOR YOU TO GAIN EXPERI-ENCE.
OH, RIGHT...
I'M IN TRAINING.

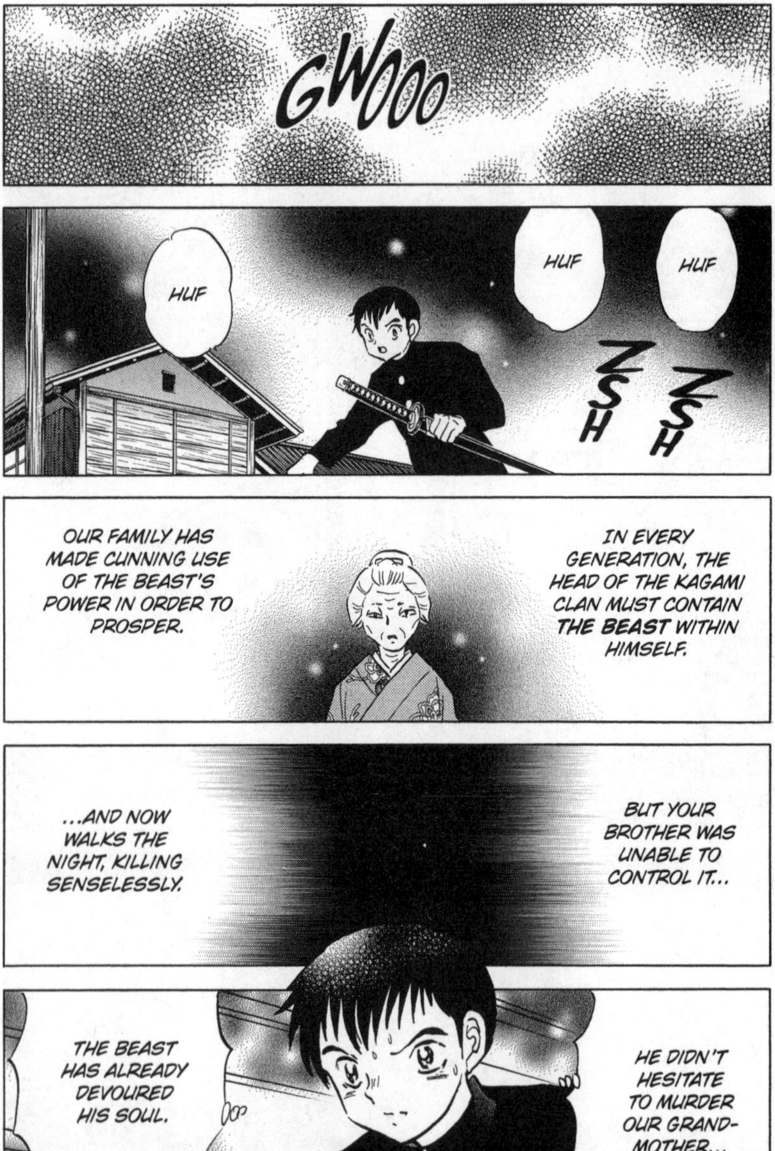
GWOOO
HUF
HUF
ZSH
ZSH
HUF
IN EVERY GENERATION, THE HEAD OF THE KAGAMI CLAN MUST CONTAIN **THE BEAST** WITHIN HIMSELF.
OUR FAMILY HAS MADE CUNNING USE OF THE BEAST'S POWER IN ORDER TO PROSPER.
BUT YOUR BROTHER WAS UNABLE TO CONTROL IT...
...AND NOW WALKS THE NIGHT, KILLING SENSELESSLY.
HE DIDN'T HESITATE TO MURDER OUR GRAND-MOTHER...
THE BEAST HAS ALREADY DEVOURED HIS SOUL.

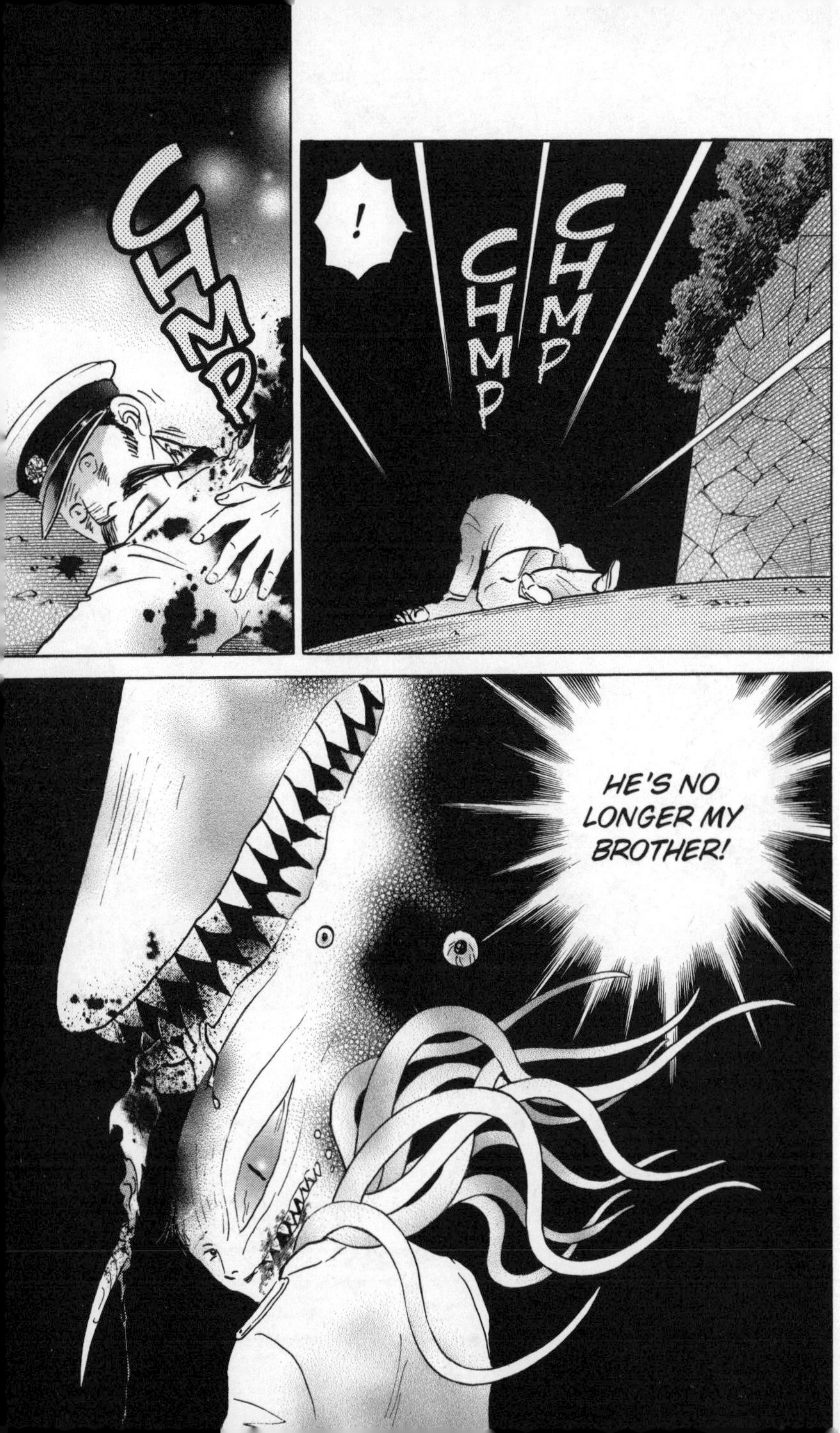
!
CHMP
CHMP
CHMP
HE'S NO LONGER MY BROTHER!

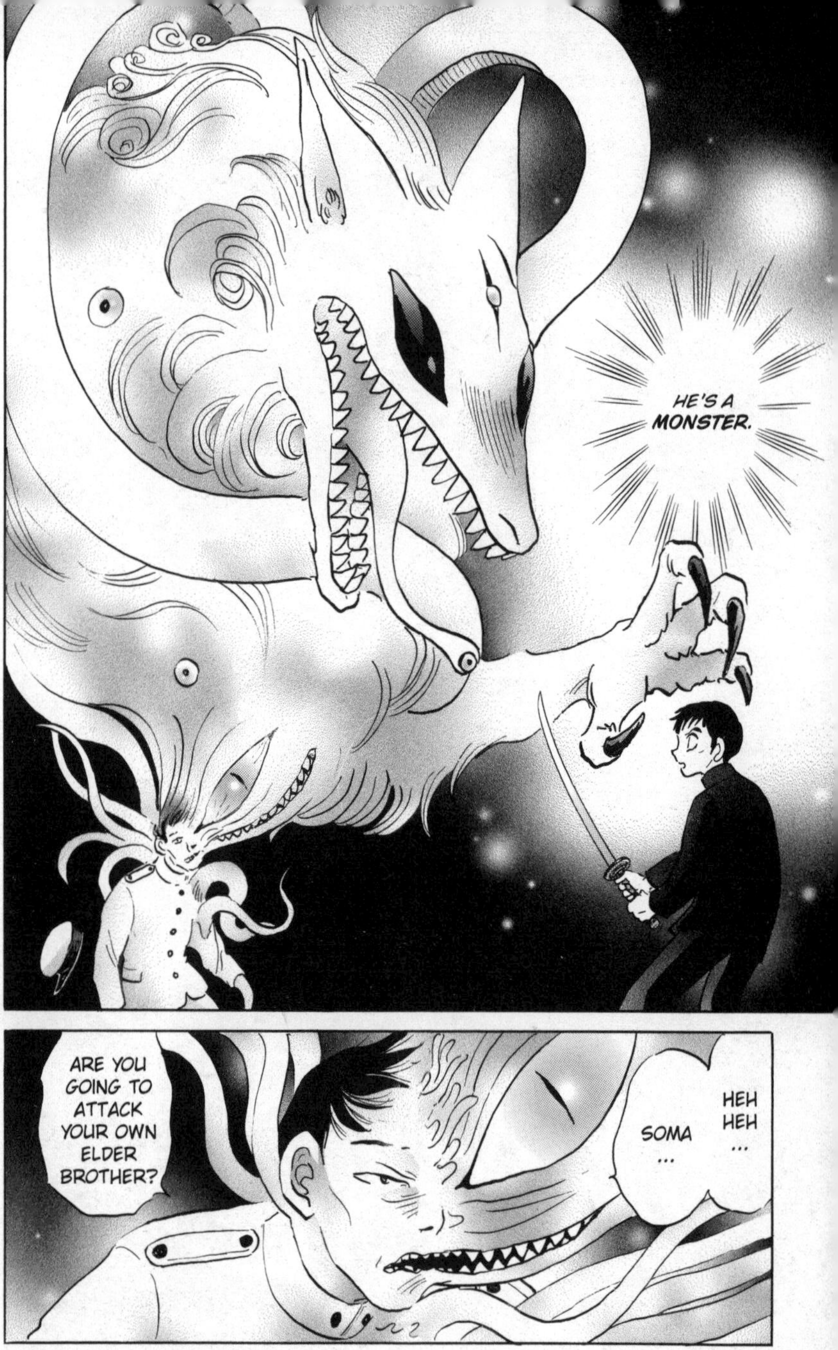
HE'S A MONSTER.
HEH HEH ...
SOMA ...
ARE YOU GOING TO ATTACK YOUR OWN ELDER BROTHER?

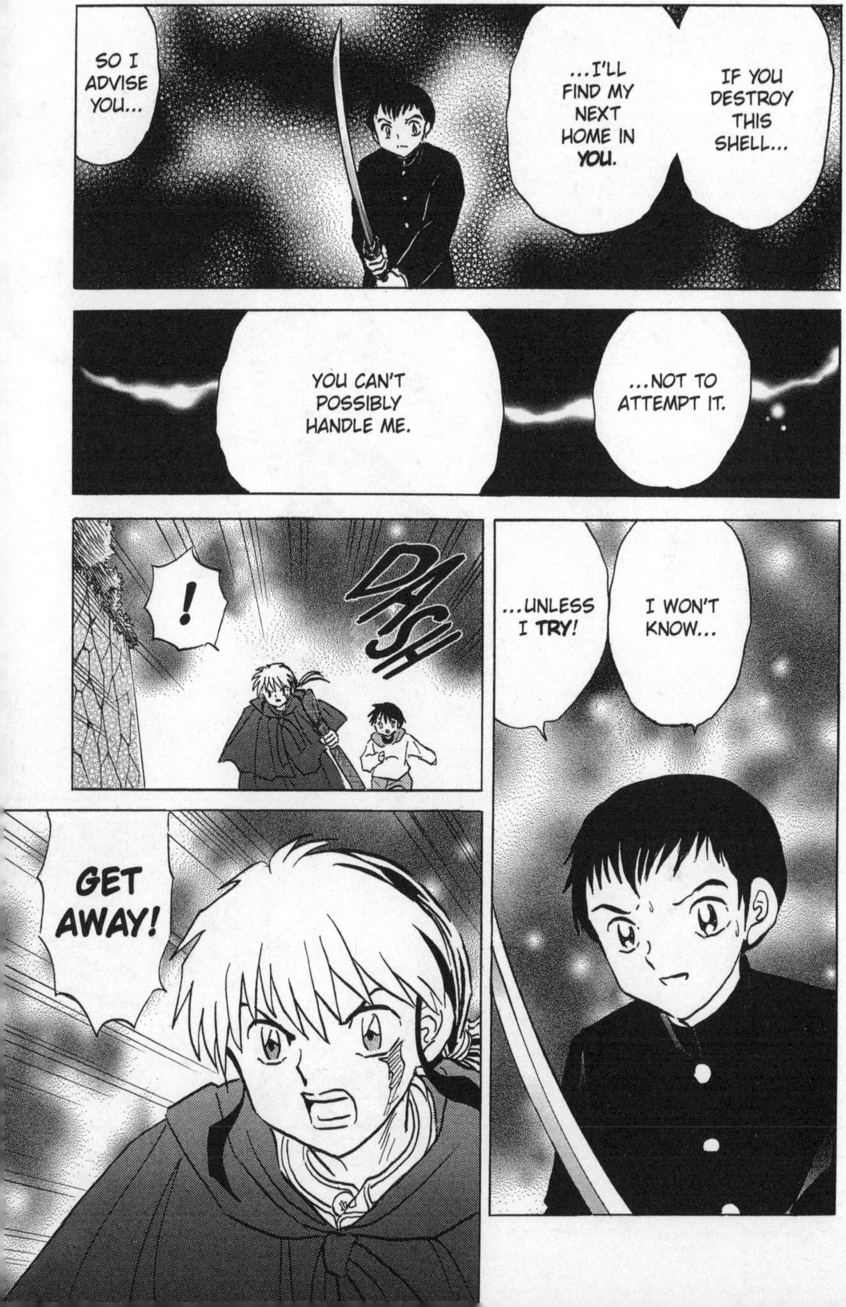
IF YOU DESTROY THIS SHELL...
...I'LL FIND MY NEXT HOME IN YOU.
SO I ADVISE YOU...
...NOT TO ATTEMPT IT.
YOU CAN'T POSSIBLY HANDLE ME.
I WON'T KNOW...
...UNLESS I TRY!
!
DASH
GET AWAY!

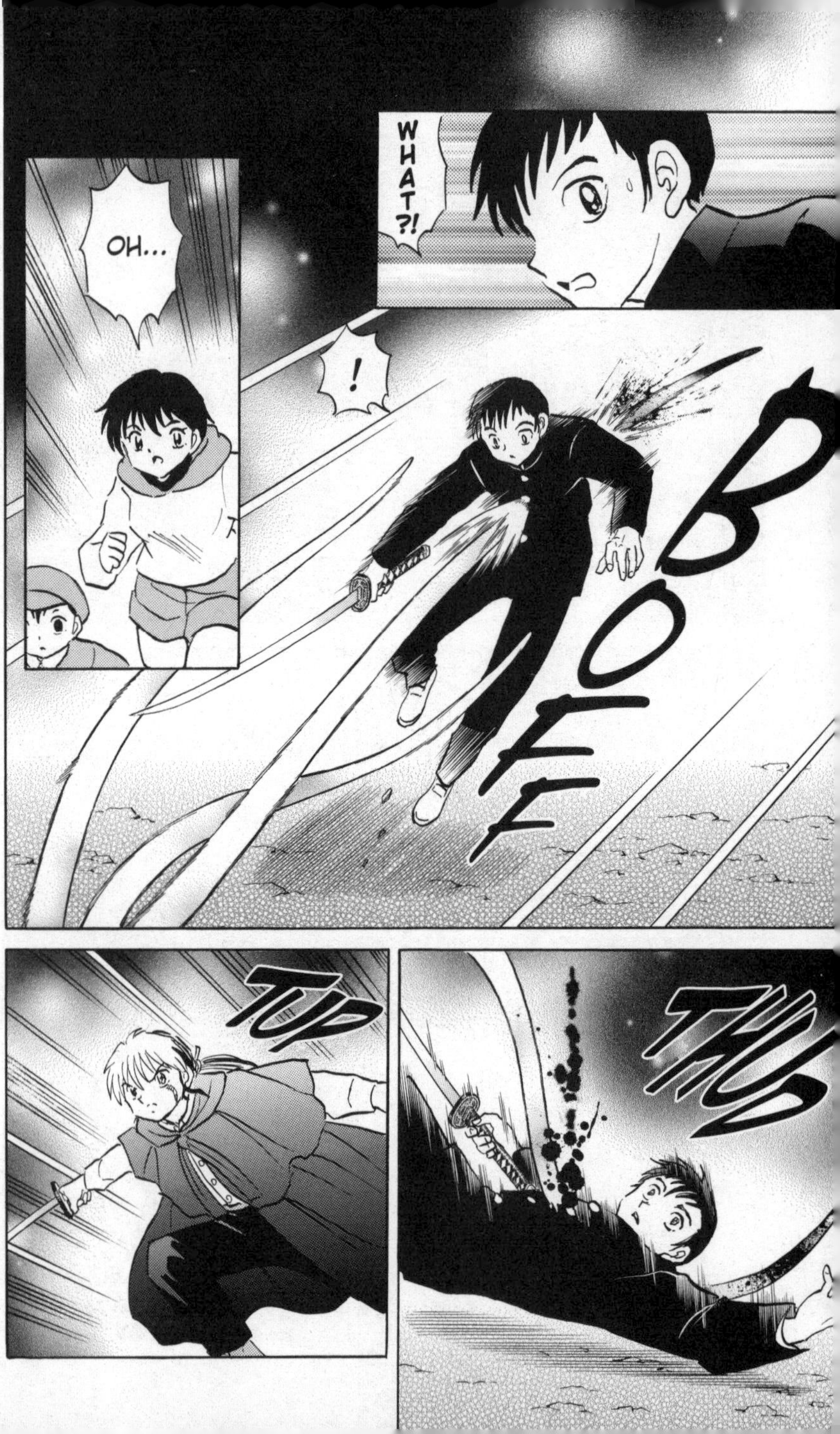
WHAT?!
OH...
!
BOFF
THUD
TUP

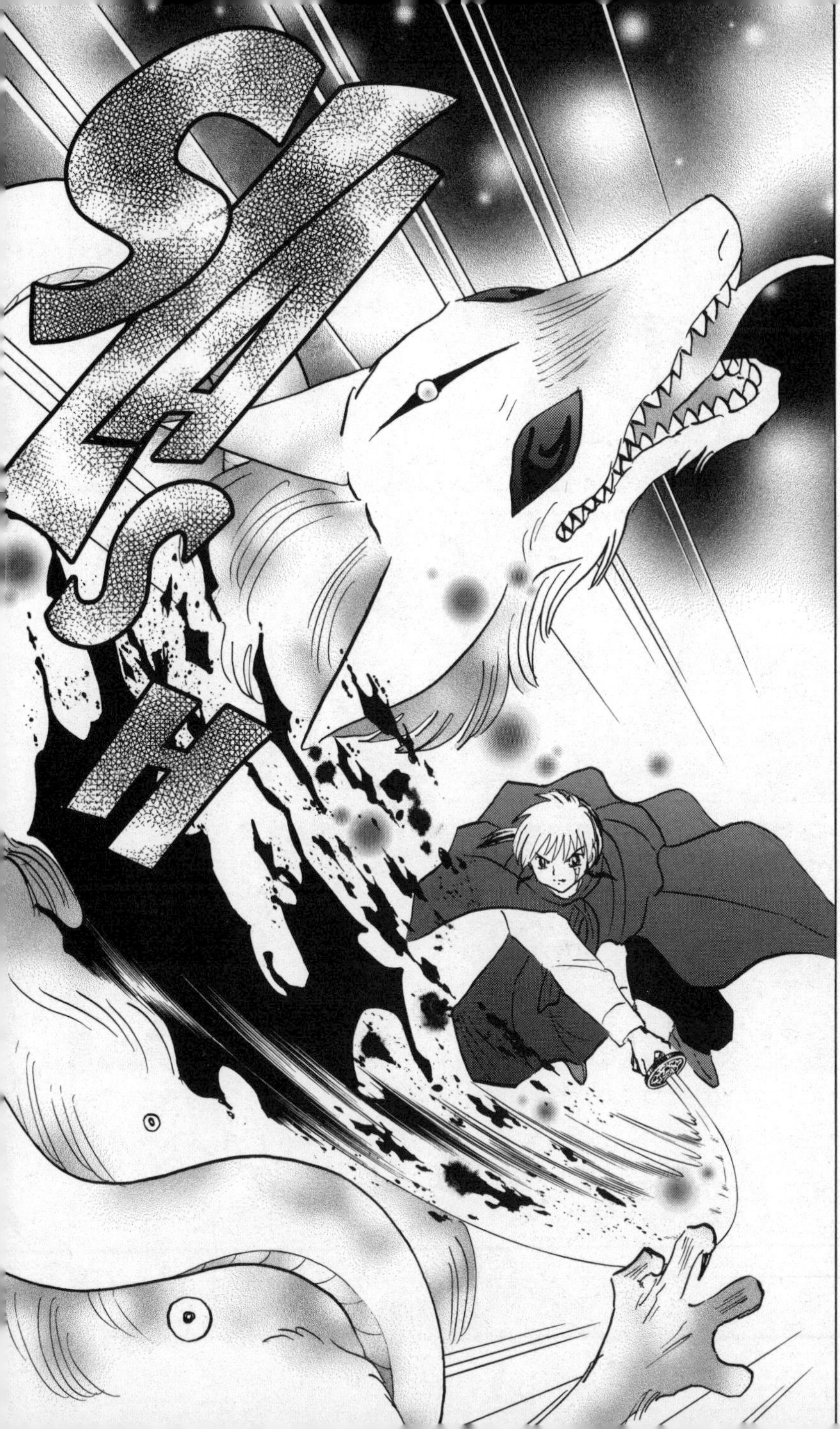
SHASH

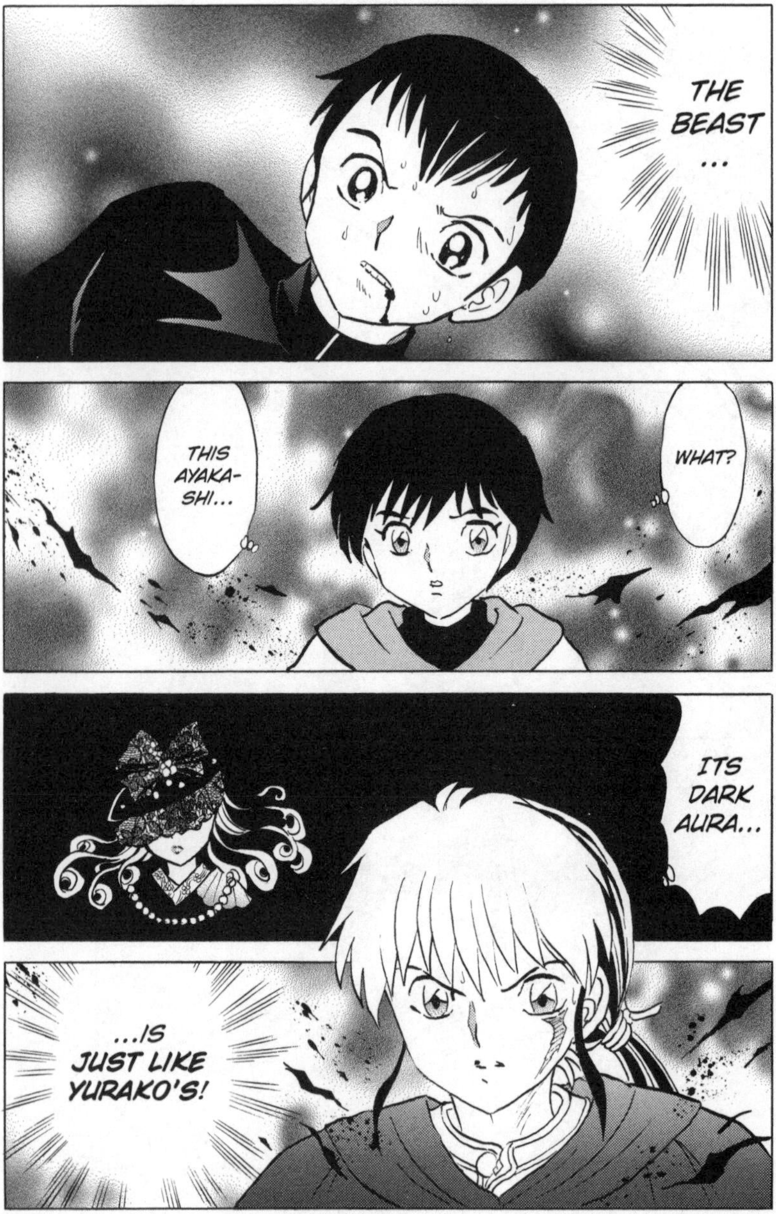
THE BEAST ...
WHAT?
THIS AYAKA-SHI...
ITS DARK AURA...
...IS JUST LIKE YURAKO'S!

Chapter 4: Beast

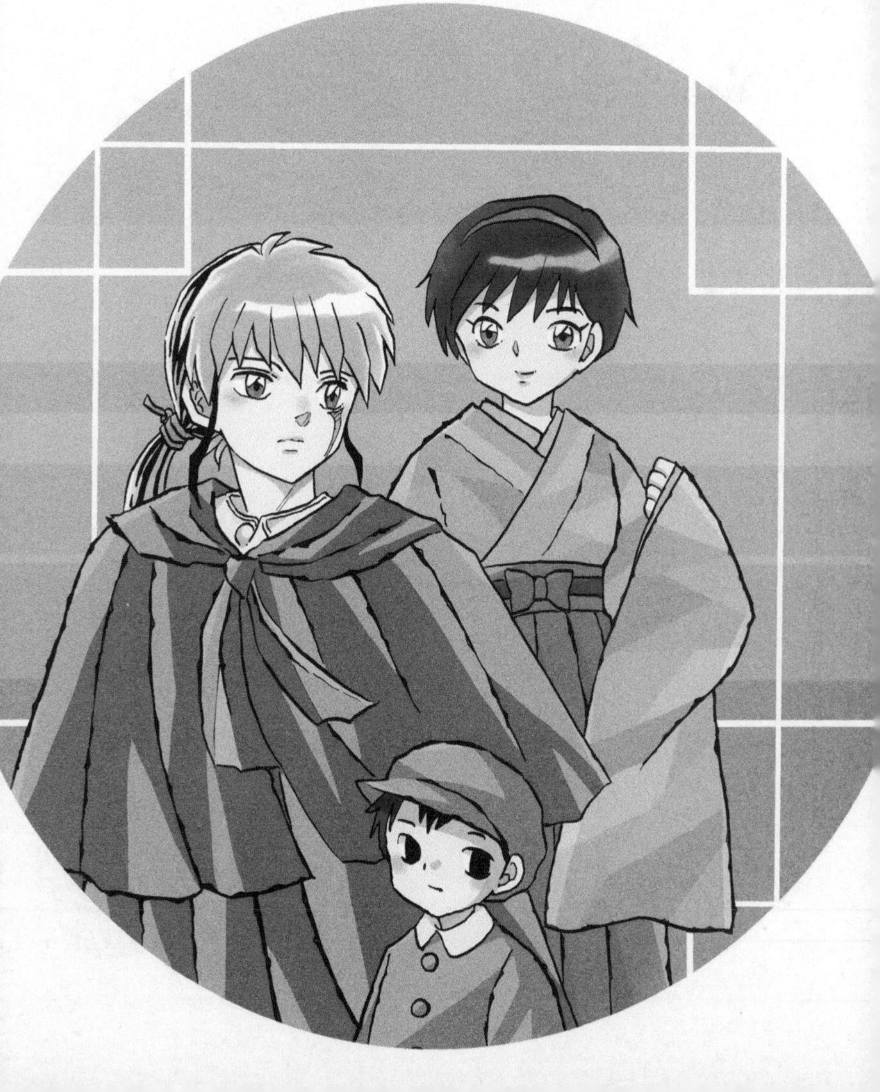

MAO

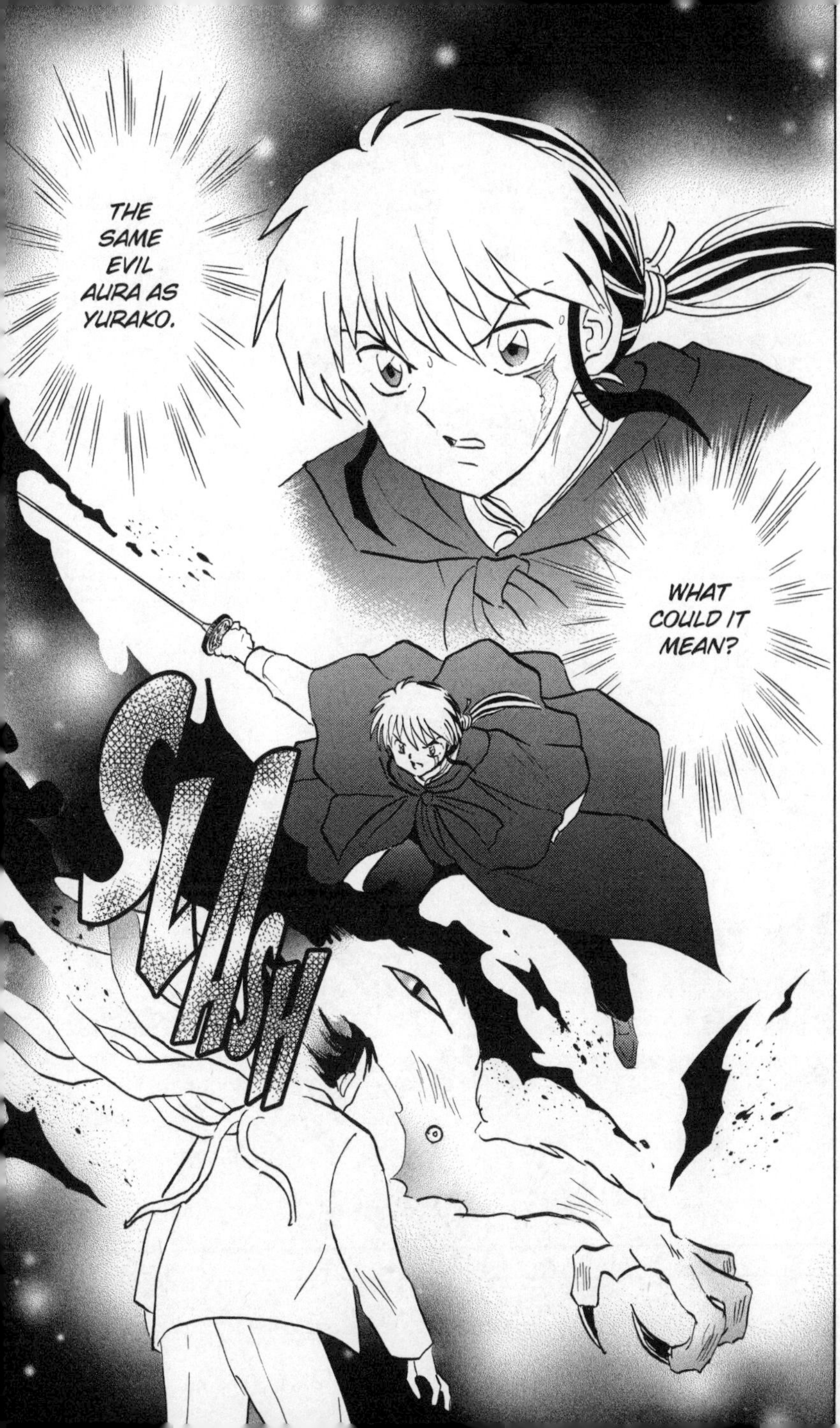
THE SAME EVIL AURA AS YURAKO.
WHAT COULD IT MEAN?
SLASH

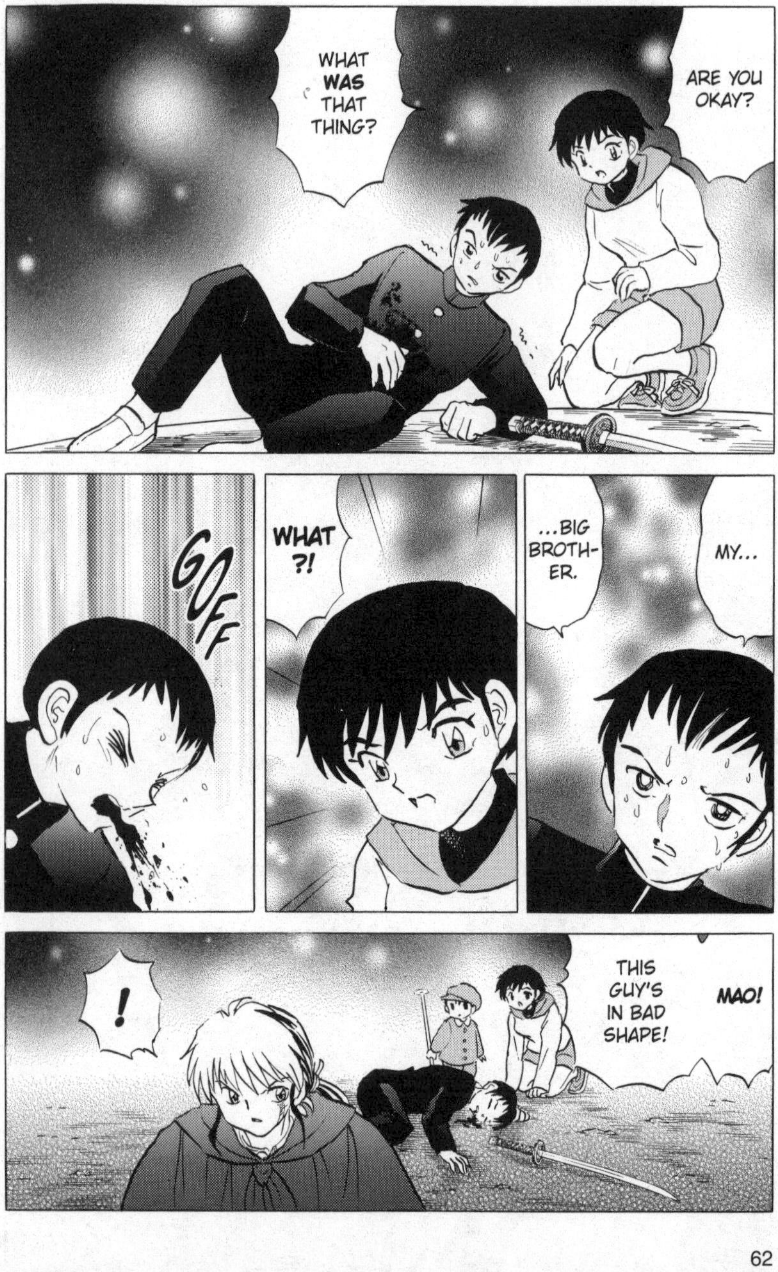
ARE YOU OKAY?
WHAT WAS THAT THING?
MY...
...BIG BROTH-ER.
WHAT ?!
GOFF
MAO!
THIS GUY'S IN BAD SHAPE!
!

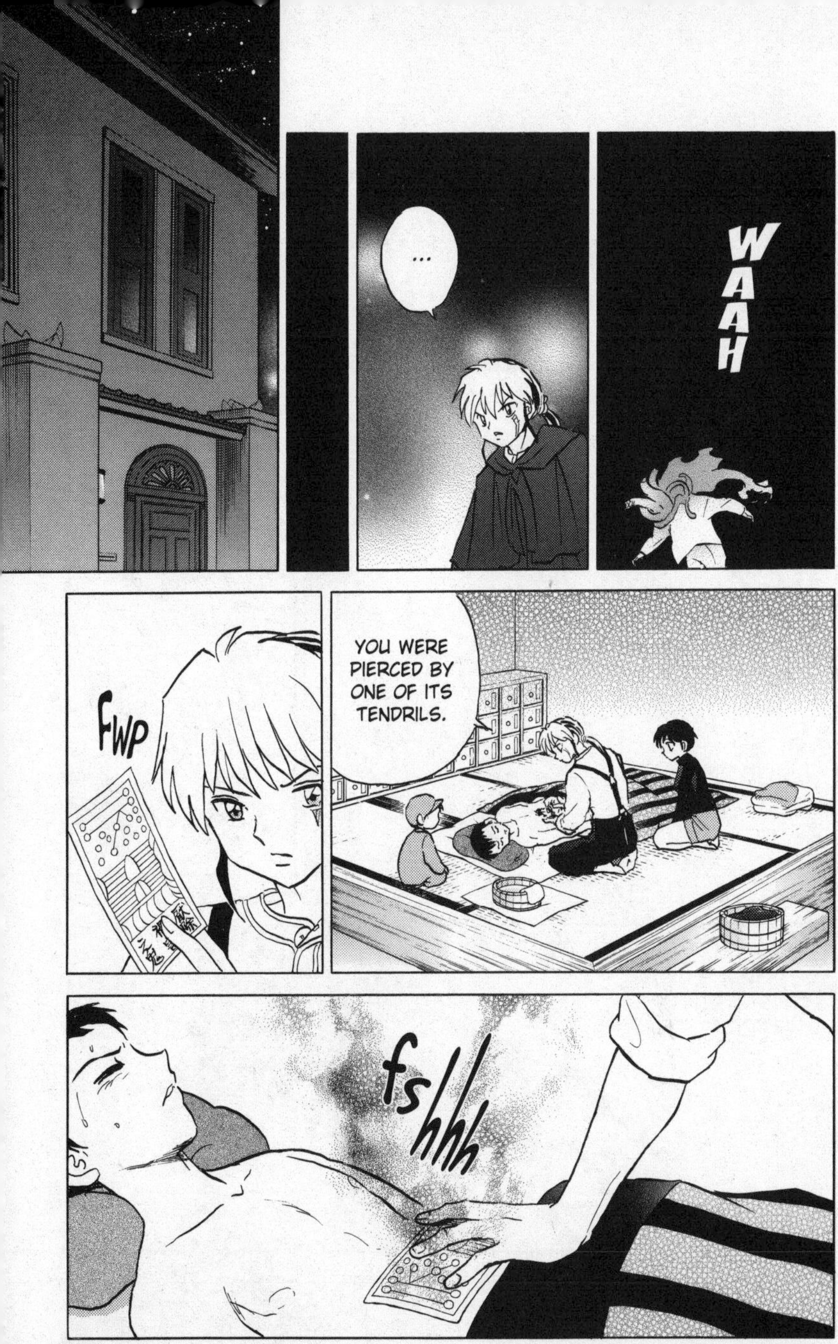
WAAH
...
YOU WERE PIERCED BY ONE OF ITS TENDRILS.
FWP
fshhh

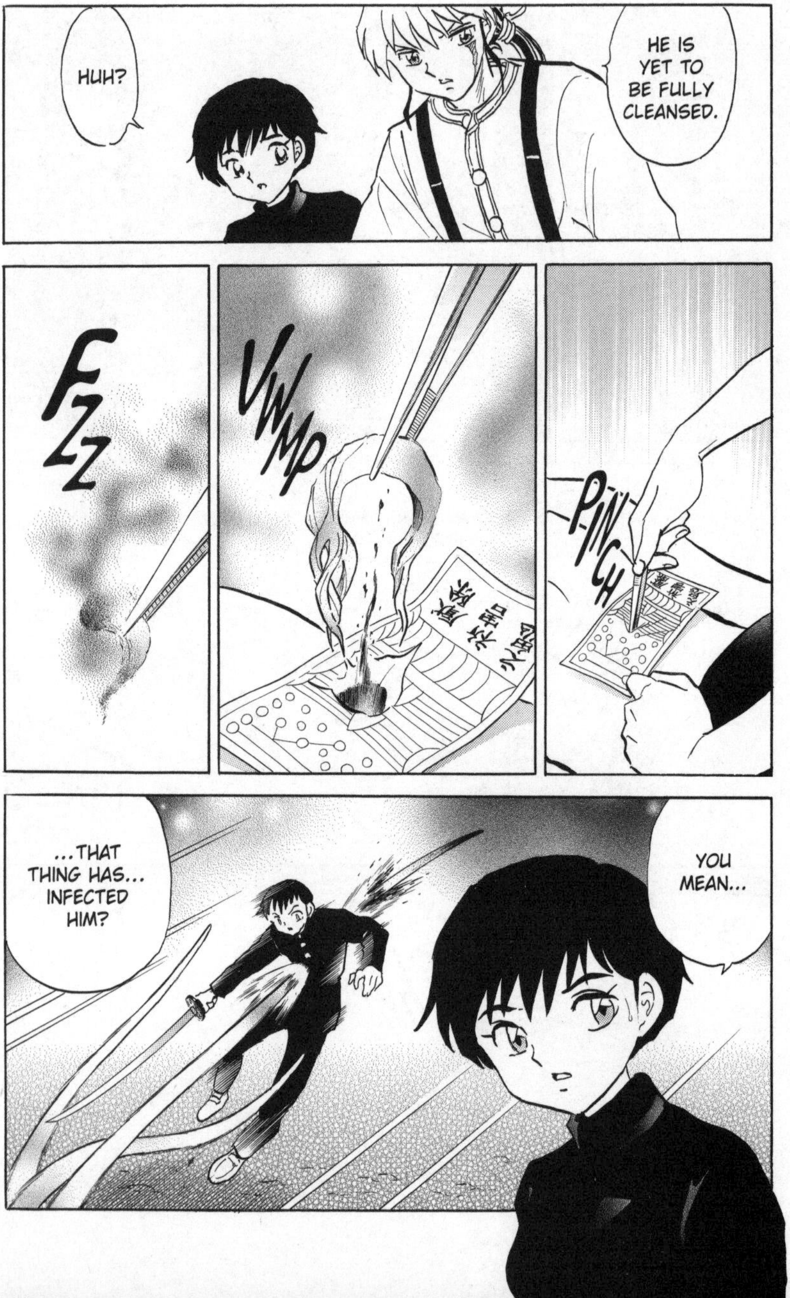
HE IS YET TO BE FULLY CLEANSED.
HUH?
PINCH
VWMP
FZZ
YOU MEAN...
...THAT THING HAS... INFECTED HIM?

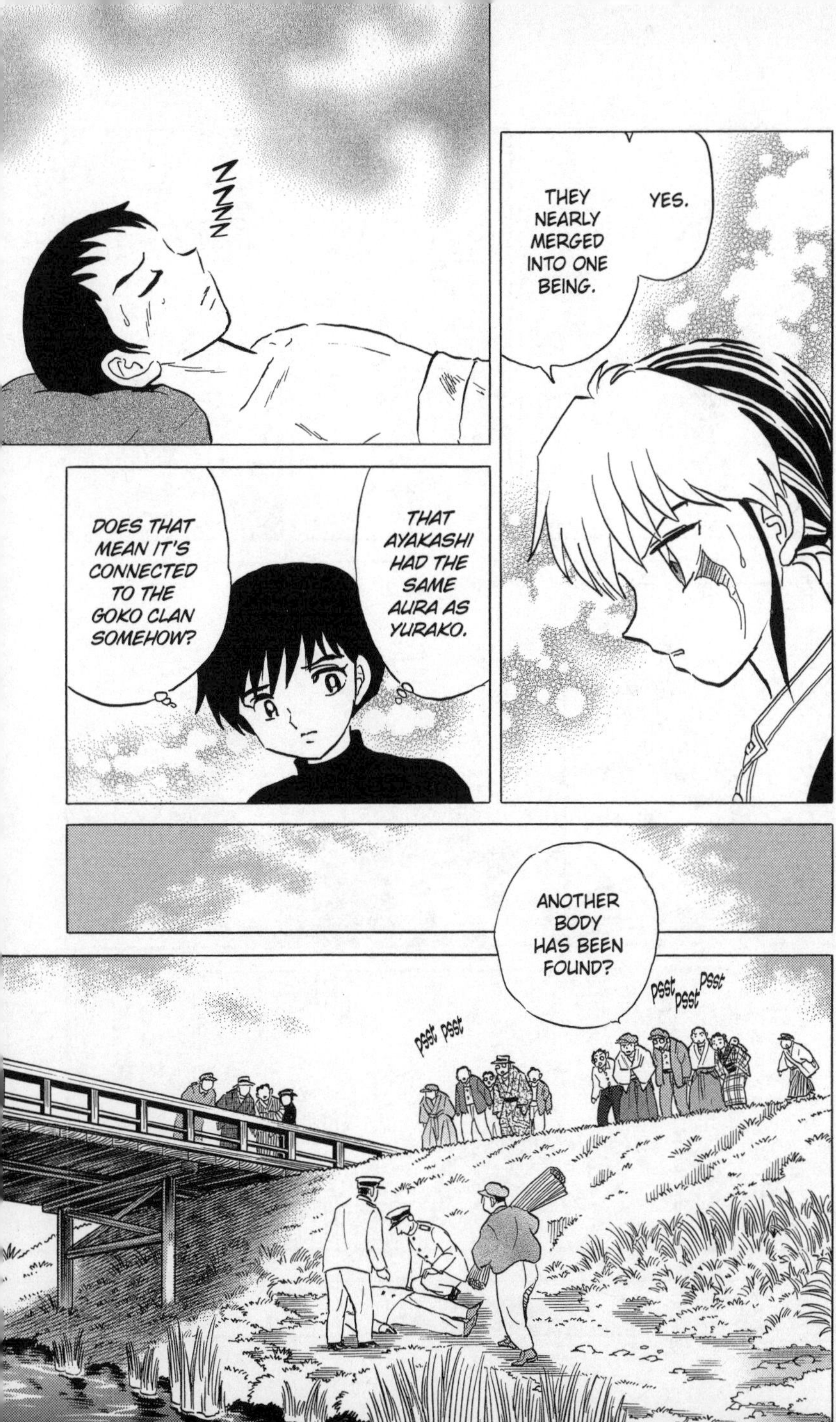
YES.
THEY NEARLY MERGED INTO ONE BEING.
ZZZZ
THAT AYAKASHI HAD THE SAME AURA AS YURAKO.
DOES THAT MEAN IT'S CONNECTED TO THE GOKO CLAN SOMEHOW?
ANOTHER BODY HAS BEEN FOUND?
psst psst psst
psst psst

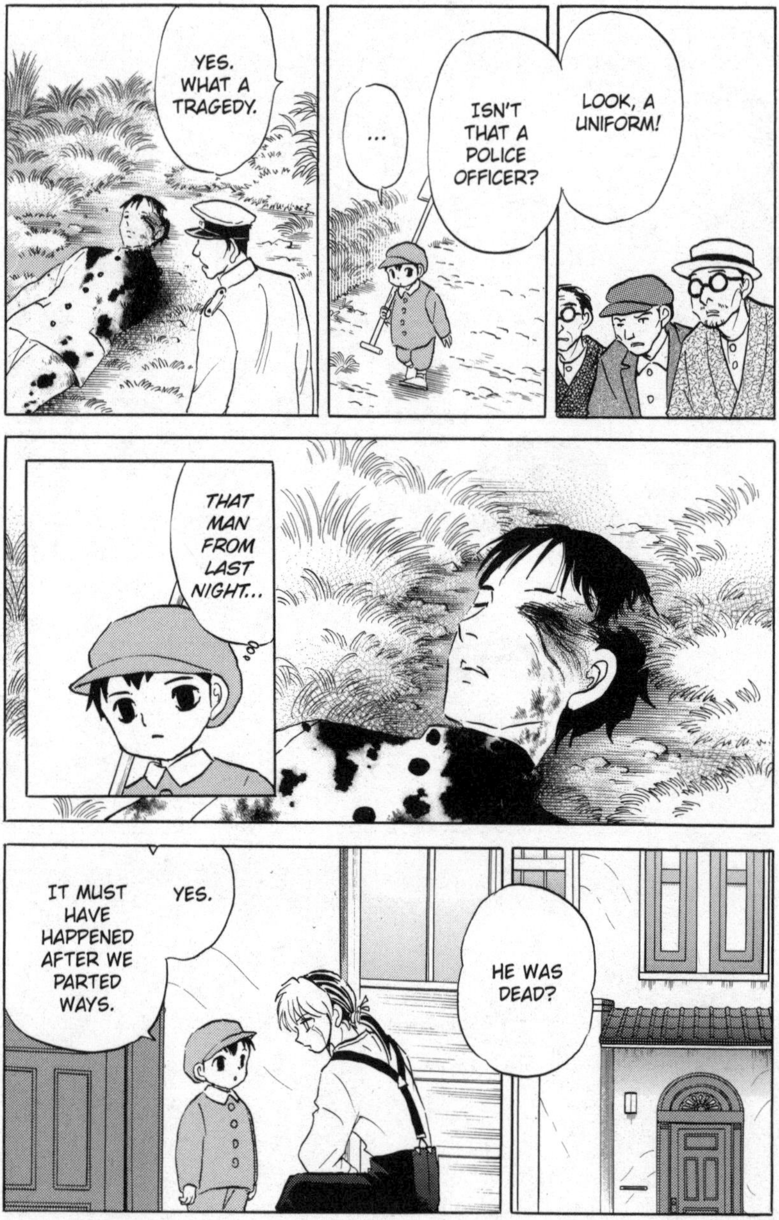
LOOK, A UNIFORM!
ISN'T THAT A POLICE OFFICER?
...
YES. WHAT A TRAGEDY.
THAT MAN FROM LAST NIGHT...
HE WAS DEAD?
YES.
IT MUST HAVE HAPPENED AFTER WE PARTED WAYS.

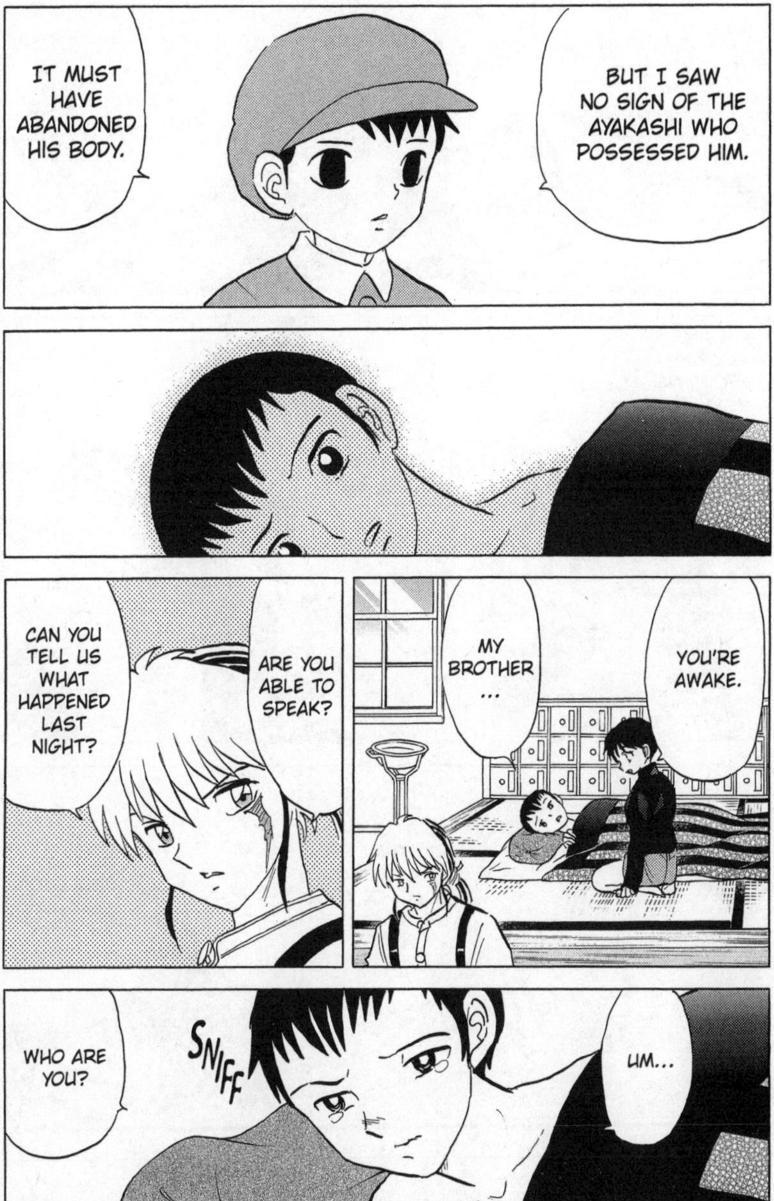
BUT I SAW NO SIGN OF THE AYAKASHI WHO POSSESSED HIM.
IT MUST HAVE ABANDONED HIS BODY.
YOU'RE AWAKE.
MY BROTHER ...
ARE YOU ABLE TO SPEAK?
CAN YOU TELL US WHAT HAPPENED LAST NIGHT?
UM...
SNIFF
WHO ARE YOU?

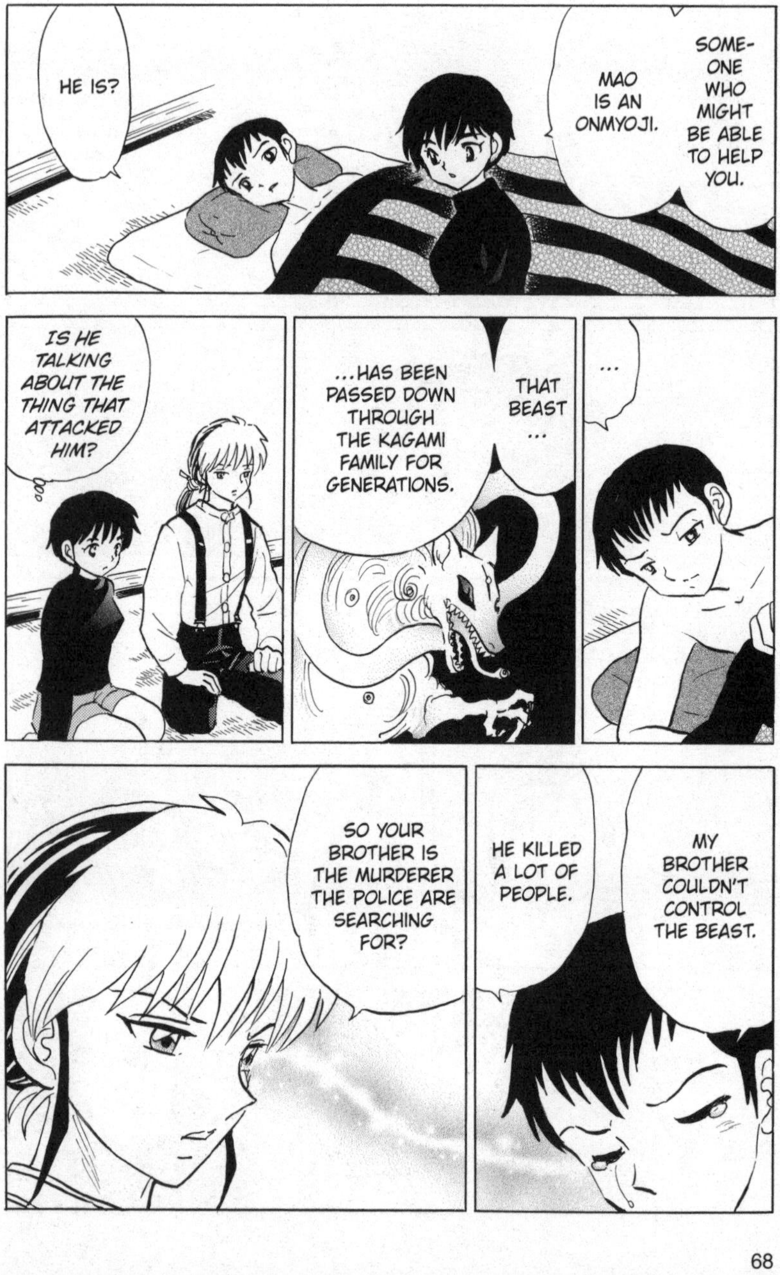
SOMEONE WHO MIGHT BE ABLE TO HELP YOU.
MAO IS AN ONMYOJI.
HE IS?
...
THAT BEAST ...
...HAS BEEN PASSED DOWN THROUGH THE KAGAMI FAMILY FOR GENERATIONS.
IS HE TALKING ABOUT THE THING THAT ATTACKED HIM?
MY BROTHER COULDN'T CONTROL THE BEAST.
HE KILLED A LOT OF PEOPLE.
SO YOUR BROTHER IS THE MURDERER THE POLICE ARE SEARCHING FOR?

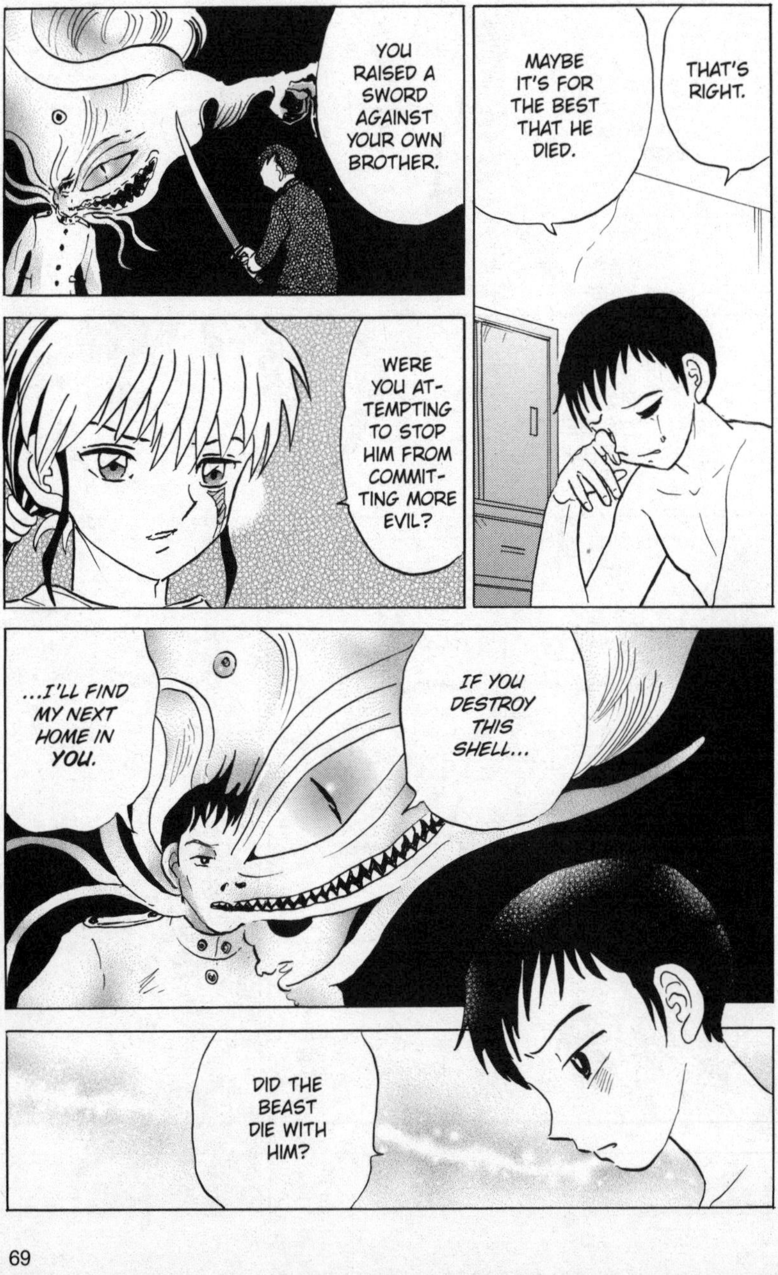
THAT'S RIGHT.
MAYBE IT'S FOR THE BEST THAT HE DIED.
YOU RAISED A SWORD AGAINST YOUR OWN BROTHER.
WERE YOU AT-TEMPTING TO STOP HIM FROM COMMIT-TING MORE EVIL?
IF YOU DESTROY THIS SHELL...
...I'LL FIND MY NEXT HOME IN YOU.
DID THE BEAST DIE WITH HIM?

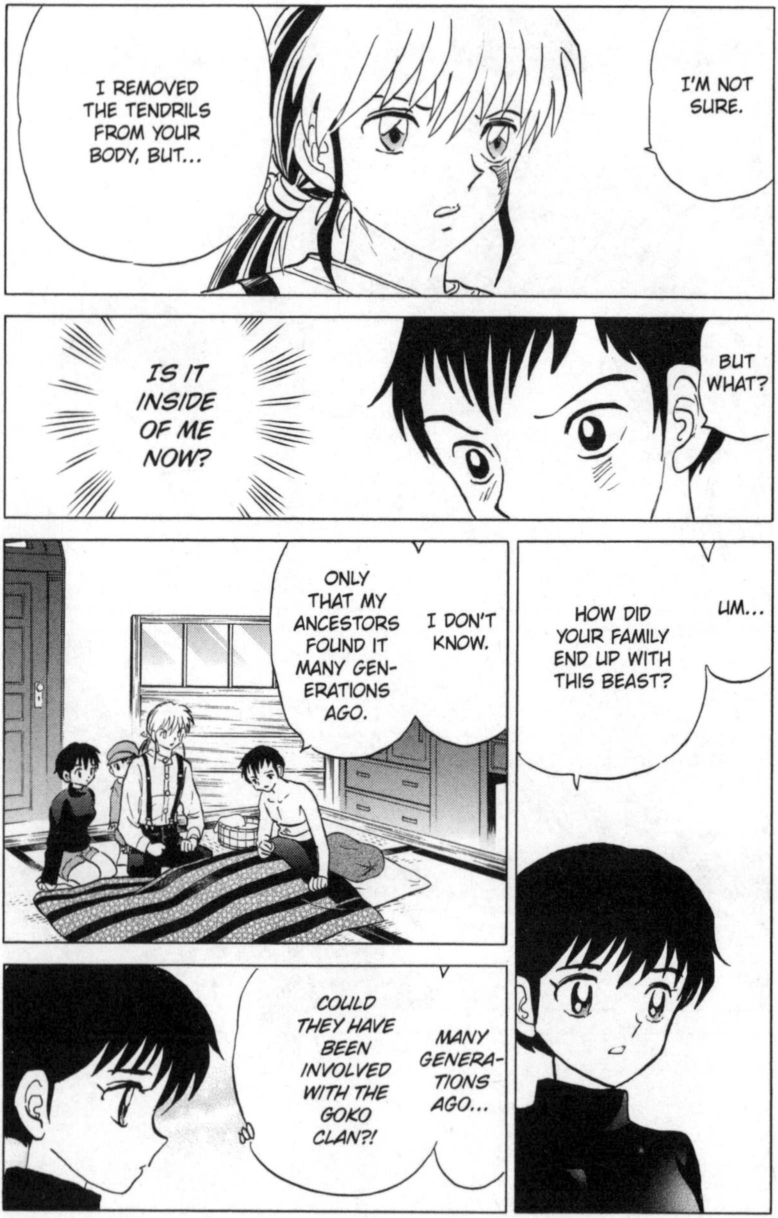
I'M NOT SURE.
I REMOVED THE TENDRILS FROM YOUR BODY, BUT...
BUT WHAT?
IS IT INSIDE OF ME NOW?
UM...
HOW DID YOUR FAMILY END UP WITH THIS BEAST?
I DON'T KNOW.
ONLY THAT MY ANCESTORS FOUND IT MANY GEN-ERATIONS AGO.
MANY GENERA-TIONS AGO...
COULD THEY HAVE BEEN INVOLVED WITH THE GOKO CLAN?!

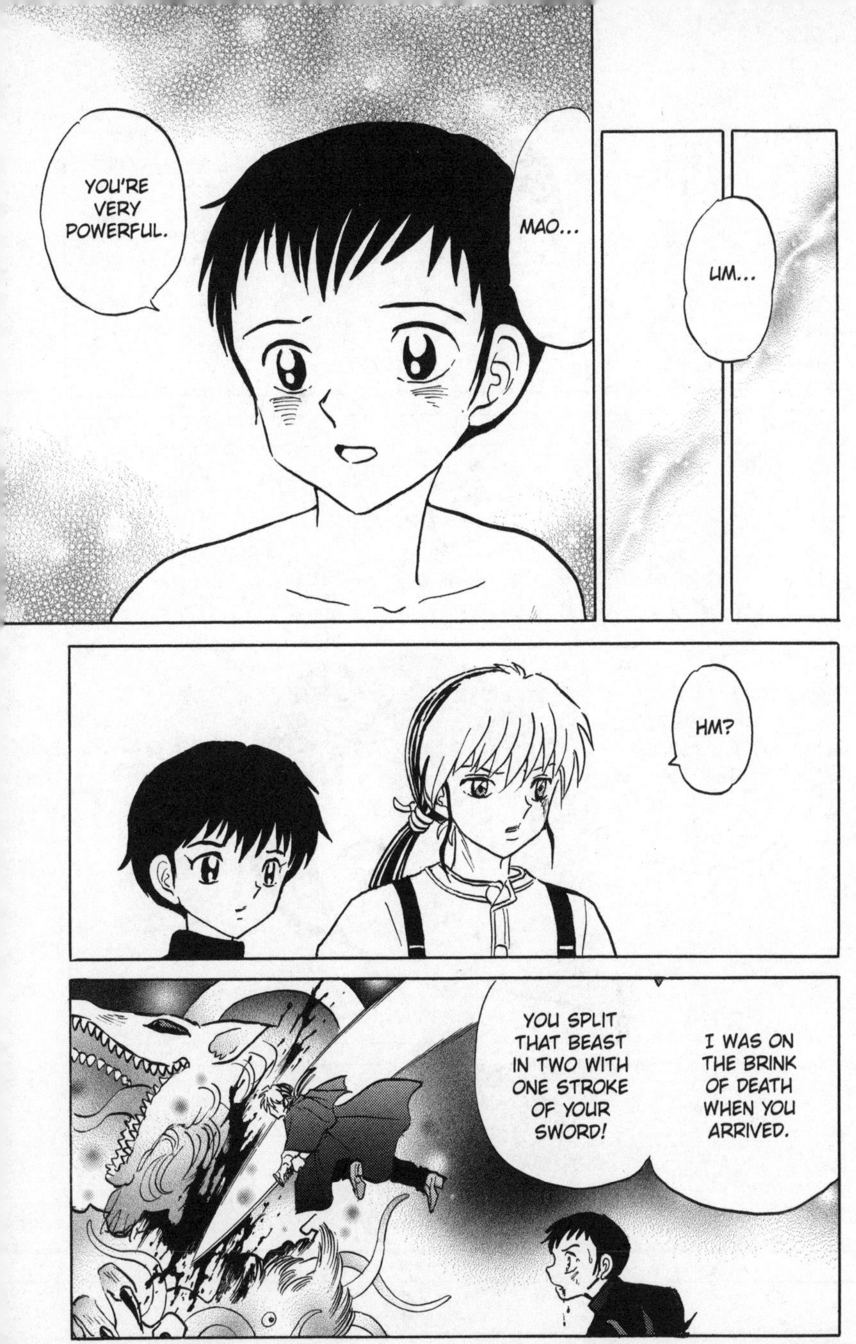
UM...
MAO...
YOU'RE VERY POWERFUL.
HM?
I WAS ON THE BRINK OF DEATH WHEN YOU ARRIVED.
YOU SPLIT THAT BEAST IN TWO WITH ONE STROKE OF YOUR SWORD!

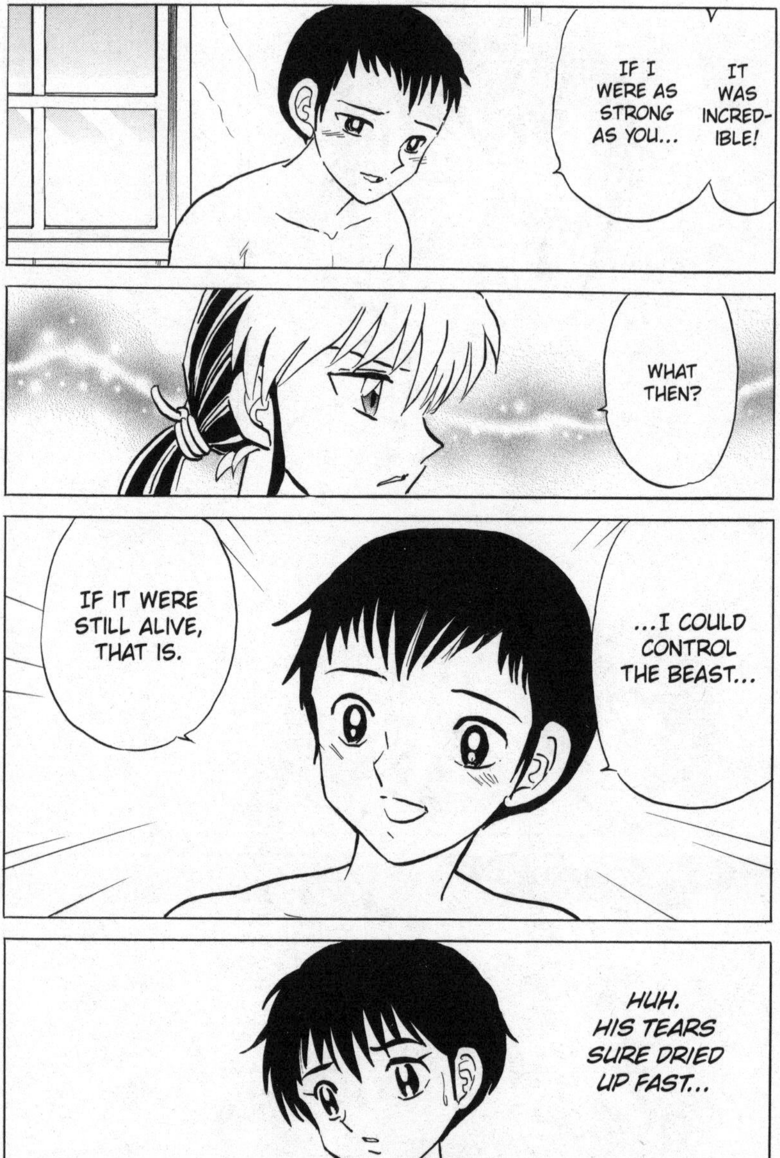
IT WAS INCREDIBLE!
IF I WERE AS STRONG AS YOU...
WHAT THEN?
...I COULD CONTROL THE BEAST...
IF IT WERE STILL ALIVE, THAT IS.
HUH. HIS TEARS SURE DRIED UP FAST...

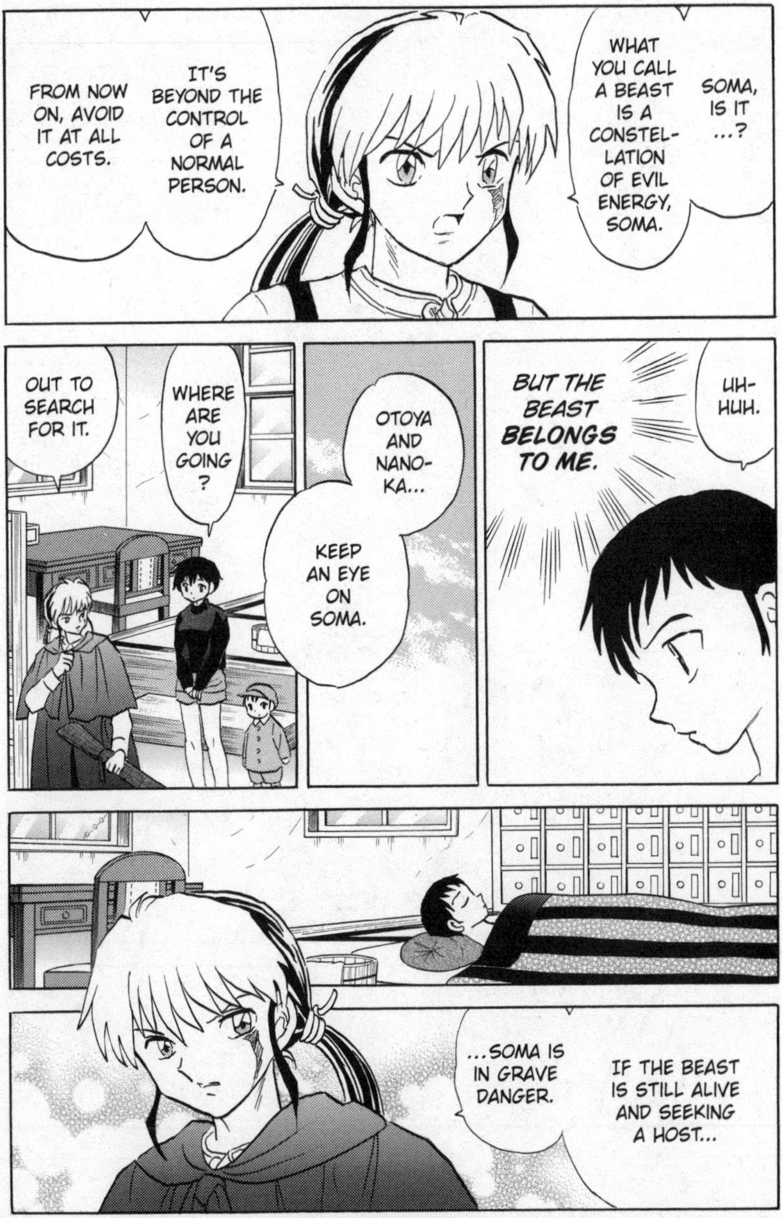
SOMA, IS IT ...?
WHAT YOU CALL A BEAST IS A CONSTELLATION OF EVIL ENERGY, SOMA.
IT'S BEYOND THE CONTROL OF A NORMAL PERSON.
FROM NOW ON, AVOID IT AT ALL COSTS.
UH-HUH.
BUT THE BEAST BELONGS TO ME.
OTOYA AND NANOKA...
KEEP AN EYE ON SOMA.
WHERE ARE YOU GOING?
OUT TO SEARCH FOR IT.
IF THE BEAST IS STILL ALIVE AND SEEKING A HOST...
...SOMA IS IN GRAVE DANGER.

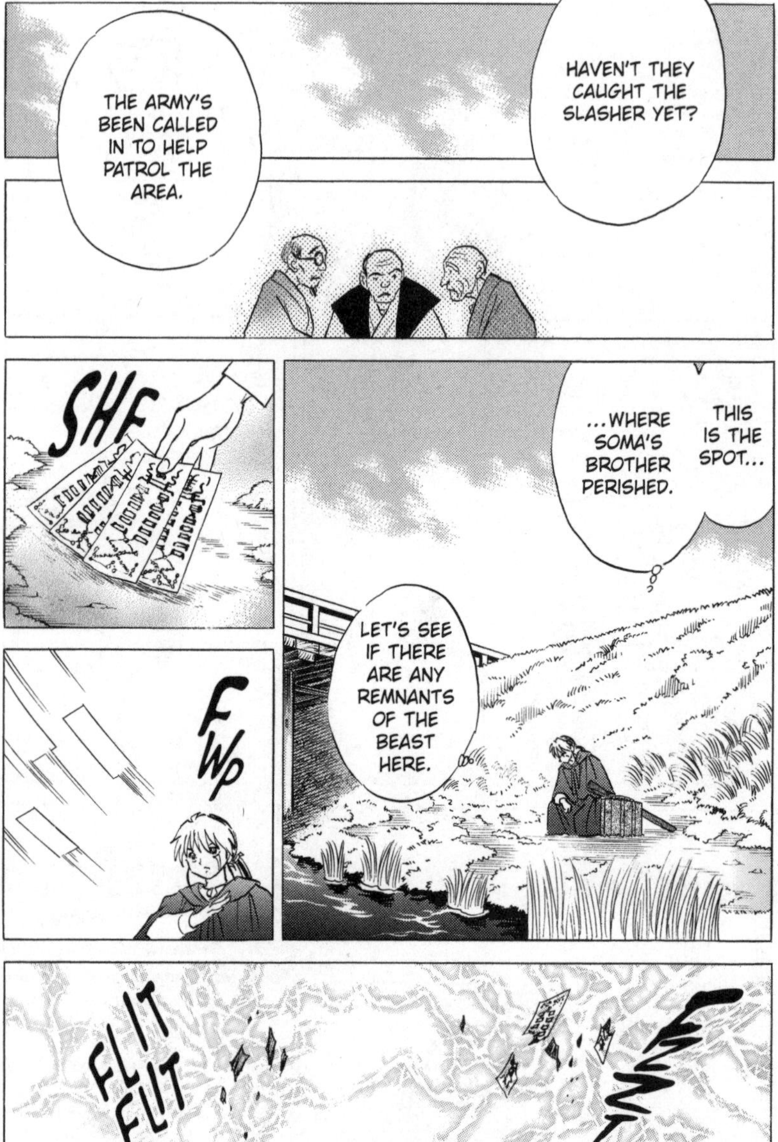
HAVEN'T THEY CAUGHT THE SLASHER YET?
THE ARMY'S BEEN CALLED IN TO HELP PATROL THE AREA.
THIS IS THE SPOT...
...WHERE SOMA'S BROTHER PERISHED.
LET'S SEE IF THERE ARE ANY REMNANTS OF THE BEAST HERE.
SHF
FWP
FLIT FLIT

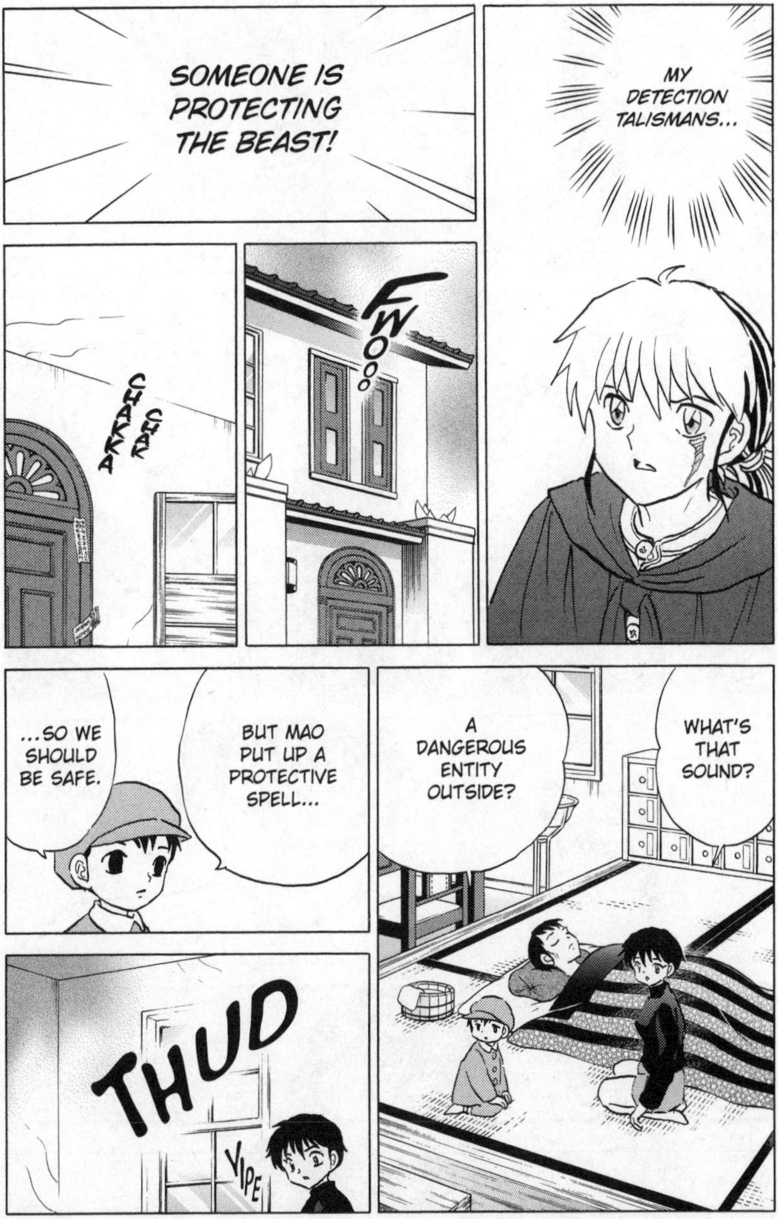
MY DETECTION TALISMANS...
SOMEONE IS PROTECTING THE BEAST!
FWOOOO
CHAKKA CHAK
WHAT'S THAT SOUND?
A DANGEROUS ENTITY OUTSIDE?
BUT MAO PUT UP A PROTECTIVE SPELL...
...SO WE SHOULD BE SAFE.
THUD
YIPE

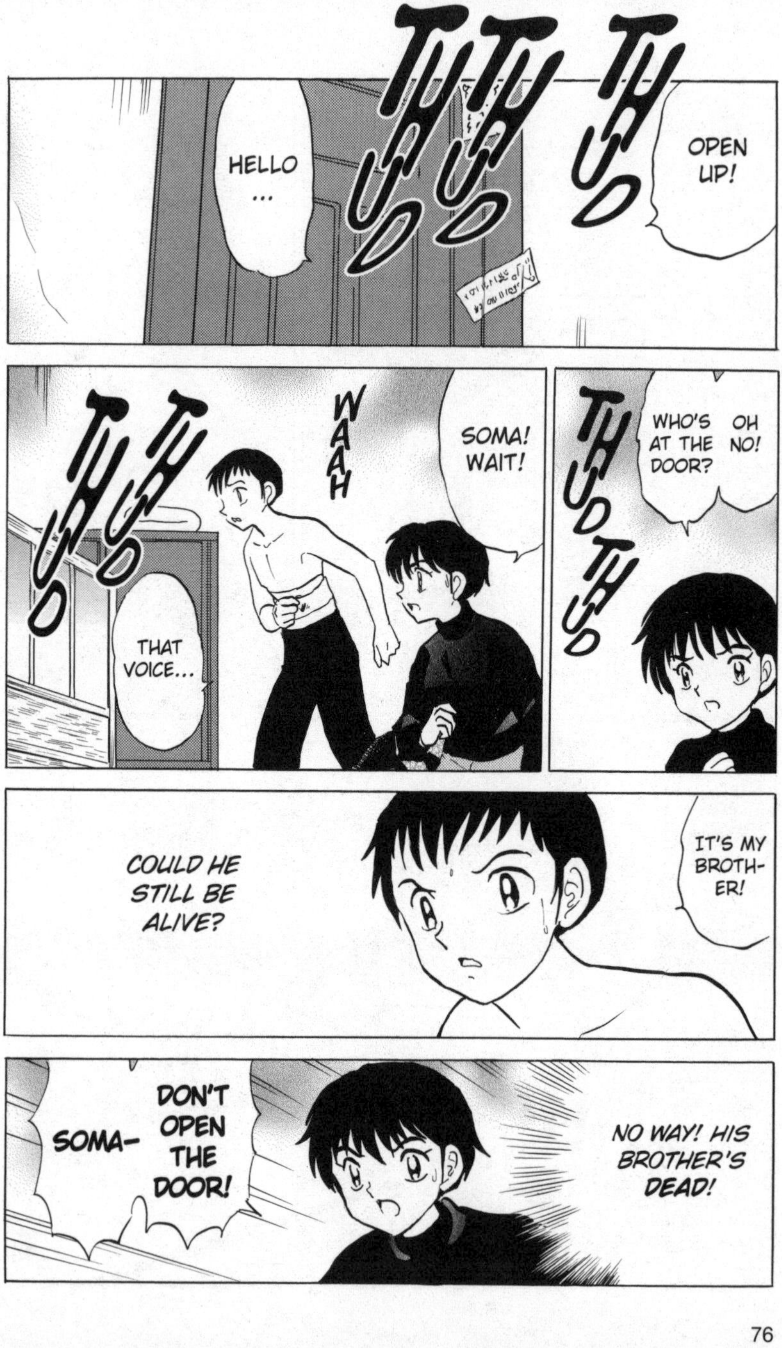
OPEN UP!
THUD
THUD
THUD
HELLO ...
OH NO!
WHO'S AT THE DOOR?
THUD THUD
SOMA! WAIT!
WAAH
THUD
THUD
THAT VOICE...
IT'S MY BROTHER!
COULD HE STILL BE ALIVE?
NO WAY! HIS BROTHER'S DEAD!
SOMA- DON'T OPEN THE DOOR!

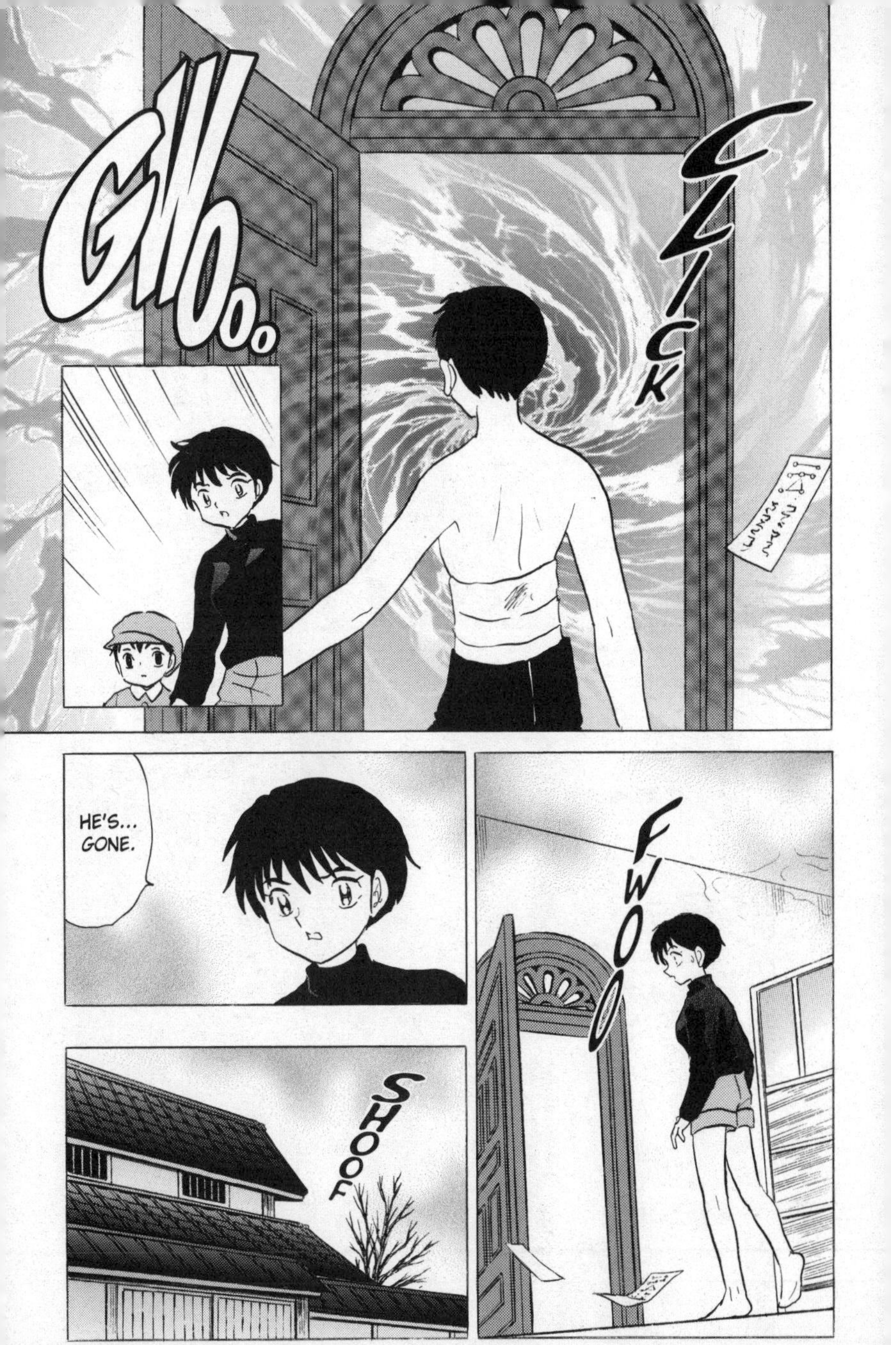
CLICK
GWOOo
FWOO
HE'S... GONE.
SHOOOF

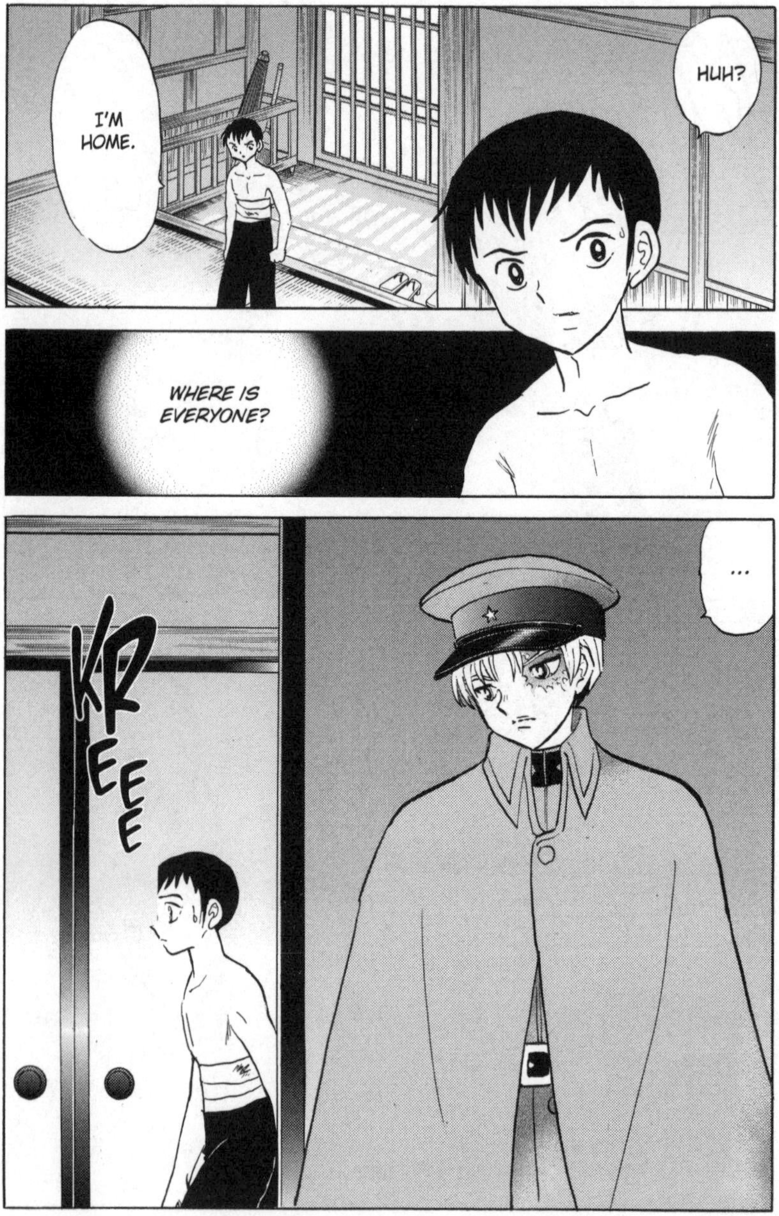
HUH?
I'M HOME.
WHERE IS EVERYONE?
...
KREEEE

Chapter 5:
The Kagami Treasure

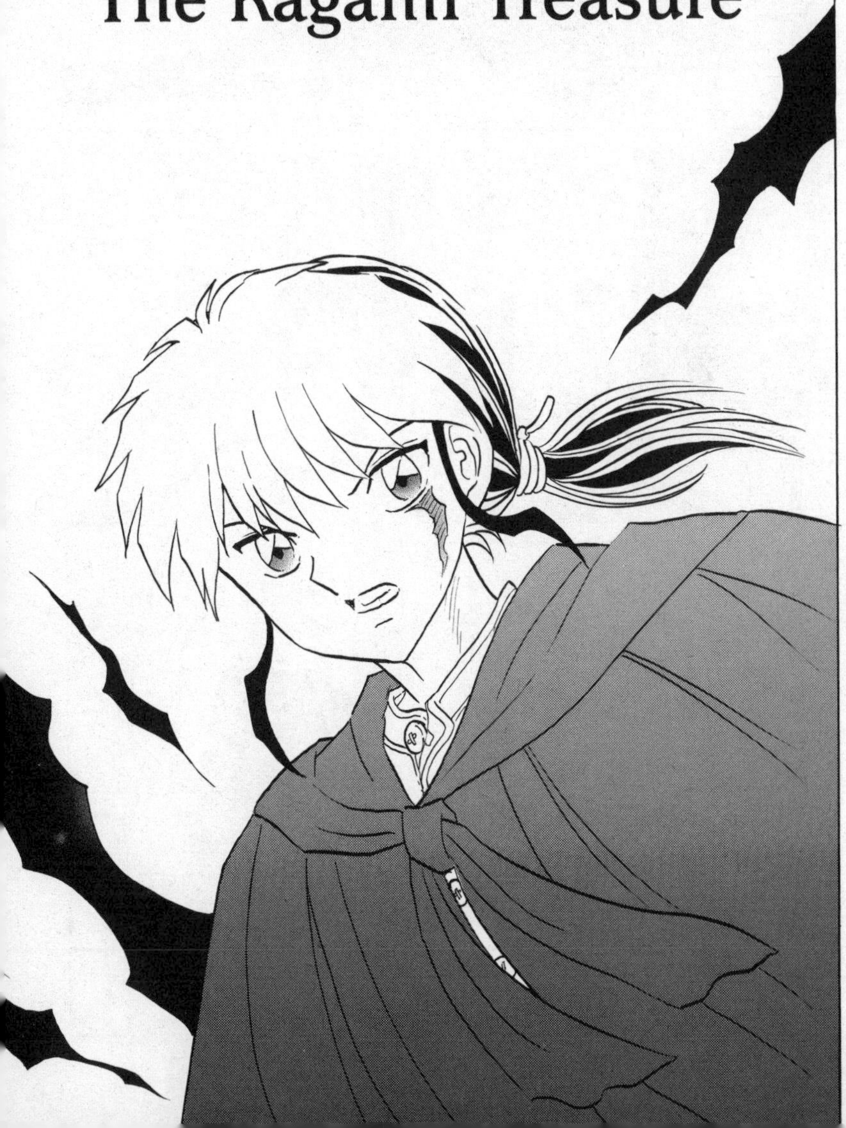

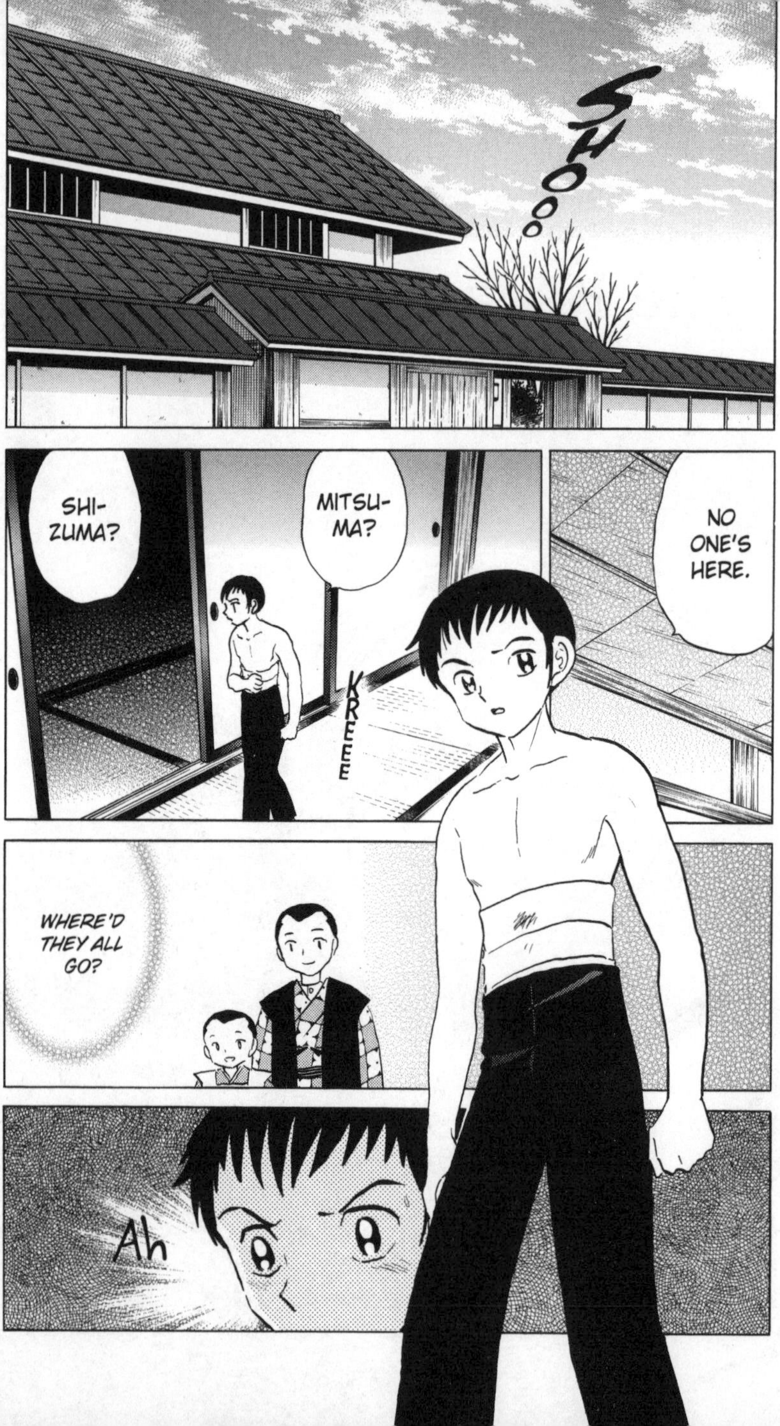
SHOOOO
NO ONE'S HERE.
MITSU-MA?
SHI-ZUMA?
KREEE
WHERE'D THEY ALL GO?
Ah

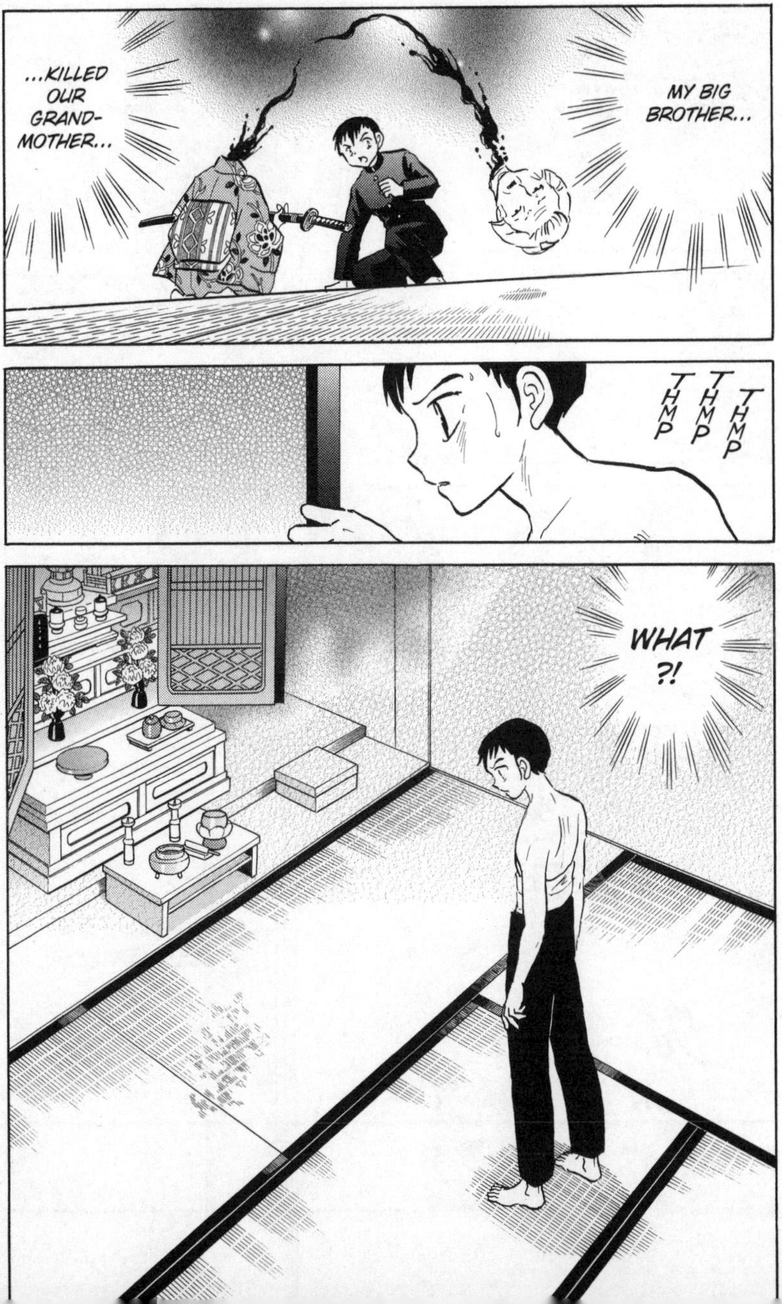
MY BIG BROTHER...
...KILLED OUR GRAND-MOTHER...
THMP THMP THMP
WHAT?!

HER BODY'S GONE.

LIKE NOTHING EVER HAPPENED...

NO! IT WASN'T JUST A DREAM!

THMP
THMP
THMP

OUR TREASURE!

SOMEONE'S BEEN IN OUR HOUSE!

DASH

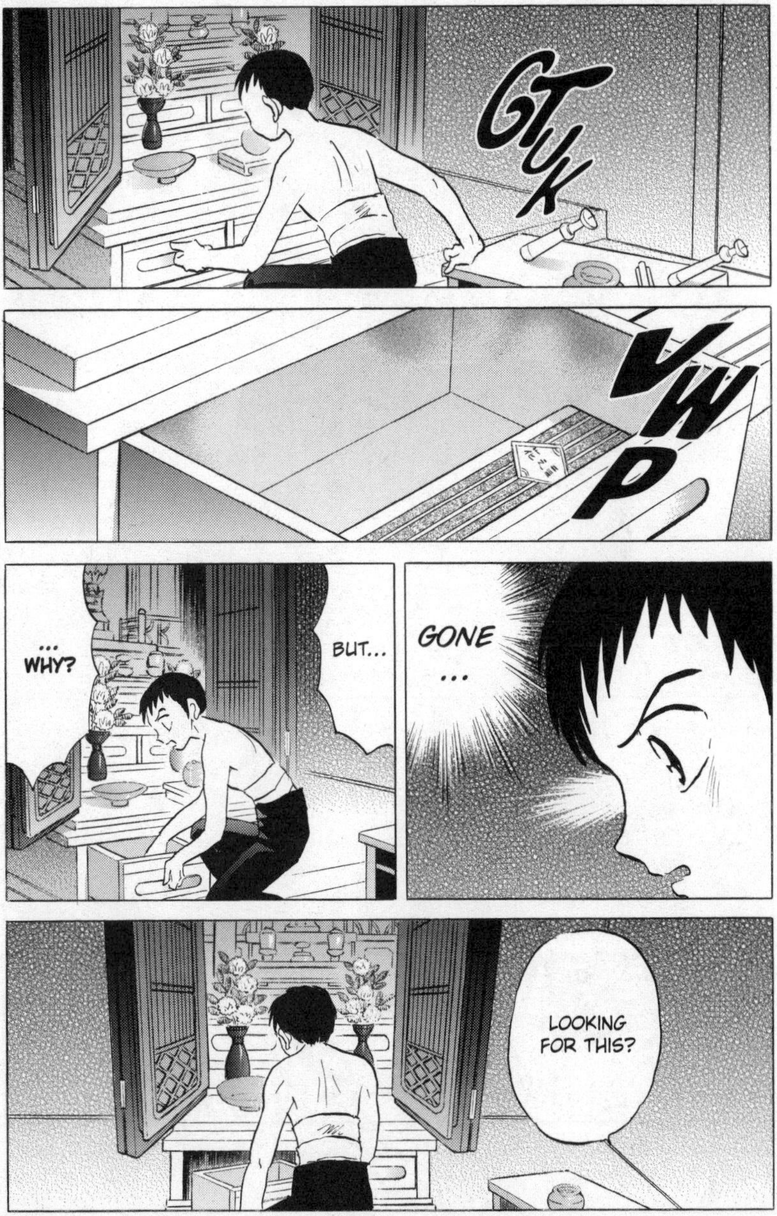
GTUK
VWP
GONE ...
BUT...
... WHY?
LOOKING FOR THIS?

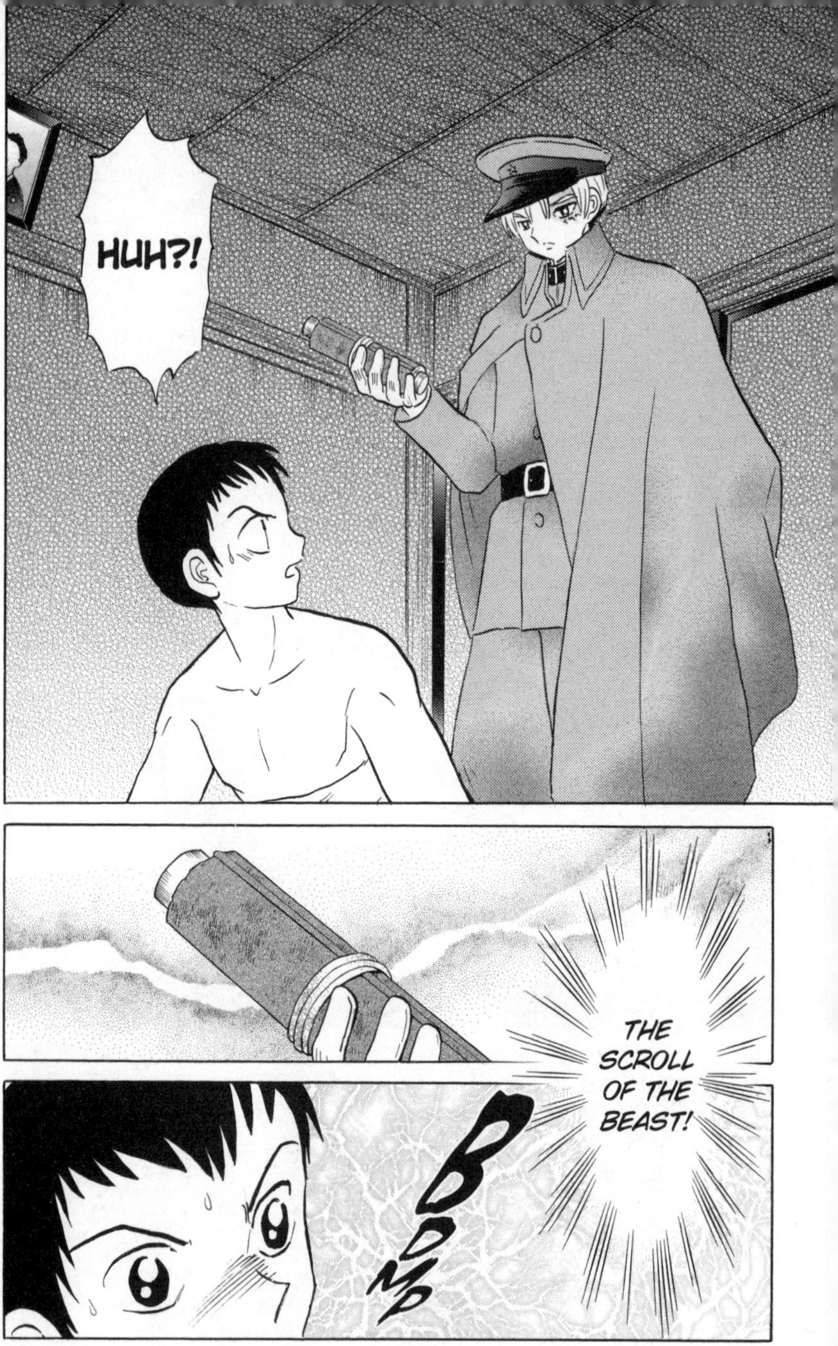
HUH?!
THE SCROLL OF THE BEAST!
BDOMP

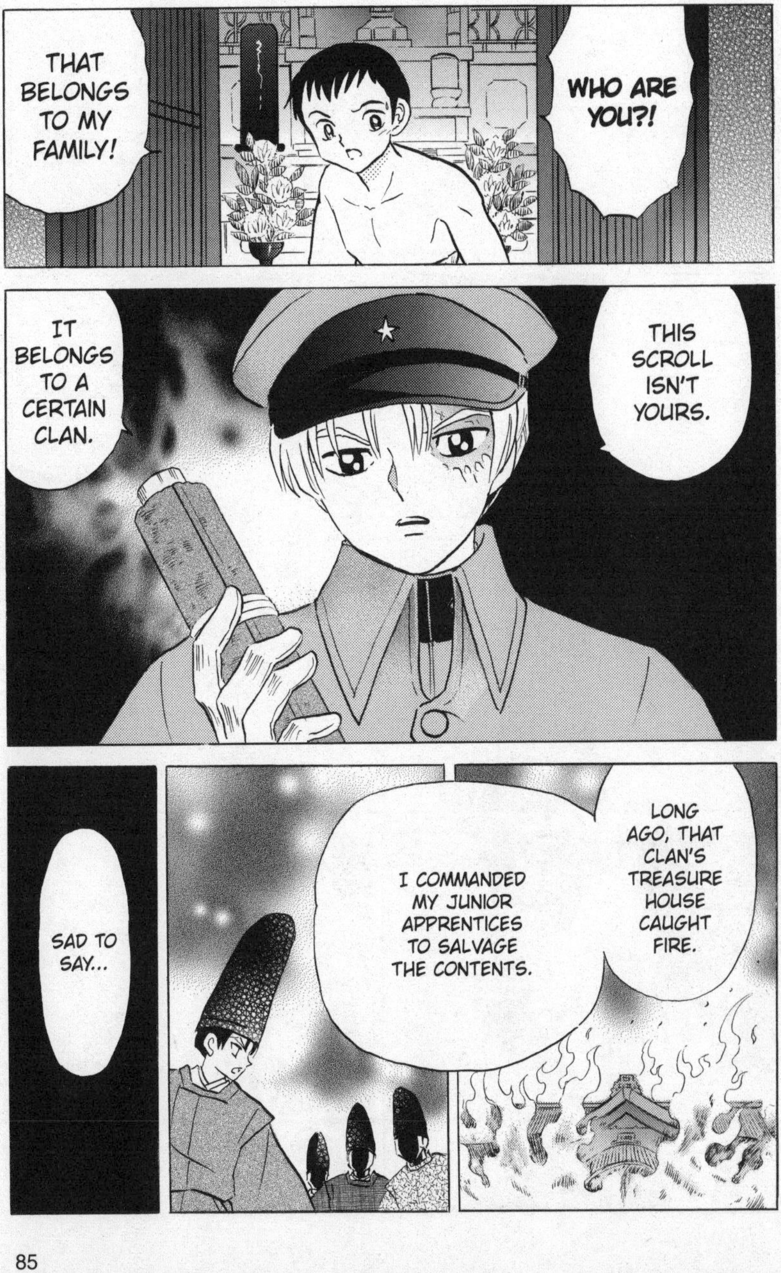
WHO ARE YOU?!
THAT BELONGS TO MY FAMILY!
THIS SCROLL ISN'T YOURS.
IT BELONGS TO A CERTAIN CLAN.
LONG AGO, THAT CLAN'S TREASURE HOUSE CAUGHT FIRE.
I COMMANDED MY JUNIOR APPRENTICES TO SALVAGE THE CONTENTS.
SAD TO SAY...

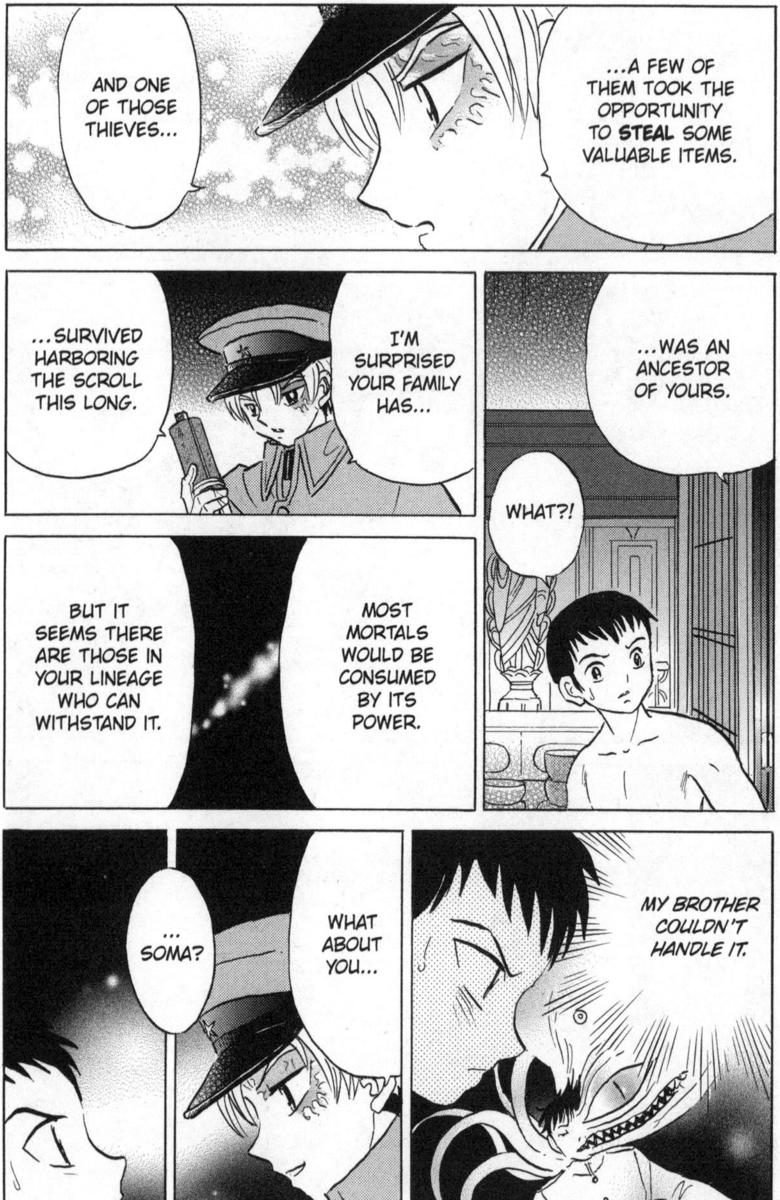
...A FEW OF THEM TOOK THE OPPORTUNITY TO **STEAL** SOME VALUABLE ITEMS.
AND ONE OF THOSE THIEVES...
...WAS AN ANCESTOR OF YOURS.
WHAT?!
I'M SURPRISED YOUR FAMILY HAS...
...SURVIVED HARBORING THE SCROLL THIS LONG.
MOST MORTALS WOULD BE CONSUMED BY ITS POWER.
BUT IT SEEMS THERE ARE THOSE IN YOUR LINEAGE WHO CAN WITHSTAND IT.
MY BROTHER COULDN'T HANDLE IT.
WHAT ABOUT YOU...
... SOMA?

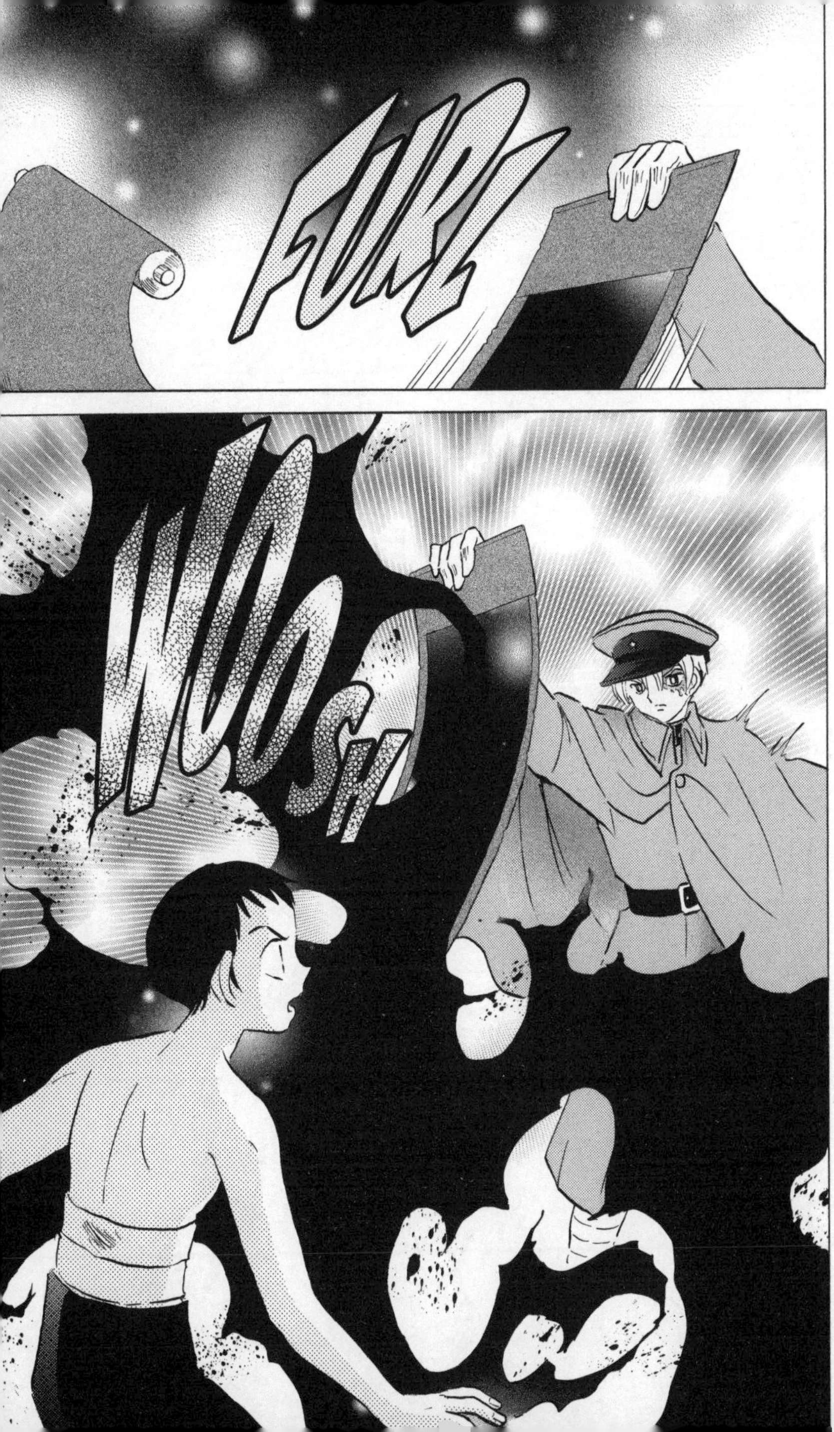
FURL
WOOSH

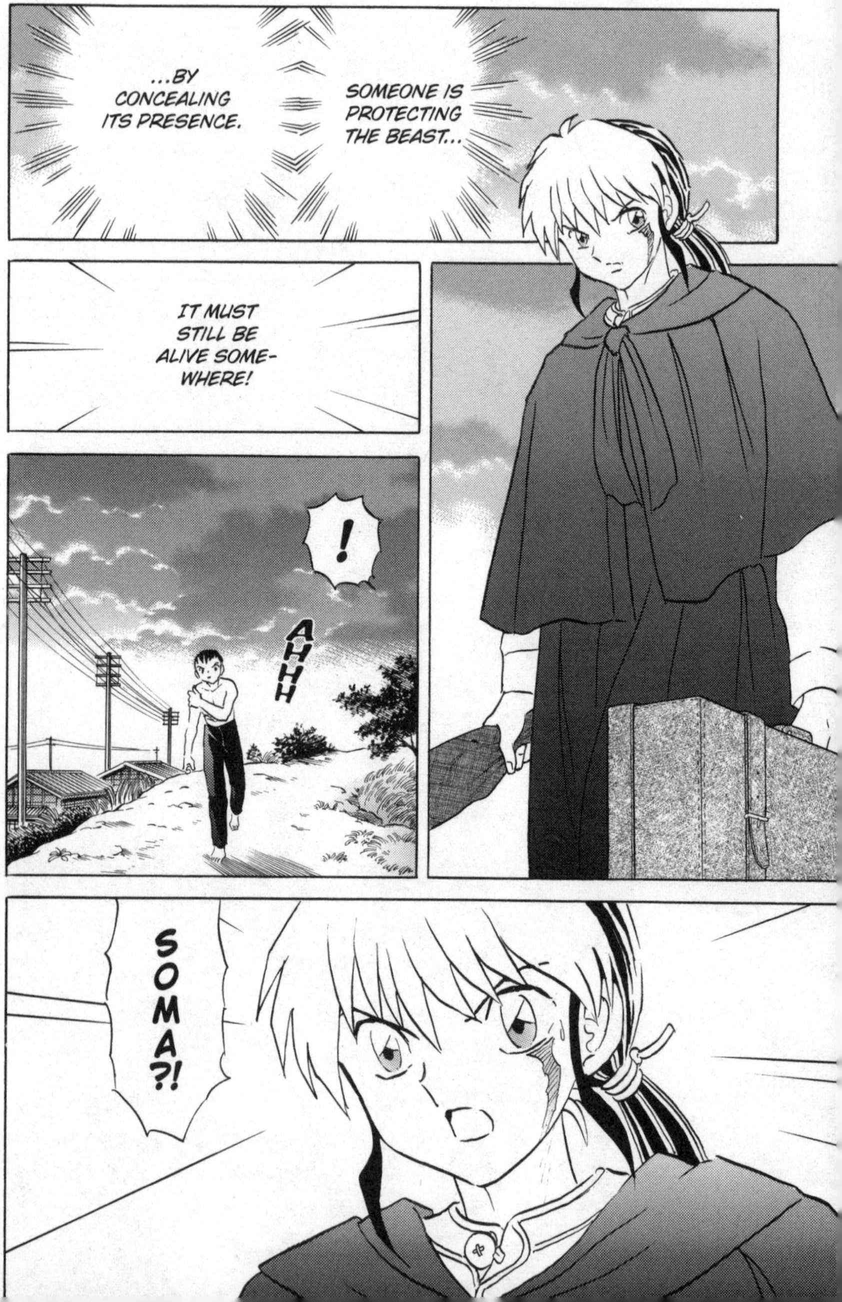
SOMEONE IS PROTECTING THE BEAST...
...BY CONCEALING ITS PRESENCE.
IT MUST STILL BE ALIVE SOME-WHERE!
!
AHHHH
SOMA?!

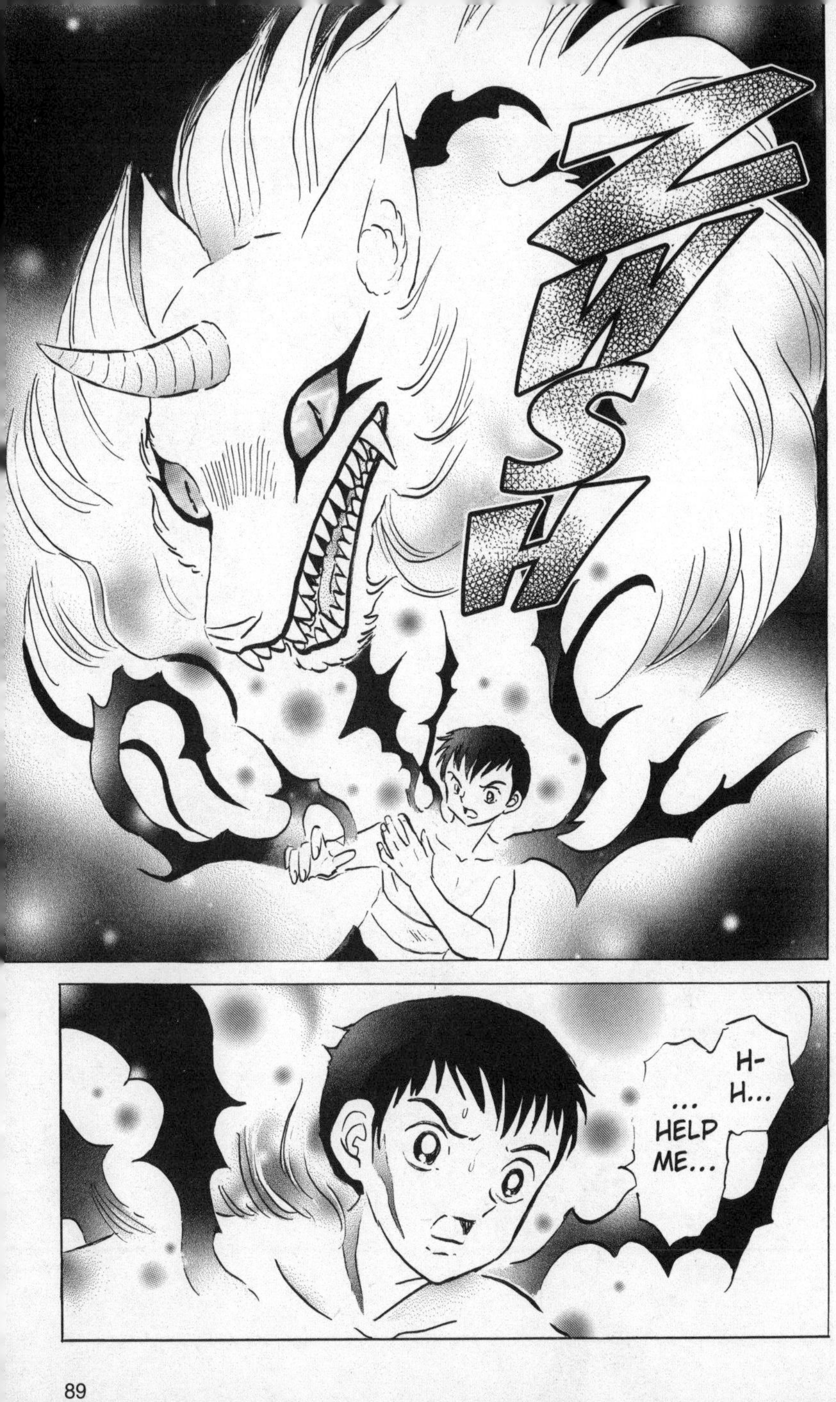
WHSH
H-H...
...HELP ME...

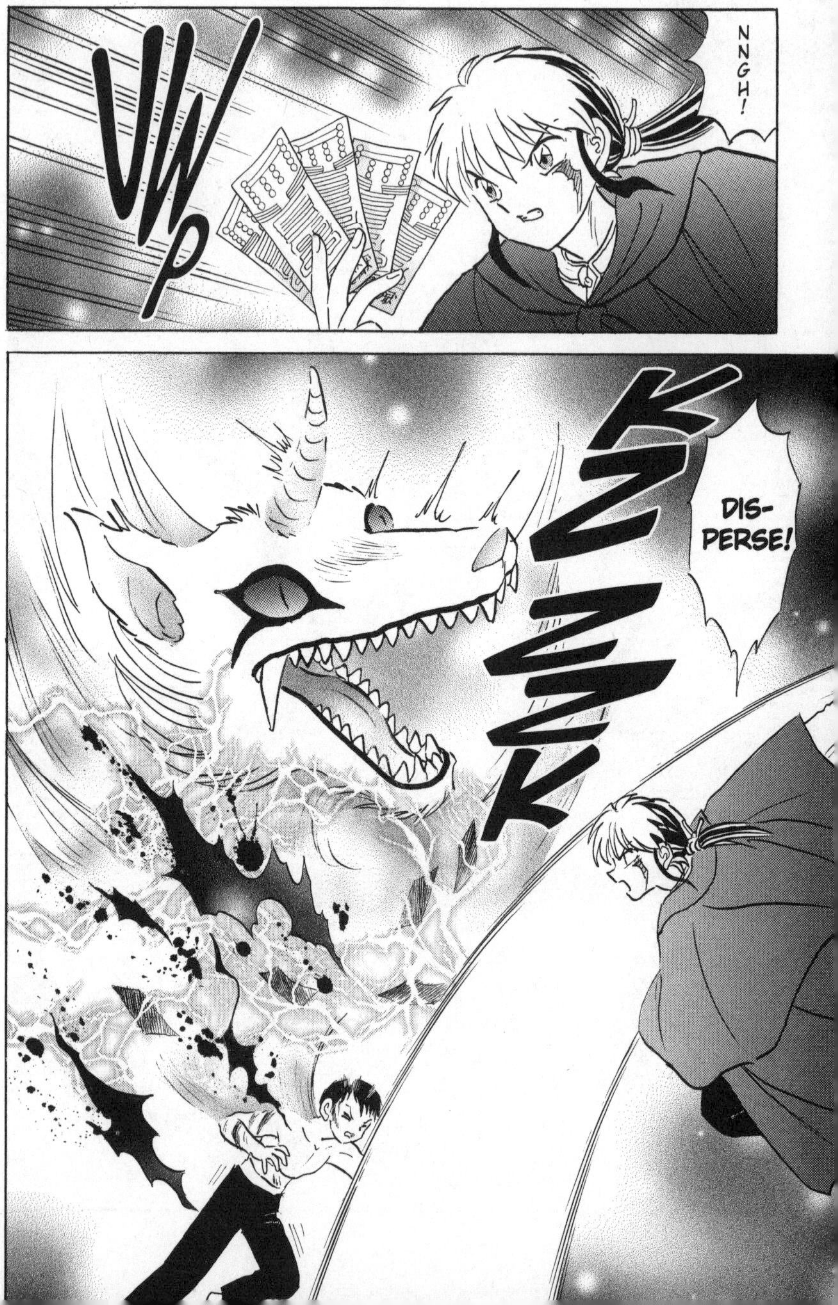
NNGH!
VWP
DIS-
PERSE!
KSSSSK

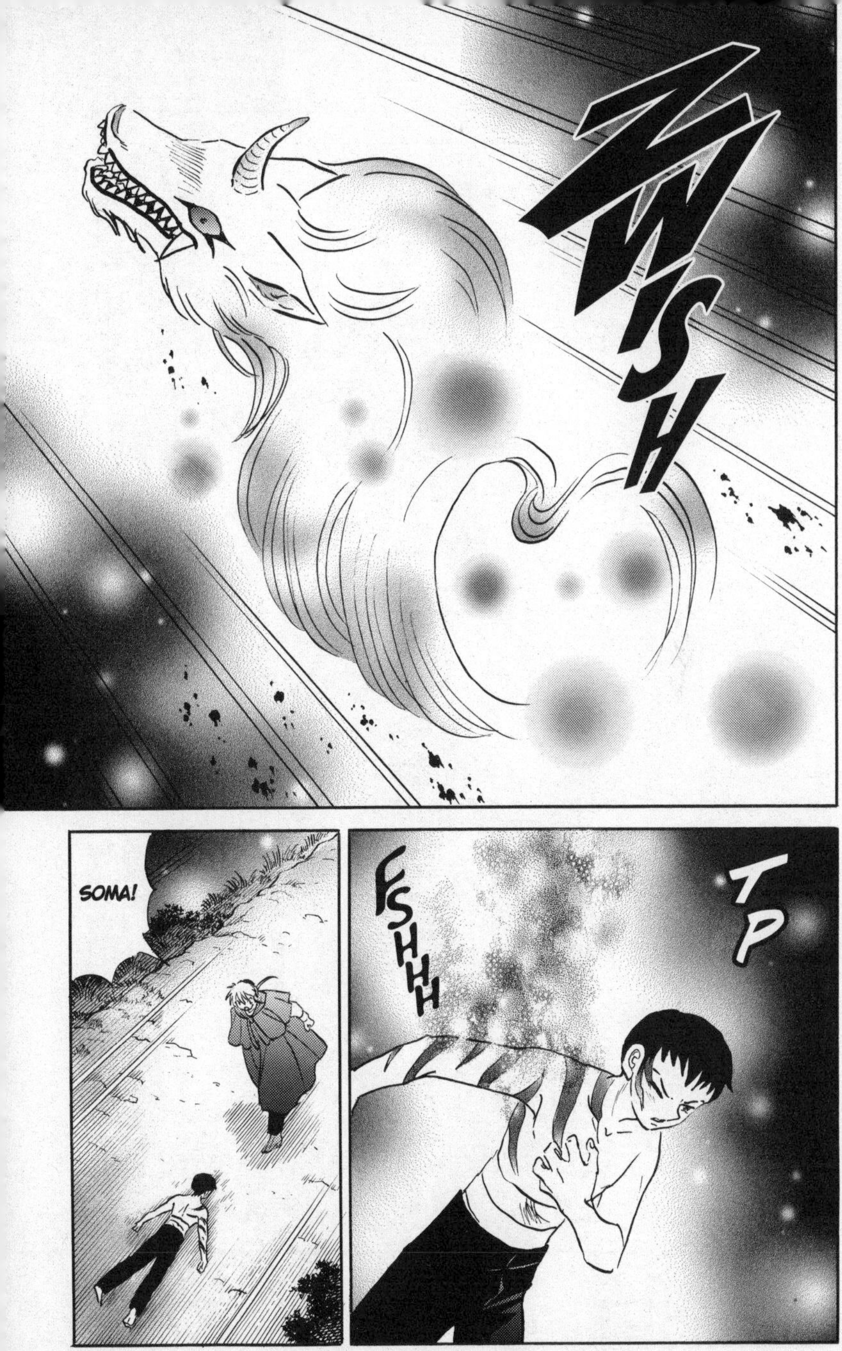
WHSH
TP
FSHHH
SOMA!

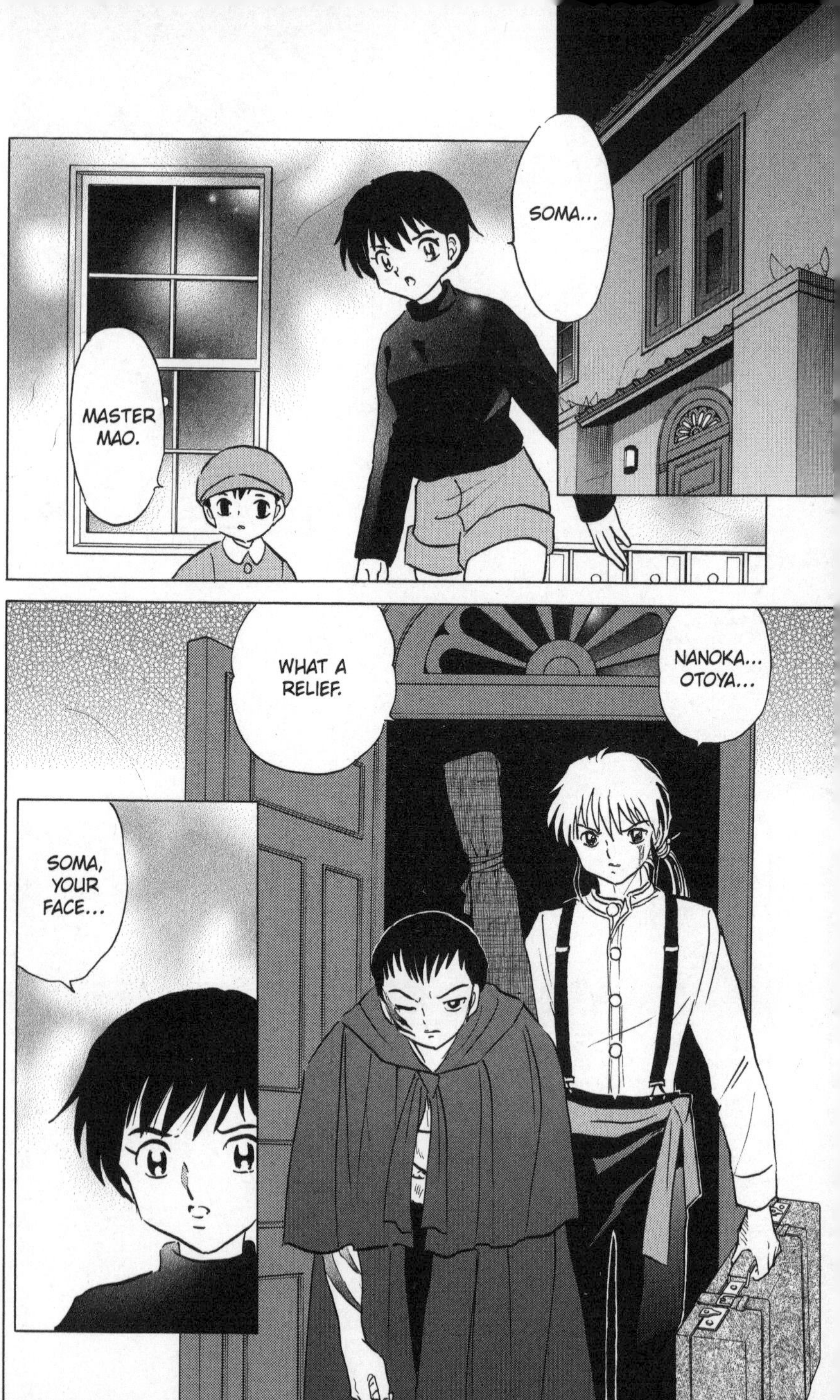
SOMA...
MASTER MAO.
NANOKA... OTOYA...
WHAT A RELIEF.
SOMA, YOUR FACE...

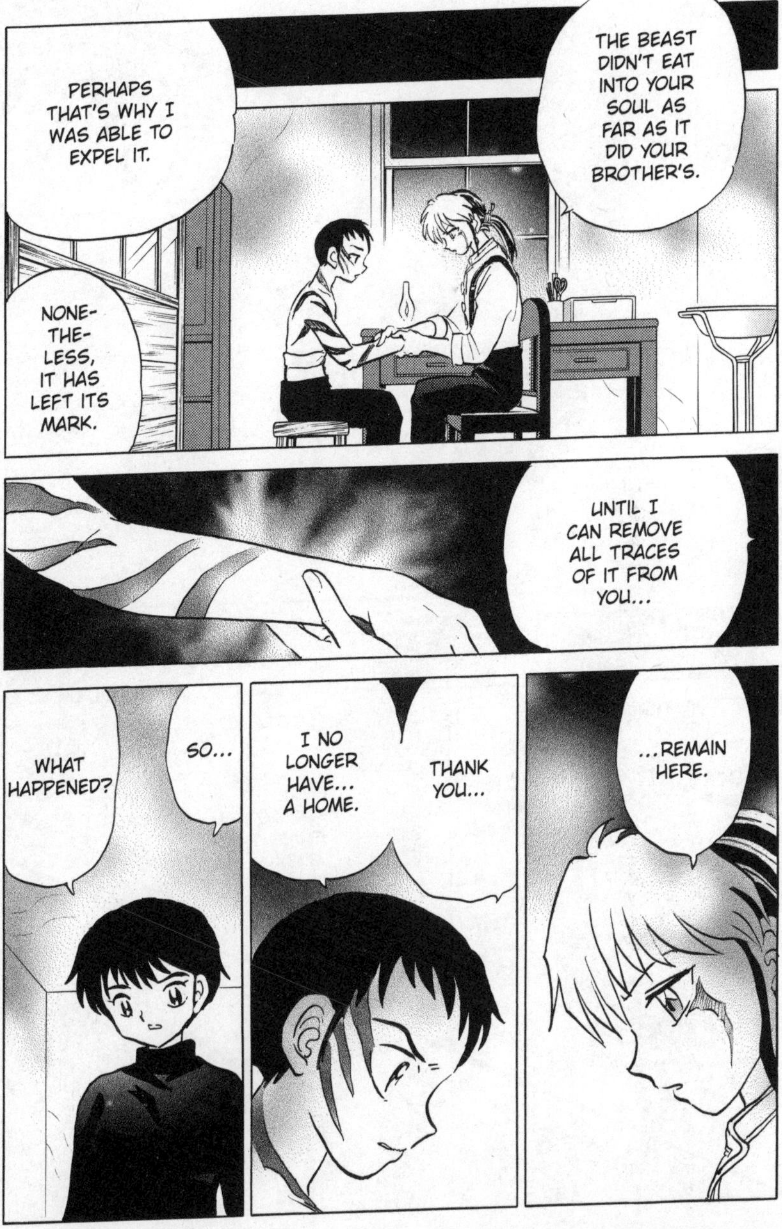
THE BEAST DIDN'T EAT INTO YOUR SOUL AS FAR AS IT DID YOUR BROTHER'S.
PERHAPS THAT'S WHY I WAS ABLE TO EXPEL IT.
NONE-THE-LESS, IT HAS LEFT ITS MARK.
UNTIL I CAN REMOVE ALL TRACES OF IT FROM YOU...
...REMAIN HERE.
THANK YOU...
I NO LONGER HAVE... A HOME.
SO...
WHAT HAPPENED?

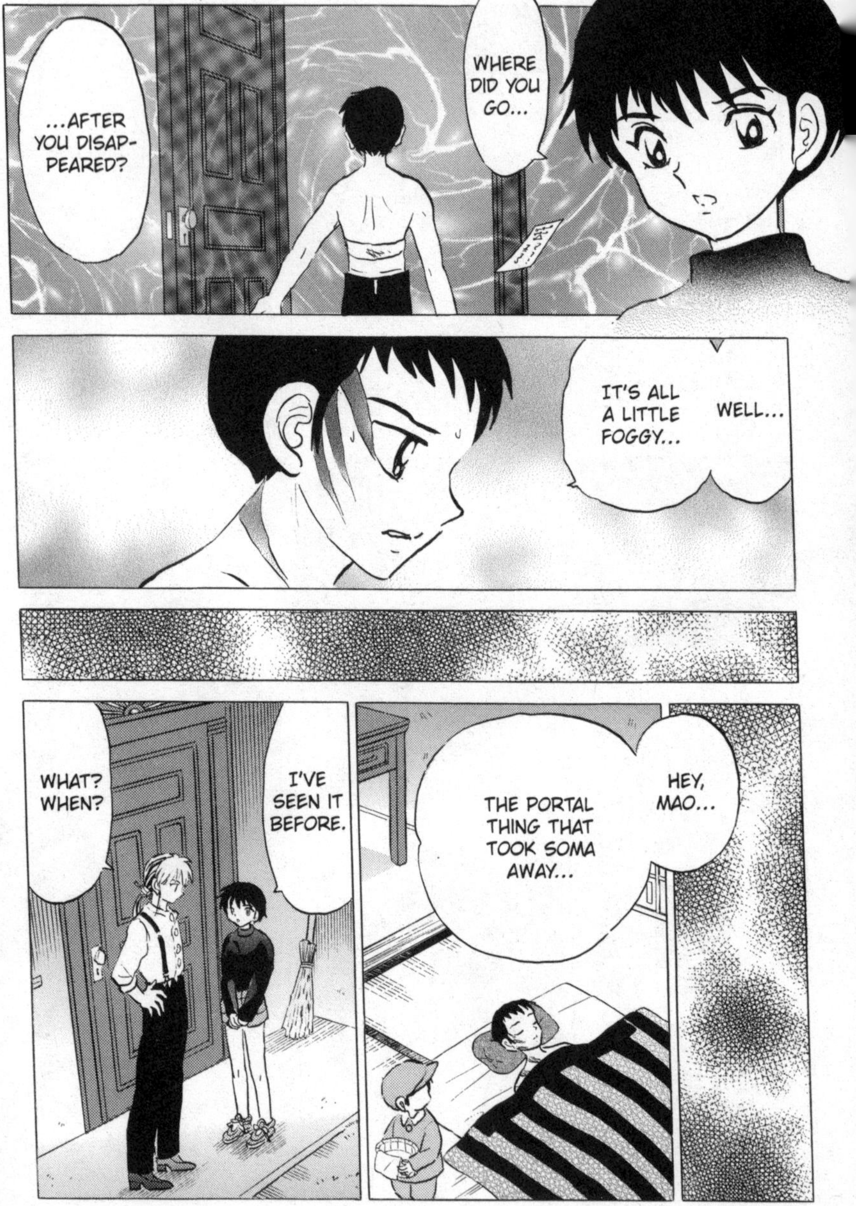
WHERE DID YOU GO...
...AFTER YOU DISAP-PEARED?
WELL...
IT'S ALL A LITTLE FOGGY...
HEY, MAO...
THE PORTAL THING THAT TOOK SOMA AWAY...
I'VE SEEN IT BEFORE.
WHAT? WHEN?

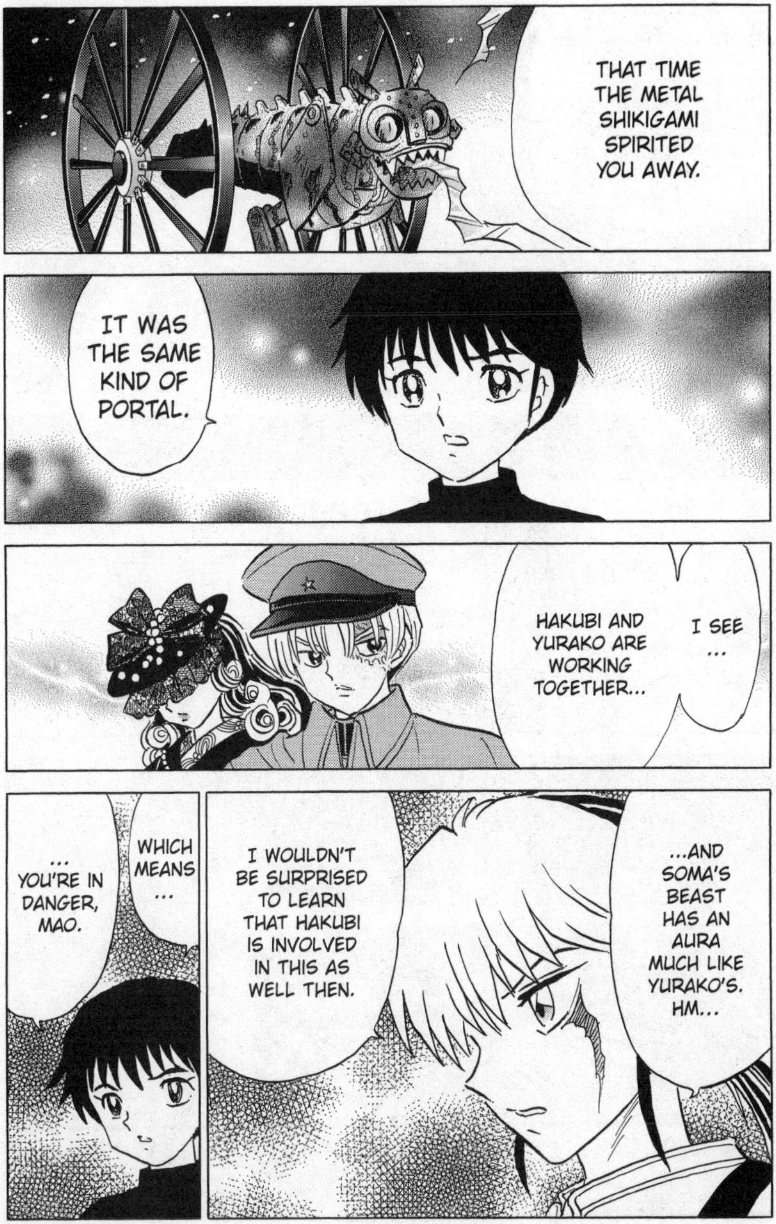
THAT TIME THE METAL SHIKIGAMI SPIRITED YOU AWAY.
IT WAS THE SAME KIND OF PORTAL.
I SEE ...
HAKUBI AND YURAKO ARE WORKING TOGETHER...
...AND SOMA'S BEAST HAS AN AURA MUCH LIKE YURAKO'S. HM...
I WOULDN'T BE SURPRISED TO LEARN THAT HAKUBI IS INVOLVED IN THIS AS WELL THEN.
WHICH MEANS ...
... YOU'RE IN DANGER, MAO.

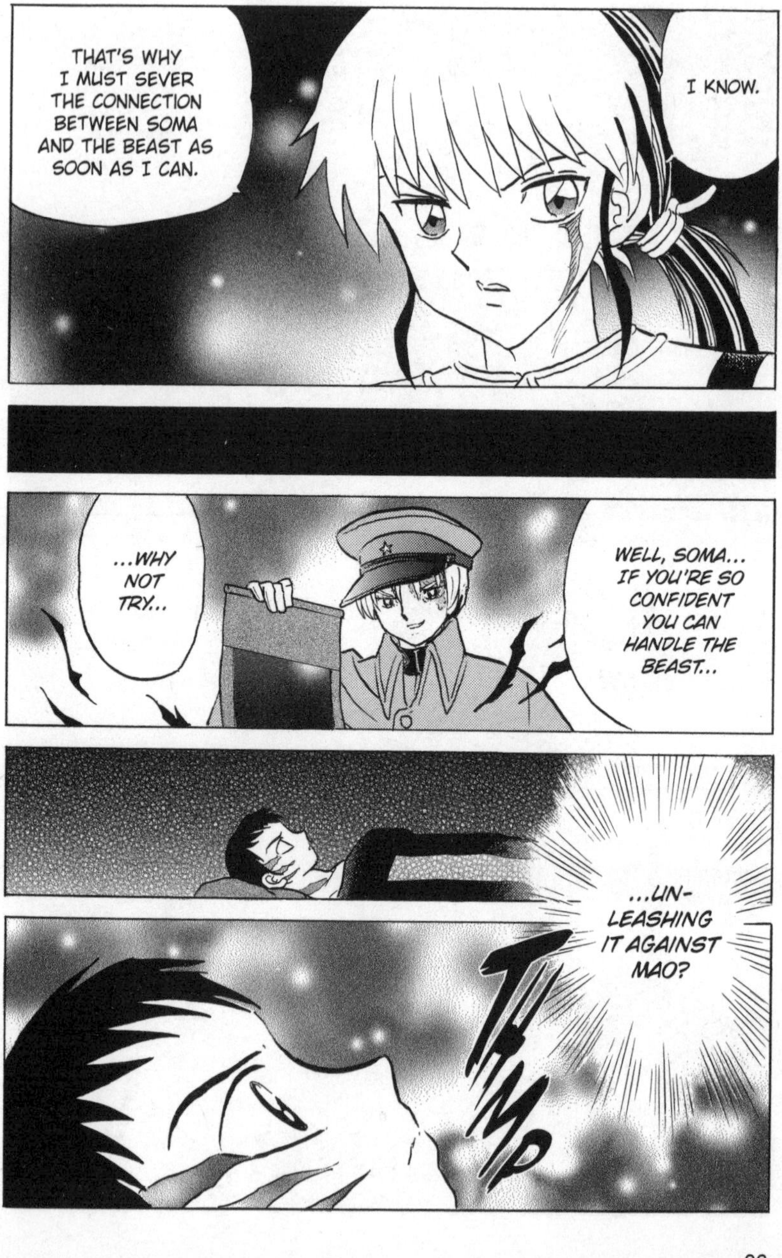
I KNOW.
THAT'S WHY I MUST SEVER THE CONNECTION BETWEEN SOMA AND THE BEAST AS SOON AS I CAN.
WELL, SOMA... IF YOU'RE SO CONFIDENT YOU CAN HANDLE THE BEAST...
...WHY NOT TRY...
...UN-LEASHING IT AGAINST MAO?
THMP

Chapter 6:
Soma's Desire

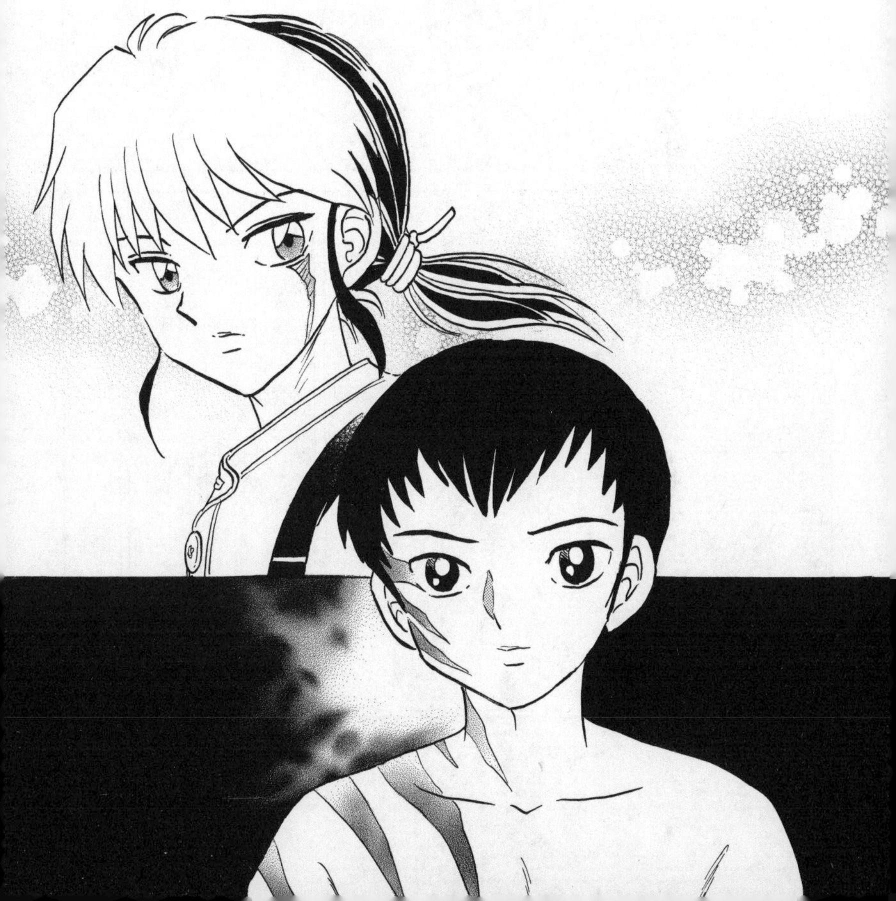

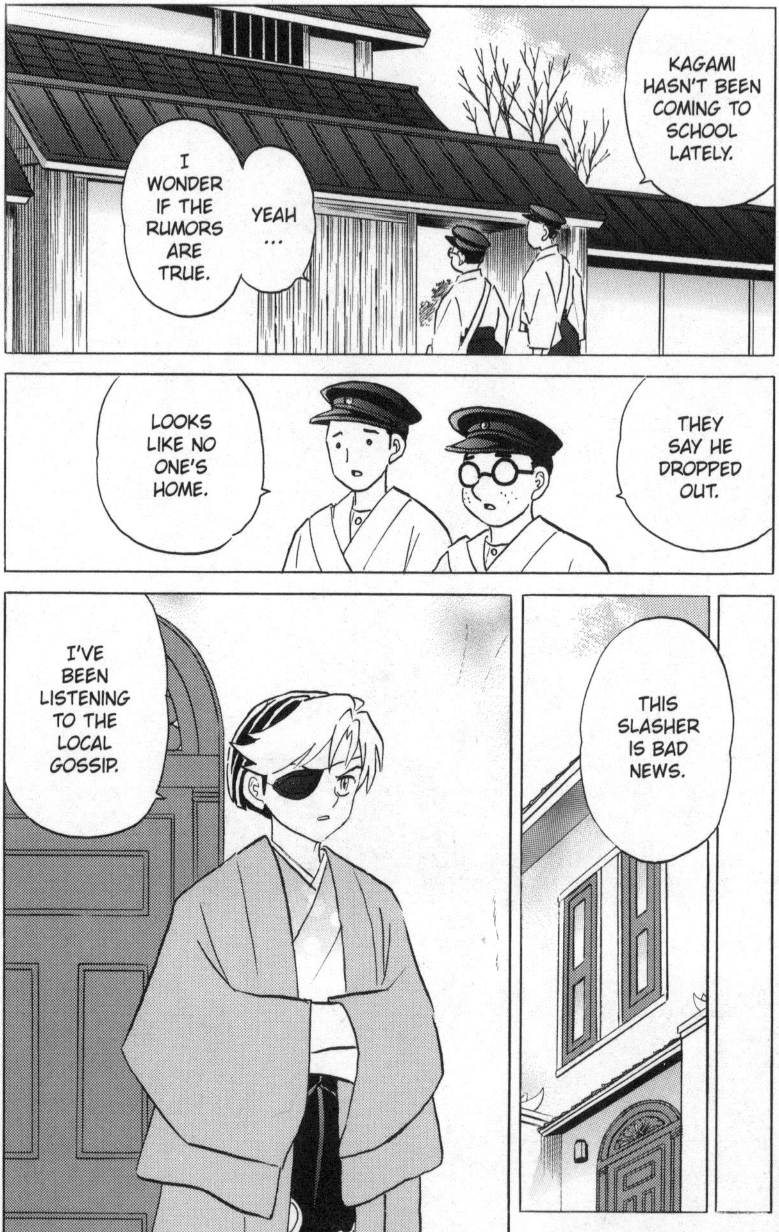
KAGAMI HASN'T BEEN COMING TO SCHOOL LATELY.
YEAH ...
I WONDER IF THE RUMORS ARE TRUE.
THEY SAY HE DROPPED OUT.
LOOKS LIKE NO ONE'S HOME.
THIS SLASHER IS BAD NEWS.
I'VE BEEN LISTENING TO THE LOCAL GOSSIP.

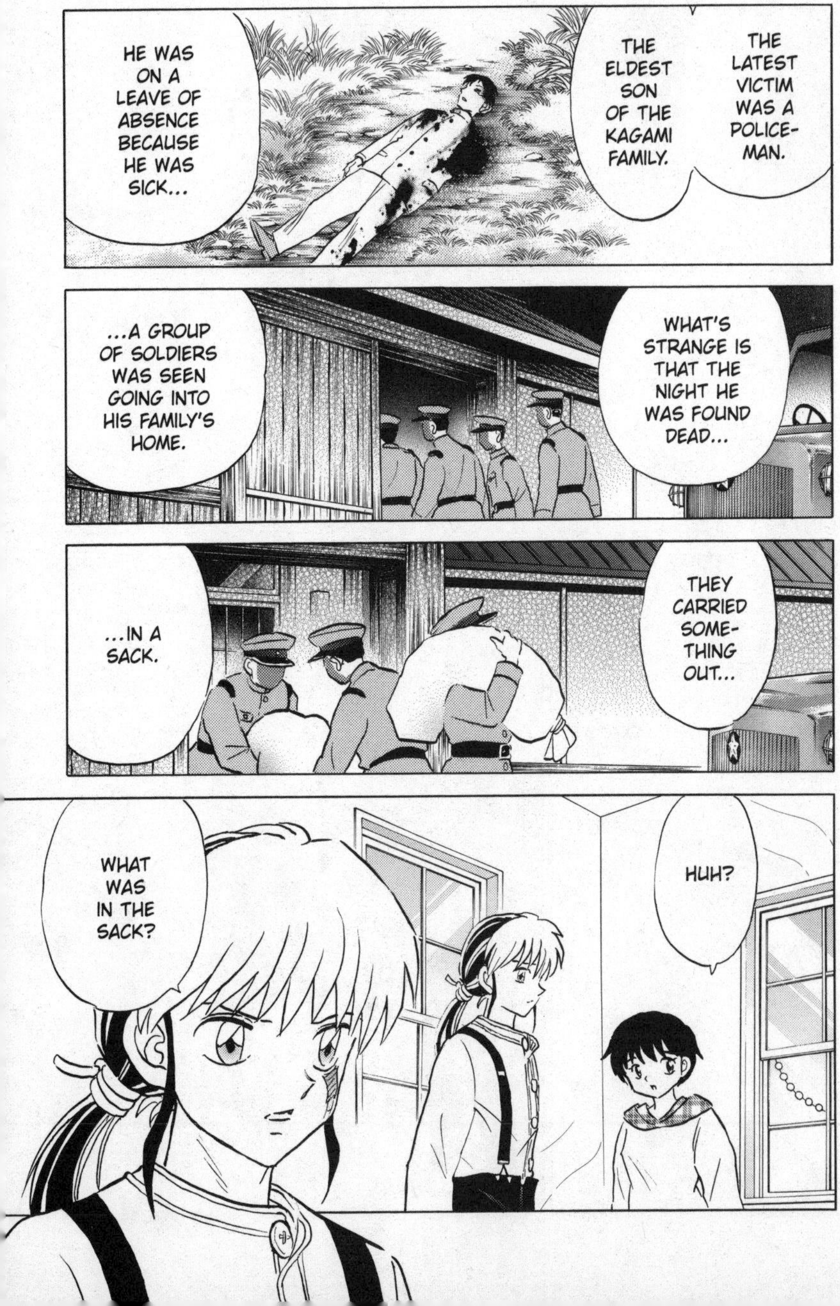
THE LATEST VICTIM WAS A POLICE-MAN.
THE ELDEST SON OF THE KAGAMI FAMILY.
HE WAS ON A LEAVE OF ABSENCE BECAUSE HE WAS SICK...
WHAT'S STRANGE IS THAT THE NIGHT HE WAS FOUND DEAD...
...A GROUP OF SOLDIERS WAS SEEN GOING INTO HIS FAMILY'S HOME.
THEY CARRIED SOME-THING OUT...
...IN A SACK.
HUH?
WHAT WAS IN THE SACK?

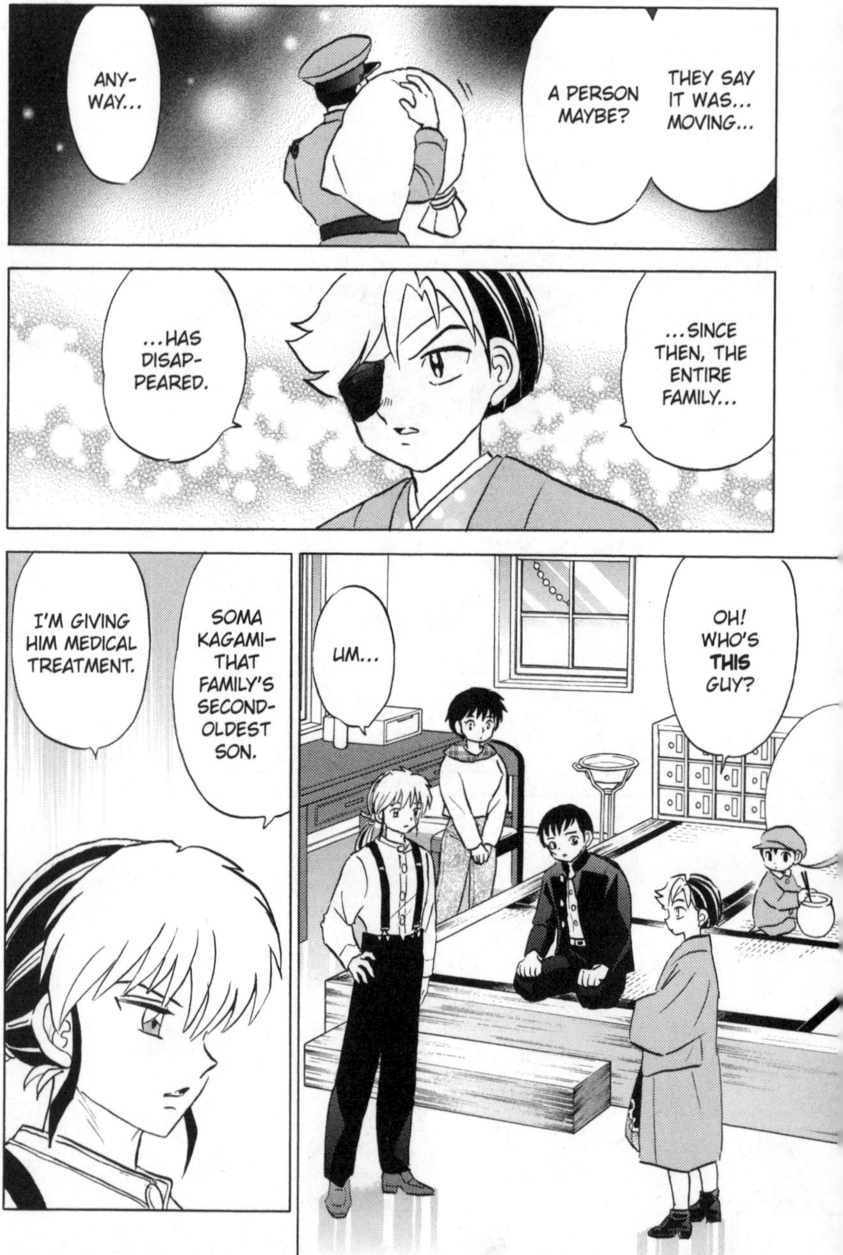
THEY SAY IT WAS... MOVING...
A PERSON MAYBE?
ANY-WAY...
...SINCE THEN, THE ENTIRE FAMILY...
...HAS DISAP-PEARED.
OH! WHO'S **THIS** GUY?
UM...
SOMA KAGAMI- THAT FAMILY'S SECOND-OLDEST SON.
I'M GIVING HIM MEDICAL TREATMENT.

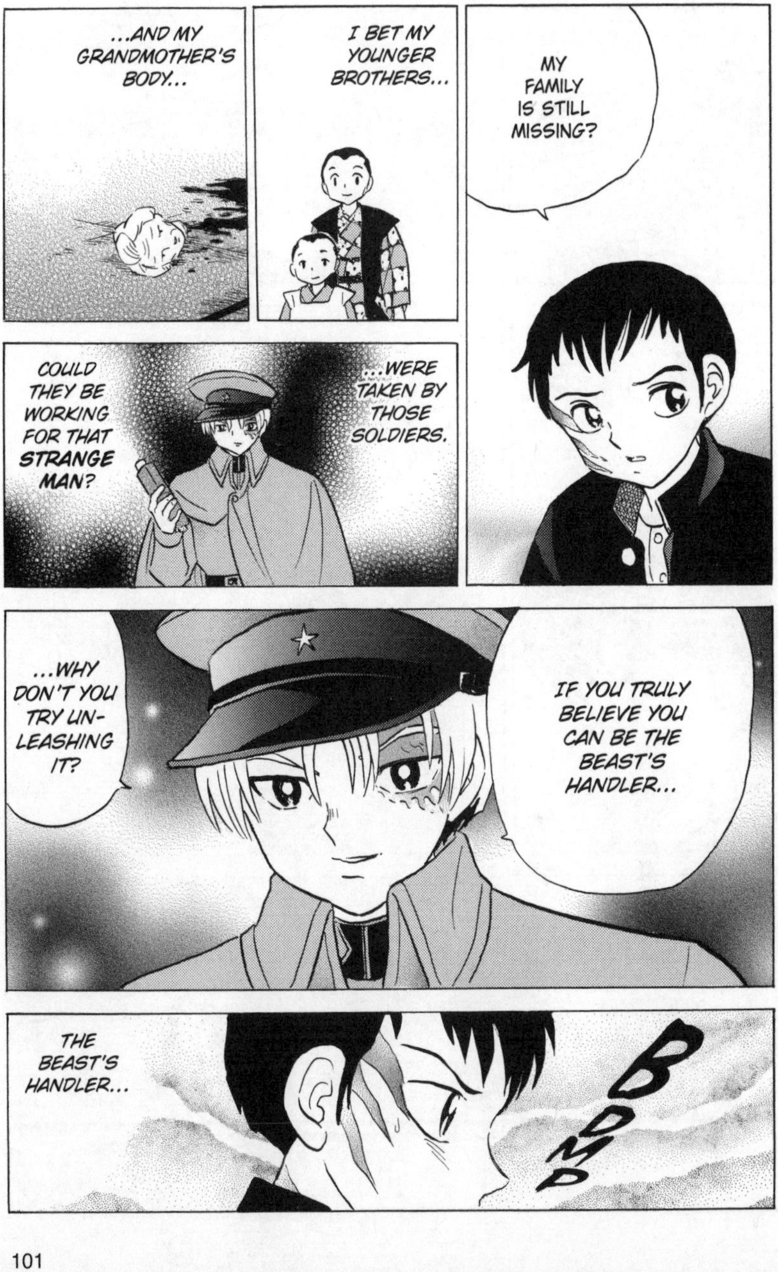
MY FAMILY IS STILL MISSING?
I BET MY YOUNGER BROTHERS...
...AND MY GRANDMOTHER'S BODY...
...WERE TAKEN BY THOSE SOLDIERS.
COULD THEY BE WORKING FOR THAT **STRANGE MAN**?
IF YOU TRULY BELIEVE YOU CAN BE THE BEAST'S HANDLER...
...WHY DON'T YOU TRY UN-LEASHING IT?
BDMP
THE BEAST'S HANDLER...

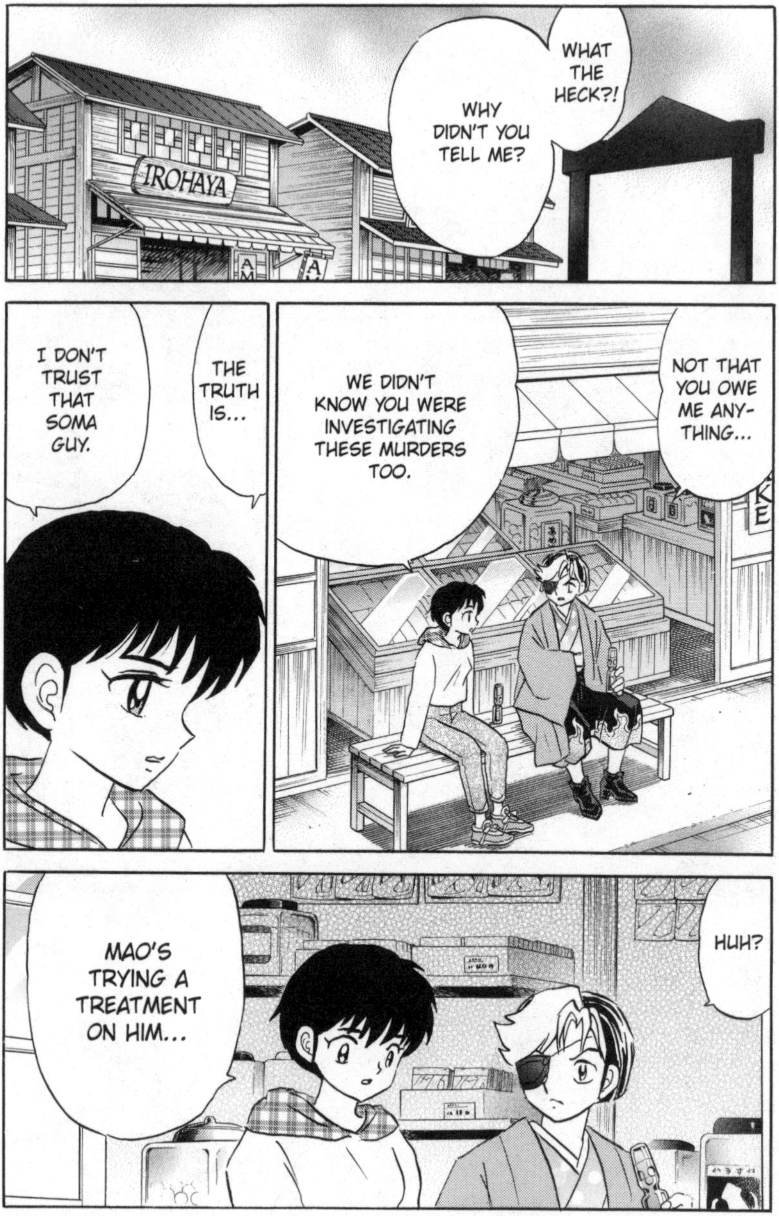
IROHAYA
WHAT THE HECK?!
WHY DIDN'T YOU TELL ME?
NOT THAT YOU OWE ME ANY-THING...
WE DIDN'T KNOW YOU WERE INVESTIGATING THESE MURDERS TOO.
THE TRUTH IS...
I DON'T TRUST THAT SOMA GUY.
HUH?
MAO'S TRYING A TREATMENT ON HIM...

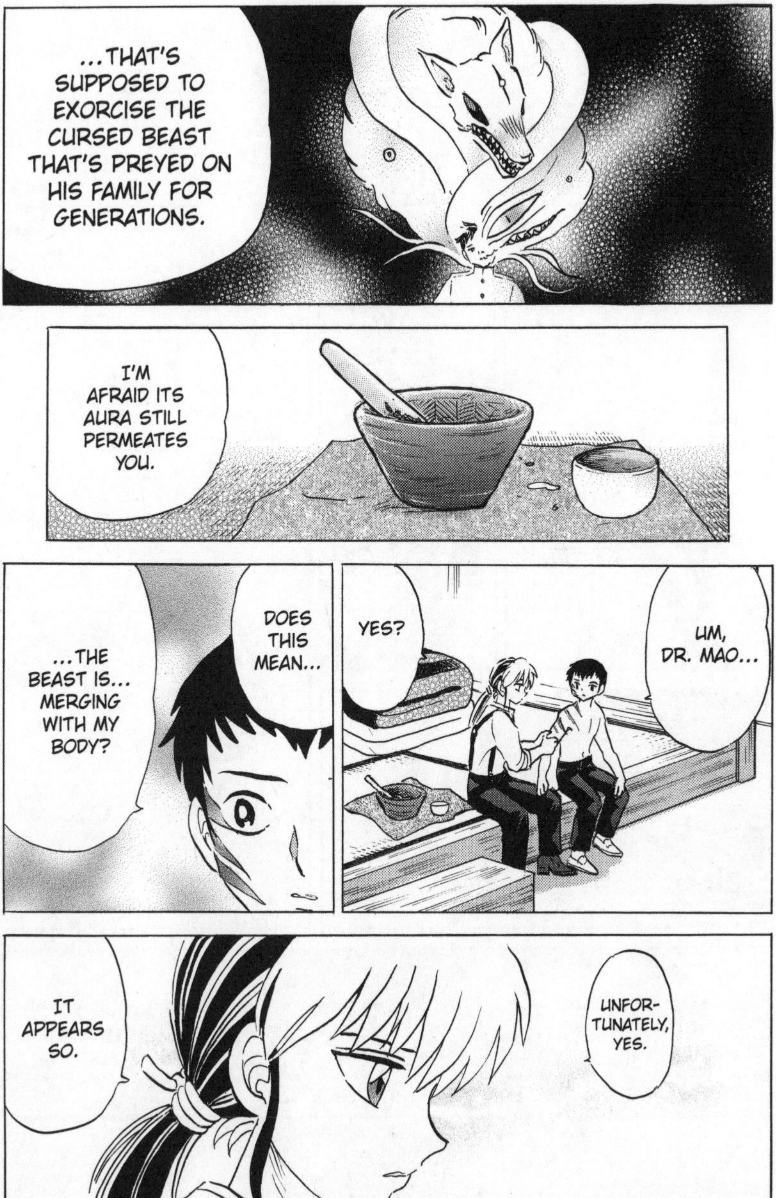
...THAT'S SUPPOSED TO EXORCISE THE CURSED BEAST THAT'S PREYED ON HIS FAMILY FOR GENERATIONS.
I'M AFRAID ITS AURA STILL PERMEATES YOU.
UM, DR. MAO...
YES?
DOES THIS MEAN...
...THE BEAST IS... MERGING WITH MY BODY?
UNFOR-TUNATELY, YES.
IT APPEARS SO.

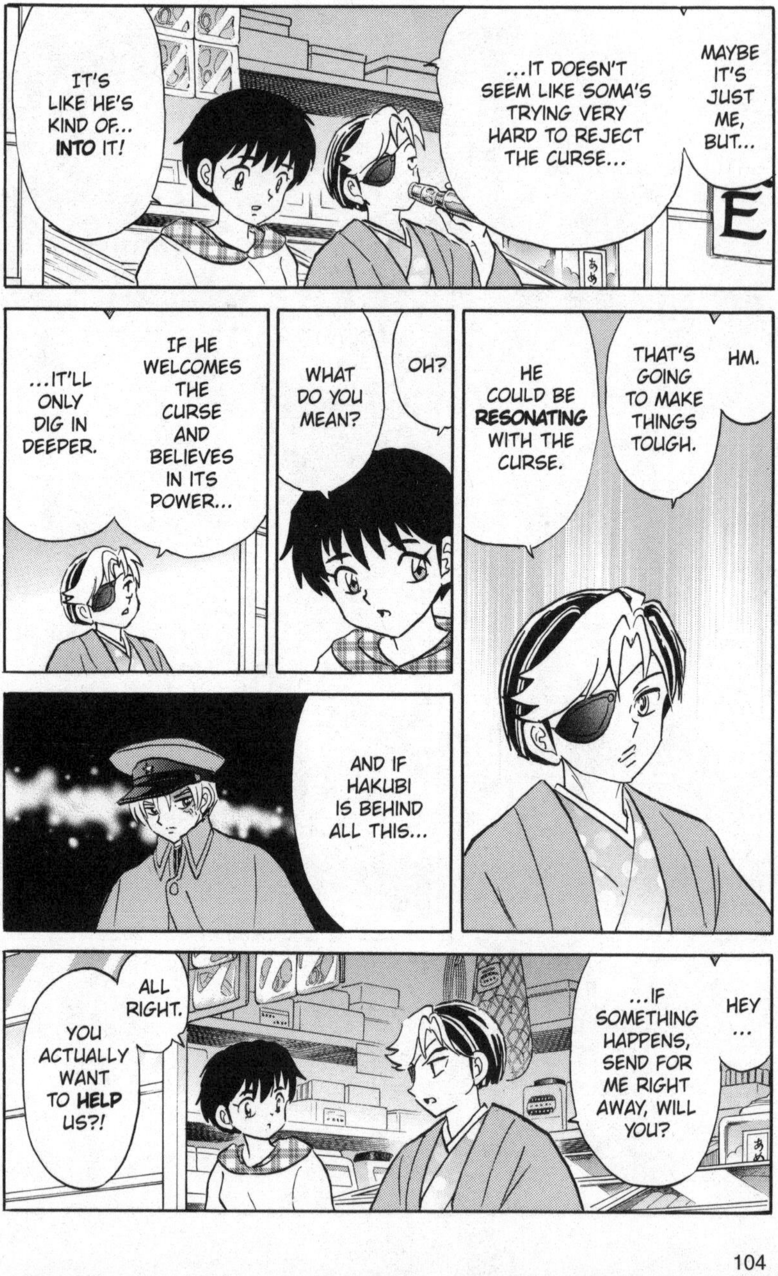
MAYBE IT'S JUST ME, BUT...
...IT DOESN'T SEEM LIKE SOMA'S TRYING VERY HARD TO REJECT THE CURSE...
IT'S LIKE HE'S KIND OF... **INTO** IT!
HM.
THAT'S GOING TO MAKE THINGS TOUGH.
HE COULD BE **RESONATING** WITH THE CURSE.
OH?
WHAT DO YOU MEAN?
IF HE WELCOMES THE CURSE AND BELIEVES IN ITS POWER...
...IT'LL ONLY DIG IN DEEPER.
AND IF HAKUBI IS BEHIND ALL THIS...
HEY...
...IF SOMETHING HAPPENS, SEND FOR ME RIGHT AWAY, WILL YOU?
ALL RIGHT.
YOU ACTUALLY WANT TO **HELP** US?!

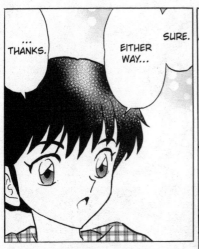

I DON'T GIVE A DAMN ABOUT MAO.
BUT I HAVE SOME SCORES TO SETTLE WITH HAKUBI.
SURE.
EITHER WAY...
...THANKS.
I DON'T NEED YOUR GRATITUDE.
COME ON. YOU KNOW WE RELY ON YOU!
MAO IS EXPECTING TO HAVE...

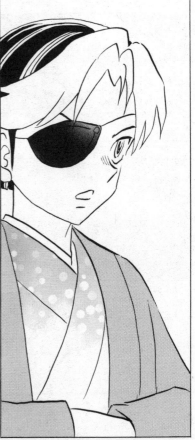

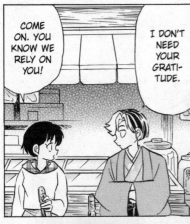

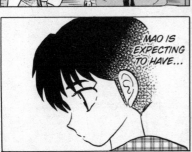

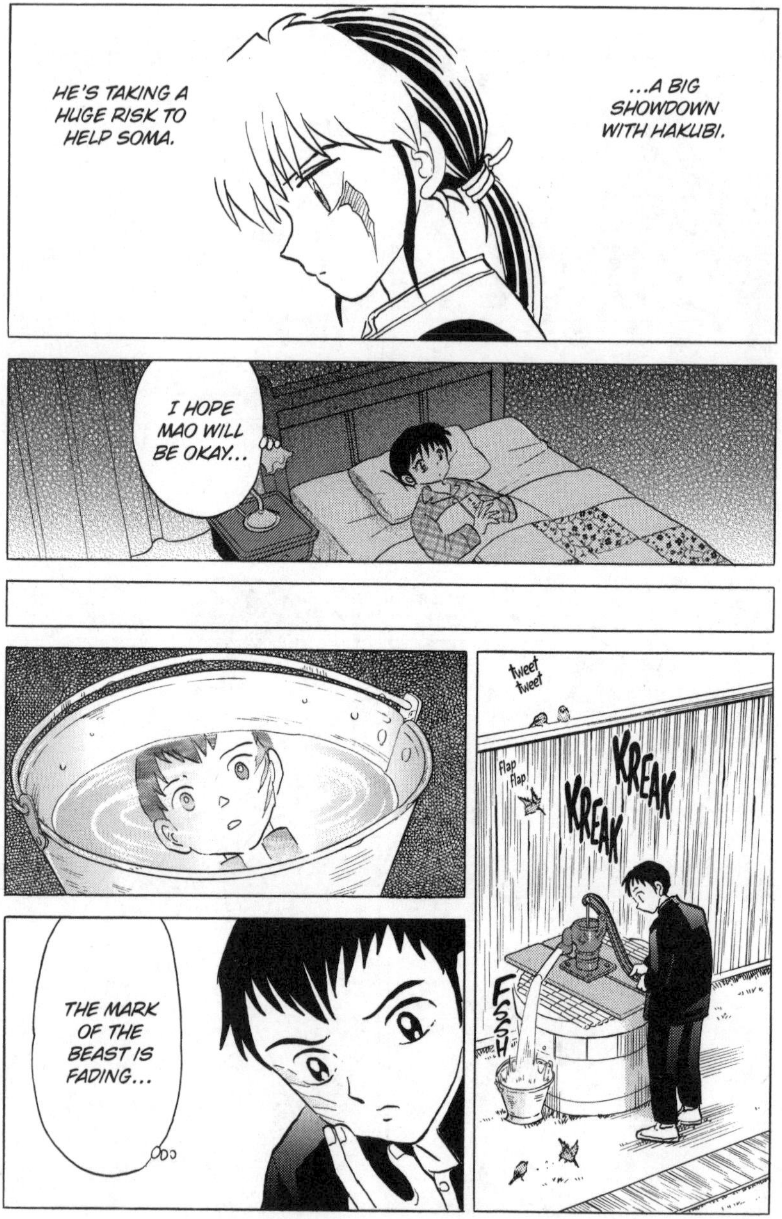

...A BIG SHOWDOWN WITH HAKUBI.
HE'S TAKING A HUGE RISK TO HELP SOMA.
I HOPE MAO WILL BE OKAY...
tweet tweet
KREAK KREAK
Flap Flap
FSSH
THE MARK OF THE BEAST IS FADING...

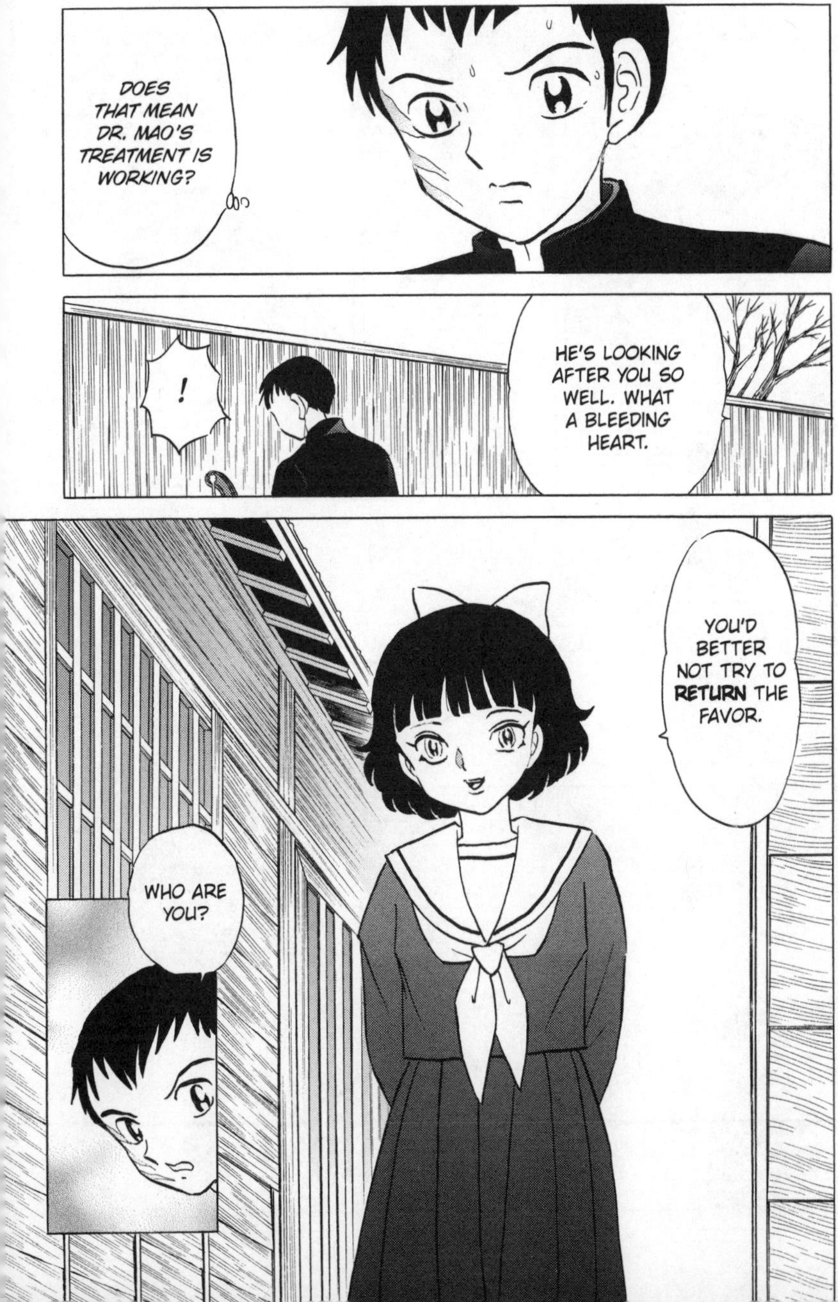
DOES THAT MEAN DR. MAO'S TREATMENT IS WORKING?
HE'S LOOKING AFTER YOU SO WELL. WHAT A BLEEDING HEART.
!
YOU'D BETTER NOT TRY TO **RETURN** THE FAVOR.
WHO ARE YOU?

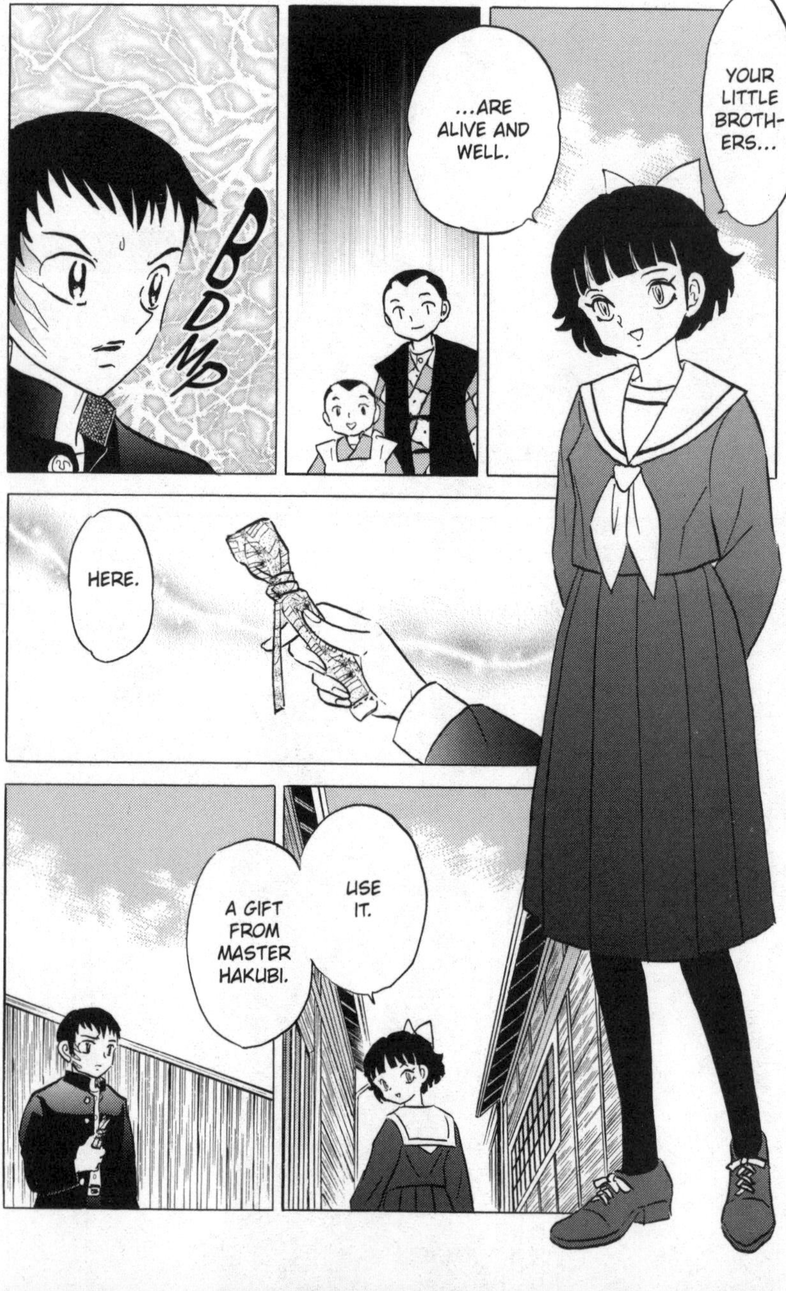
YOUR LITTLE BROTH-ERS...
...ARE ALIVE AND WELL.
BDMP
HERE.
USE IT.
A GIFT FROM MASTER HAKUBI.

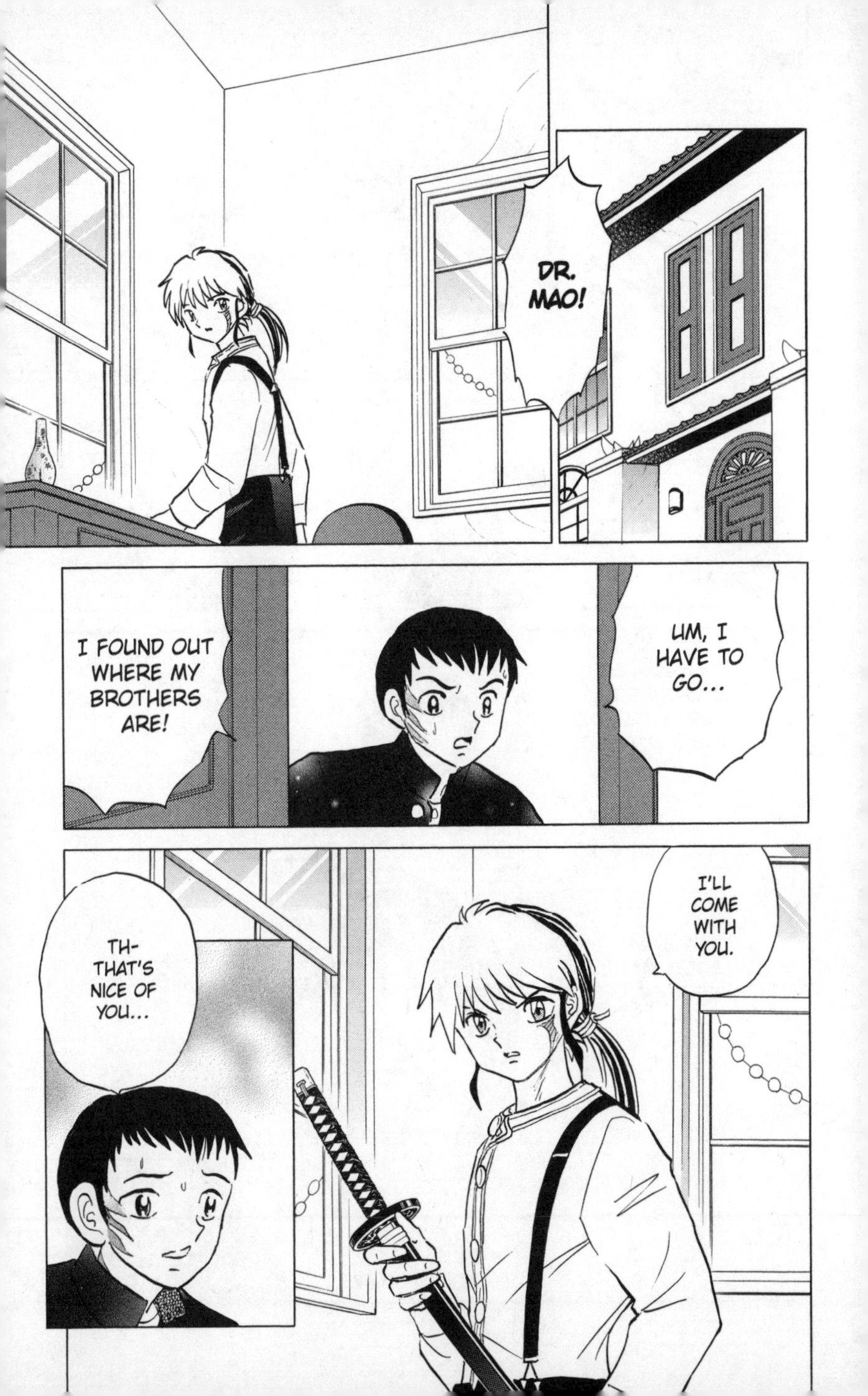
DR. MAO!
UM, I HAVE TO GO...
I FOUND OUT WHERE MY BROTHERS ARE!
I'LL COME WITH YOU.
TH- THAT'S NICE OF YOU...

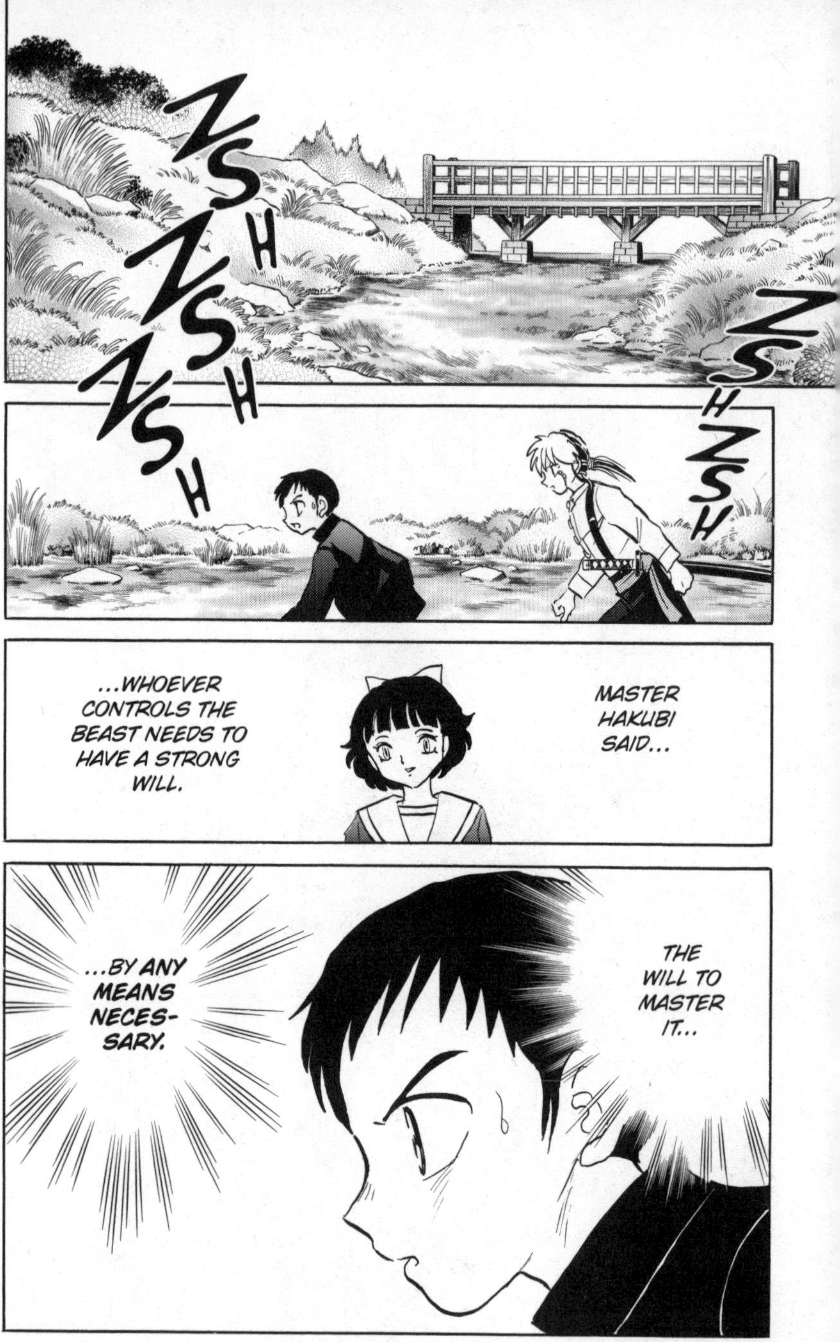
ZSH
ZSH
ZSH
ZSH
ZSH
MASTER HAKUBI SAID...
...WHOEVER CONTROLS THE BEAST NEEDS TO HAVE A STRONG WILL.
THE WILL TO MASTER IT...
...BY ANY MEANS NECES-SARY.

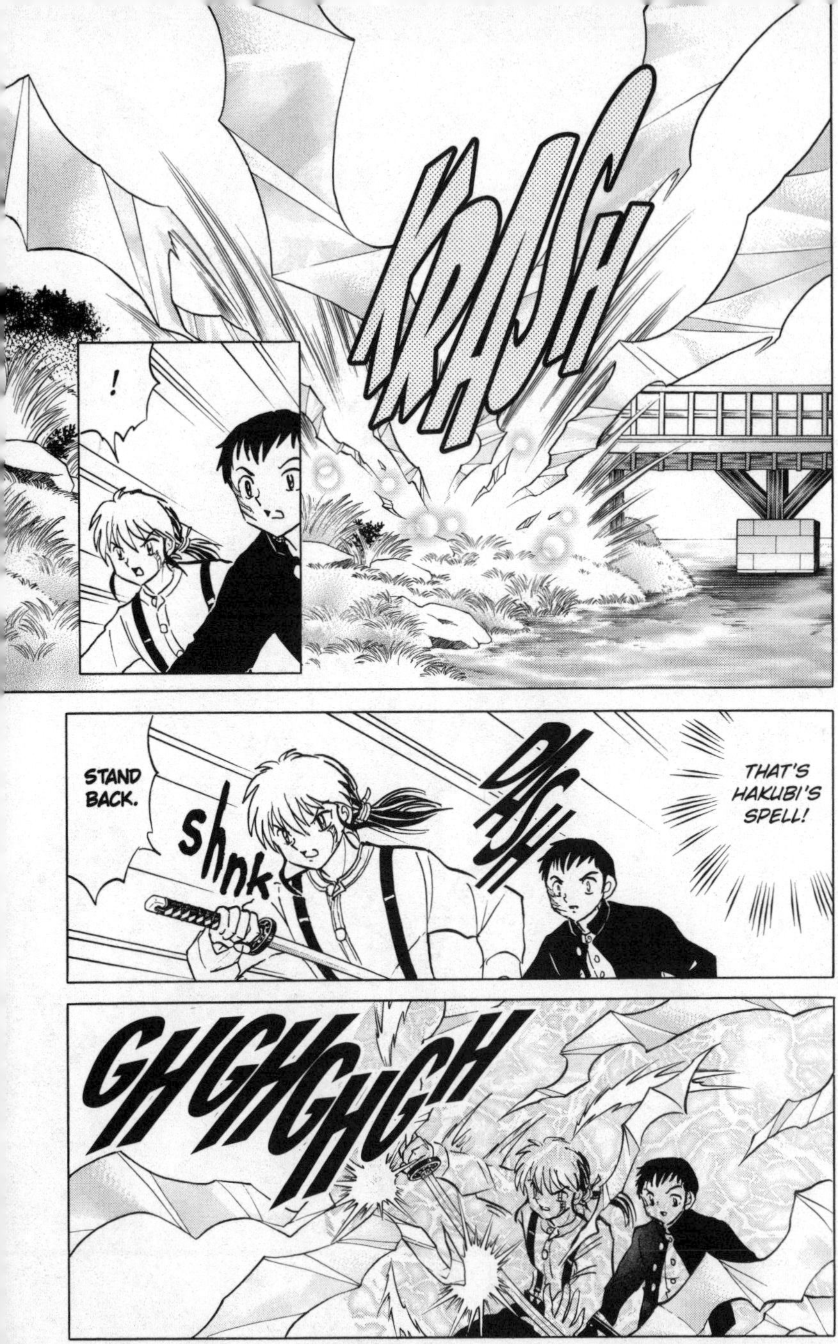
KRASH
!
THAT'S HAKUBI'S SPELL!
DASH
shnk
STAND BACK.
GHGHGHGH

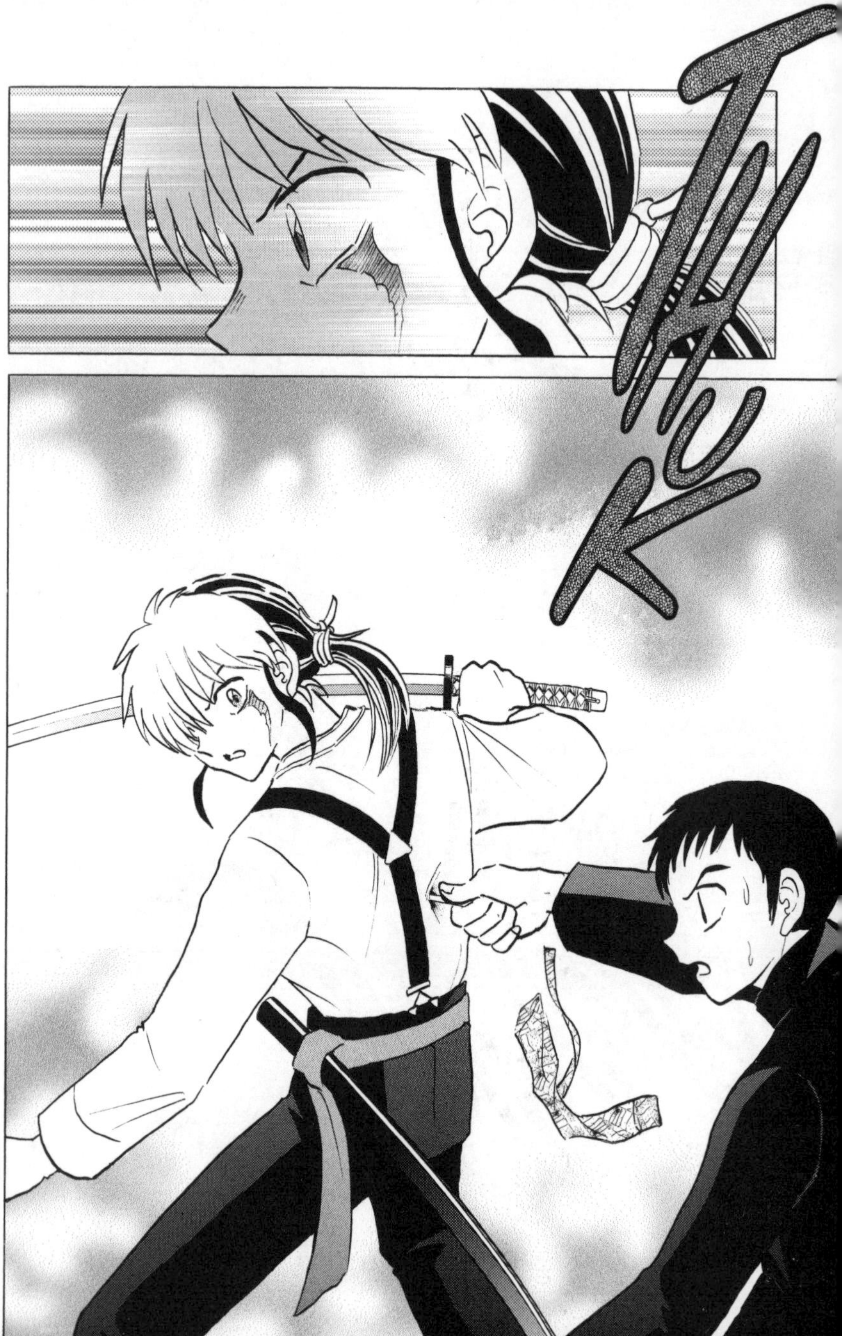
THUNK

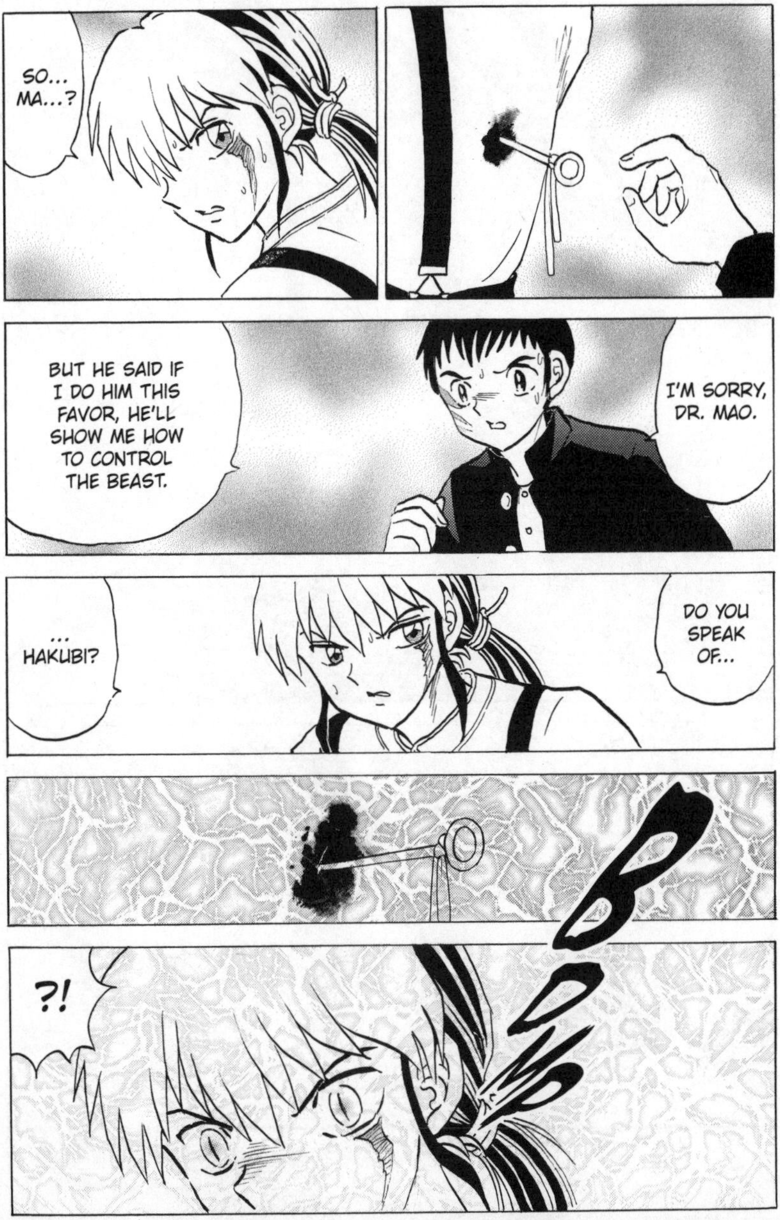
SO... MA...?
I'M SORRY, DR. MAO.
BUT HE SAID IF I DO HIM THIS FAVOR, HE'LL SHOW ME HOW TO CONTROL THE BEAST.
DO YOU SPEAK OF...
...HAKUBI?
?!

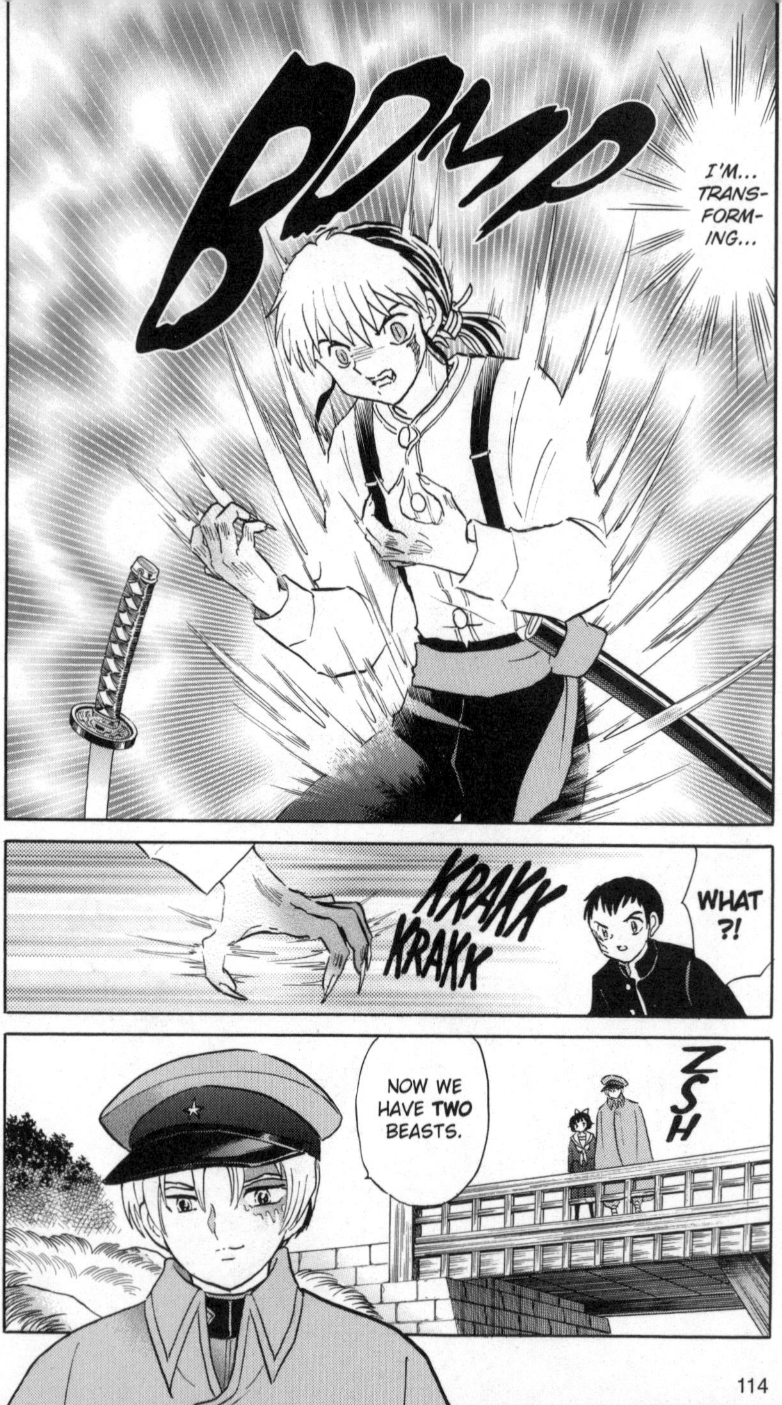
BOMP
I'M... TRANS-FORM-ING...
WHAT ?!
KRAKK KRAKK
ZSH
NOW WE HAVE TWO BEASTS.

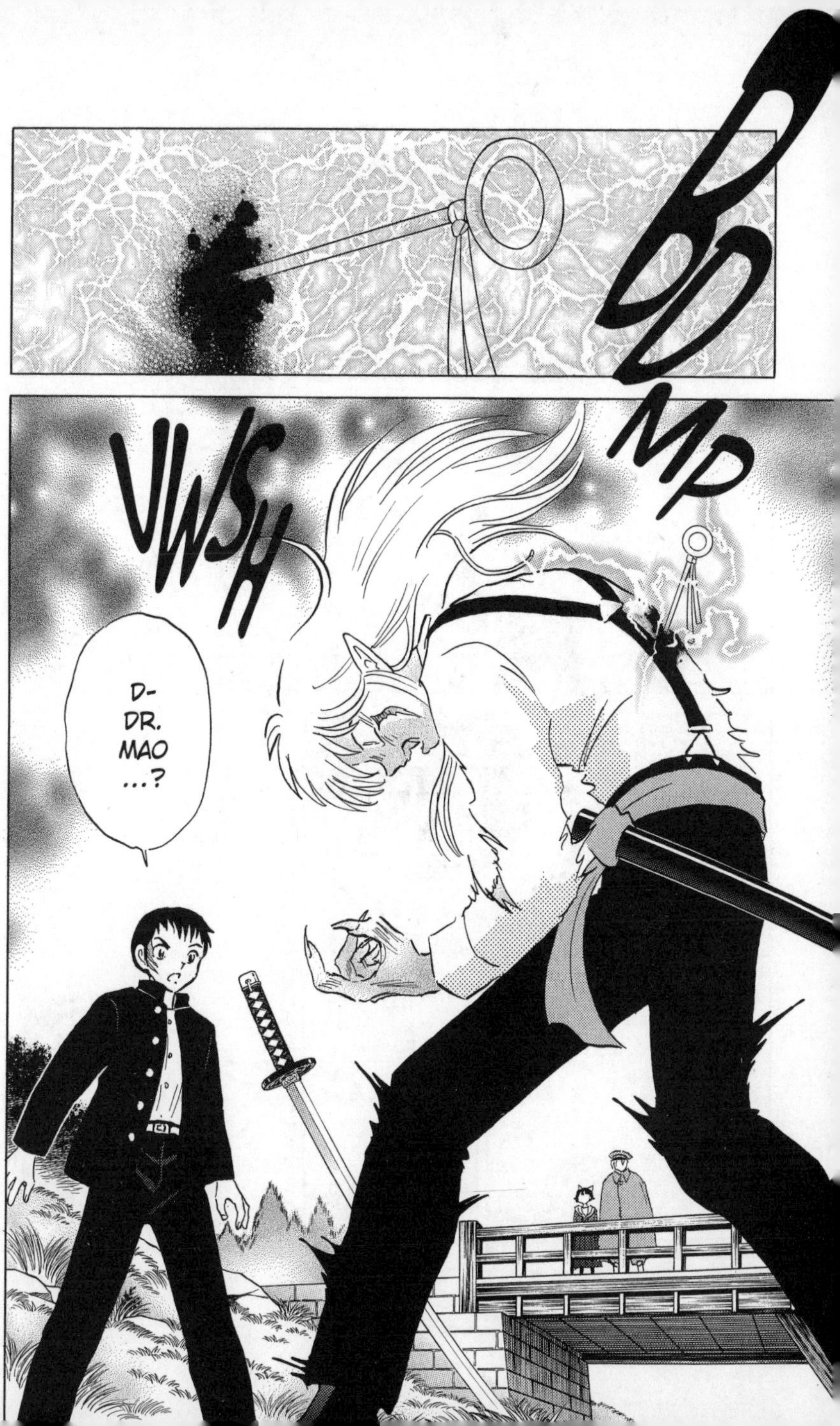

BDDMP
VWSH
D- DR. MAO ...?

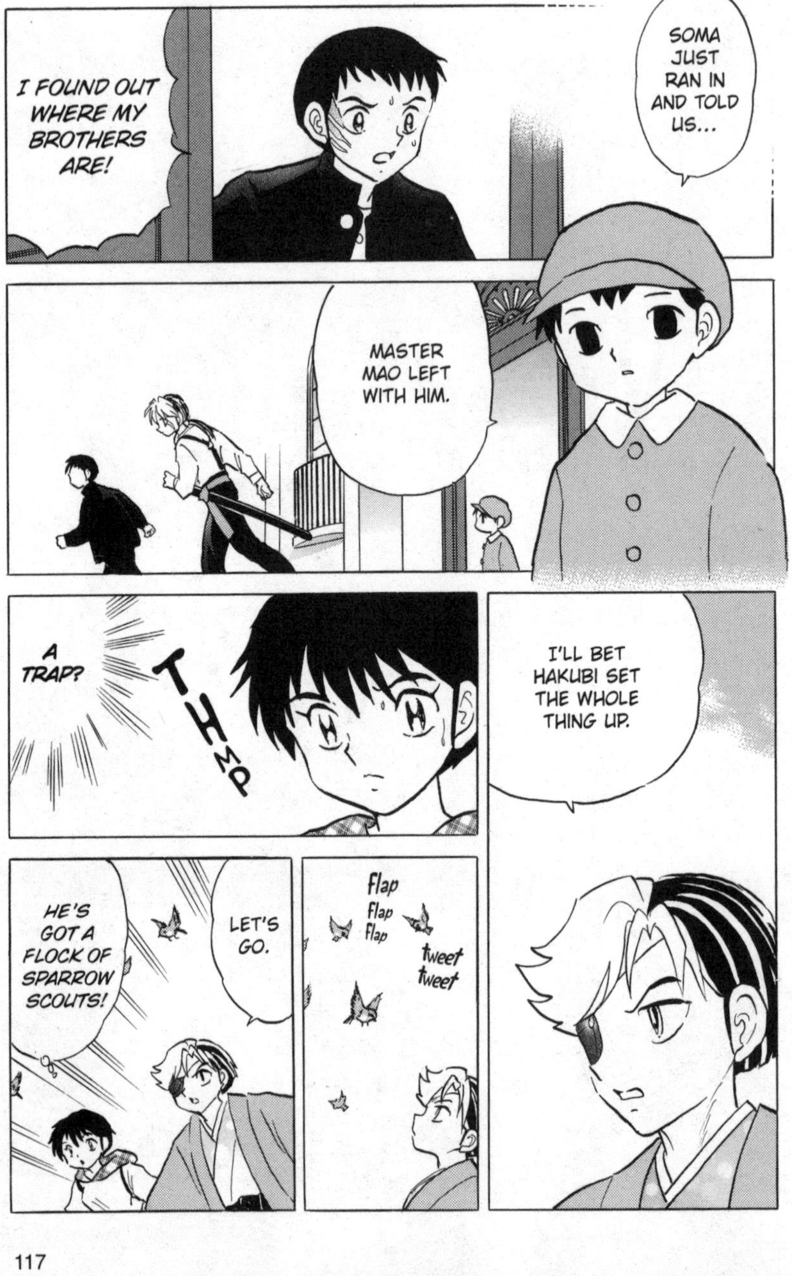
SOMA JUST RAN IN AND TOLD US...
I FOUND OUT WHERE MY BROTHERS ARE!
MASTER MAO LEFT WITH HIM.
I'LL BET HAKUBI SET THE WHOLE THING UP.
THMP
A TRAP?
Flap Flap Flap
tweet tweet
LET'S GO.
HE'S GOT A FLOCK OF SPARROW SCOUTS!

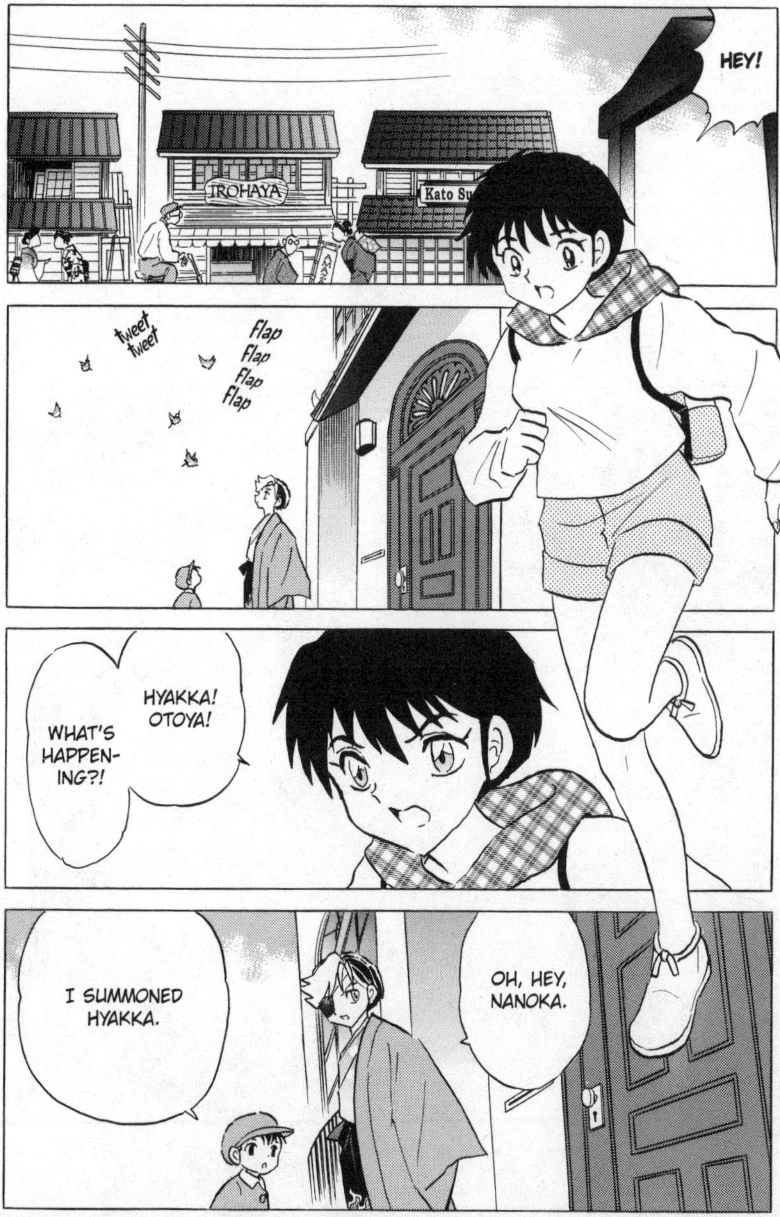
IROHAYA
HEY!
tweet tweet
Flap Flap Flap Flap
HYAKKA! OTOYA!
WHAT'S HAPPEN-ING?!
OH, HEY, NANOKA.
I SUMMONED HYAKKA.

Chapter 7:
Puppet Needle

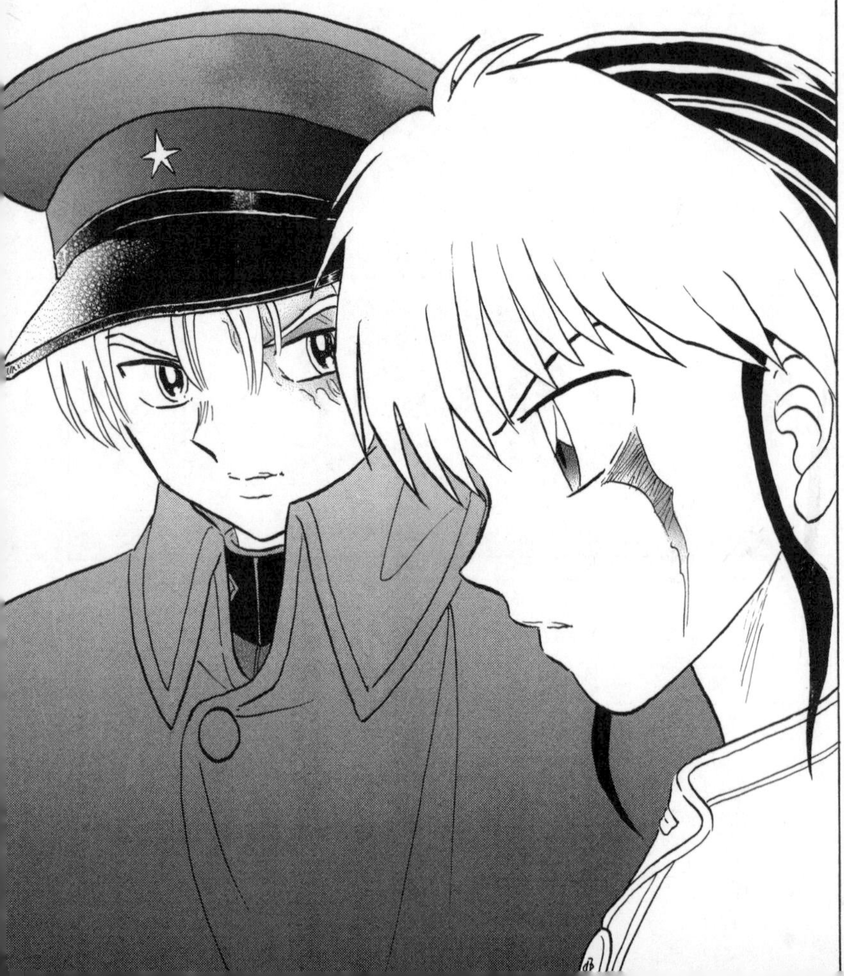

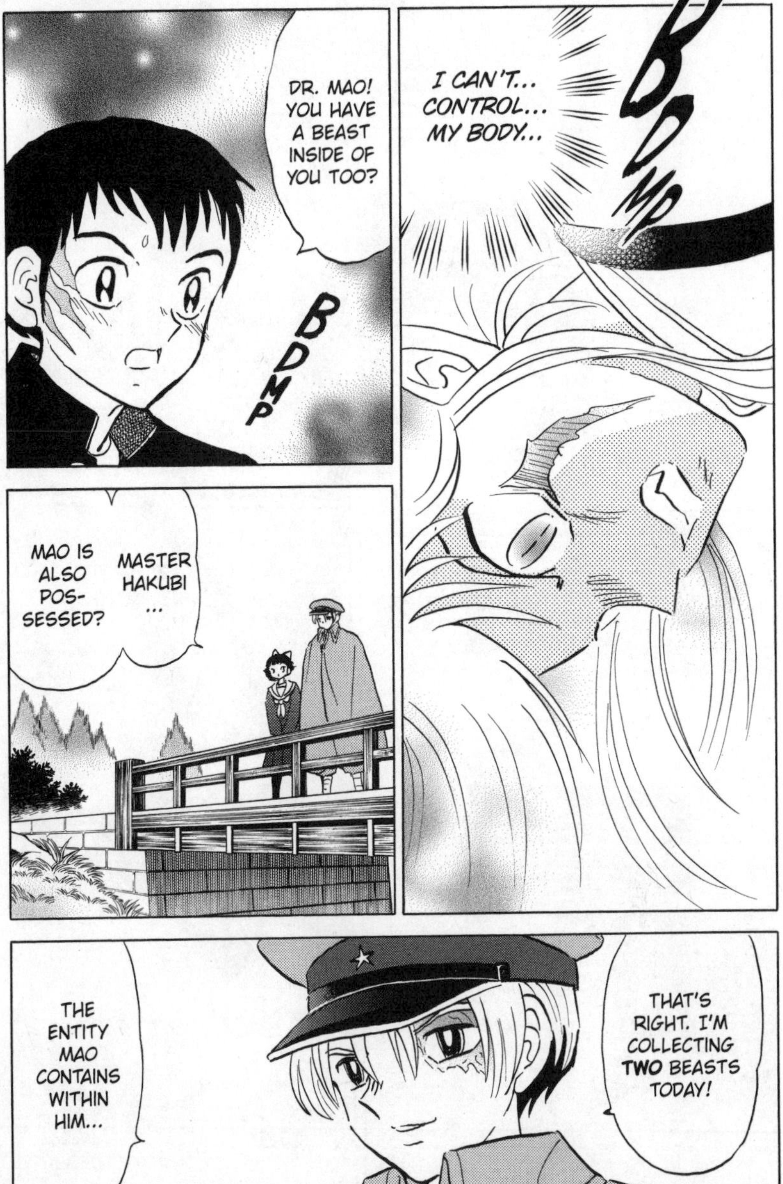
BDMP
I CAN'T... CONTROL... MY BODY...
DR. MAO! YOU HAVE A BEAST INSIDE OF YOU TOO?
BDMP
MASTER HAKUBI ...
MAO IS ALSO POS-SESSED?
THAT'S RIGHT. I'M COLLECTING **TWO** BEASTS TODAY!
THE ENTITY MAO CONTAINS WITHIN HIM...

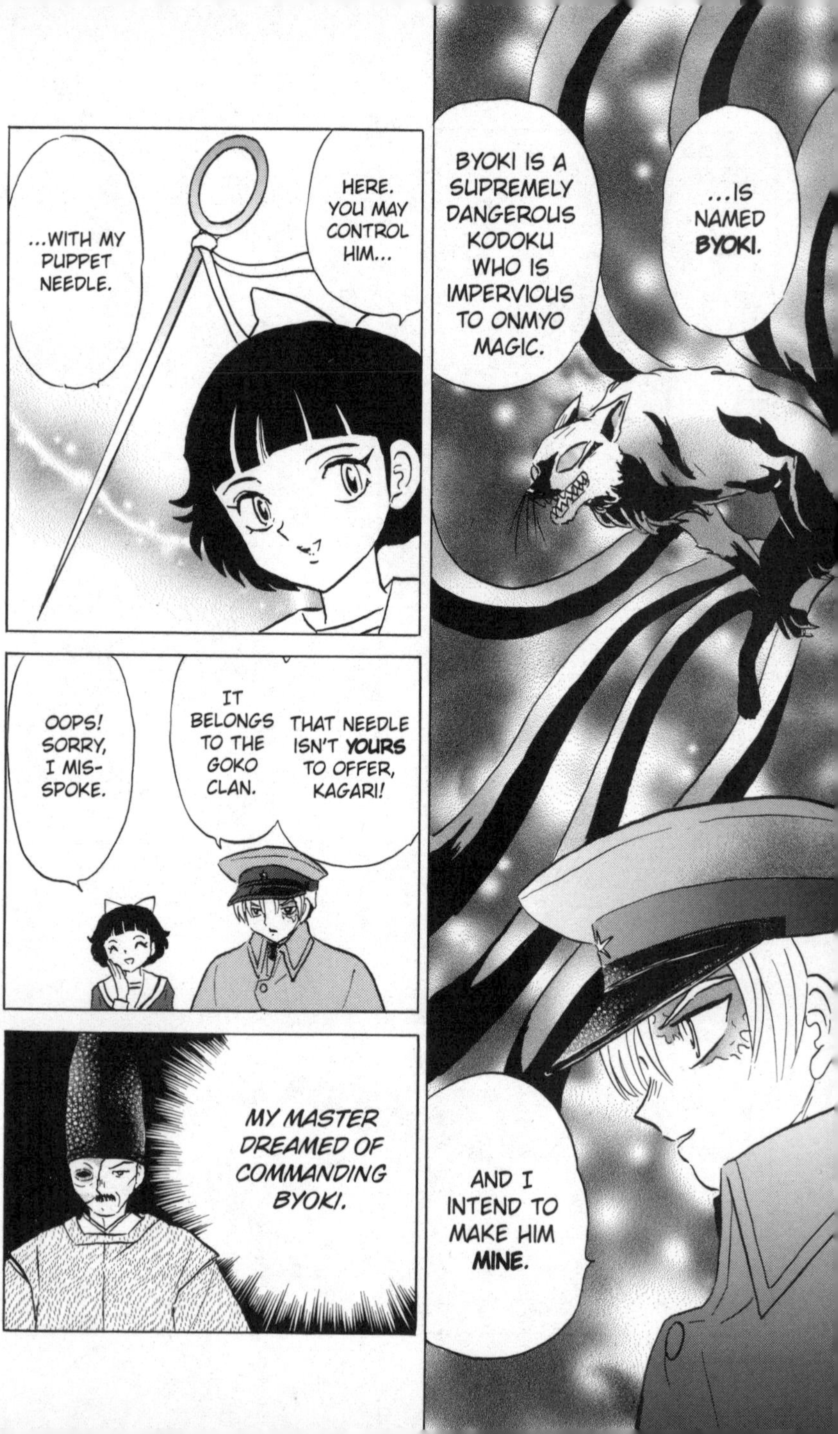
...IS NAMED **BYOKI.**
BYOKI IS A SUPREMELY DANGEROUS KODOKU WHO IS IMPERVIOUS TO ONMYO MAGIC.
AND I INTEND TO MAKE HIM **MINE.**
HERE. YOU MAY CONTROL HIM...
...WITH MY PUPPET NEEDLE.
THAT NEEDLE ISN'T **YOURS** TO OFFER, KAGARI!
IT BELONGS TO THE GOKO CLAN.
OOPS! SORRY, I MIS-SPOKE.
MY MASTER DREAMED OF COMMANDING BYOKI.

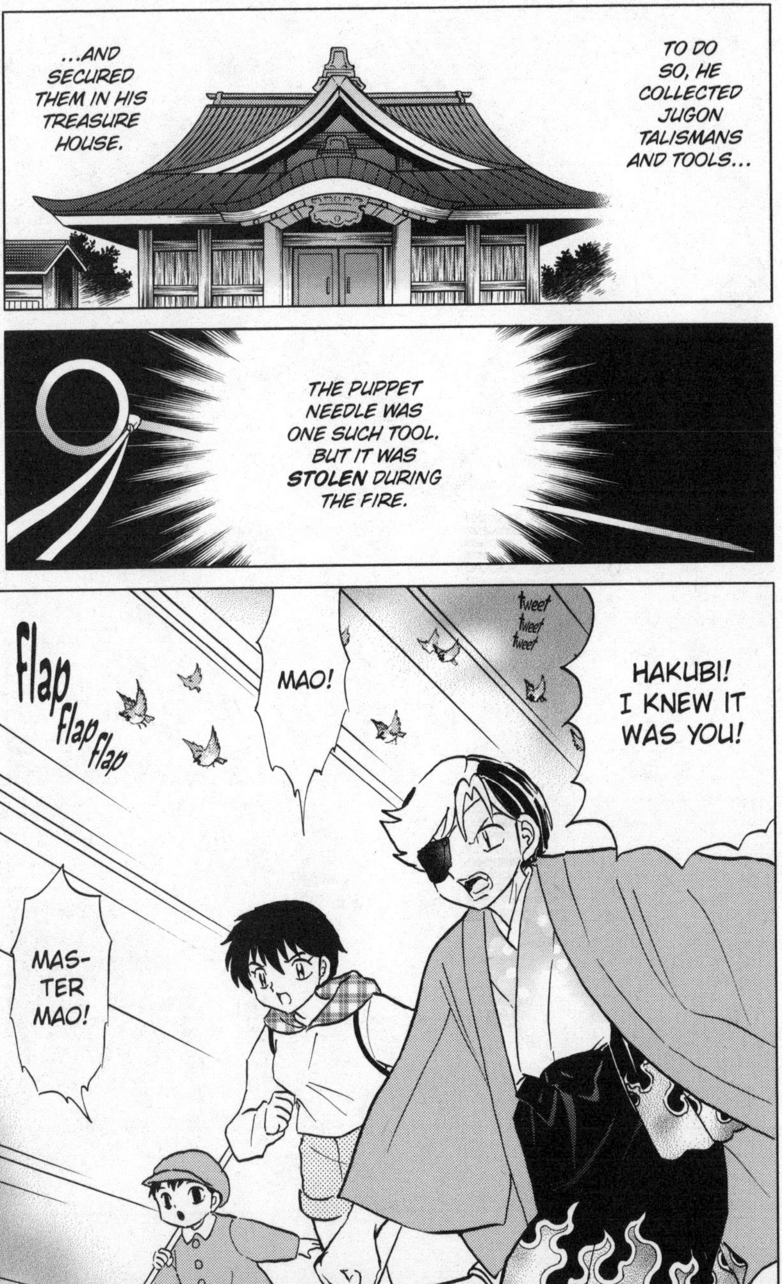
TO DO SO, HE COLLECTED JUGON TALISMANS AND TOOLS...
...AND SECURED THEM IN HIS TREASURE HOUSE.
THE PUPPET NEEDLE WAS ONE SUCH TOOL. BUT IT WAS **STOLEN** DURING THE FIRE.
HAKUBI! I KNEW IT WAS YOU!
tweet tweet tweet
MAO!
Flap Flap Flap
MAS-TER MAO!

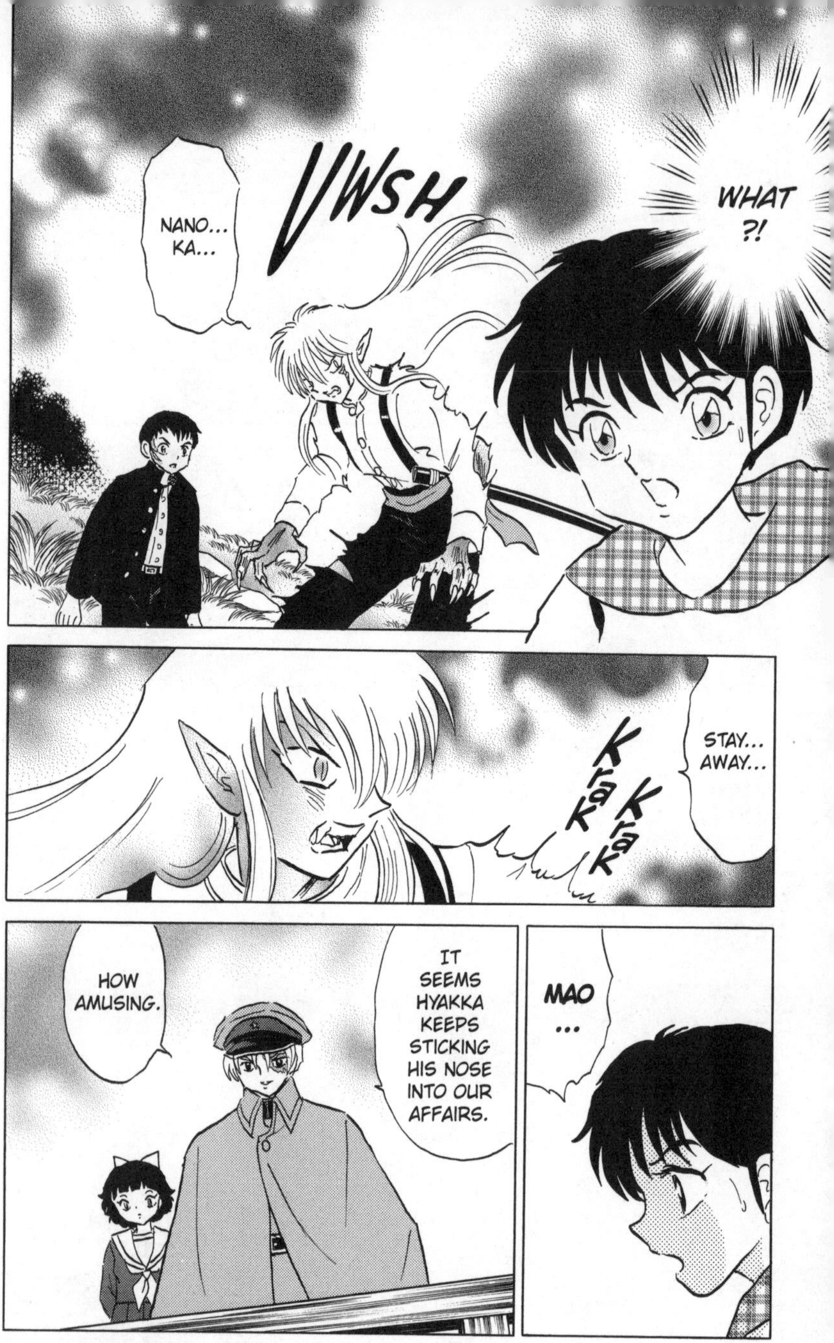
WHAT ?!
VWSH
NANO... KA...
STAY... AWAY...
Krak Krak
MAO ...
IT SEEMS HYAKKA KEEPS STICKING HIS NOSE INTO OUR AFFAIRS.
HOW AMUSING.

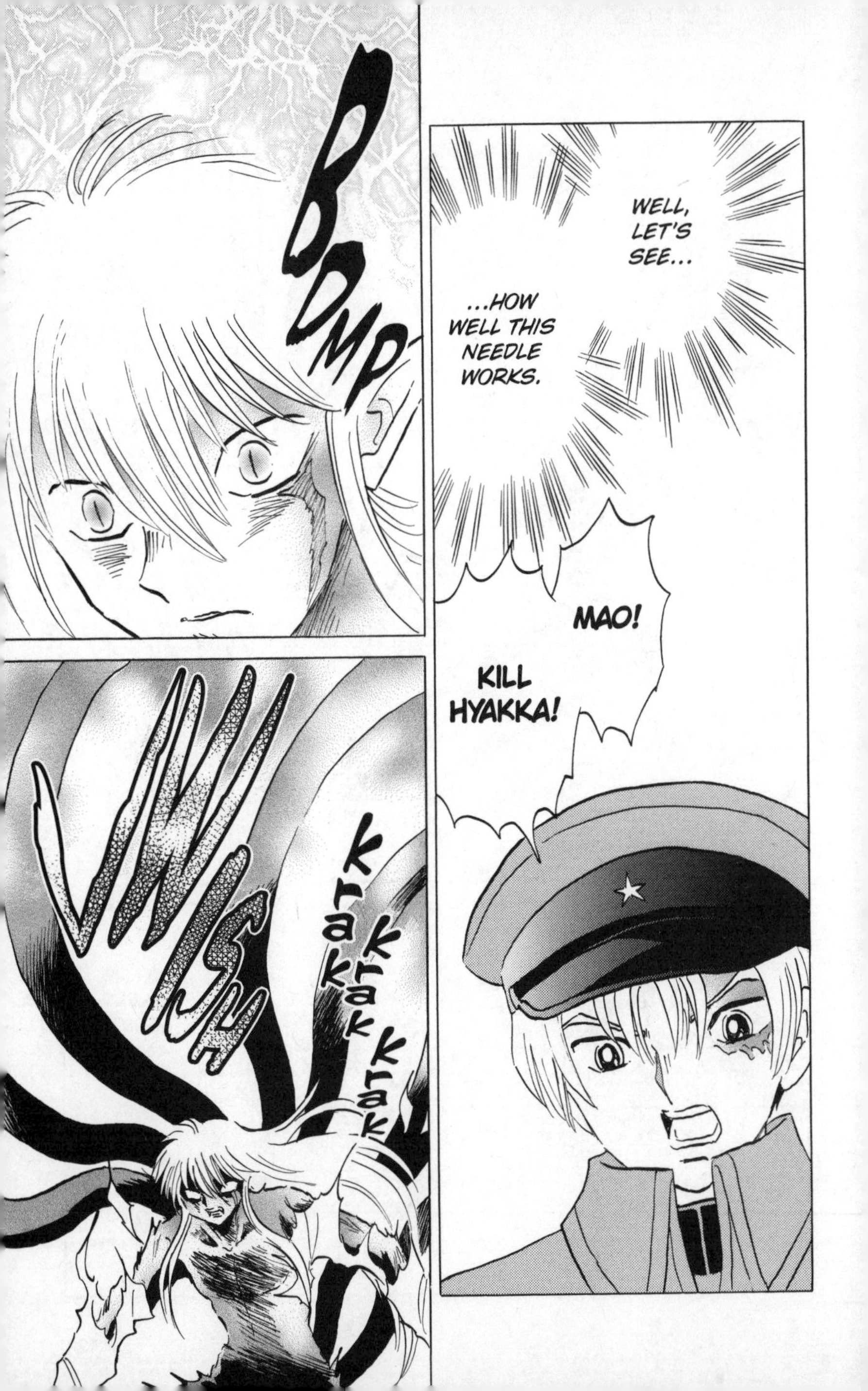
WELL, LET'S SEE...
...HOW WELL THIS NEEDLE WORKS.
MAO!
KILL HYAKKA!
BDMP
krak krak krak

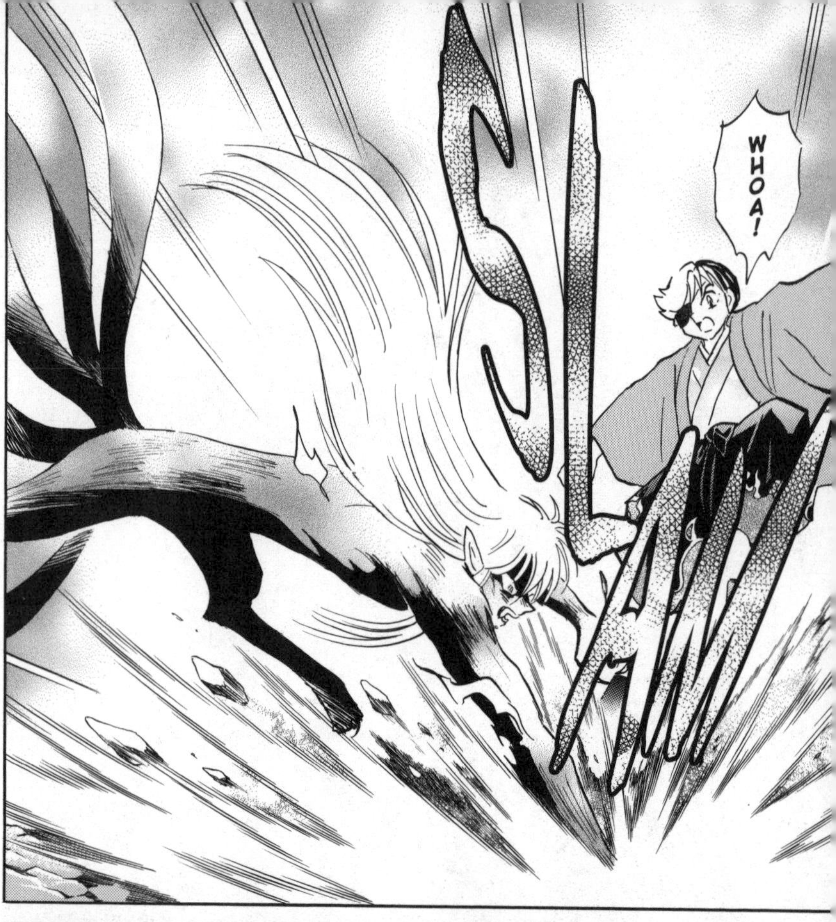
WHOA!
SLAM

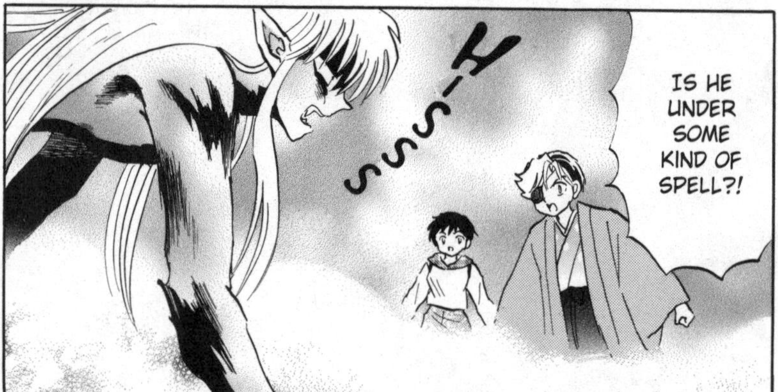
IS HE UNDER SOME KIND OF SPELL?!
SSSS–H

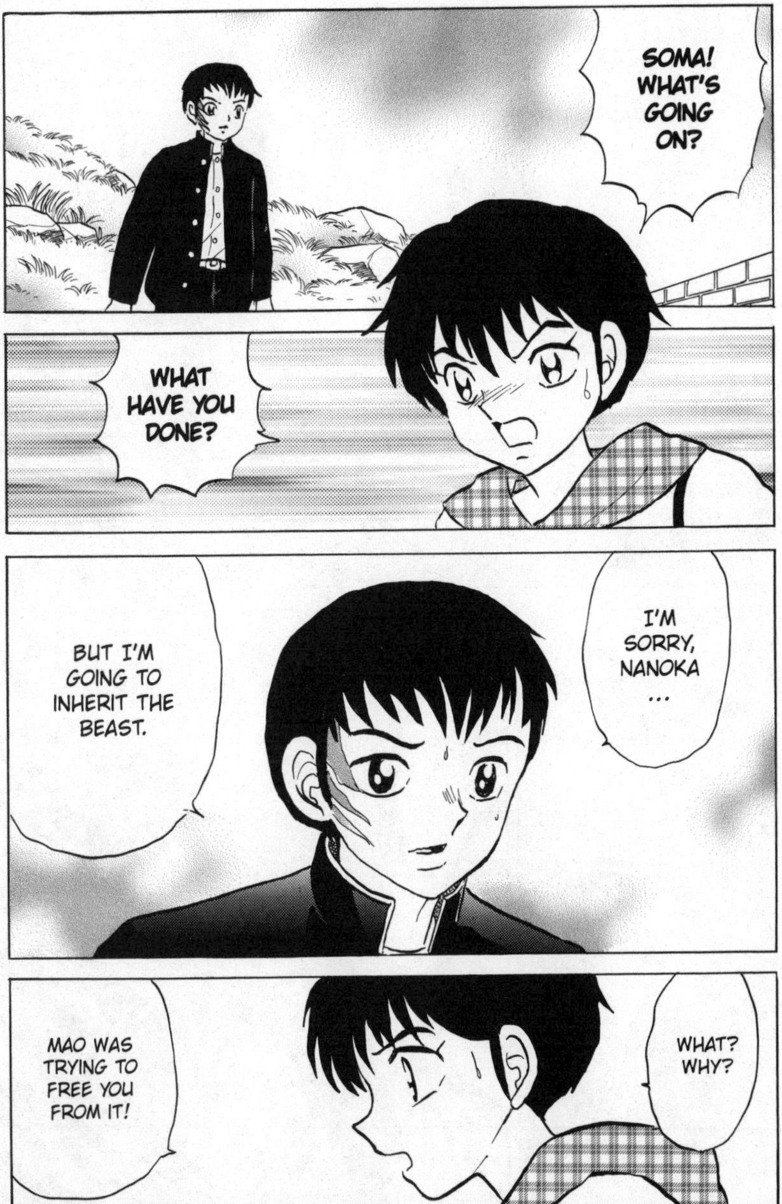
SOMA! WHAT'S GOING ON?
WHAT HAVE YOU DONE?
I'M SORRY, NANOKA ...
BUT I'M GOING TO INHERIT THE BEAST.
WHAT? WHY?
MAO WAS TRYING TO FREE YOU FROM IT!

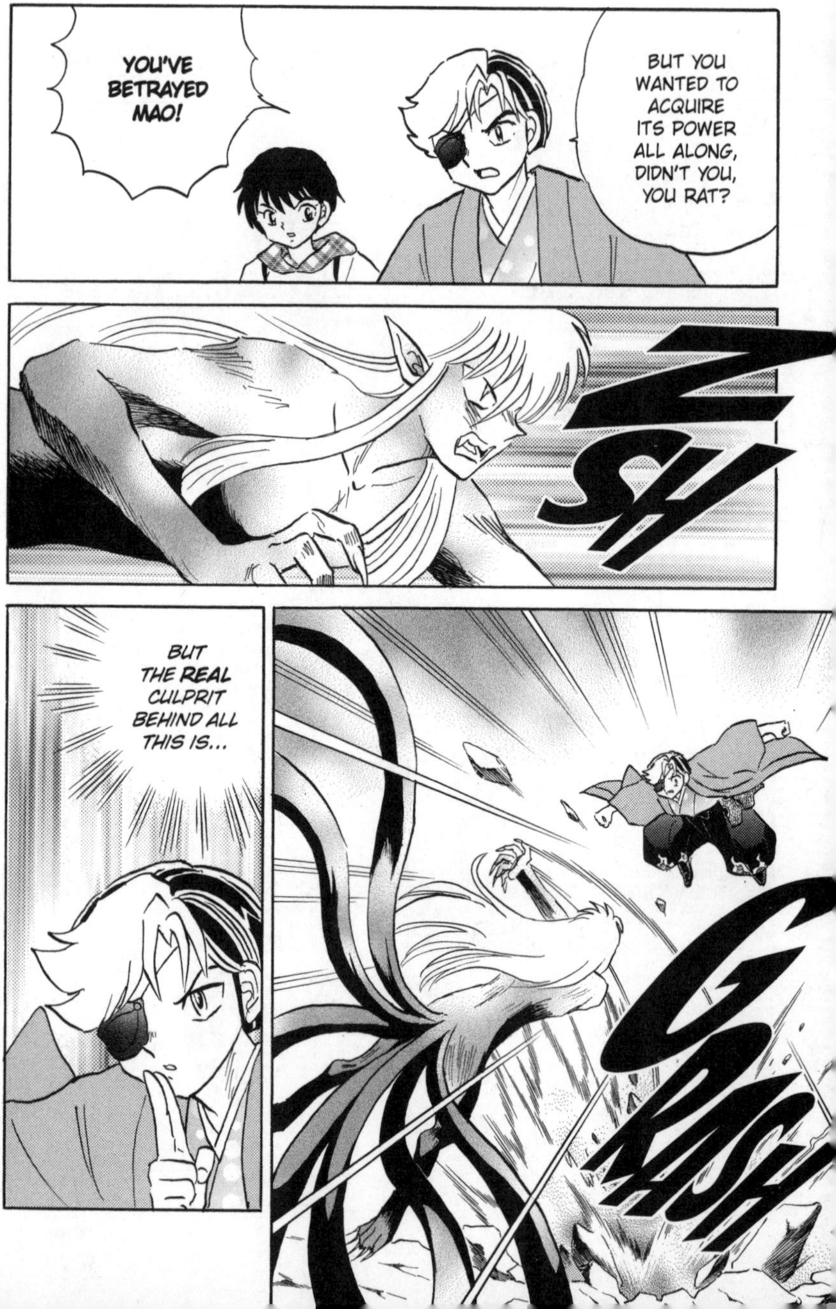
BUT YOU WANTED TO ACQUIRE ITS POWER ALL ALONG, DIDN'T YOU, YOU RAT?
YOU'VE BETRAYED MAO!
SMASH
BUT THE REAL CULPRIT BEHIND ALL THIS IS...

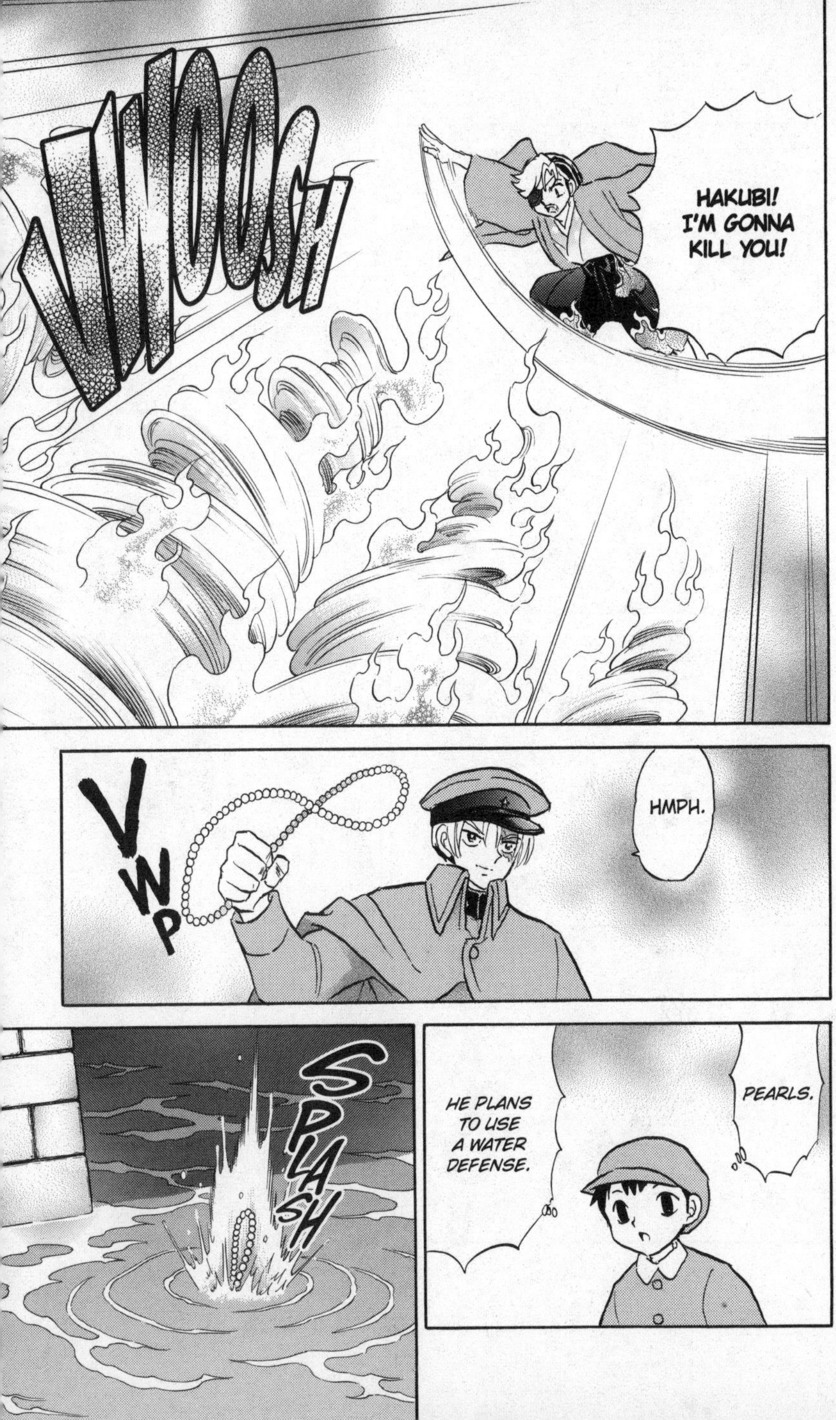
HAKUBI! I'M GONNA KILL YOU!
WHOOSH
HMPH.
VWP
PEARLS.
HE PLANS TO USE A WATER DEFENSE.
SPLASH

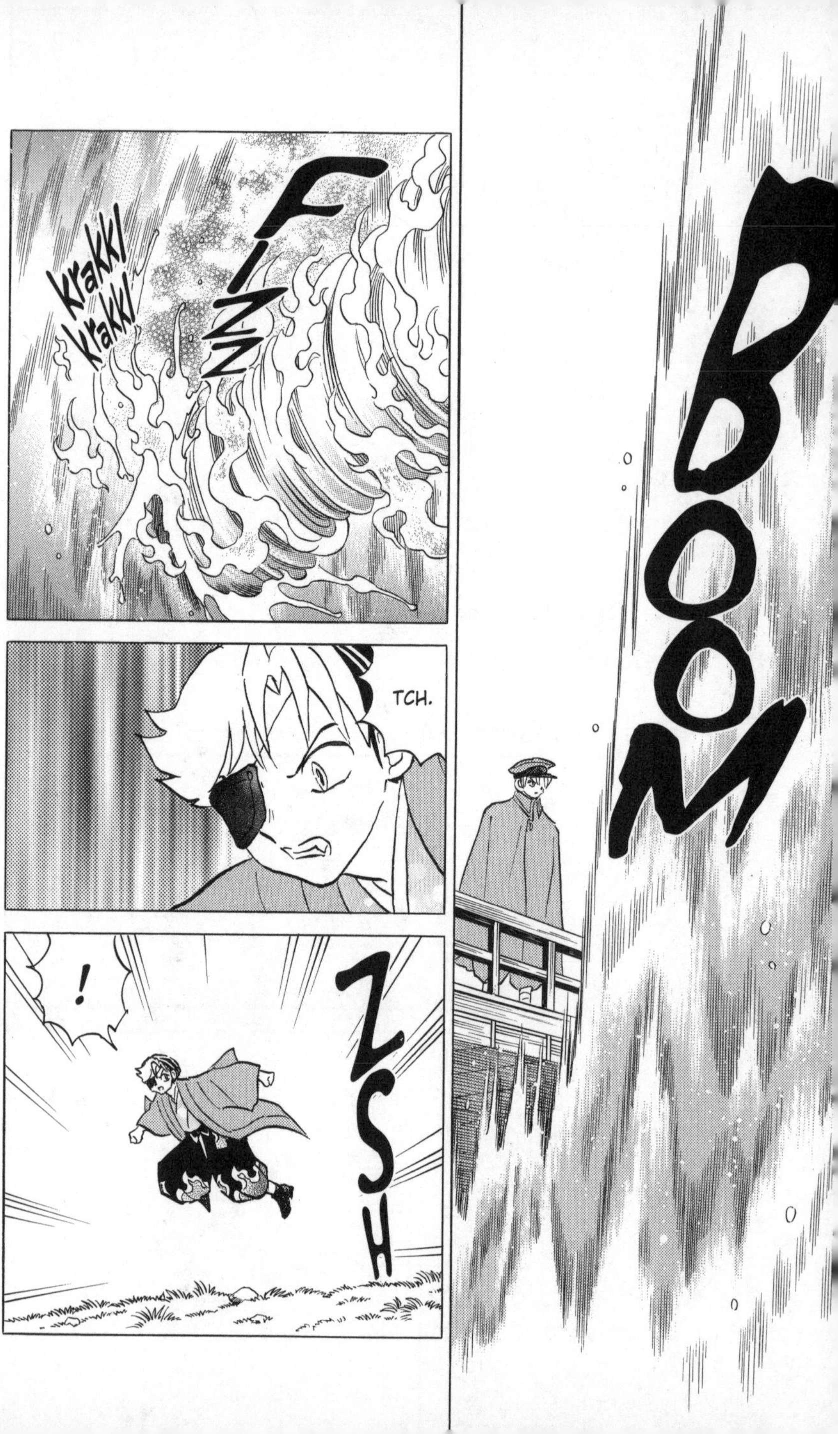
BDOOM
FIZZZ
krakkl
krakkl
TCH.
!
ZSH

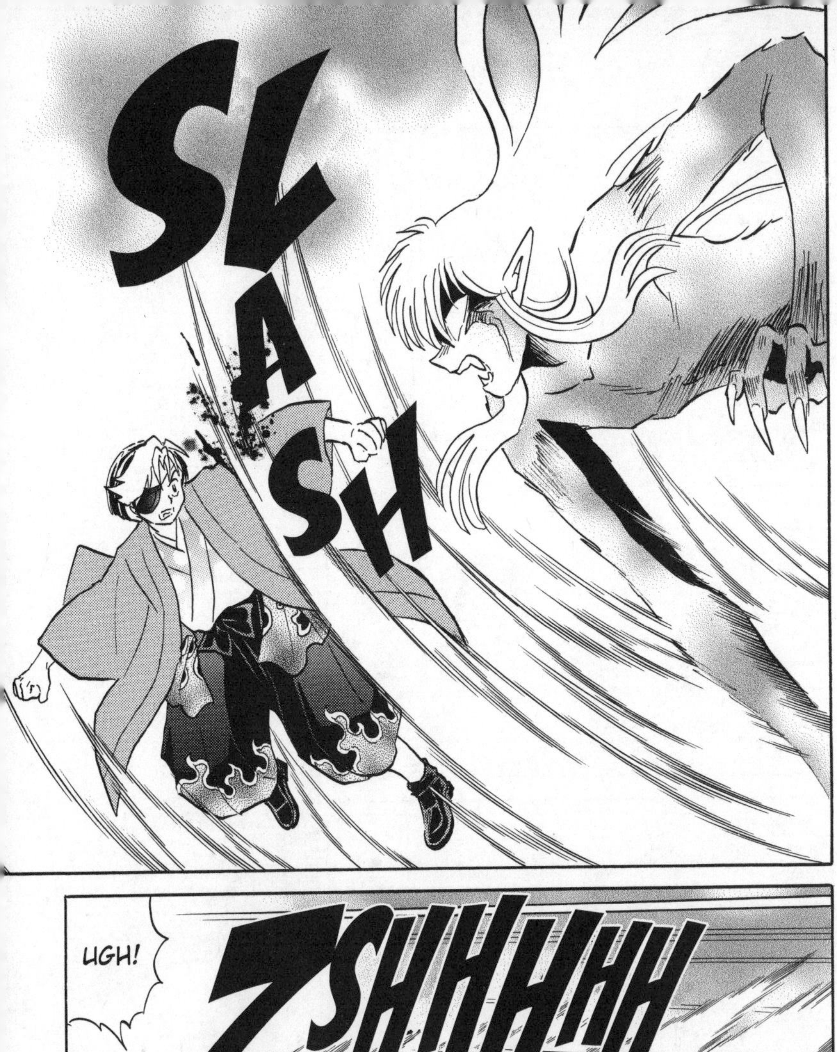
SLASH
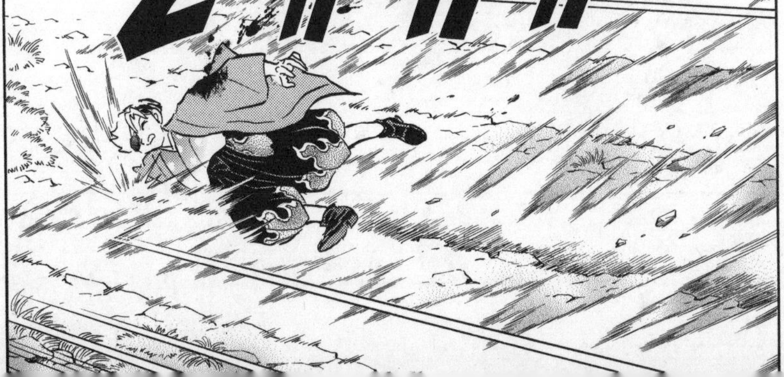
UGH!
ZSHHHHHH

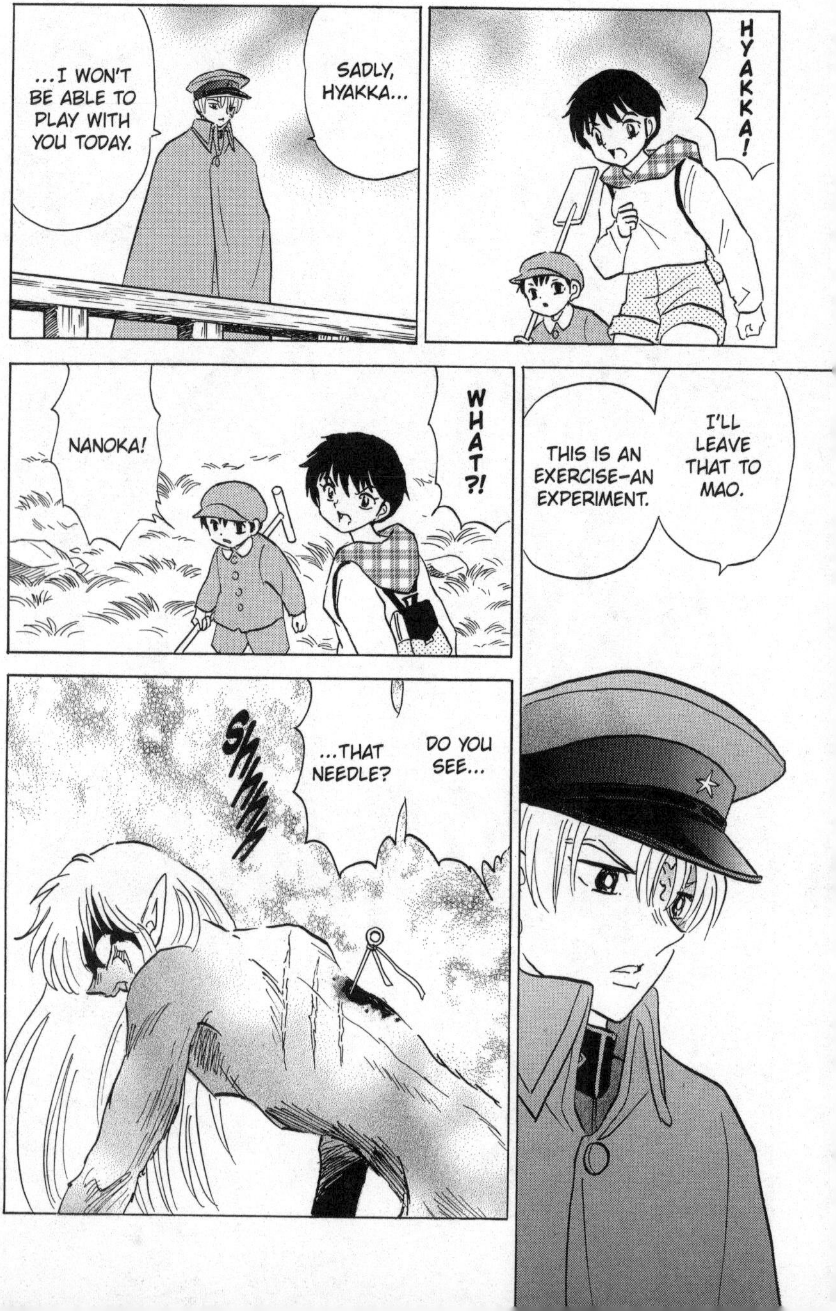
HYAKKA!
SADLY, HYAKKA...
...I WON'T BE ABLE TO PLAY WITH YOU TODAY.
I'LL LEAVE THAT TO MAO.
THIS IS AN EXERCISE—AN EXPERIMENT.
WHAT?!
NANOKA!
DO YOU SEE...
...THAT NEEDLE?

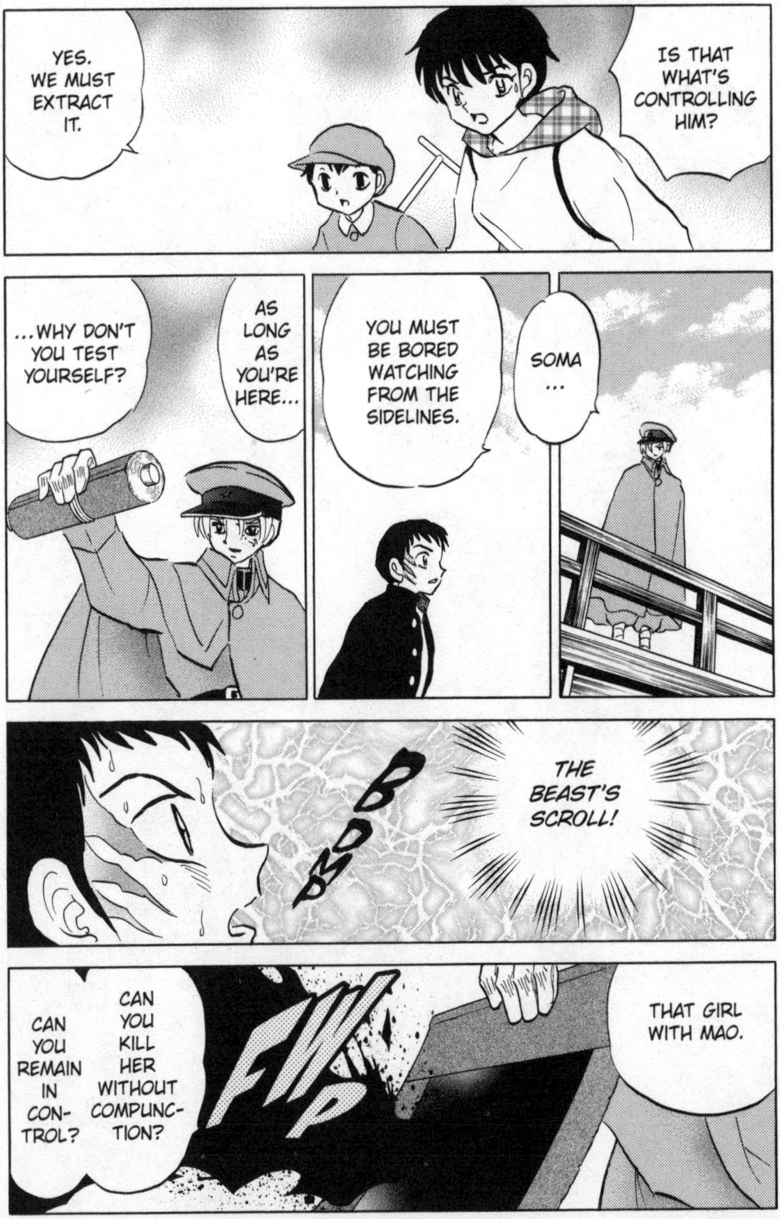
IS THAT WHAT'S CONTROLLING HIM?
YES. WE MUST EXTRACT IT.
SOMA ...
YOU MUST BE BORED WATCHING FROM THE SIDELINES.
AS LONG AS YOU'RE HERE...
...WHY DON'T YOU TEST YOURSELF?
THE BEAST'S SCROLL!
BDMP
THAT GIRL WITH MAO.
CAN YOU KILL HER WITHOUT COMPUNCTION?
CAN YOU REMAIN IN CONTROL?
FWP

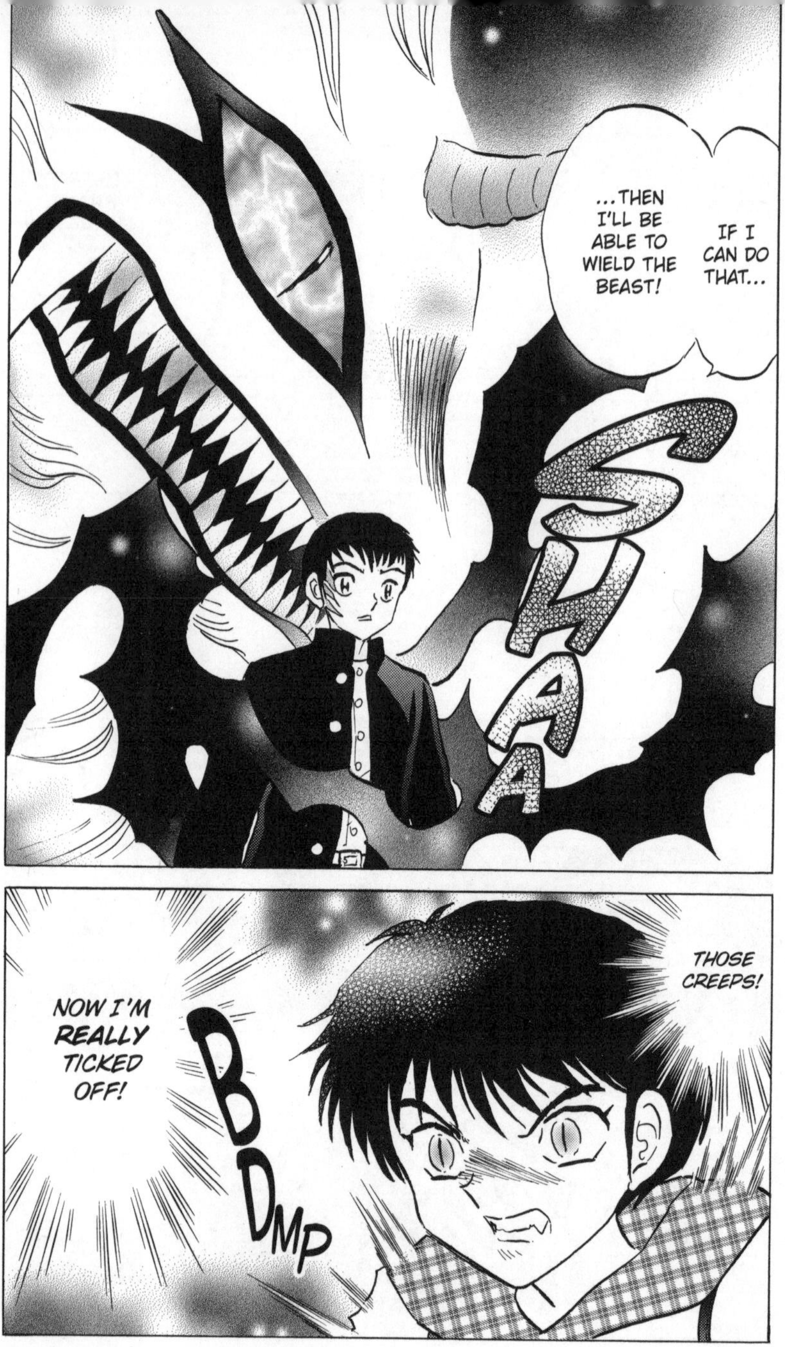
IF I CAN DO THAT...
...THEN I'LL BE ABLE TO WIELD THE BEAST!
SHAA
THOSE CREEPS!
BDMP
NOW I'M **REALLY** TICKED OFF!

Chapter 8: Strike the Beast

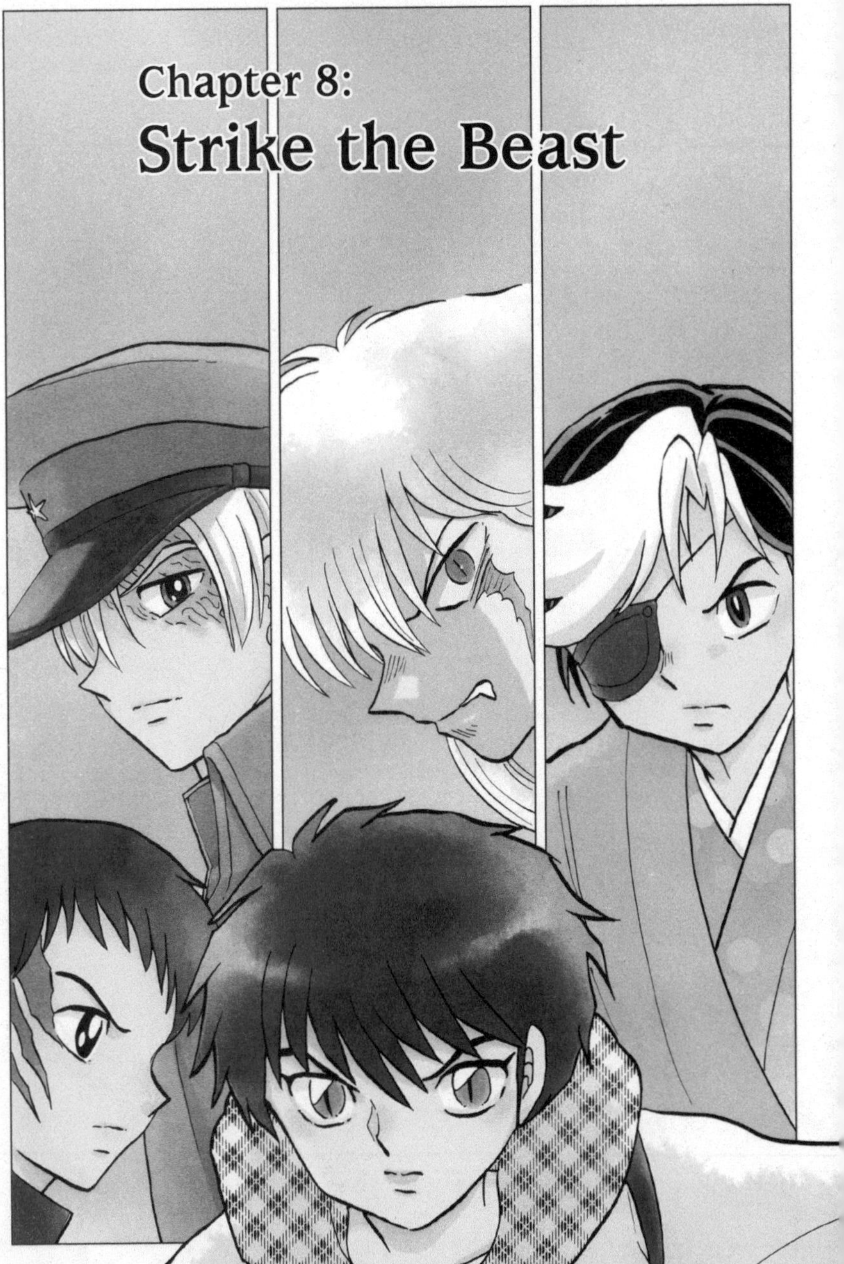

MAO

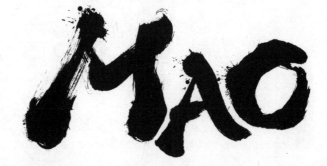

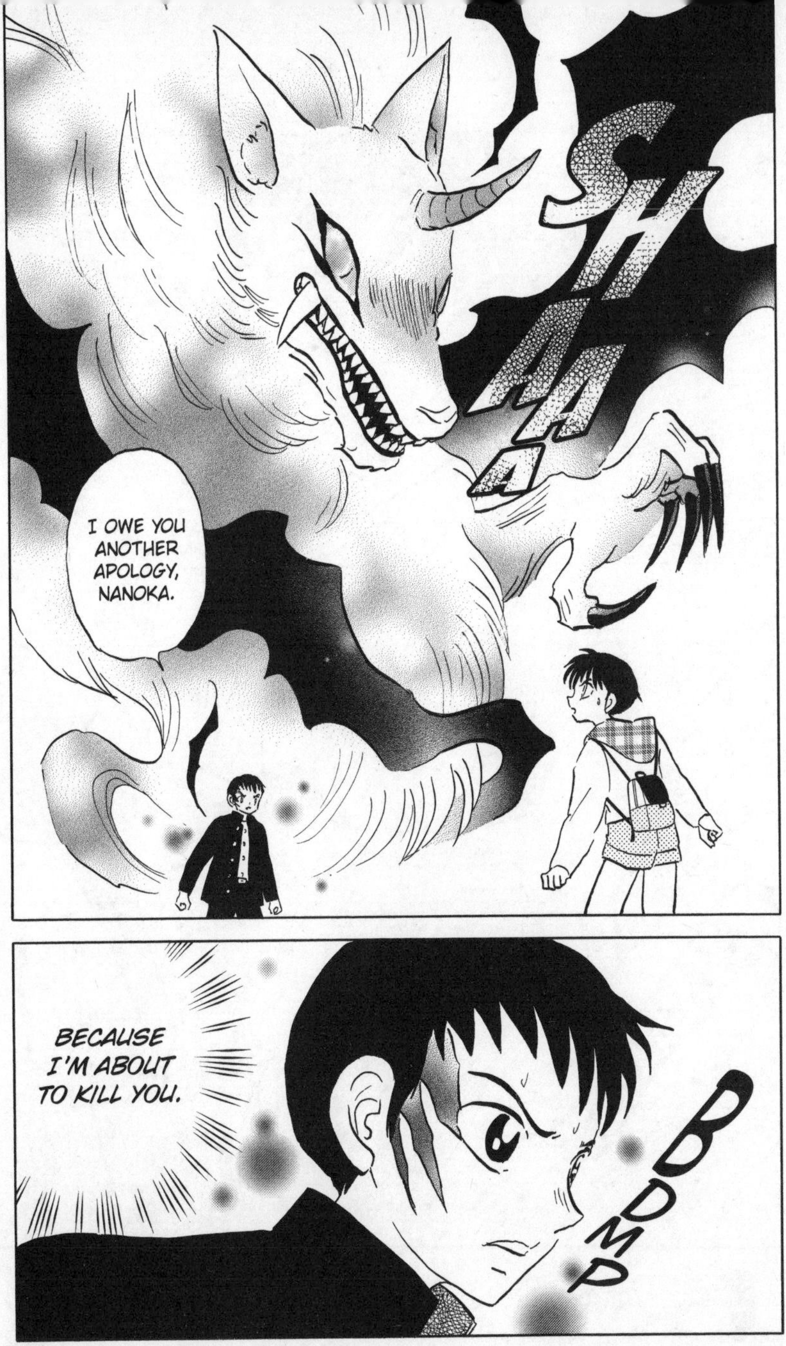
SHAAA
I OWE YOU ANOTHER APOLOGY, NANOKA.
BECAUSE I'M ABOUT TO KILL YOU.
BDDMP

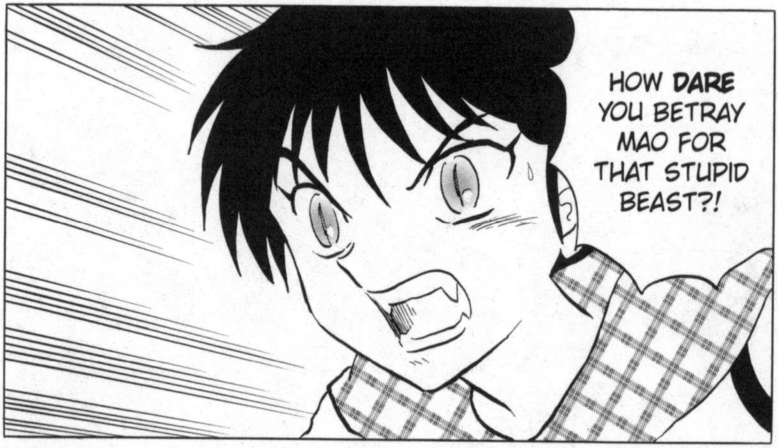
HOW **DARE** YOU BETRAY MAO FOR THAT STUPID BEAST?!
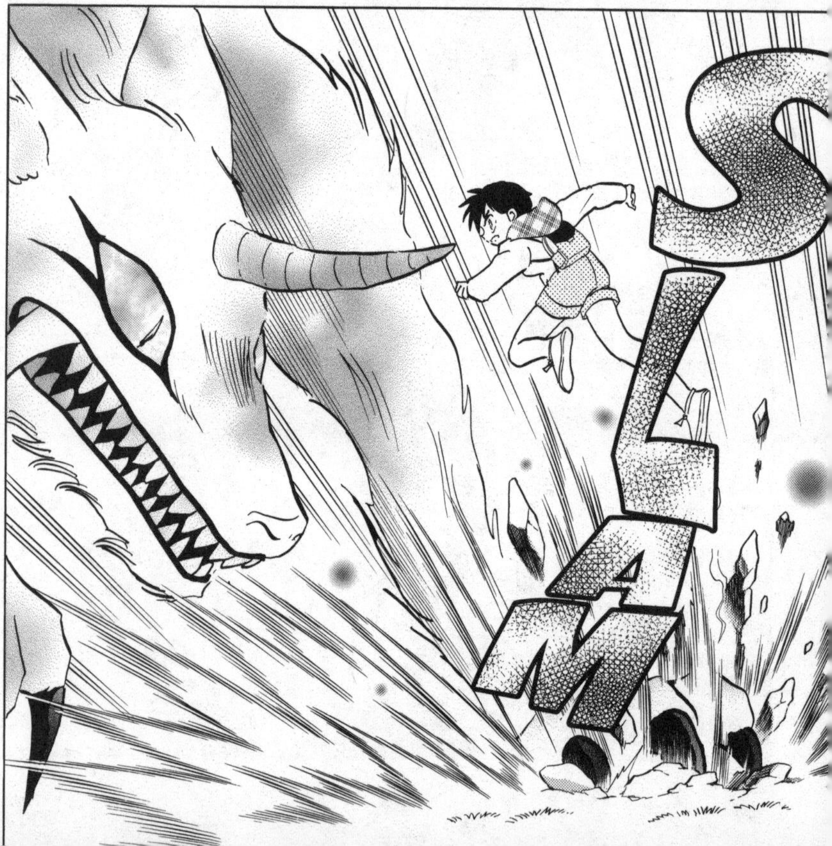
SLAM

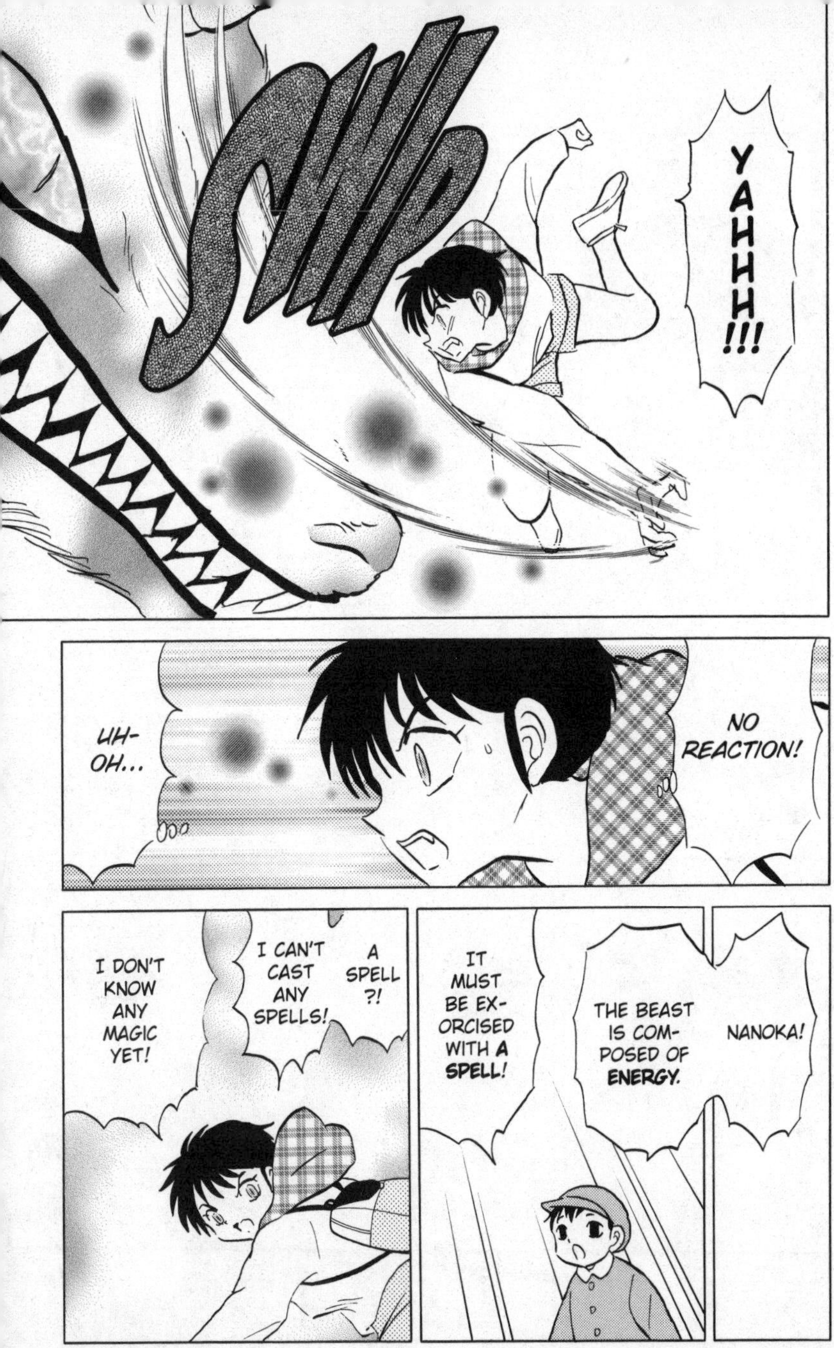
YAHHH!!!
NO REACTION!
UH-OH...
NANOKA!
THE BEAST IS COMPOSED OF **ENERGY**.
IT MUST BE EXORCISED WITH **A SPELL**!
A SPELL?!
I CAN'T CAST ANY SPELLS!
I DON'T KNOW ANY MAGIC YET!

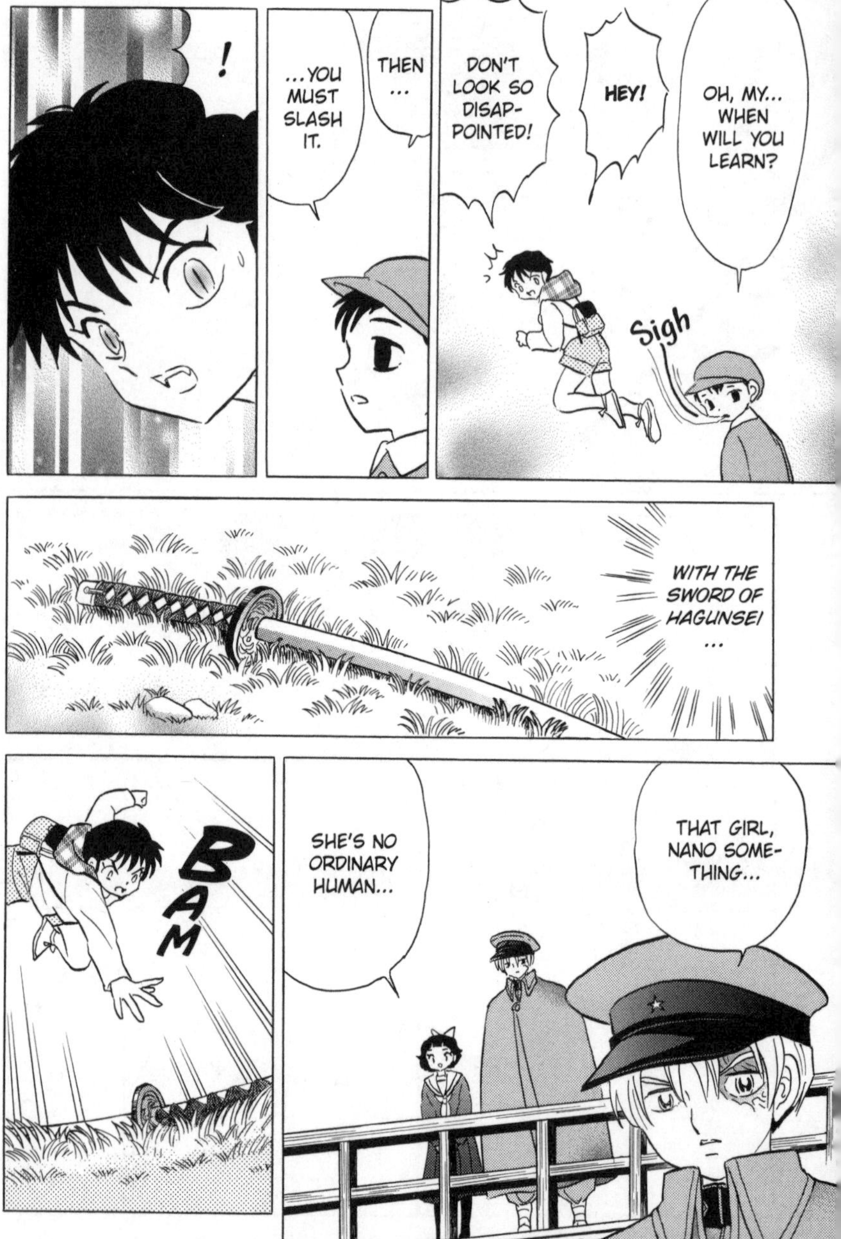
OH, MY... WHEN WILL YOU LEARN?
Sigh
HEY!
DON'T LOOK SO DISAP-POINTED!
THEN ...
...YOU MUST SLASH IT.
!
WITH THE SWORD OF HAGUNSEI ...
THAT GIRL, NANO SOME-THING...
SHE'S NO ORDINARY HUMAN...
BAM

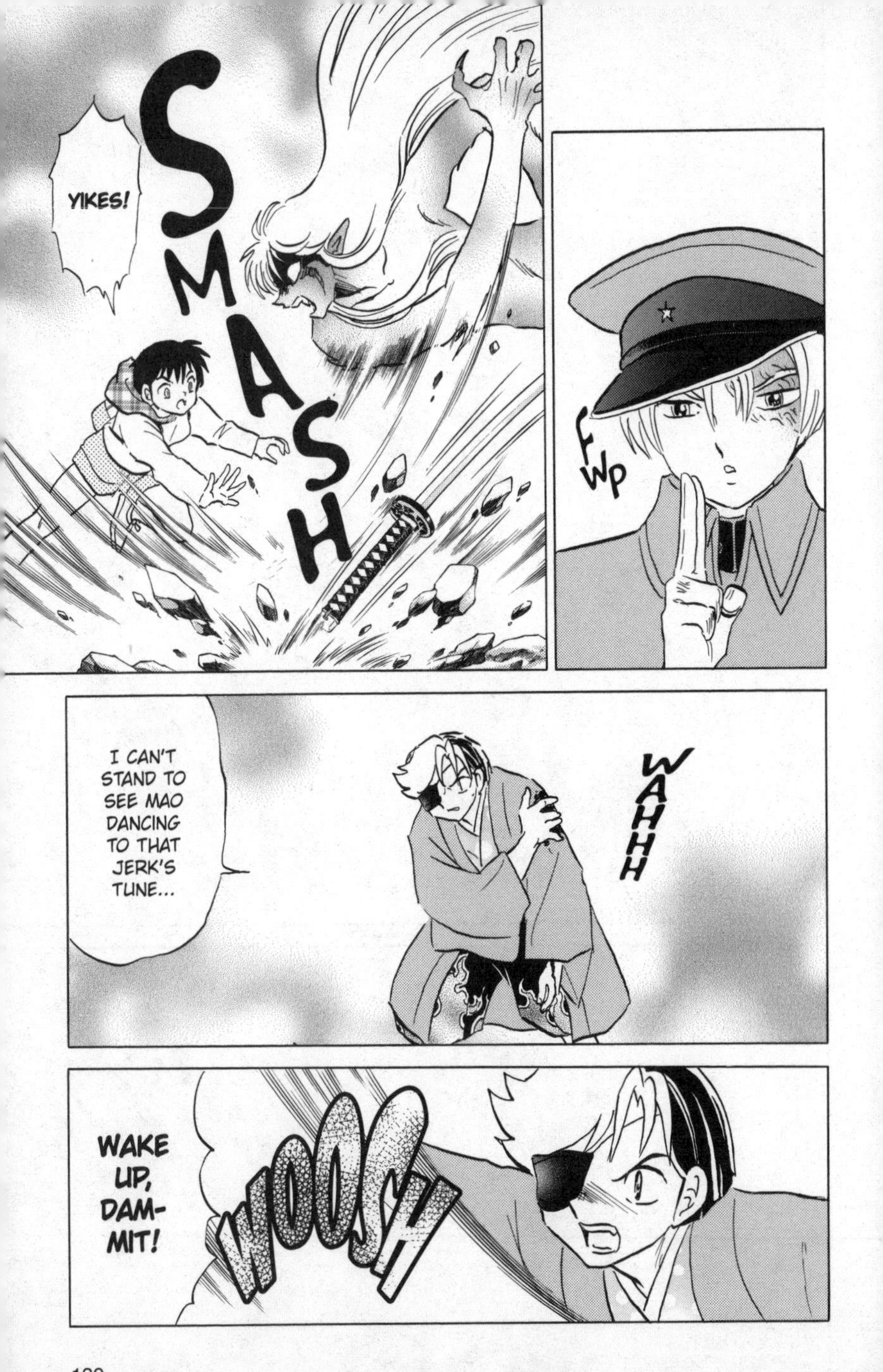
FWP
YIKES!
SMASH
I CAN'T STAND TO SEE MAO DANCING TO THAT JERK'S TUNE...
WAHHH
WAKE UP, DAM-MIT!
WOOSH

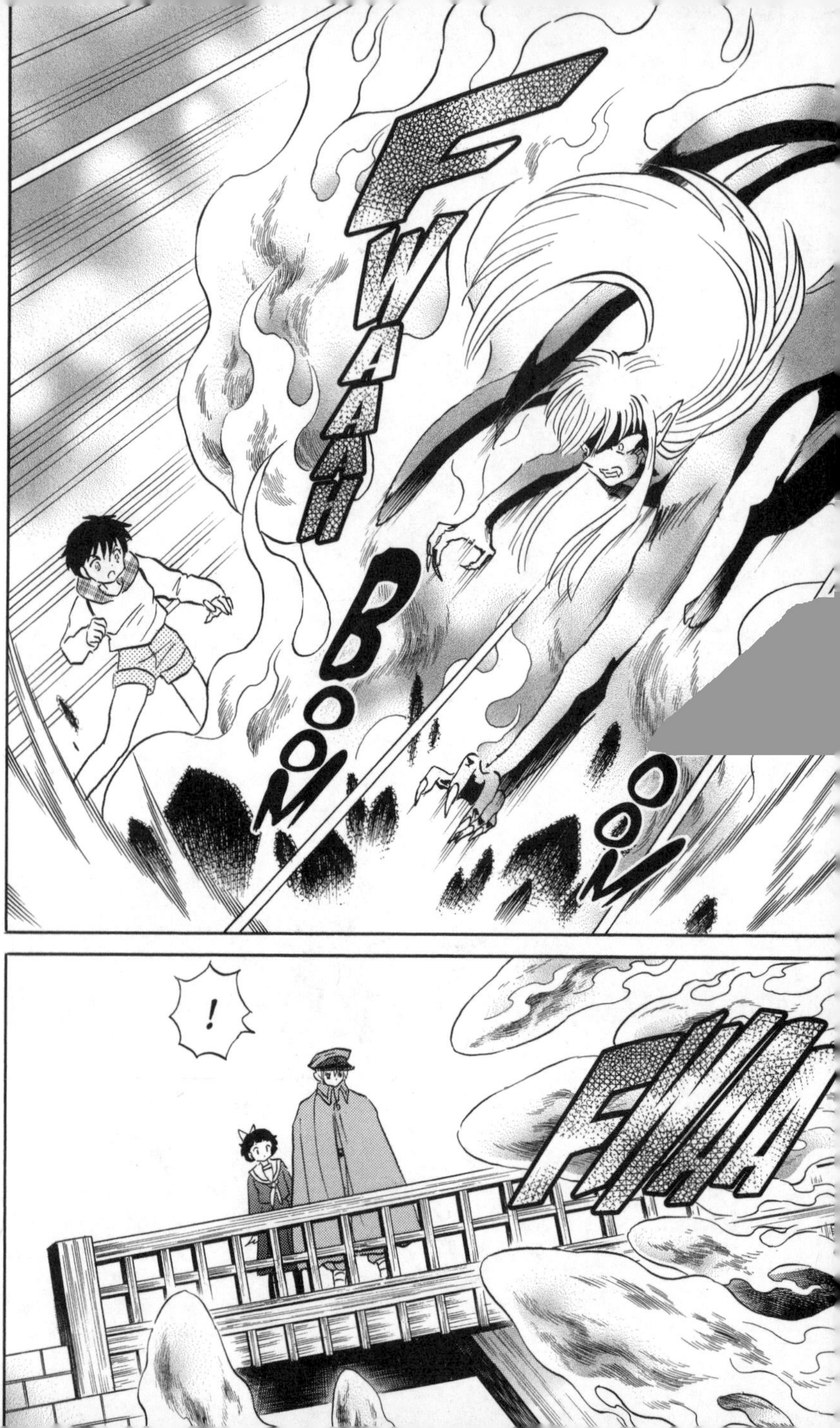
FWAAAH
BOOOM
OOOM
FWHA
!

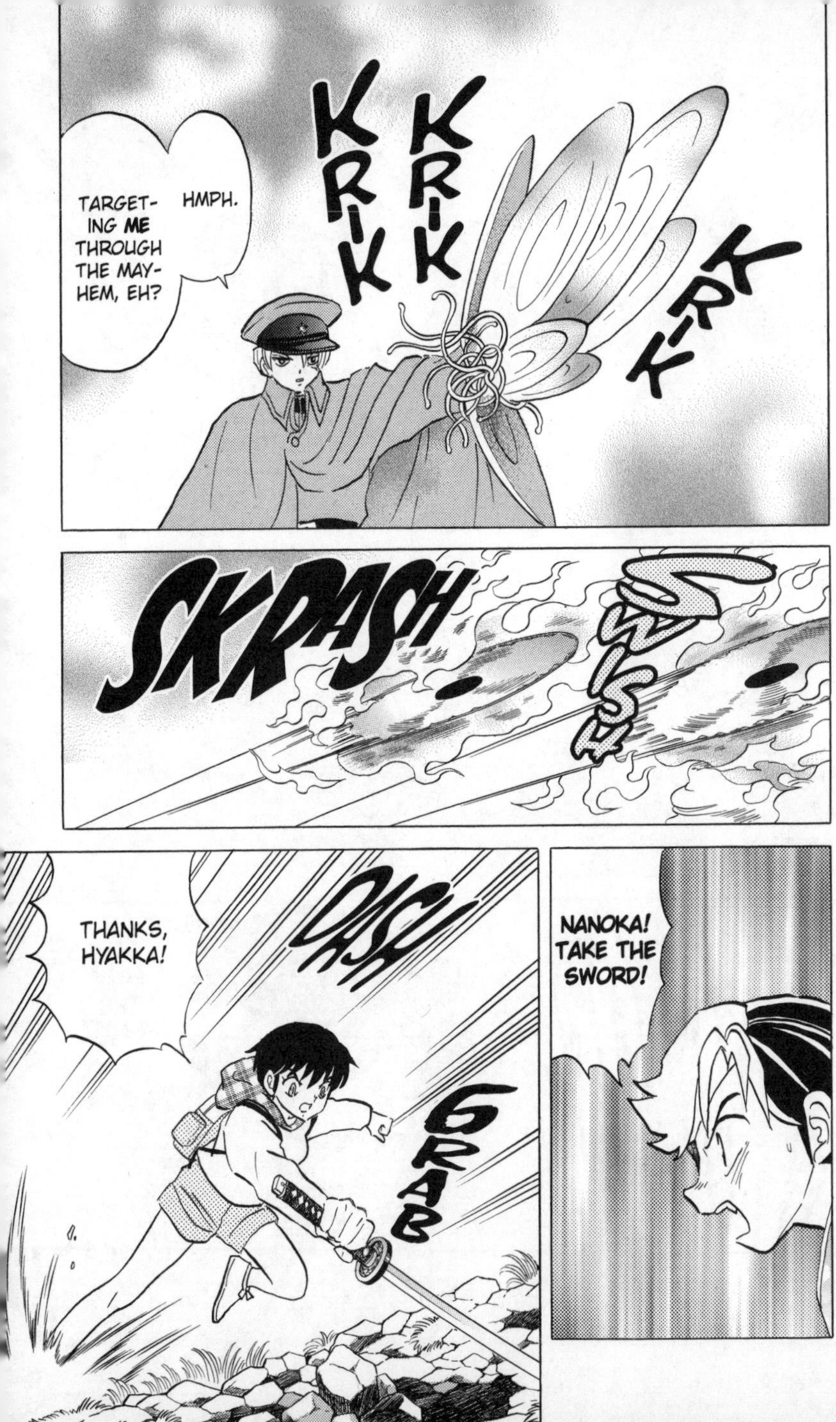
K-R-K
KRIK
KRIK
HMPH.
TARGET-ING ME THROUGH THE MAY-HEM, EH?
SWISH
SKRASH
NANOKA! TAKE THE SWORD!
DASH
THANKS, HYAKKA!
GRAB

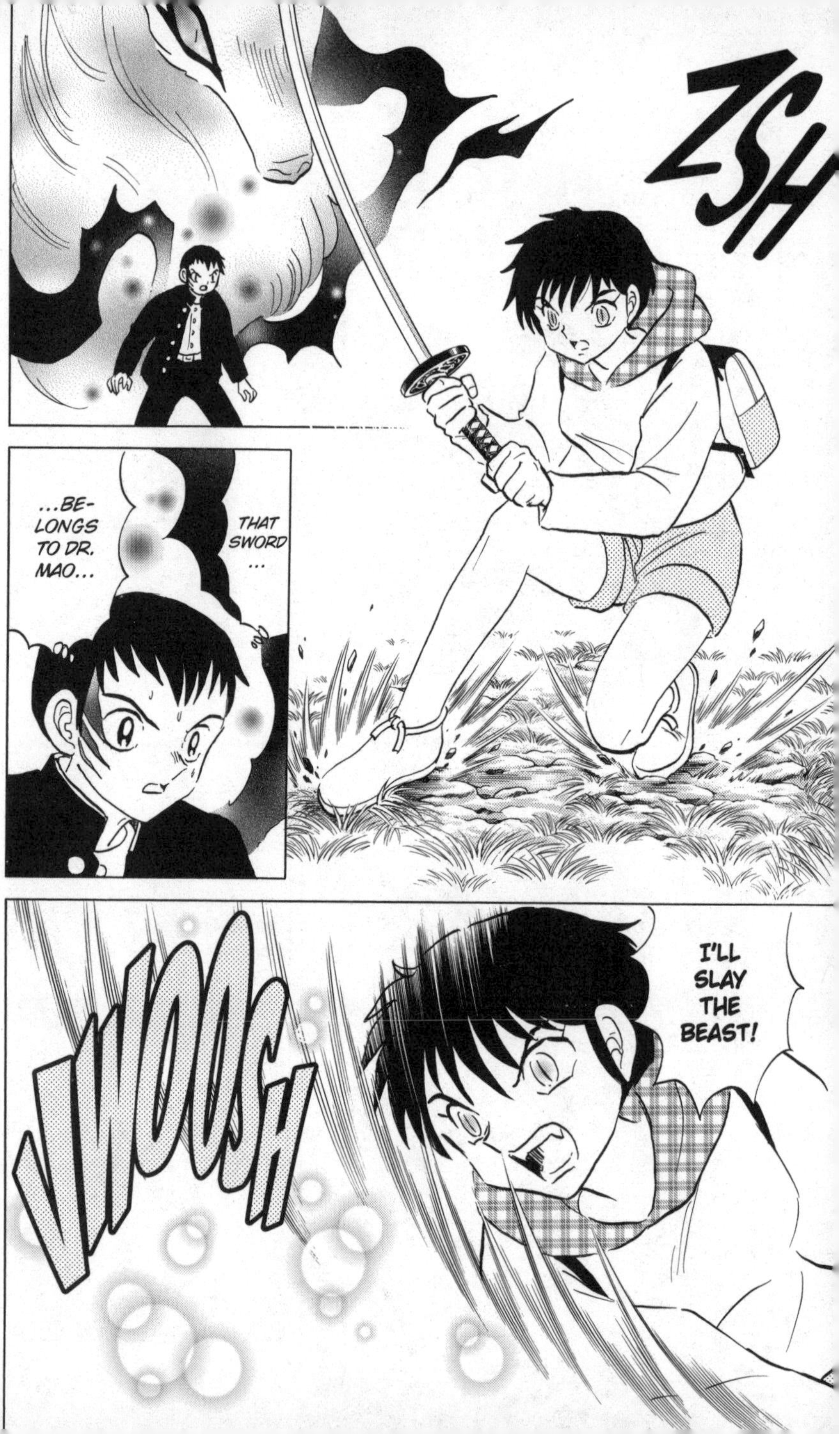
ZSH
THAT SWORD...
...BE-LONGS TO DR. MAO...
I'LL SLAY THE BEAST!
VWOOSH

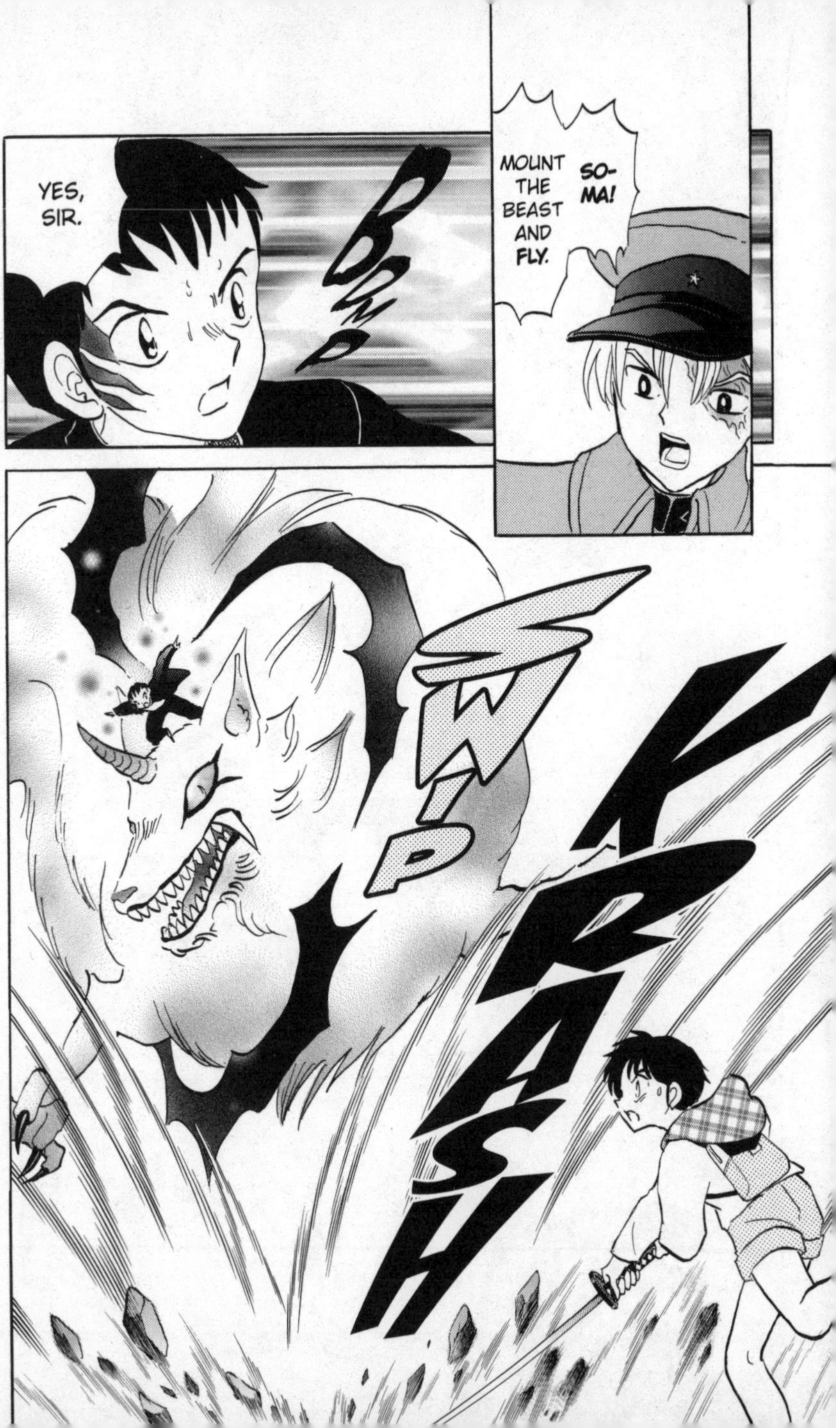
SO-MA!
MOUNT THE BEAST AND FLY.
YES, SIR.
BOOMP
SWIP
KRASH!

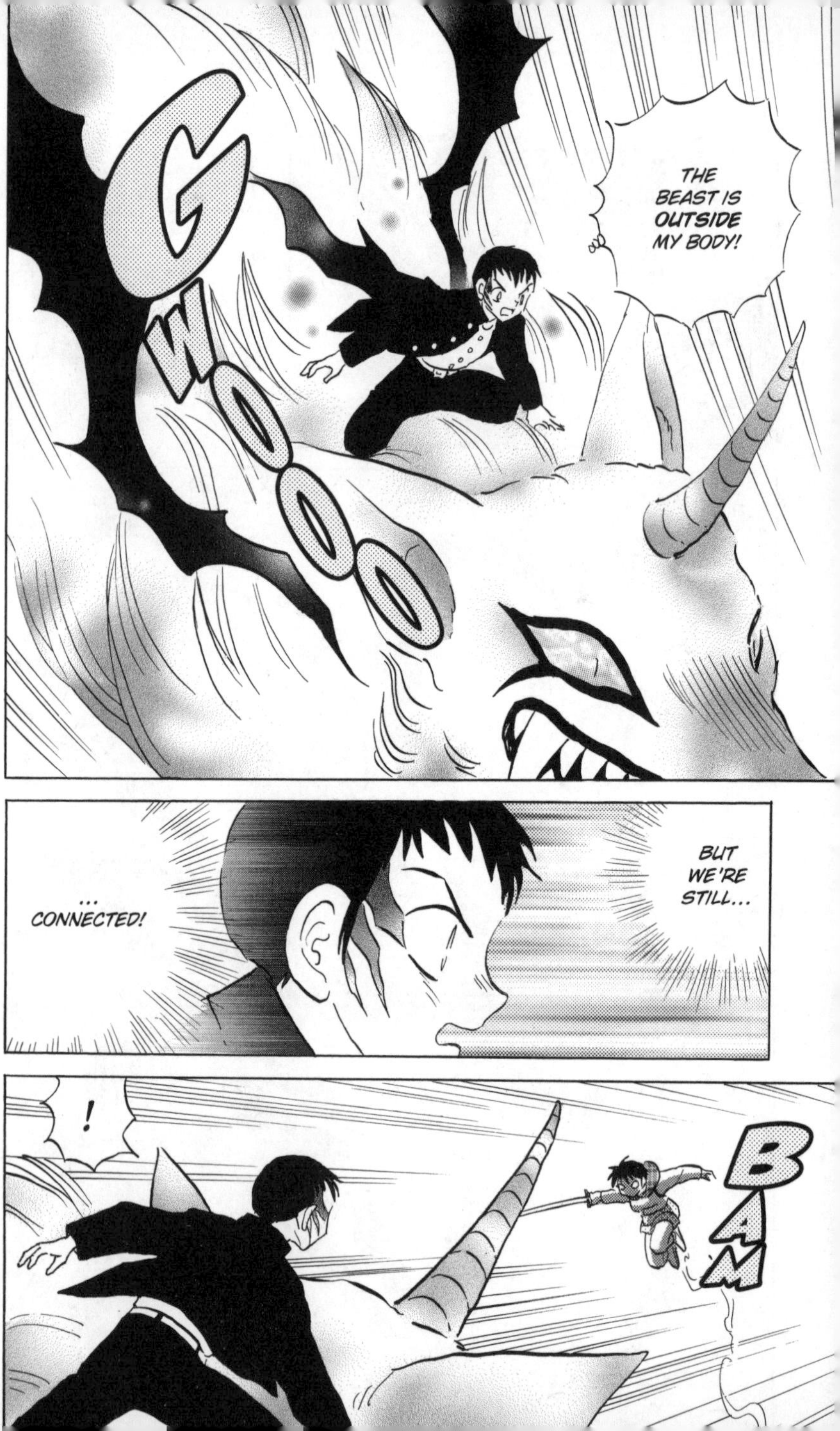
THE BEAST IS OUTSIDE MY BODY!
GWOOOOO
BUT WE'RE STILL...
...CONNECTED!
BAM
!

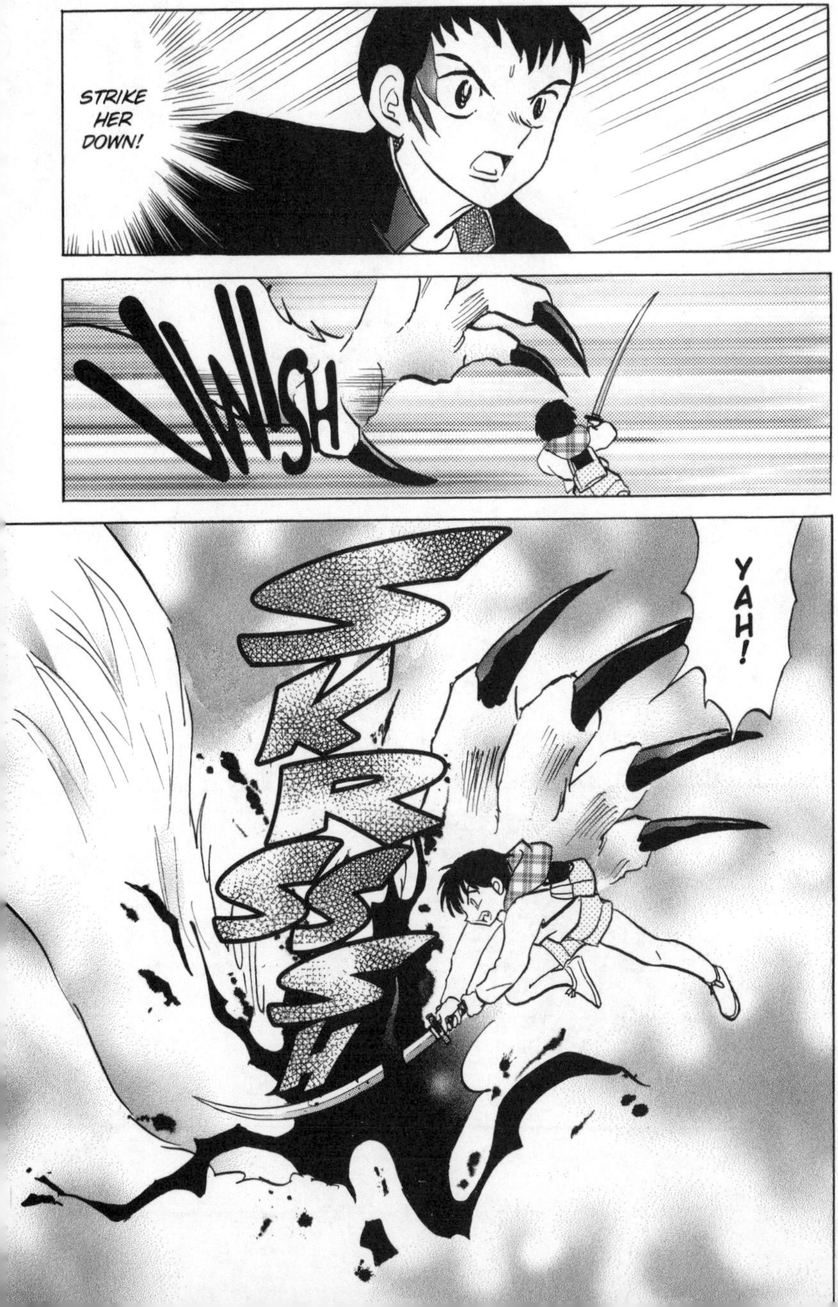
STRIKE HER DOWN!
VWISH
YAH!
SKRSSSH

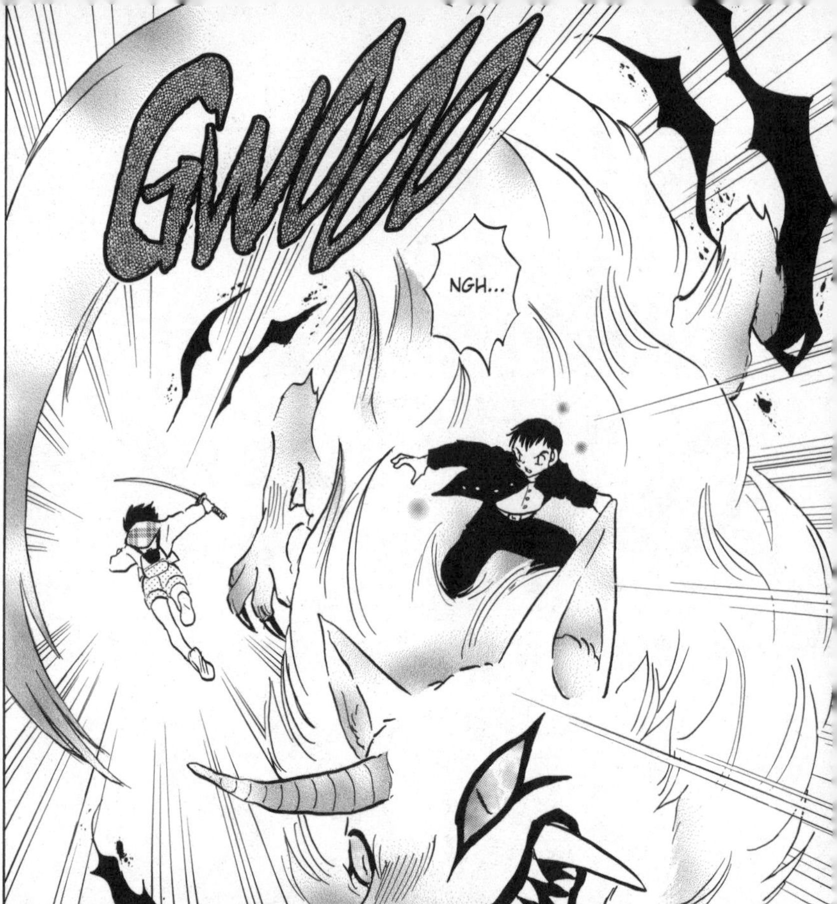
GWOM
NGH...

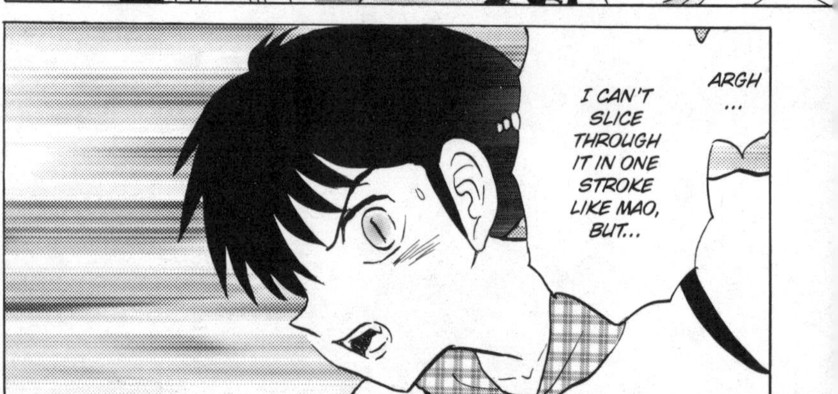
ARGH ...
I CAN'T SLICE THROUGH IT IN ONE STROKE LIKE MAO, BUT...

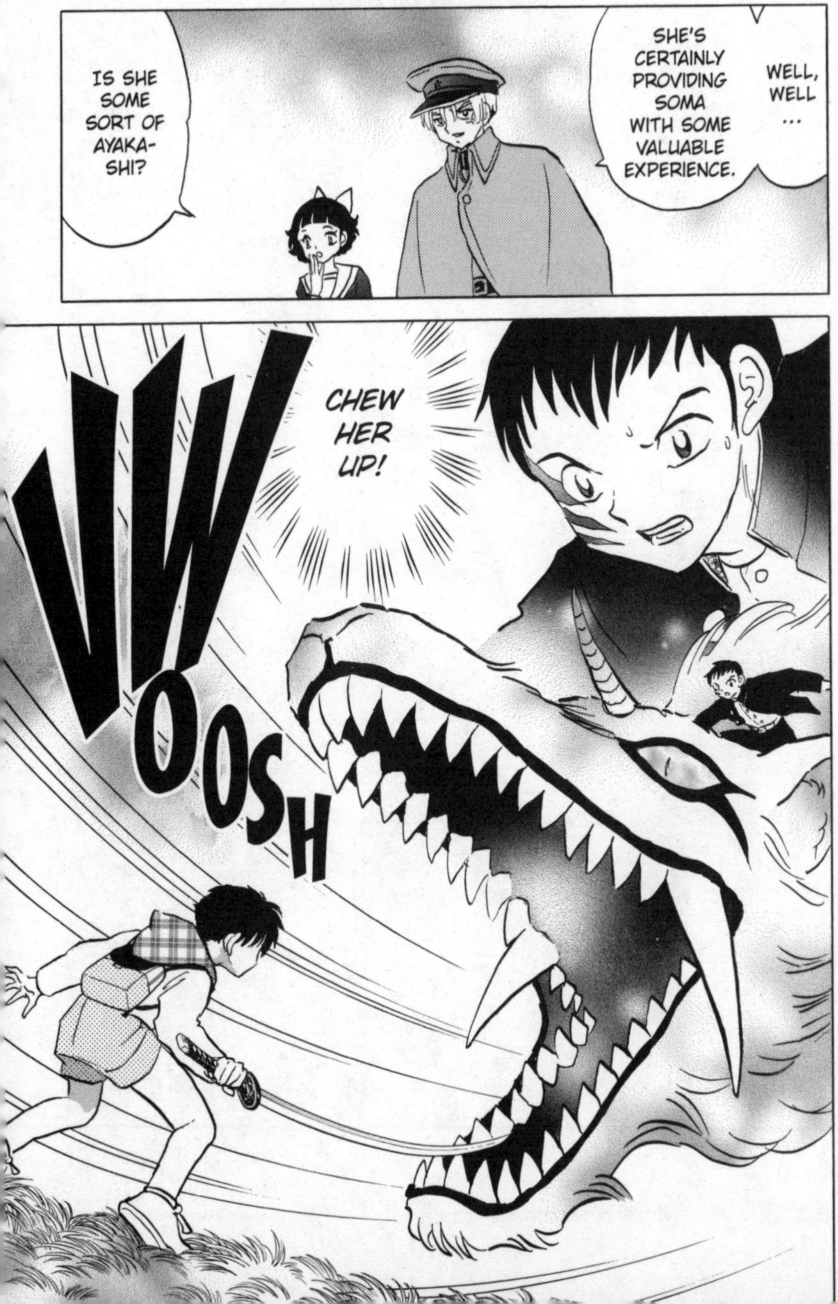
WELL, WELL ...
SHE'S CERTAINLY PROVIDING SOMA WITH SOME VALUABLE EXPERIENCE.
IS SHE SOME SORT OF AYAKA-SHI?
CHEW HER UP!
VWOOSH

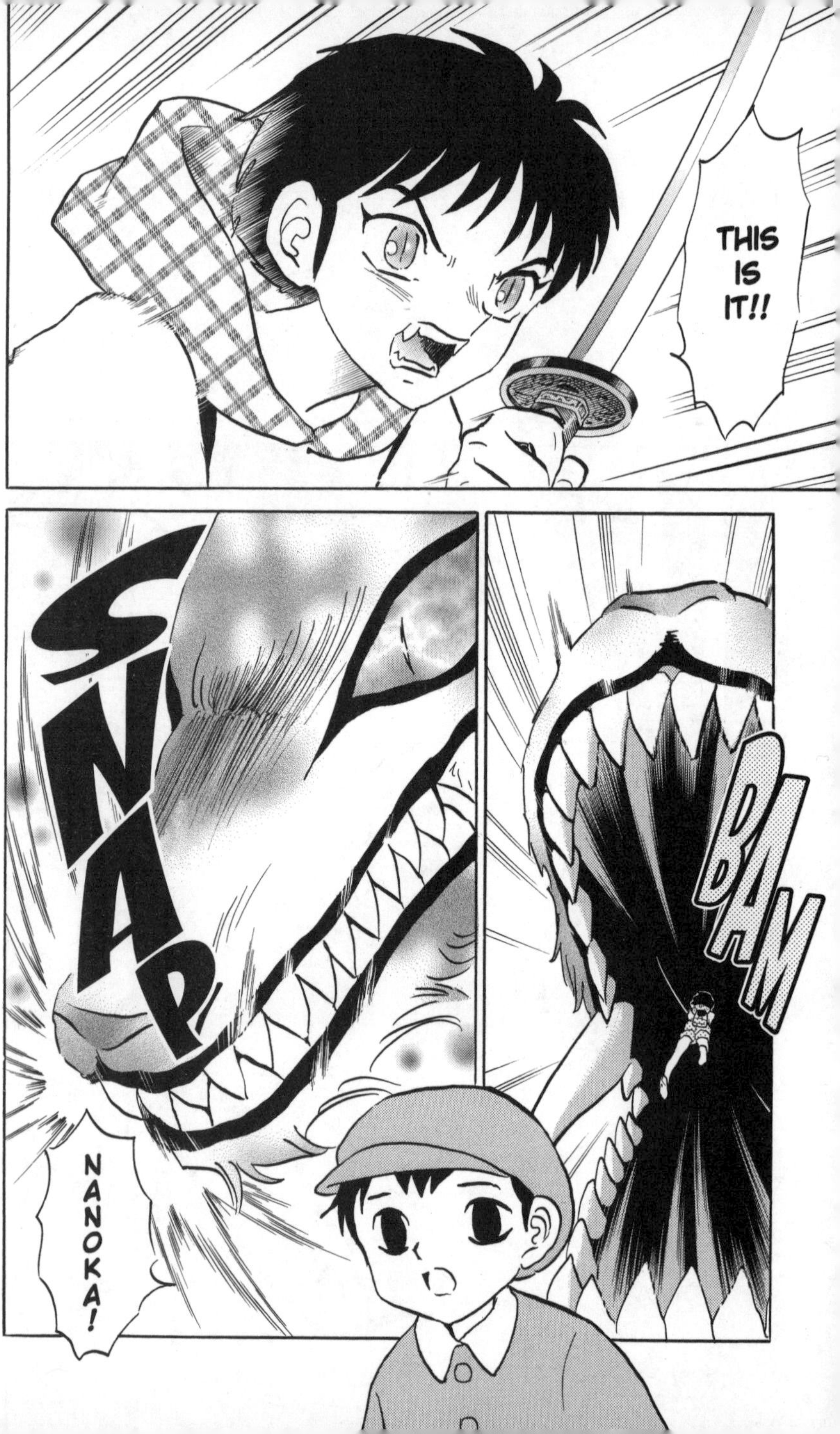
THIS IS IT!!
BAM
SNAP
NANOKA!

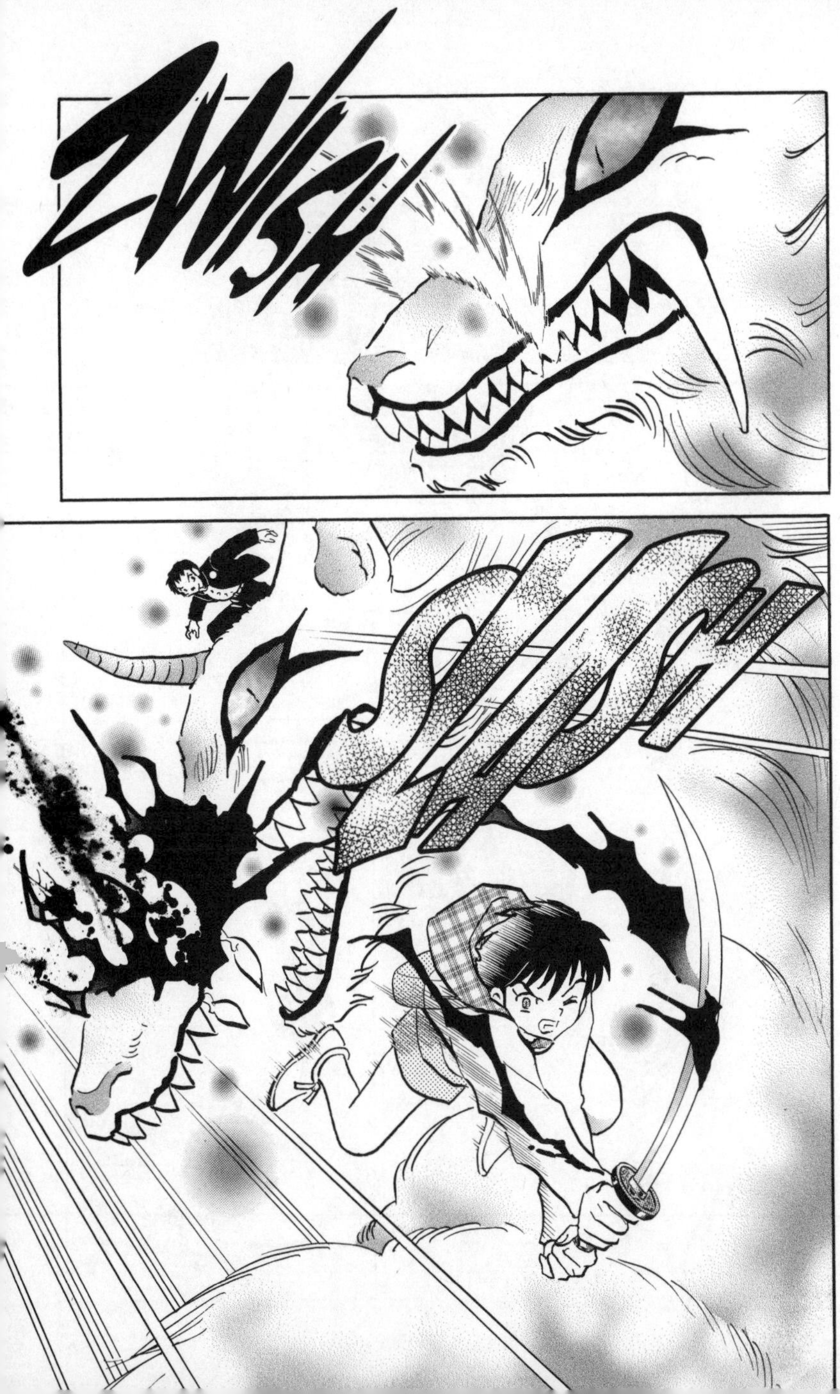
ZWISH

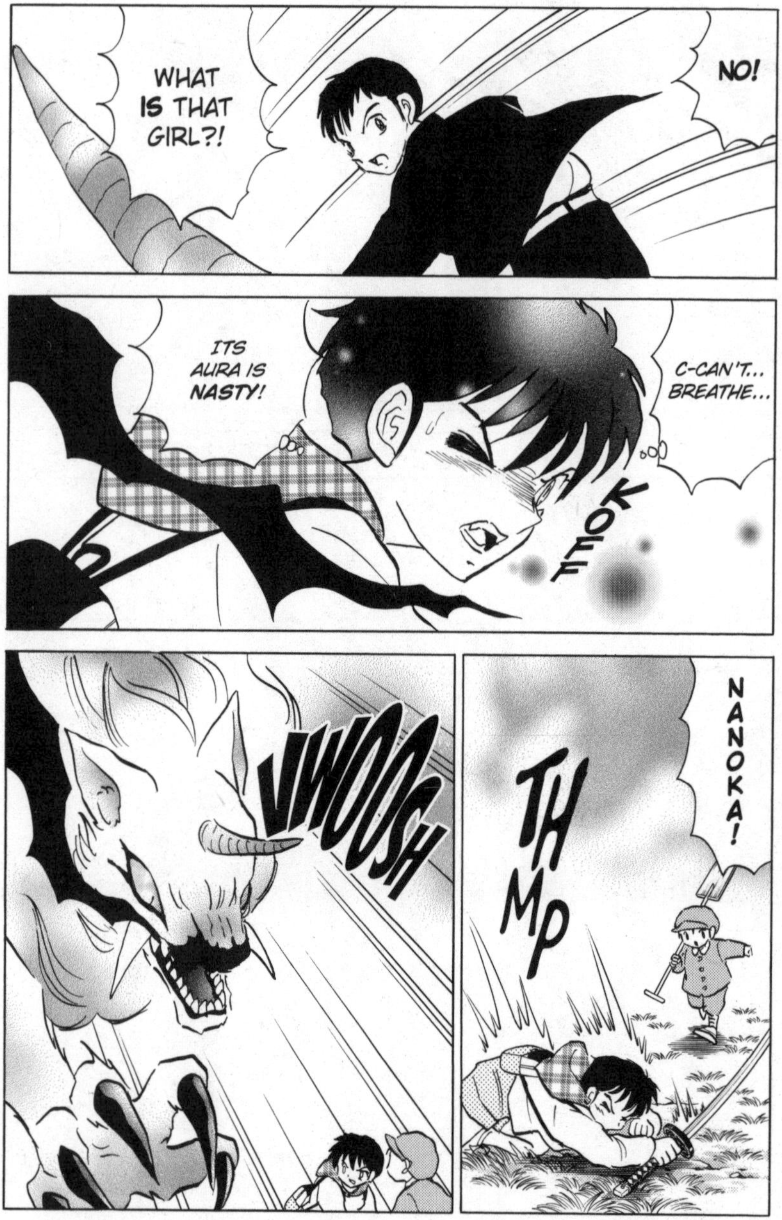
NO!
WHAT **IS** THAT GIRL?!
C-CAN'T... BREATHE...
KOFF
ITS AURA IS ***NASTY!***
NANOKA!
THMP
VWOOSH

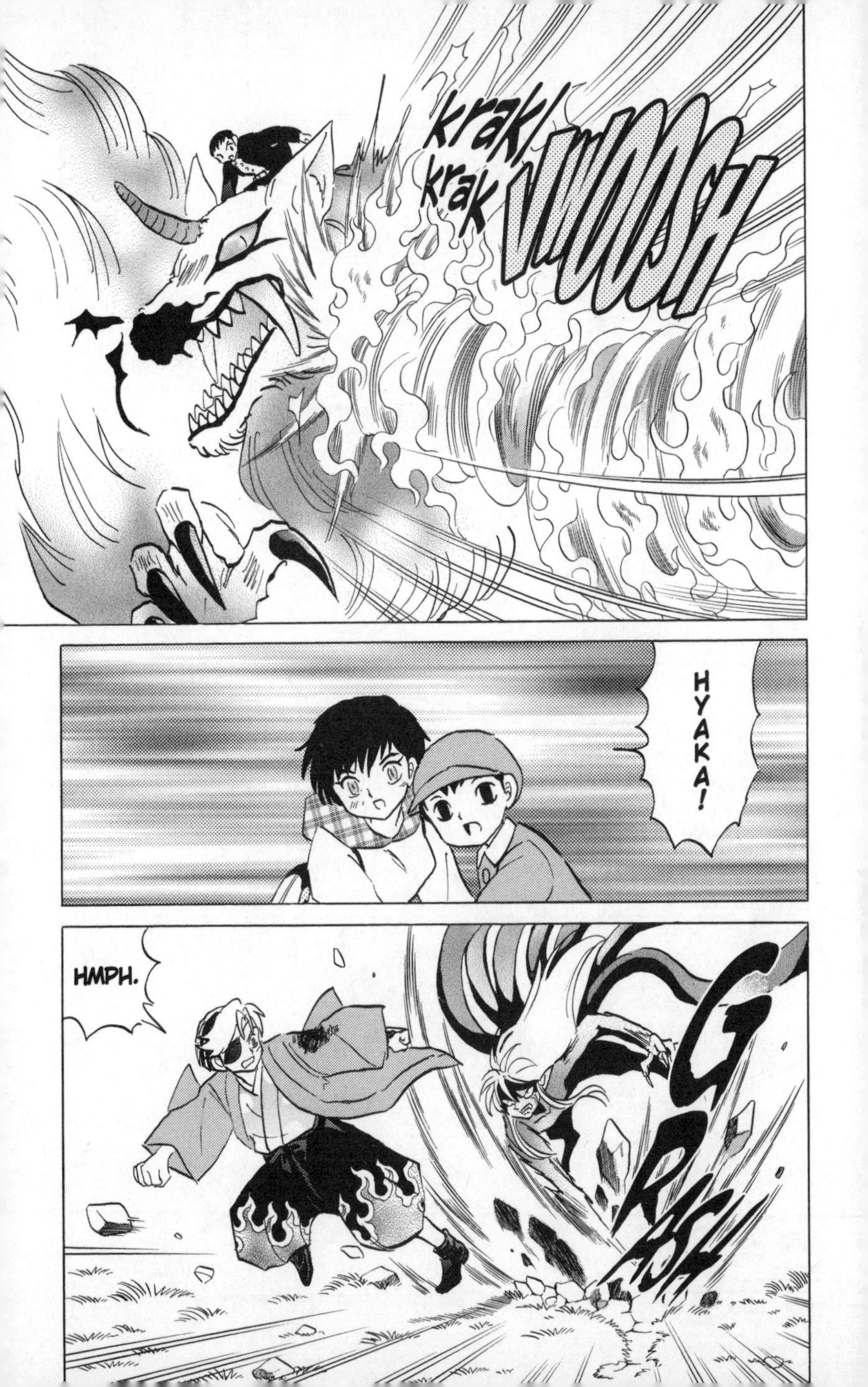
krak! krak
VWOOSH
HYAKA!
HMPH.
GRASH

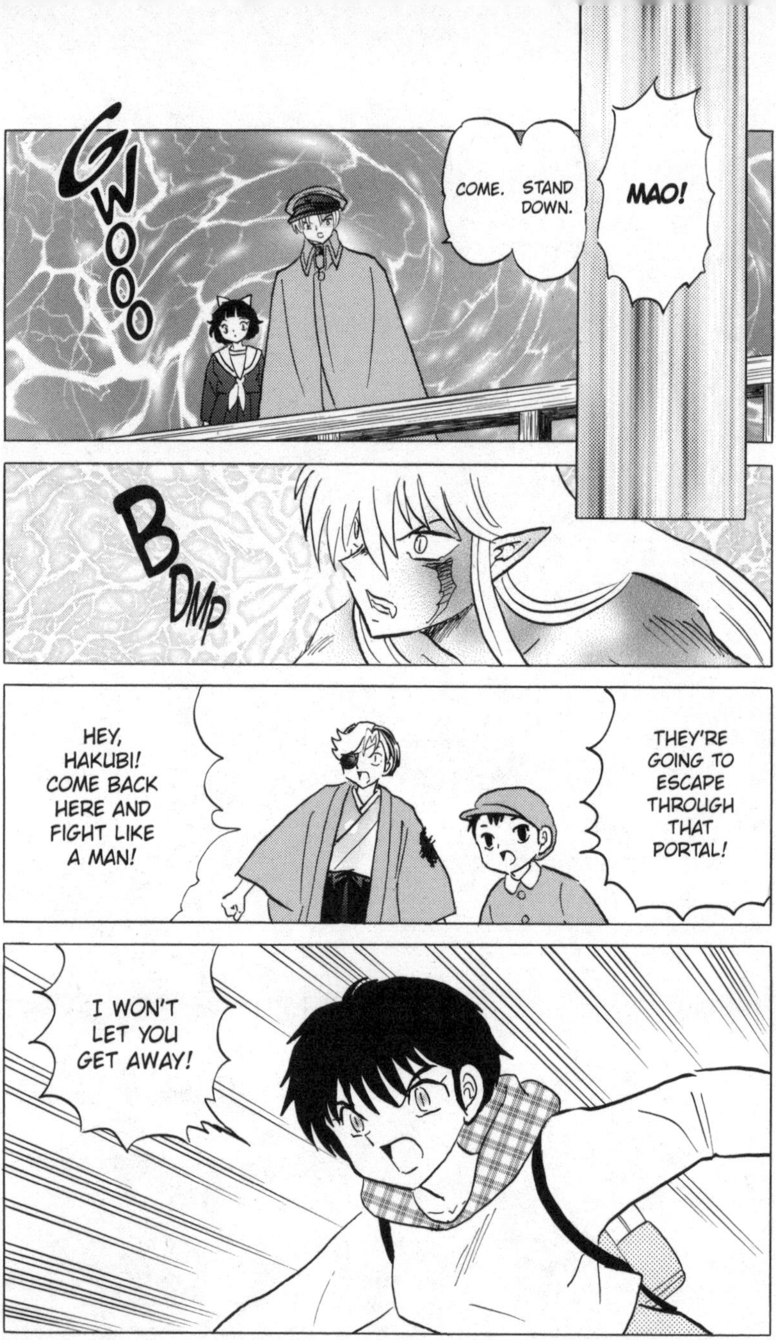
MAO!
COME. STAND DOWN.
GWOOOO
BDMP
THEY'RE GOING TO ESCAPE THROUGH THAT PORTAL!
HEY, HAKUBI! COME BACK HERE AND FIGHT LIKE A MAN!
I WON'T LET YOU GET AWAY!

Chapter 9: Risk My Life

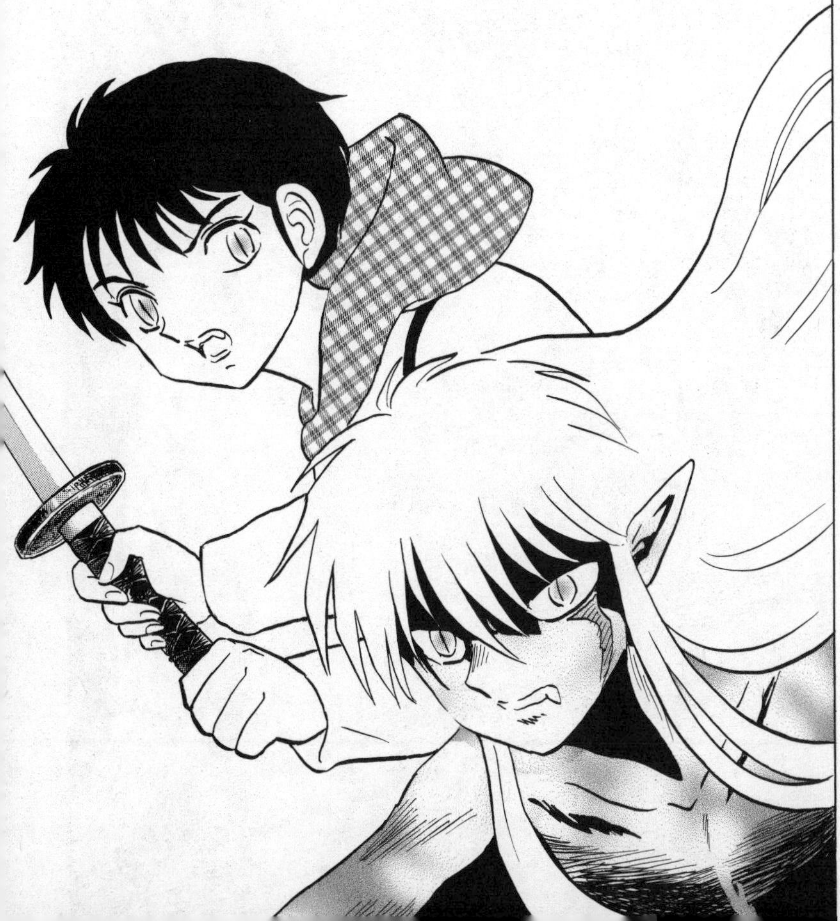

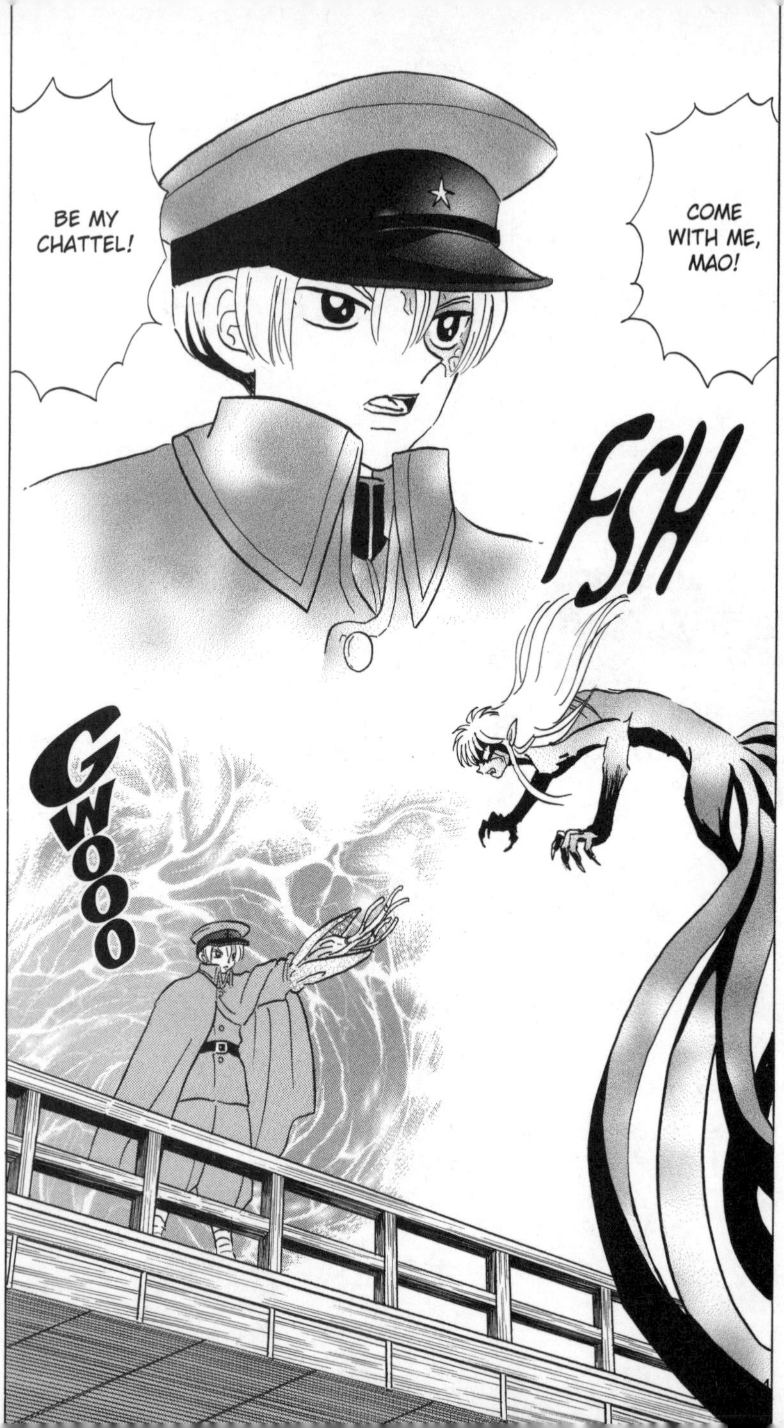
COME WITH ME, MAO!
BE MY CHATTEL!
FSH
GWOOO

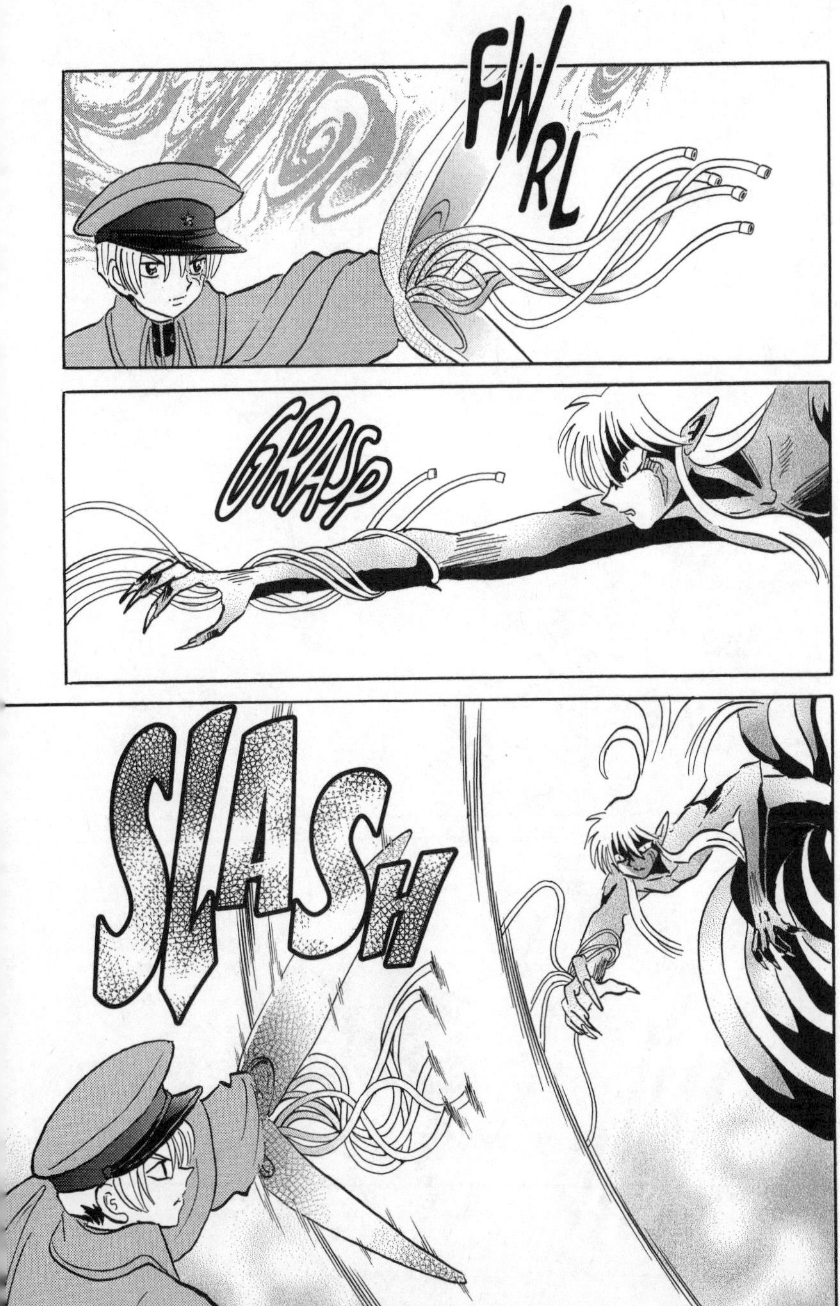
FWRL
GRASP
SLASH

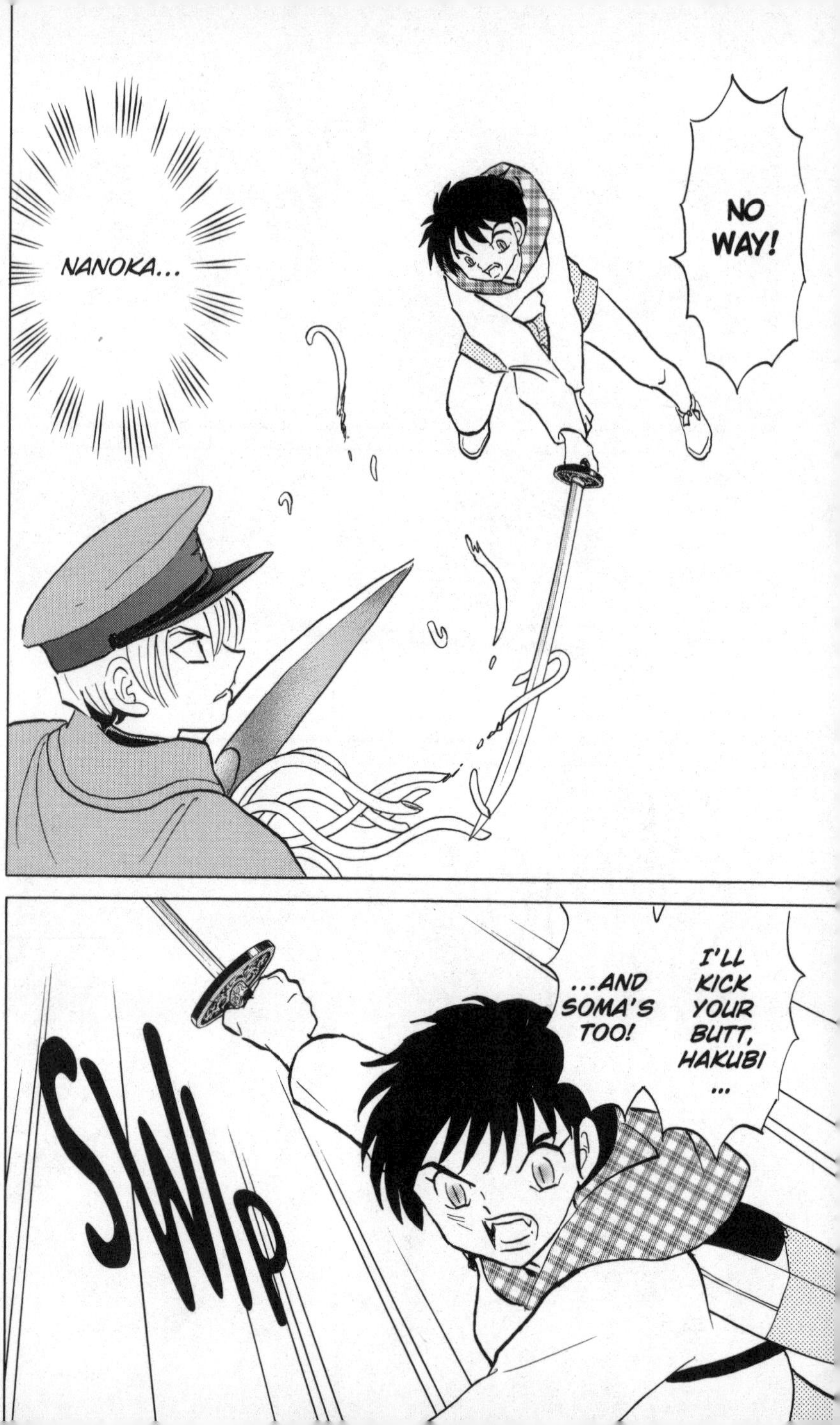
NO WAY!
NANOKA...
I'LL KICK YOUR BUTT, HAKUBI...
...AND SOMA'S TOO!
SWIP

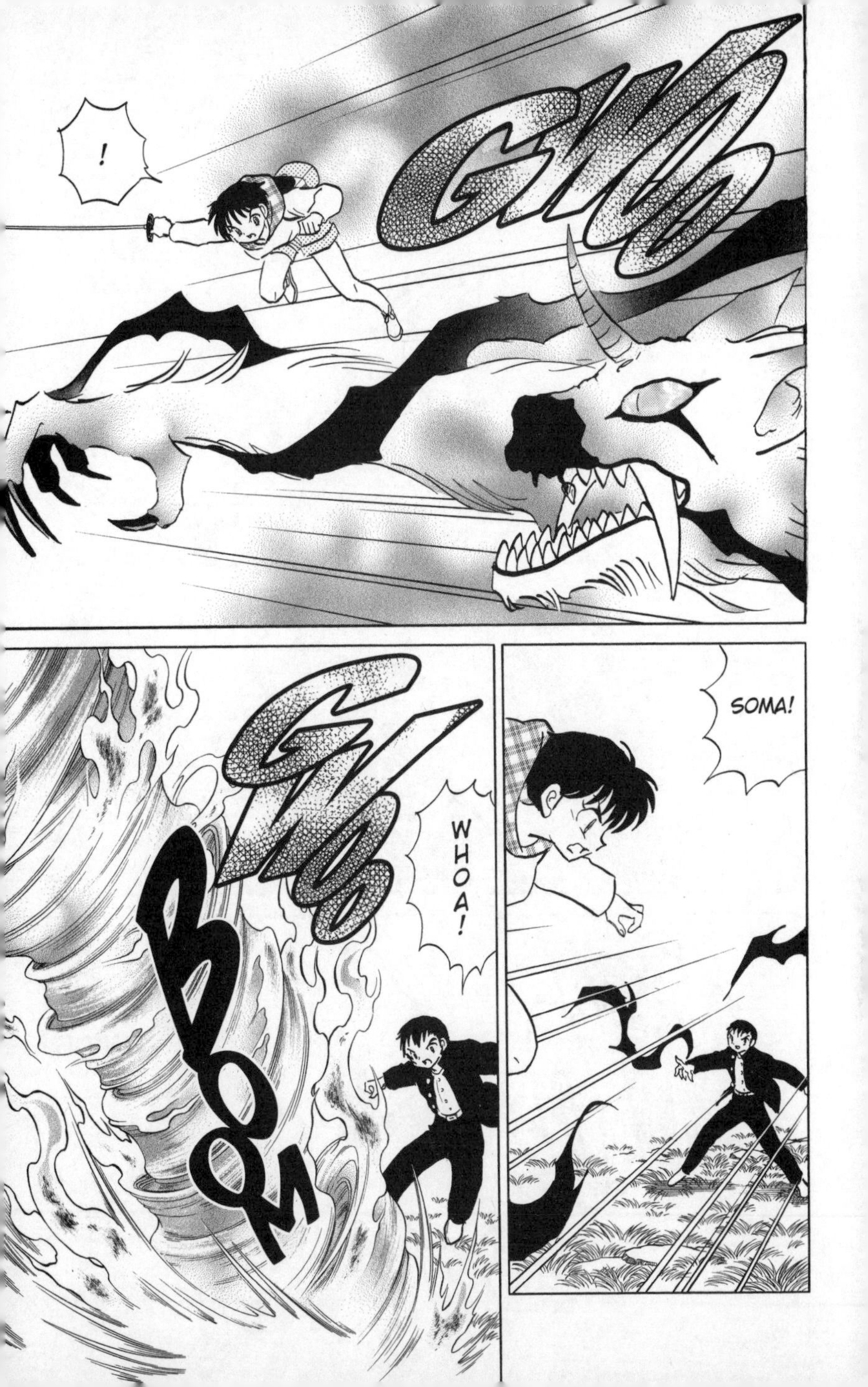
!
SOMA!
WHOA!
BOOM

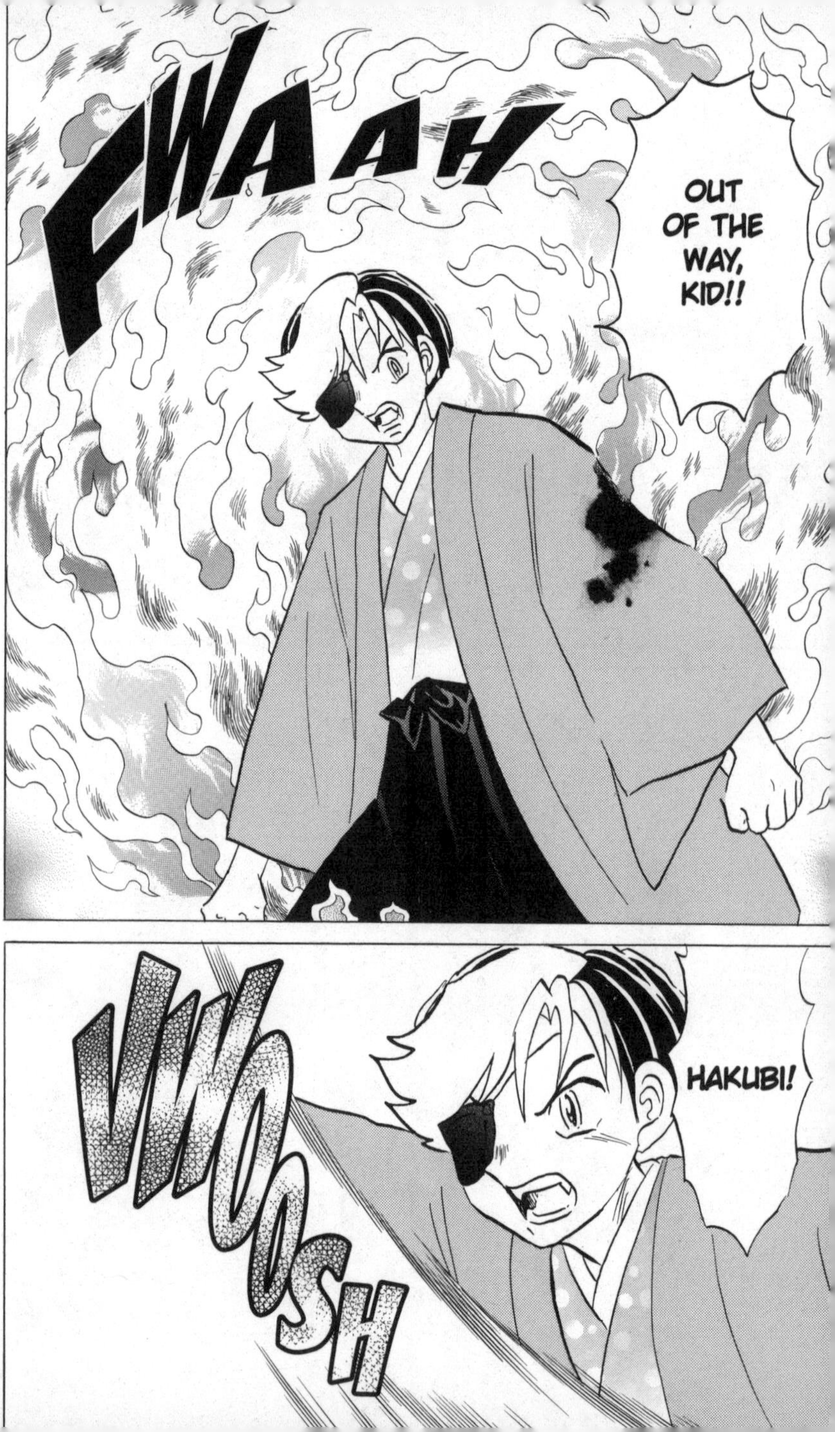
OUT OF THE WAY, KID!!
FWAAH
HAKUBI!
VWOOSH

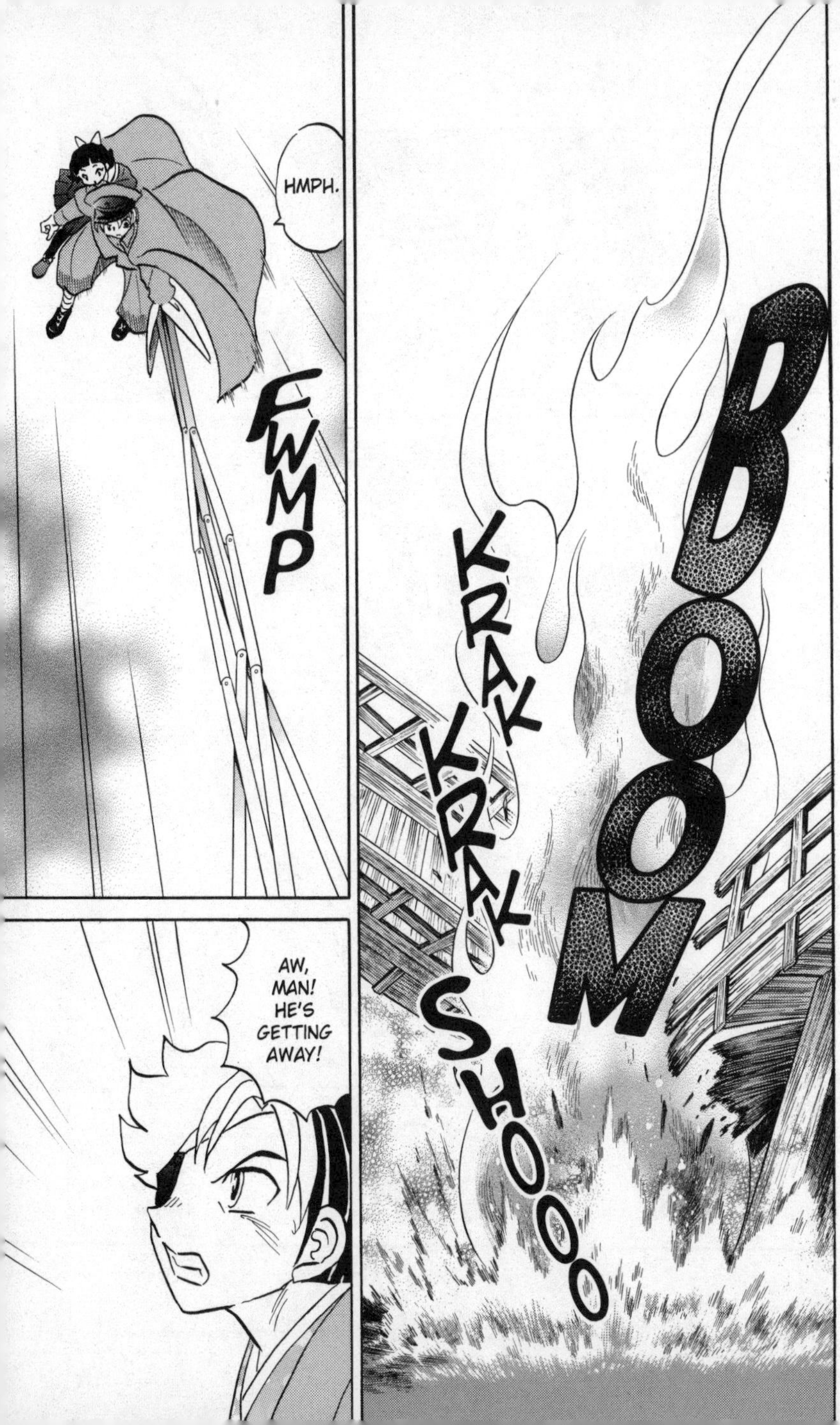
BOOM
KRAK KRAK
SHOOOO
HMPH.
FWMP
AW, MAN! HE'S GETTING AWAY!

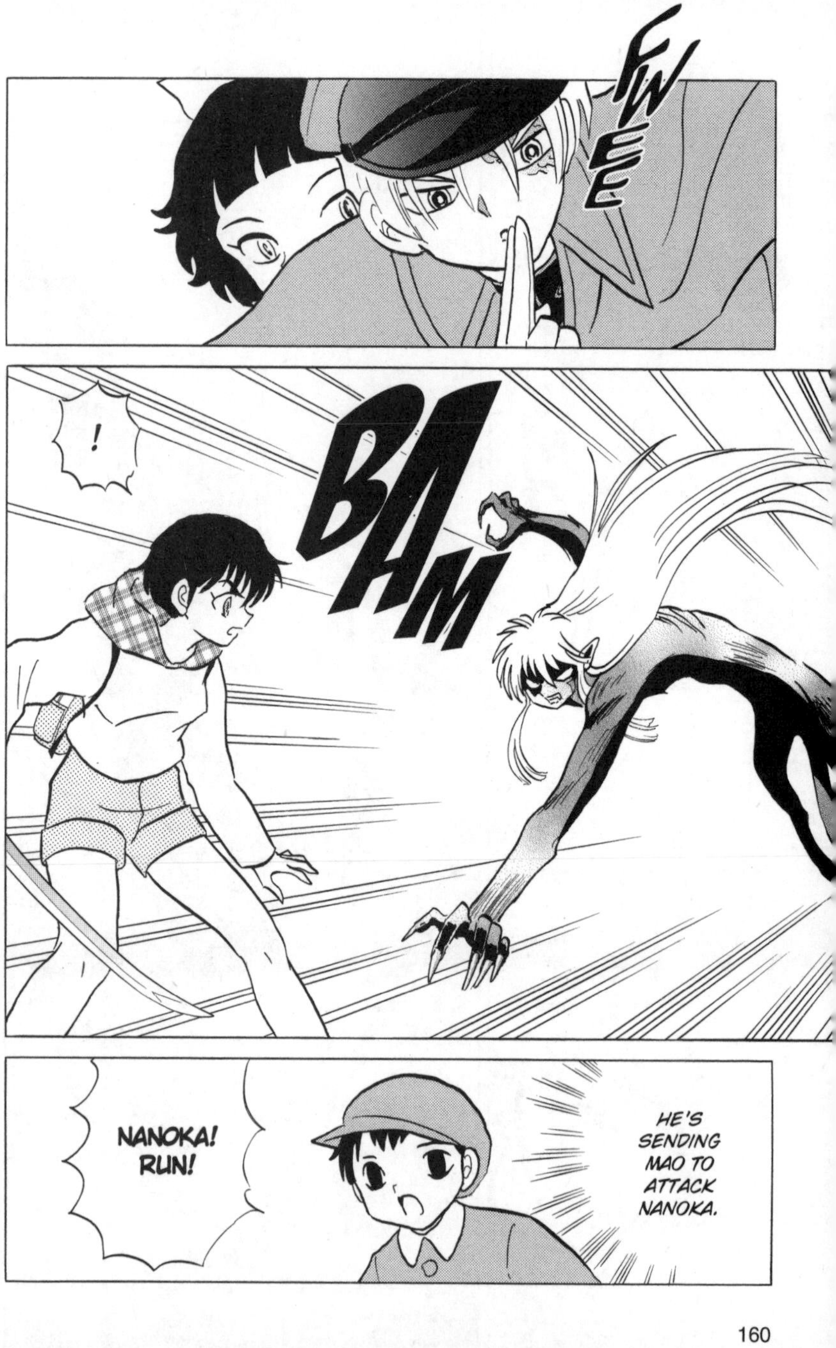
FWEE
BAM
!
HE'S SENDING MAO TO ATTACK NANOKA.
NANOKA! RUN!

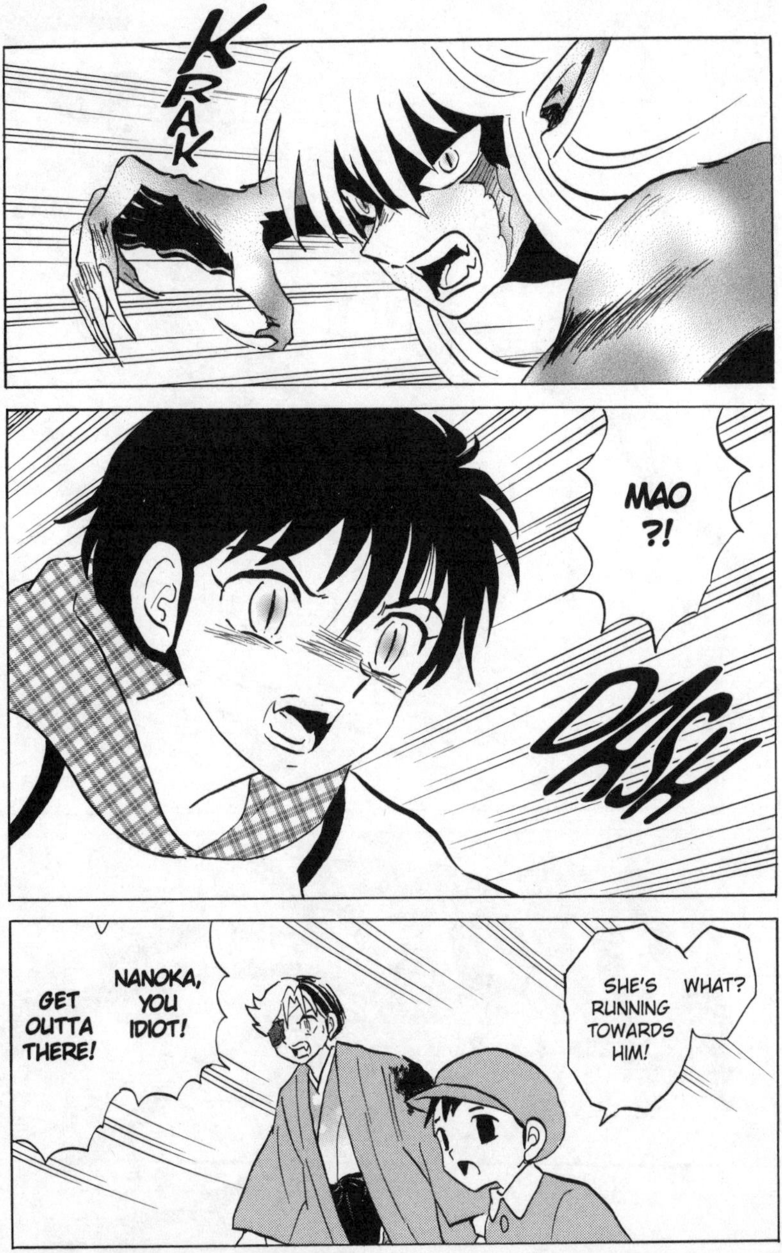
KRAK
MAO ?!
DASH
WHAT?
SHE'S RUNNING TOWARDS HIM!
NANOKA, YOU IDIOT!
GET OUTTA THERE!

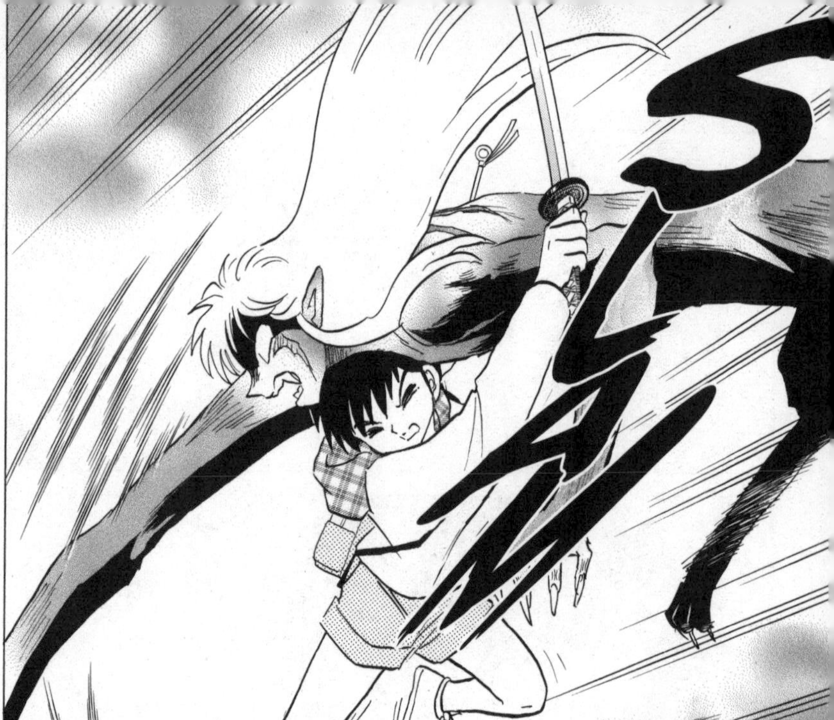
SWSH
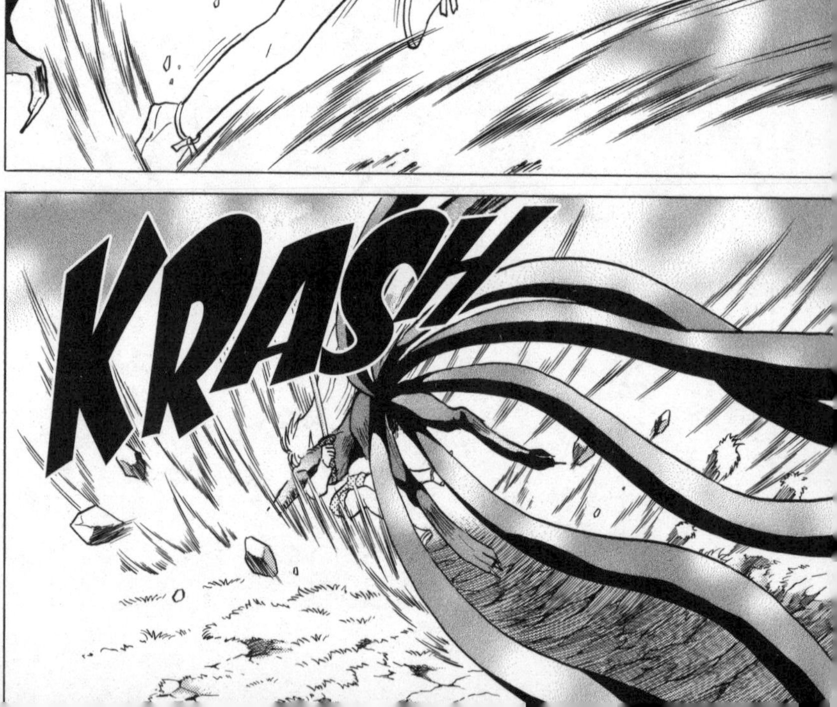
KRASH

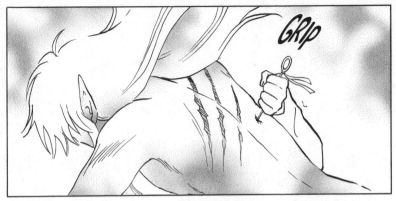

GRIP

V
W
P

MY PUPPET NEEDLE...

TCH.

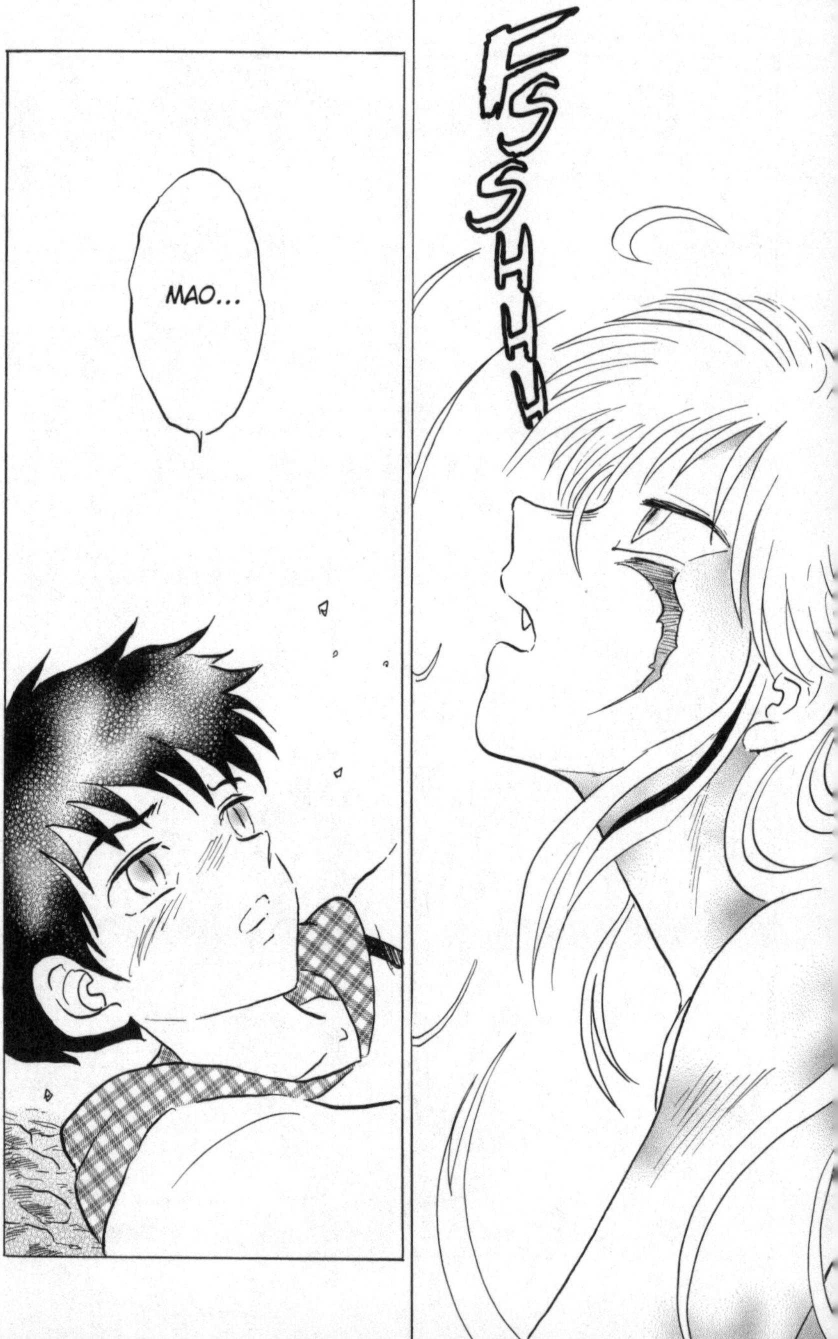
FSSHHH
MAO...

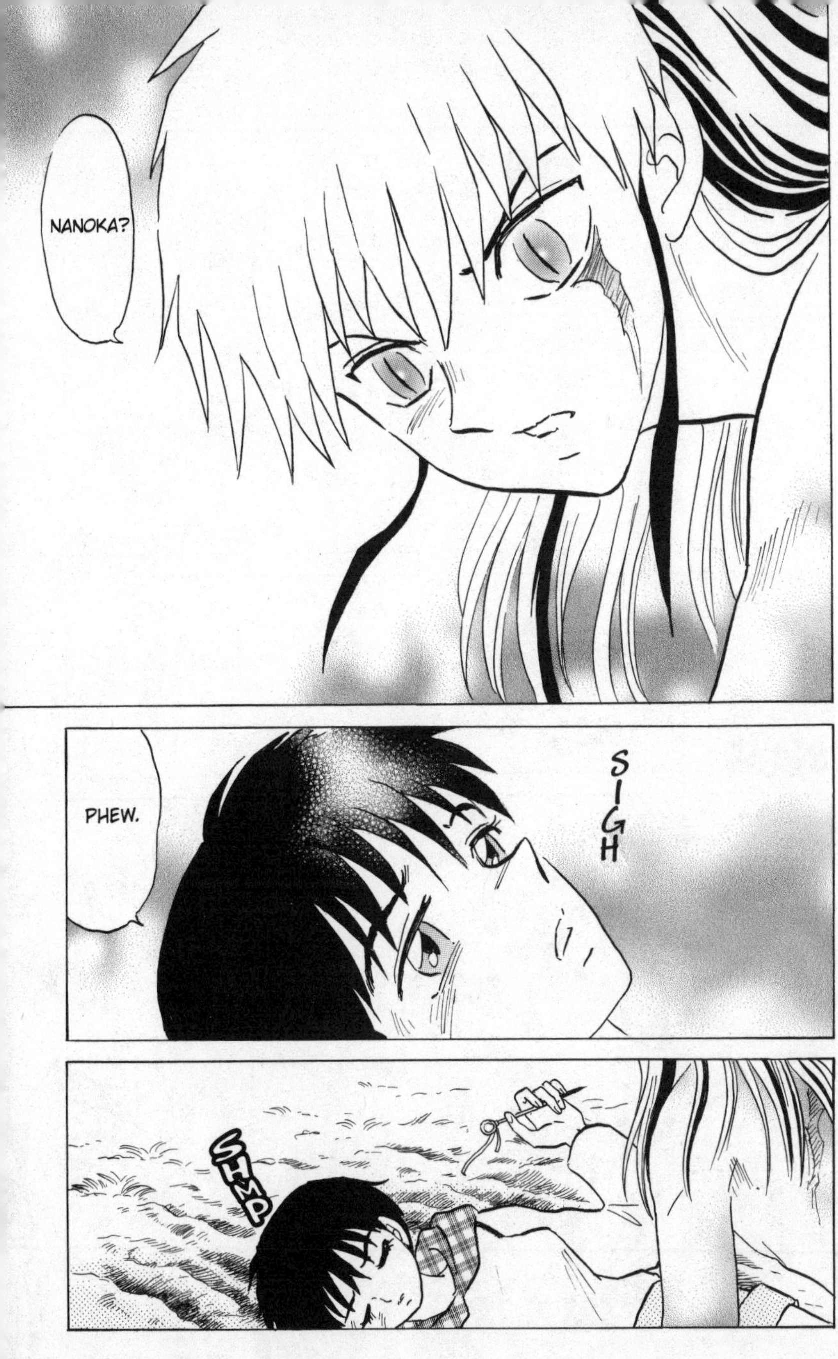
NANOKA?
PHEW.
SIGH
SHMP

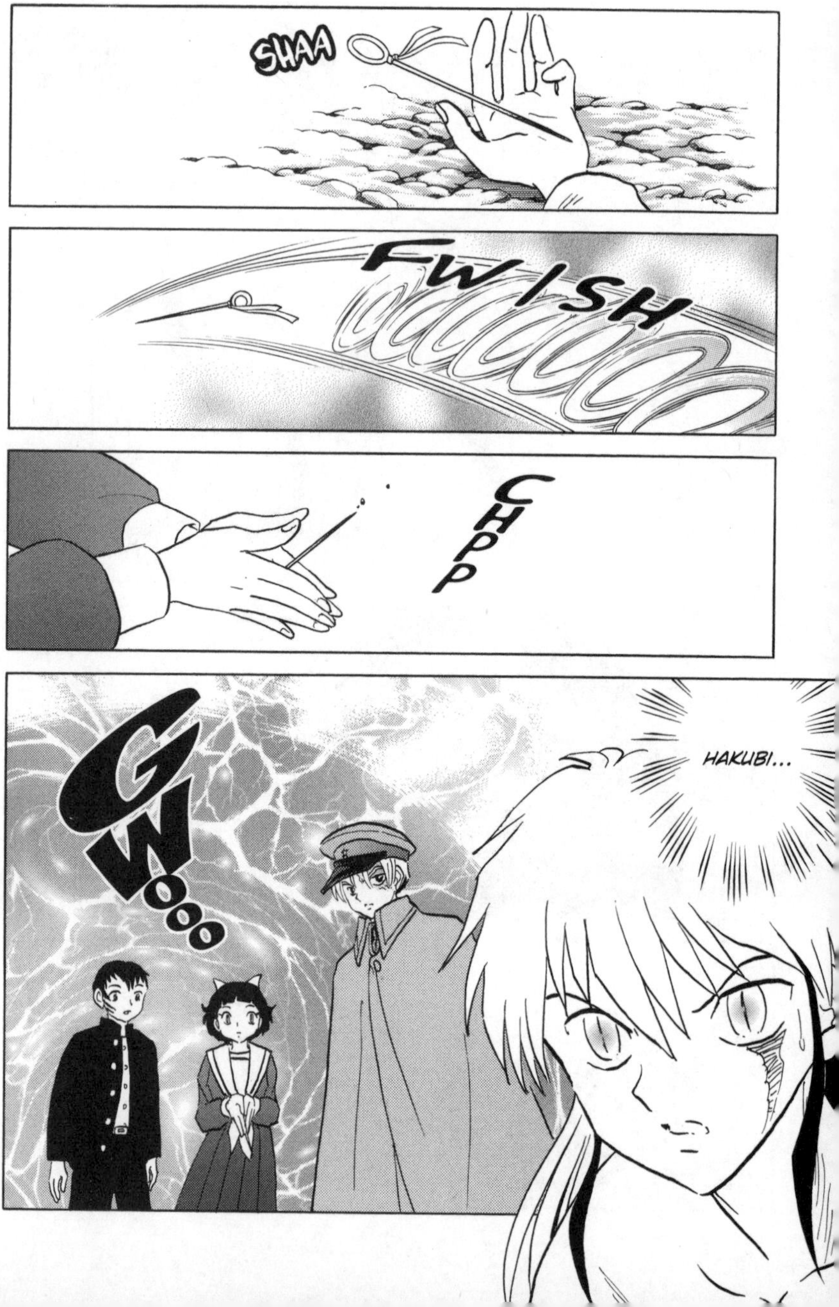
SHAA
FWISH
CHPP
HAKUBI...
GWOOO

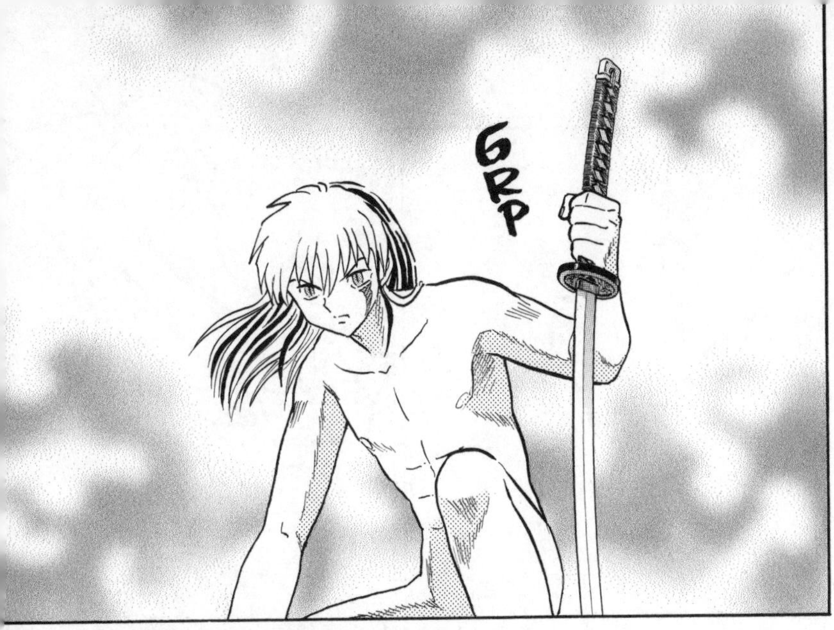
GRP
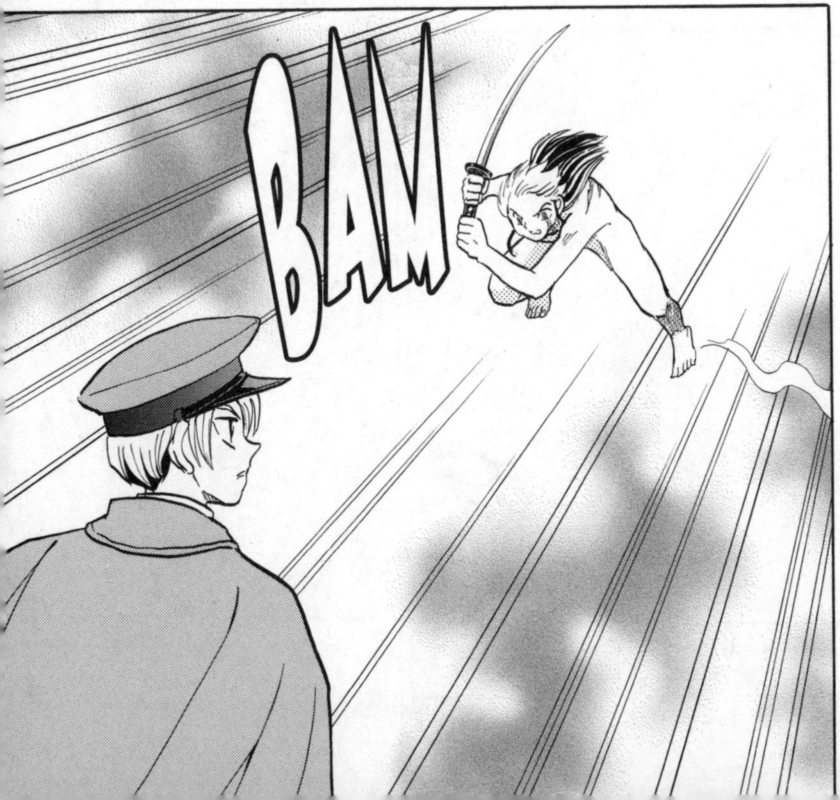
BAM

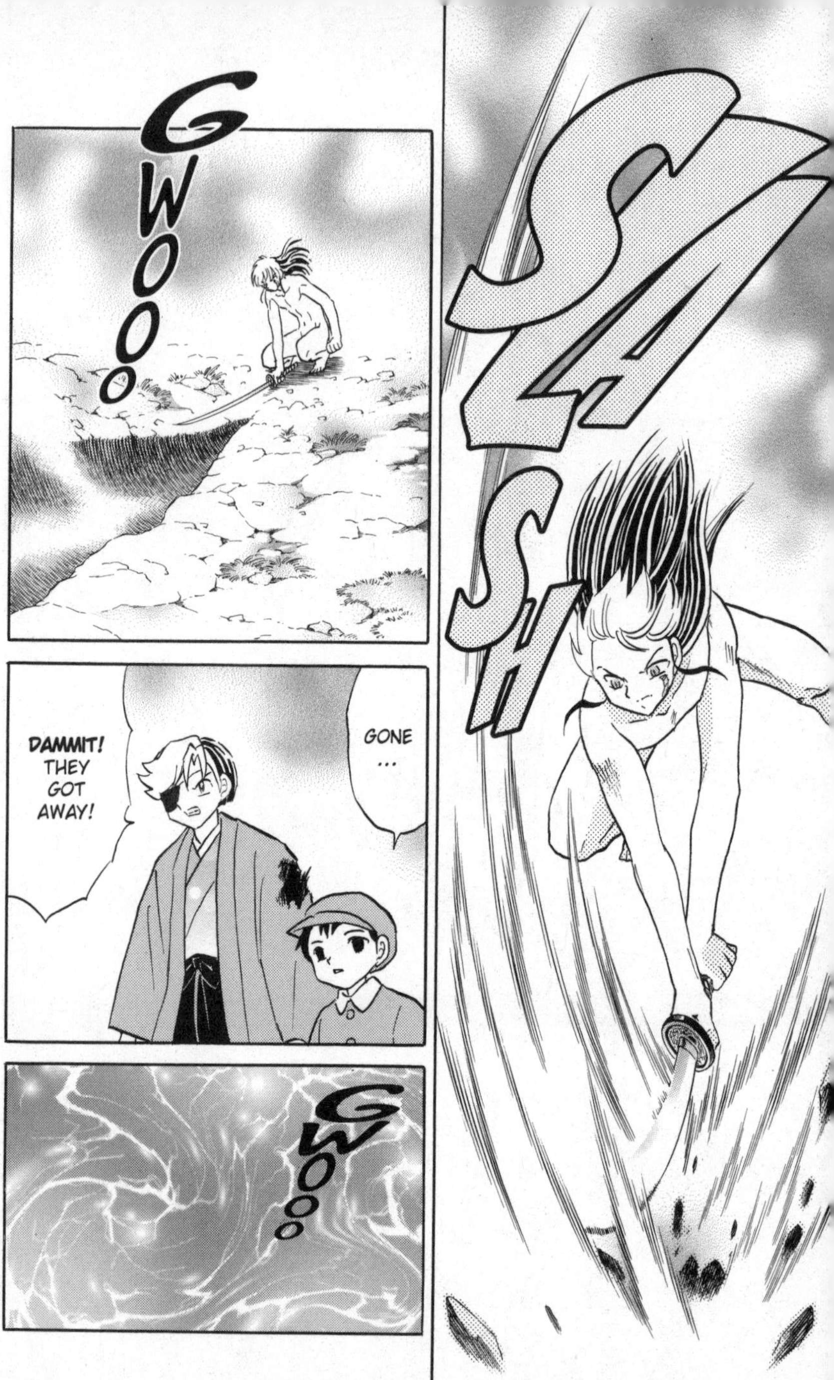
SASH
GWOOOO
GONE ...
DAMMIT! THEY GOT AWAY!
GWOOO

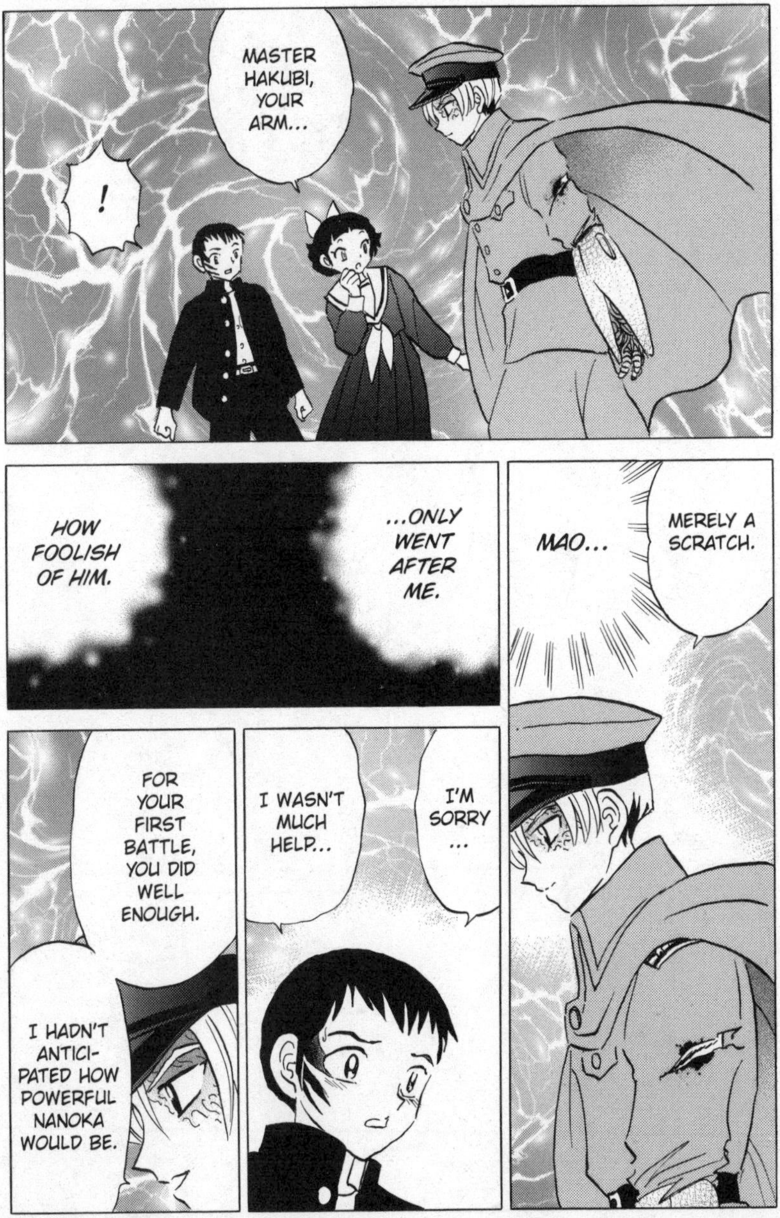
MASTER HAKUBI, YOUR ARM...
!
MERELY A SCRATCH.
MAO...
...ONLY WENT AFTER ME.
HOW FOOLISH OF HIM.
I'M SORRY ...
I WASN'T MUCH HELP...
FOR YOUR FIRST BATTLE, YOU DID WELL ENOUGH.
I HADN'T ANTICIPATED HOW POWERFUL NANOKA WOULD BE.

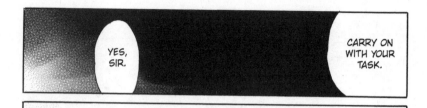

YES, SIR.

CARRY ON WITH YOUR TASK.

NANOKA ...

FWSH

IT SEEMS YOU'VE SAVED ME ONCE AGAIN.

Chapter 10:
The Sleepwalking Patient

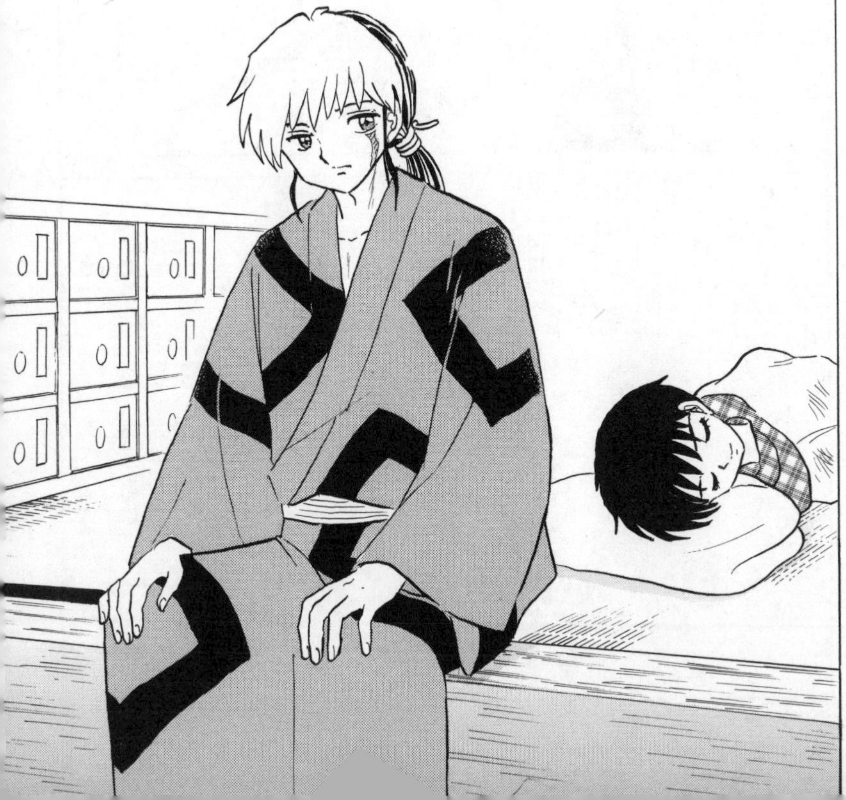

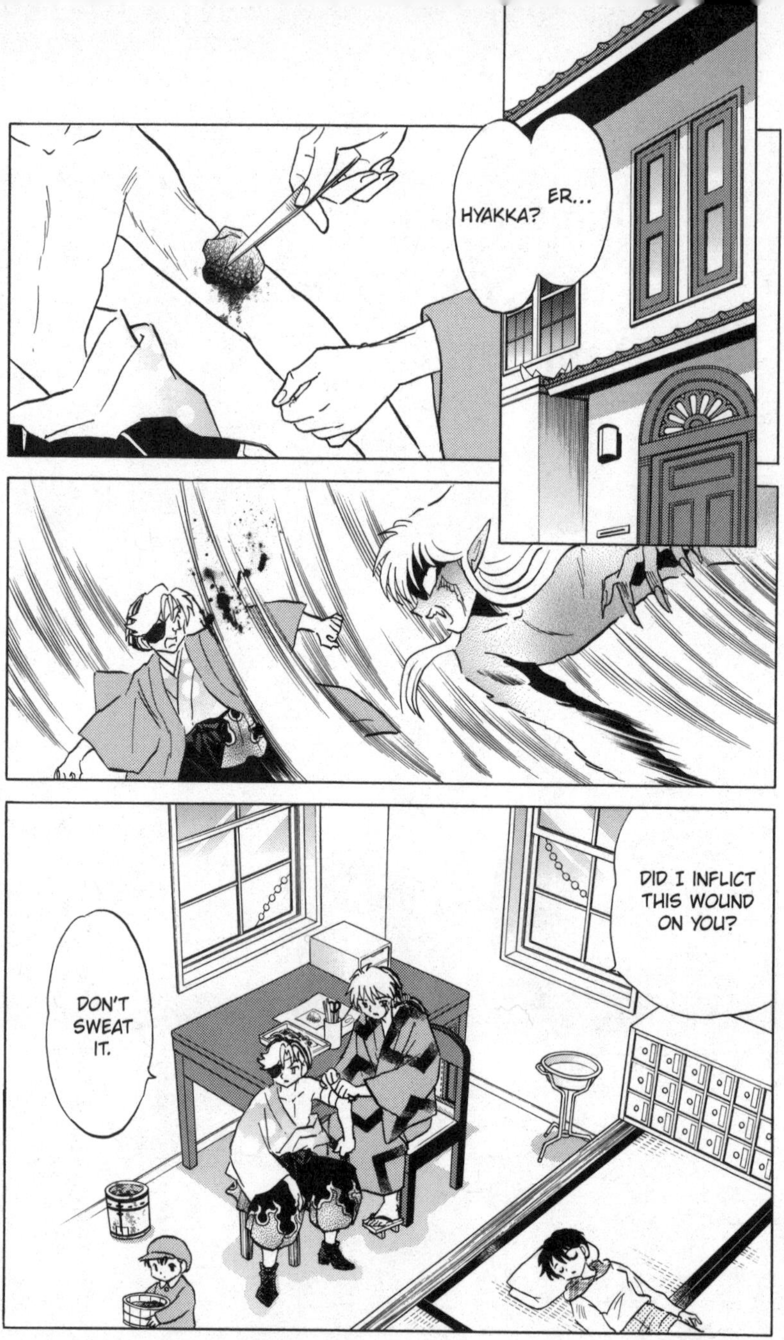
ER... HYAKKA?
DID I INFLICT THIS WOUND ON YOU?
DON'T SWEAT IT.

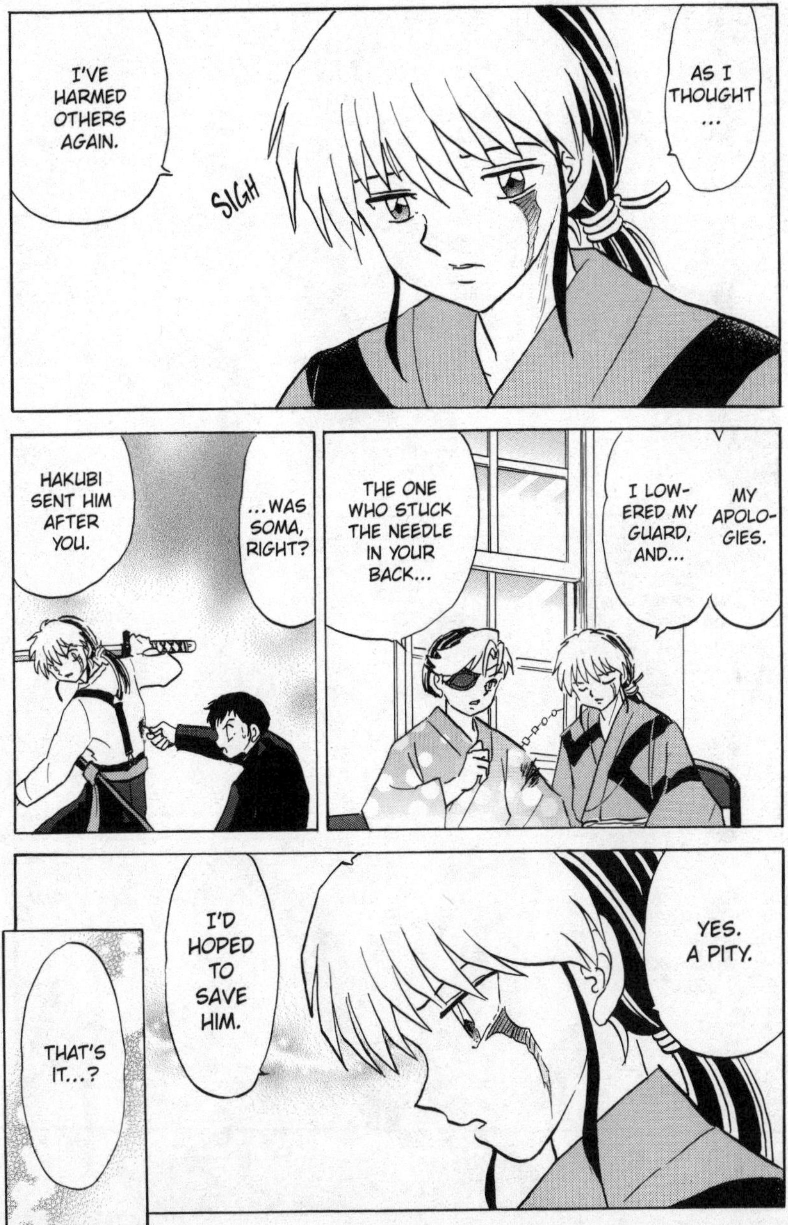
AS I THOUGHT...
I'VE HARMED OTHERS AGAIN.
SIGH
MY APOLOGIES.
I LOWERED MY GUARD, AND...
THE ONE WHO STUCK THE NEEDLE IN YOUR BACK...
...WAS SOMA, RIGHT?
HAKUBI SENT HIM AFTER YOU.
YES. A PITY.
I'D HOPED TO SAVE HIM.
THAT'S IT...?

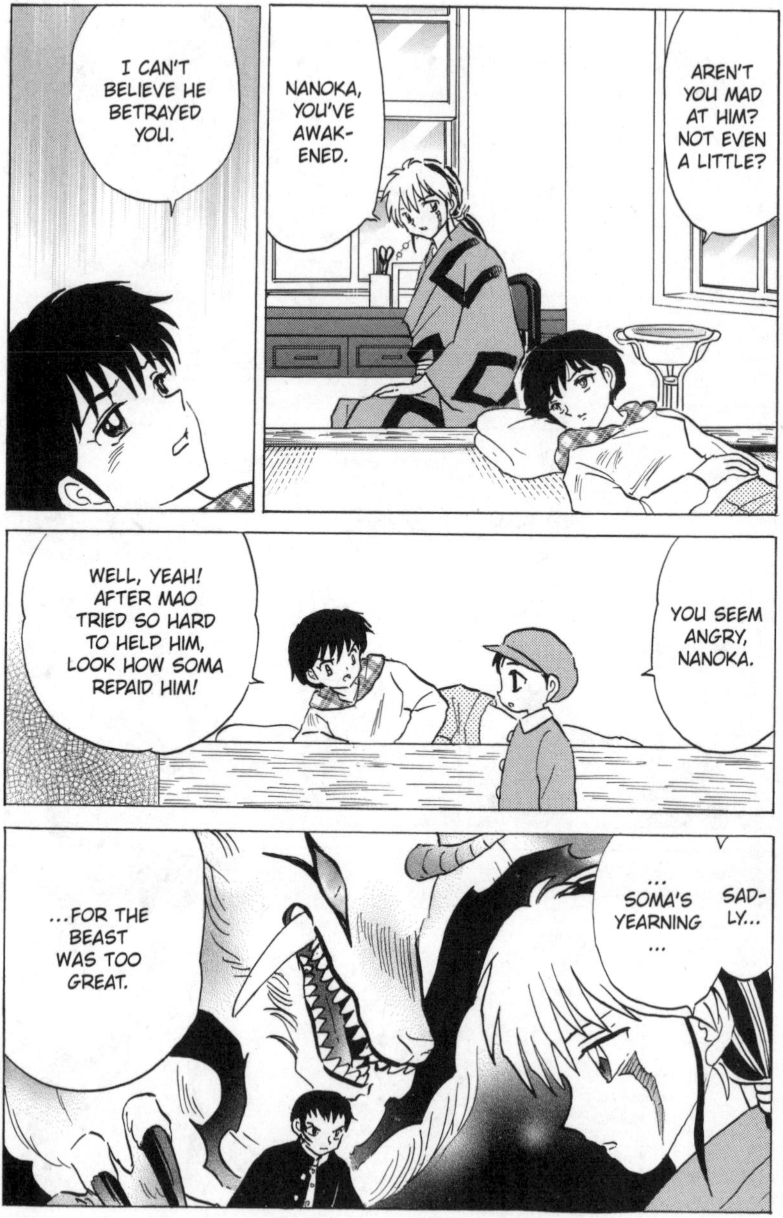
AREN'T YOU MAD AT HIM? NOT EVEN A LITTLE?
NANOKA, YOU'VE AWAK-ENED.
I CAN'T BELIEVE HE BETRAYED YOU.
YOU SEEM ANGRY, NANOKA.
WELL, YEAH! AFTER MAO TRIED SO HARD TO HELP HIM, LOOK HOW SOMA REPAID HIM!
SAD-LY...
...SOMA'S YEARNING...
...FOR THE BEAST WAS TOO GREAT.

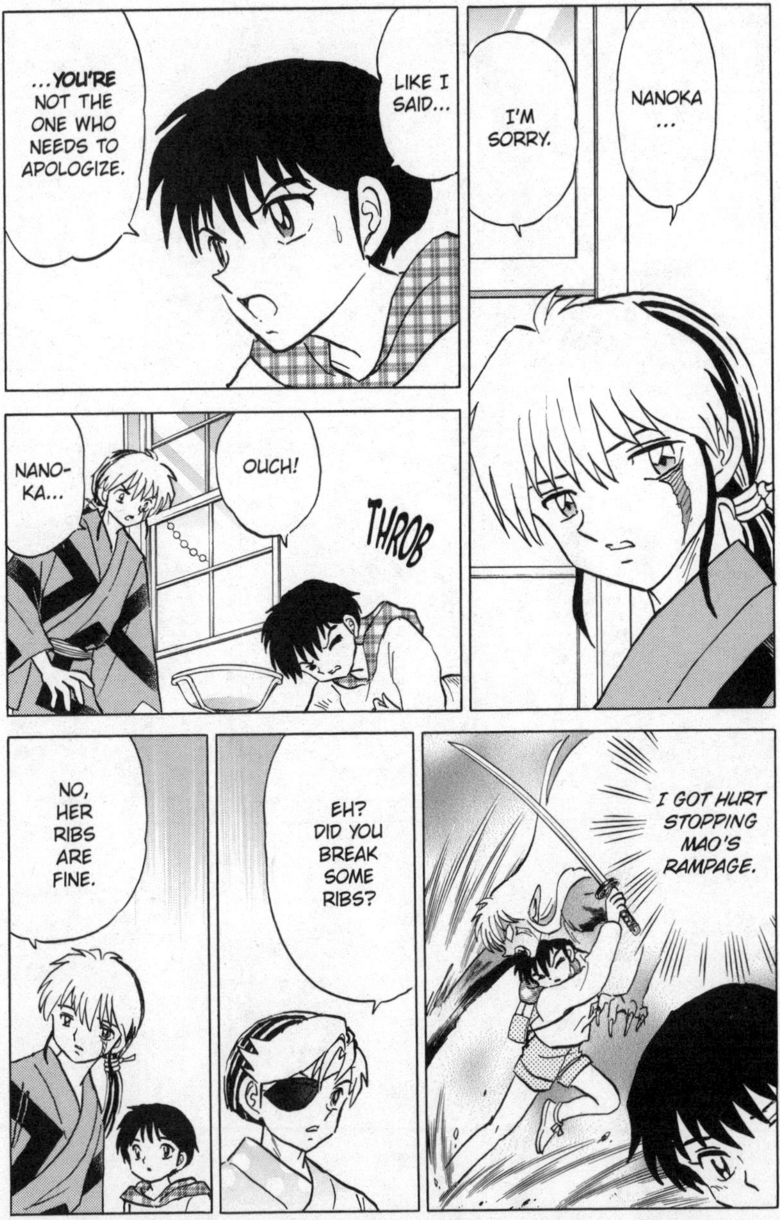
NANOKA...
I'M SORRY.
LIKE I SAID...
...YOU'RE NOT THE ONE WHO NEEDS TO APOLOGIZE.
OUCH!
THROB
NANO-KA...
I GOT HURT STOPPING MAO'S RAMPAGE.
EH? DID YOU BREAK SOME RIBS?
NO, HER RIBS ARE FINE.

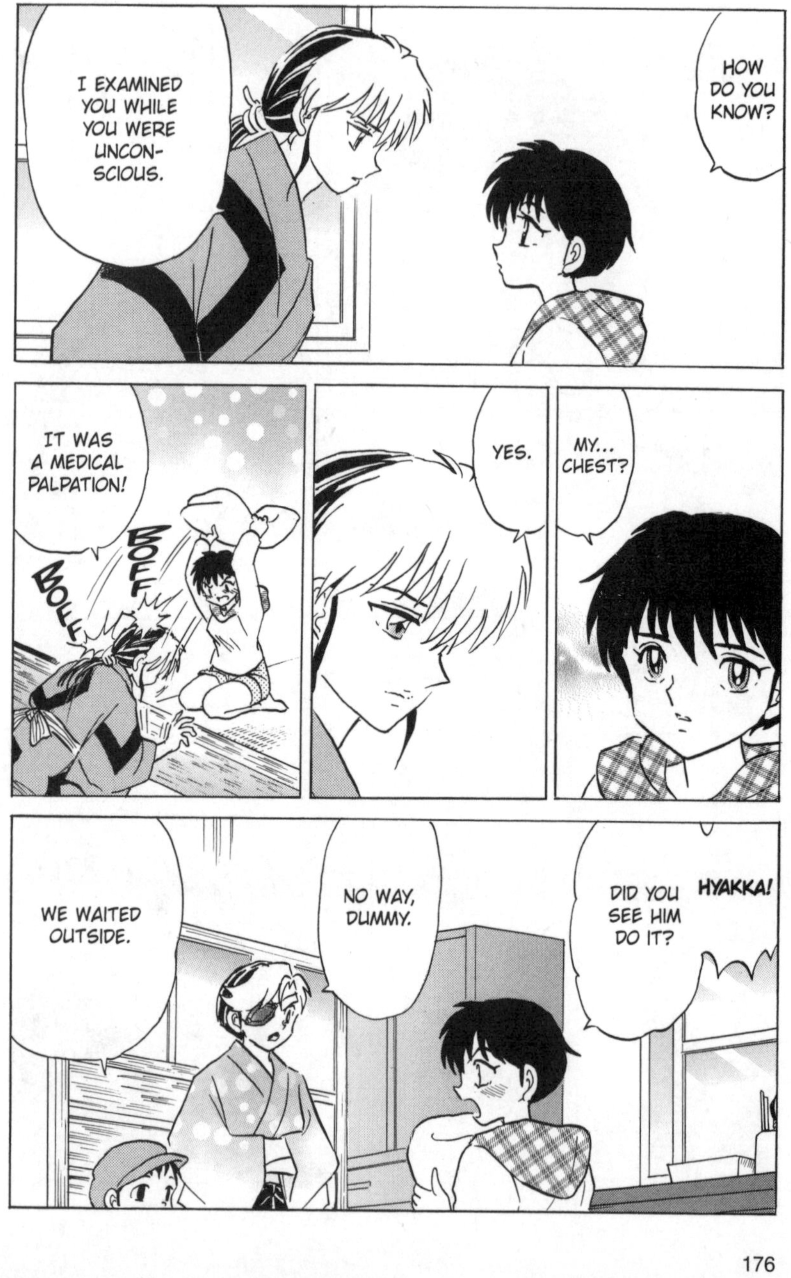
HOW DO YOU KNOW?
I EXAMINED YOU WHILE YOU WERE UNCON-SCIOUS.
MY... CHEST?
YES.
IT WAS A MEDICAL PALPATION!
BOFF
BOFF
HYAKKA!
DID YOU SEE HIM DO IT?
NO WAY, DUMMY.
WE WAITED OUTSIDE.

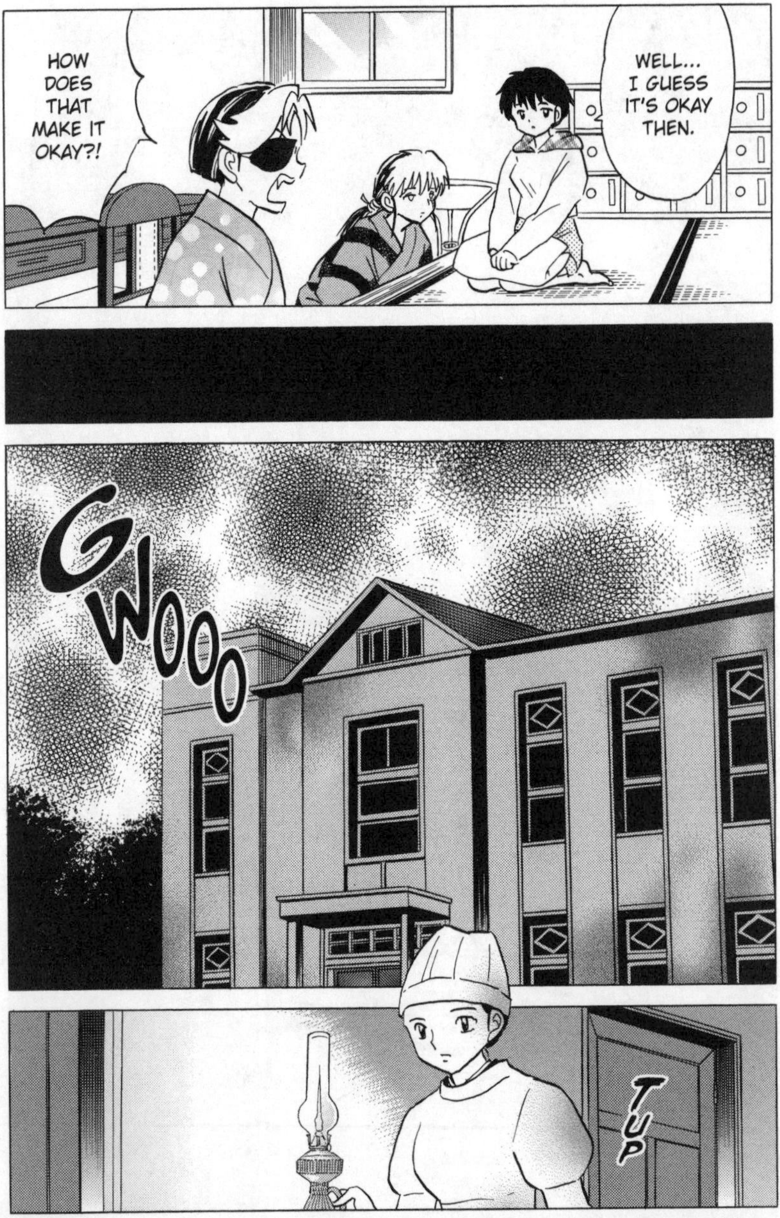
WELL... I GUESS IT'S OKAY THEN.
HOW DOES THAT MAKE IT OKAY?!
GWOOO
TUP

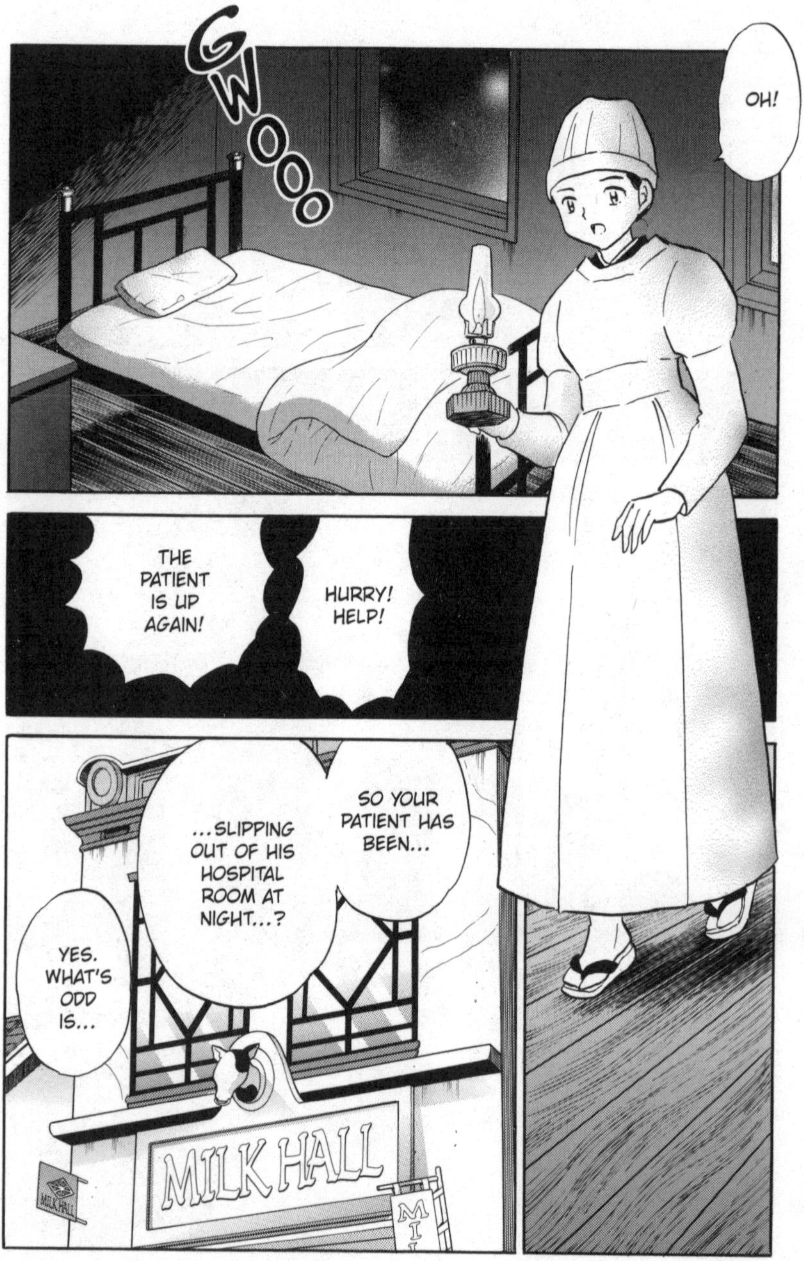
GWOOO
OH!
HURRY! HELP!
THE PATIENT IS UP AGAIN!
SO YOUR PATIENT HAS BEEN...
...SLIPPING OUT OF HIS HOSPITAL ROOM AT NIGHT...?
YES. WHAT'S ODD IS...
MILK HALL
MILK HALL

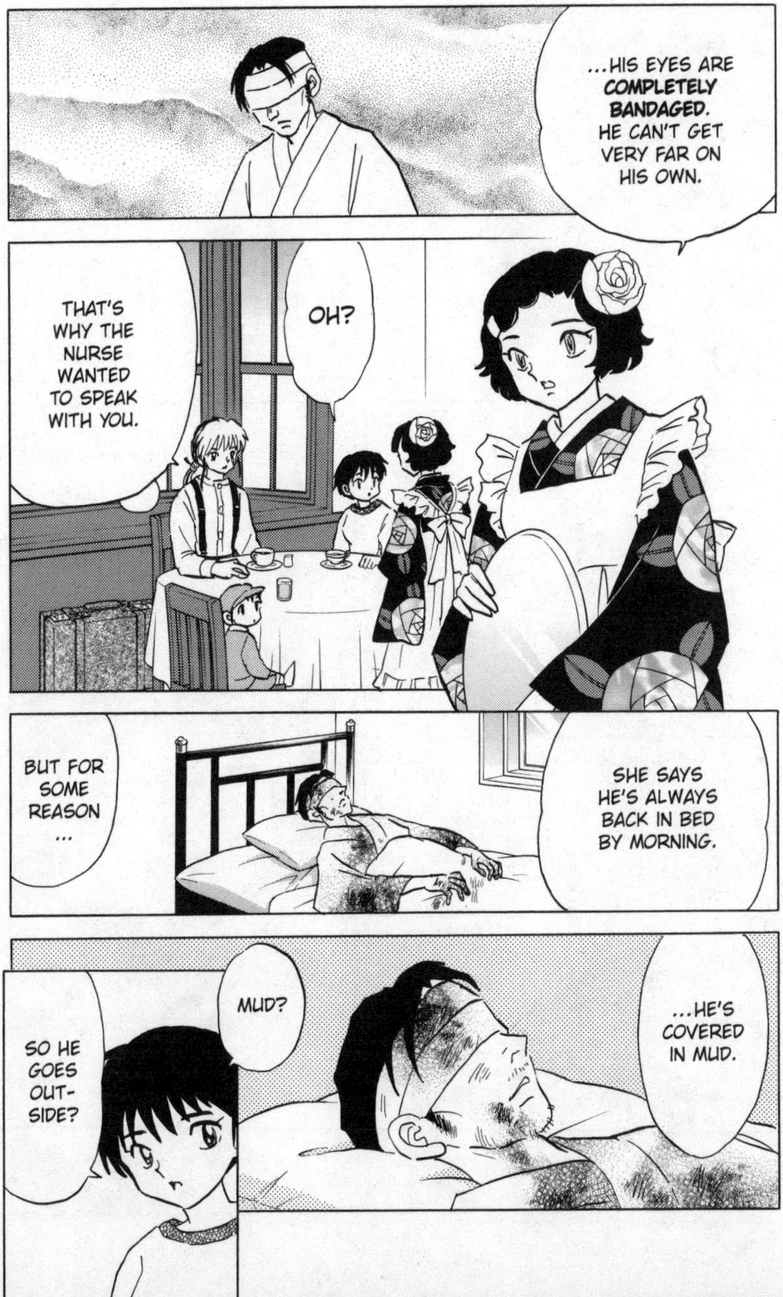
...HIS EYES ARE **COMPLETELY BANDAGED.** HE CAN'T GET VERY FAR ON HIS OWN.
OH?
THAT'S WHY THE NURSE WANTED TO SPEAK WITH YOU.
SHE SAYS HE'S ALWAYS BACK IN BED BY MORNING.
BUT FOR SOME REASON ...
...HE'S COVERED IN MUD.
MUD?
SO HE GOES OUT-SIDE?

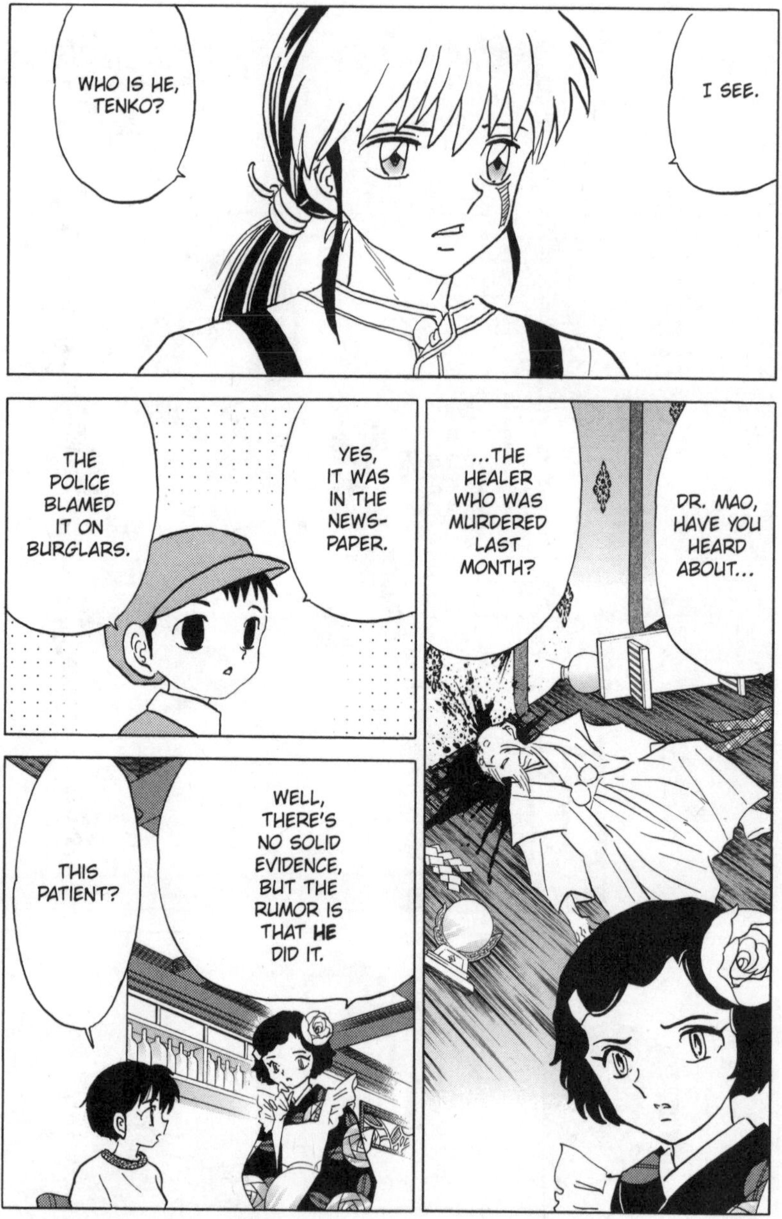
I SEE.
WHO IS HE, TENKO?
DR. MAO, HAVE YOU HEARD ABOUT...
...THE HEALER WHO WAS MURDERED LAST MONTH?
YES, IT WAS IN THE NEWSPAPER.
THE POLICE BLAMED IT ON BURGLARS.
WELL, THERE'S NO SOLID EVIDENCE, BUT THE RUMOR IS THAT **HE** DID IT.
THIS PATIENT?

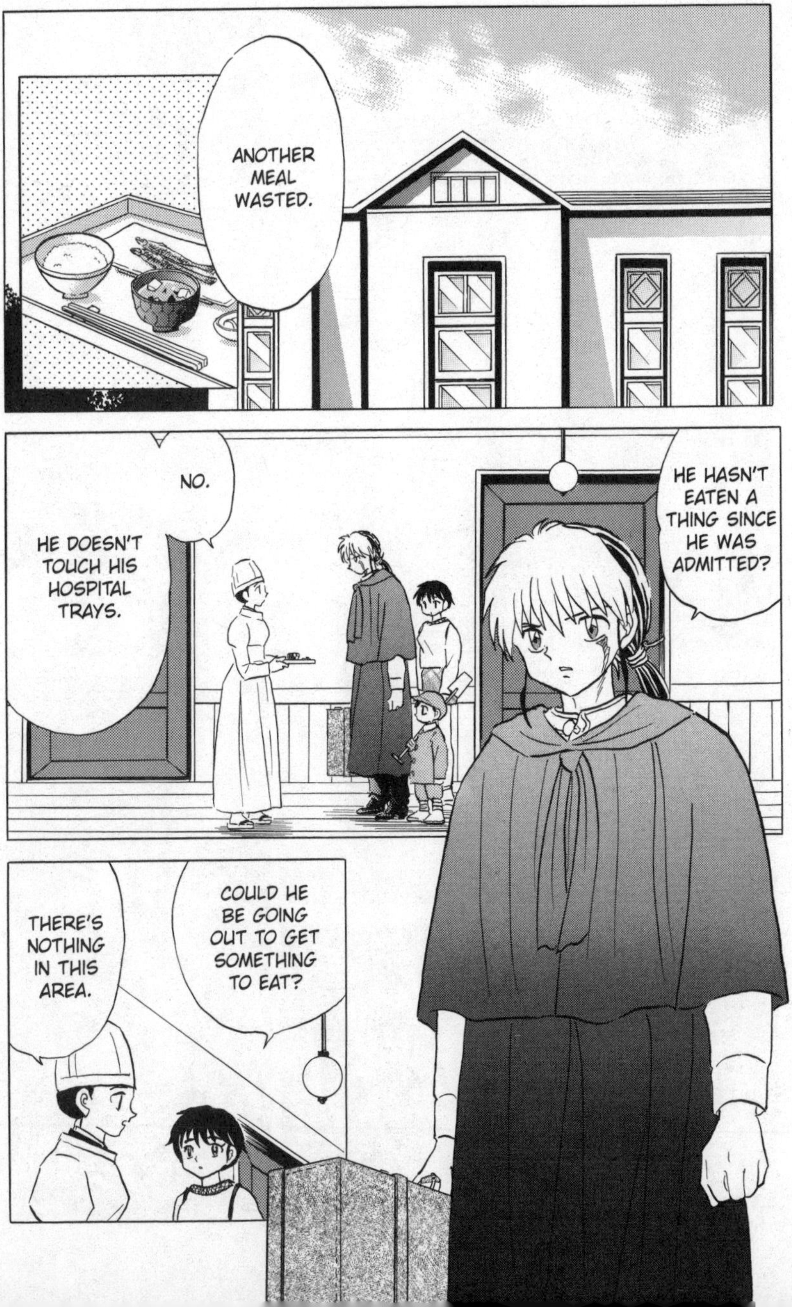
ANOTHER MEAL WASTED.
HE HASN'T EATEN A THING SINCE HE WAS ADMITTED?
NO.
HE DOESN'T TOUCH HIS HOSPITAL TRAYS.
COULD HE BE GOING OUT TO GET SOMETHING TO EAT?
THERE'S NOTHING IN THIS AREA.

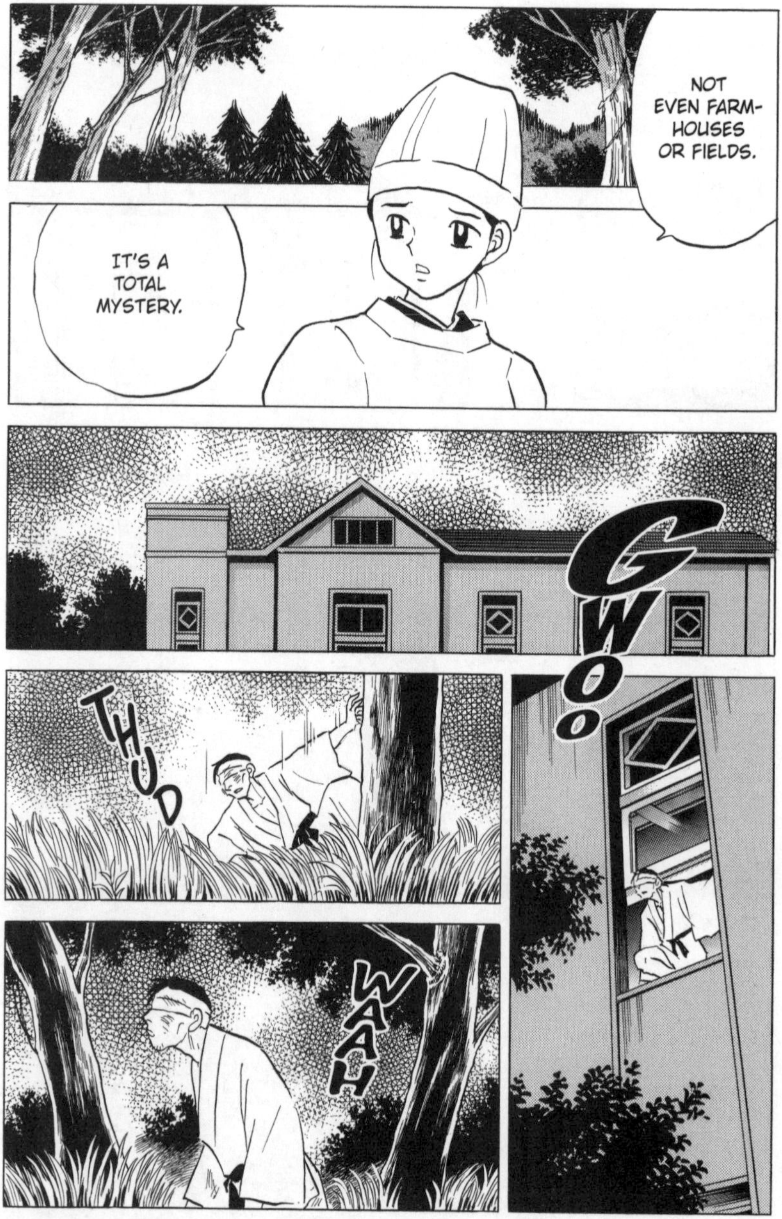
NOT EVEN FARM-HOUSES OR FIELDS.
IT'S A TOTAL MYSTERY.
GWOO
THUD
WAAH

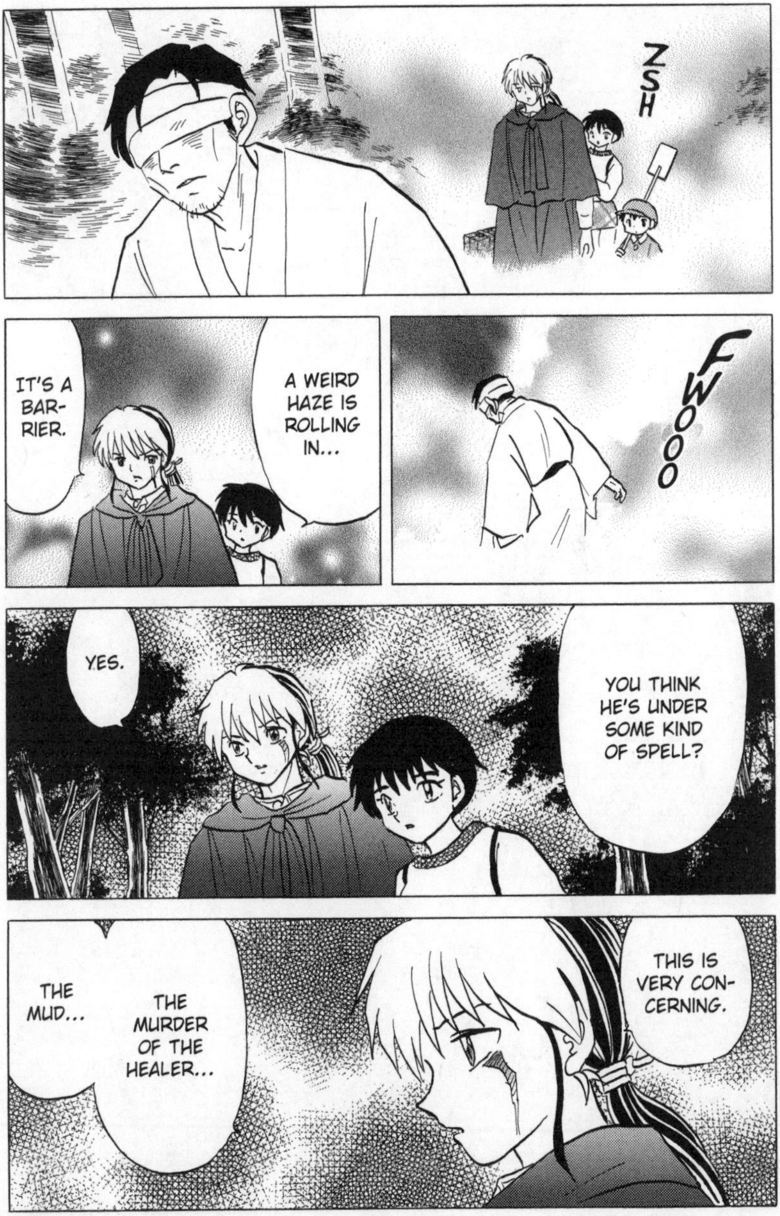
ZSH
FWOOOO
A WEIRD HAZE IS ROLLING IN...
IT'S A BARRIER.
YOU THINK HE'S UNDER SOME KIND OF SPELL?
YES.
THIS IS VERY CONCERNING.
THE MURDER OF THE HEALER...
THE MUD...

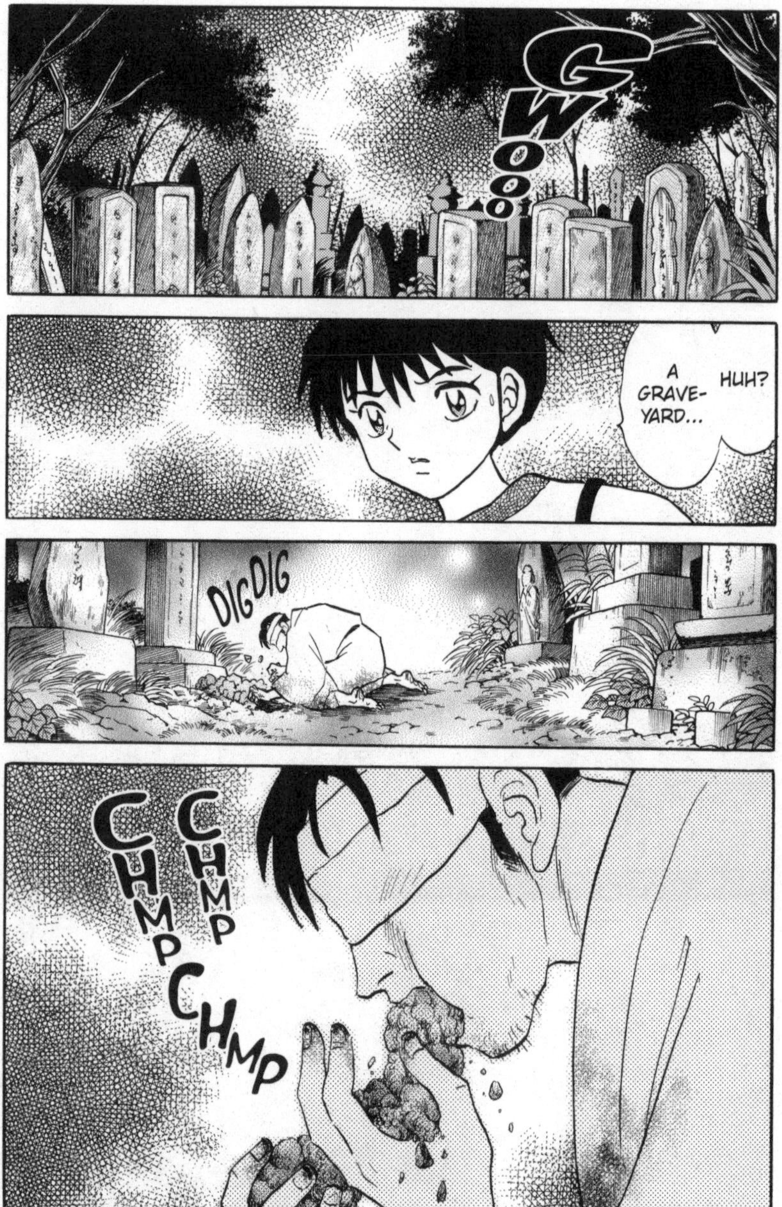
GWOOO
HUH?
A GRAVE-YARD...
DIG DIG
CHMP CHMP
CHMP CHMP

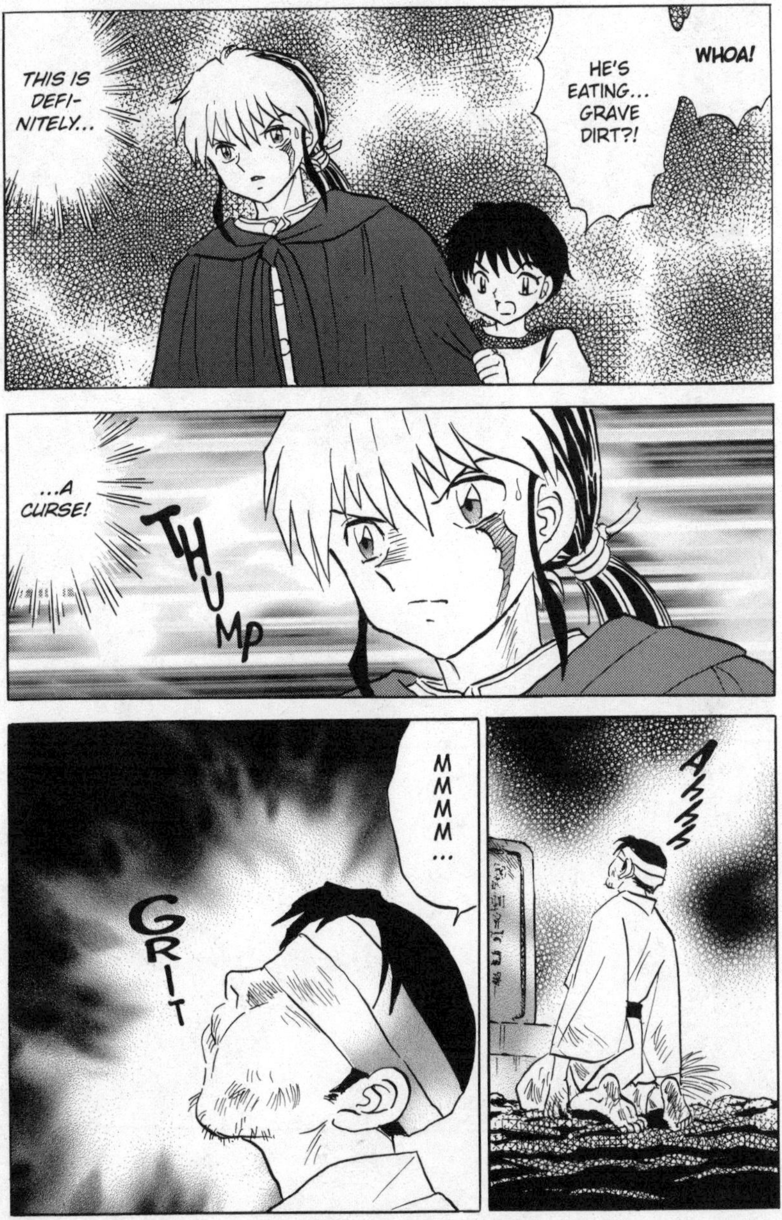
WHOA!
HE'S EATING... GRAVE DIRT?!
THIS IS DEFI-NITELY...
...A CURSE!
THUMP
MMMM...
GRIT

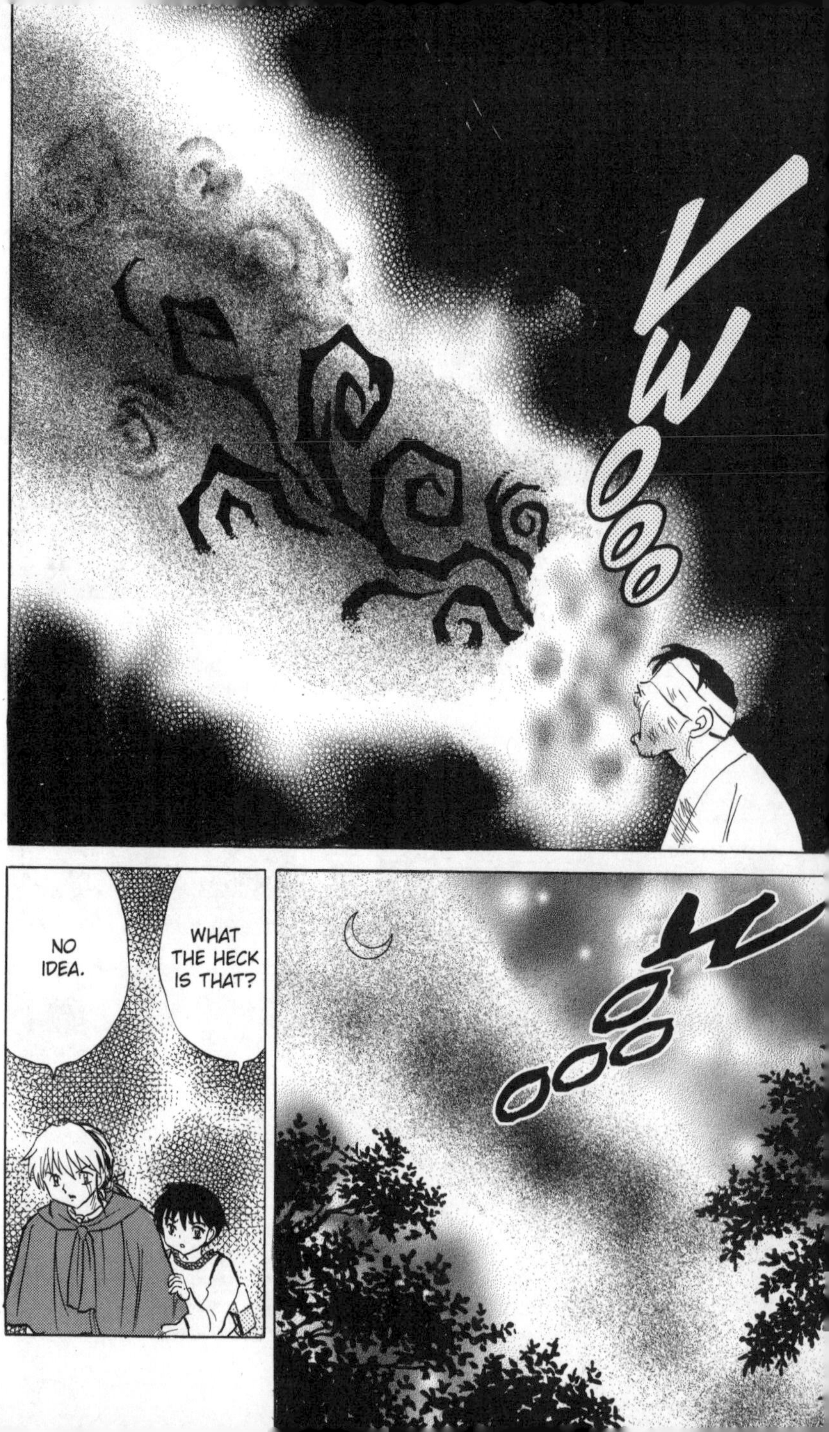
VWOOOO
VWOOOO
WHAT THE HECK IS THAT?
NO IDEA.

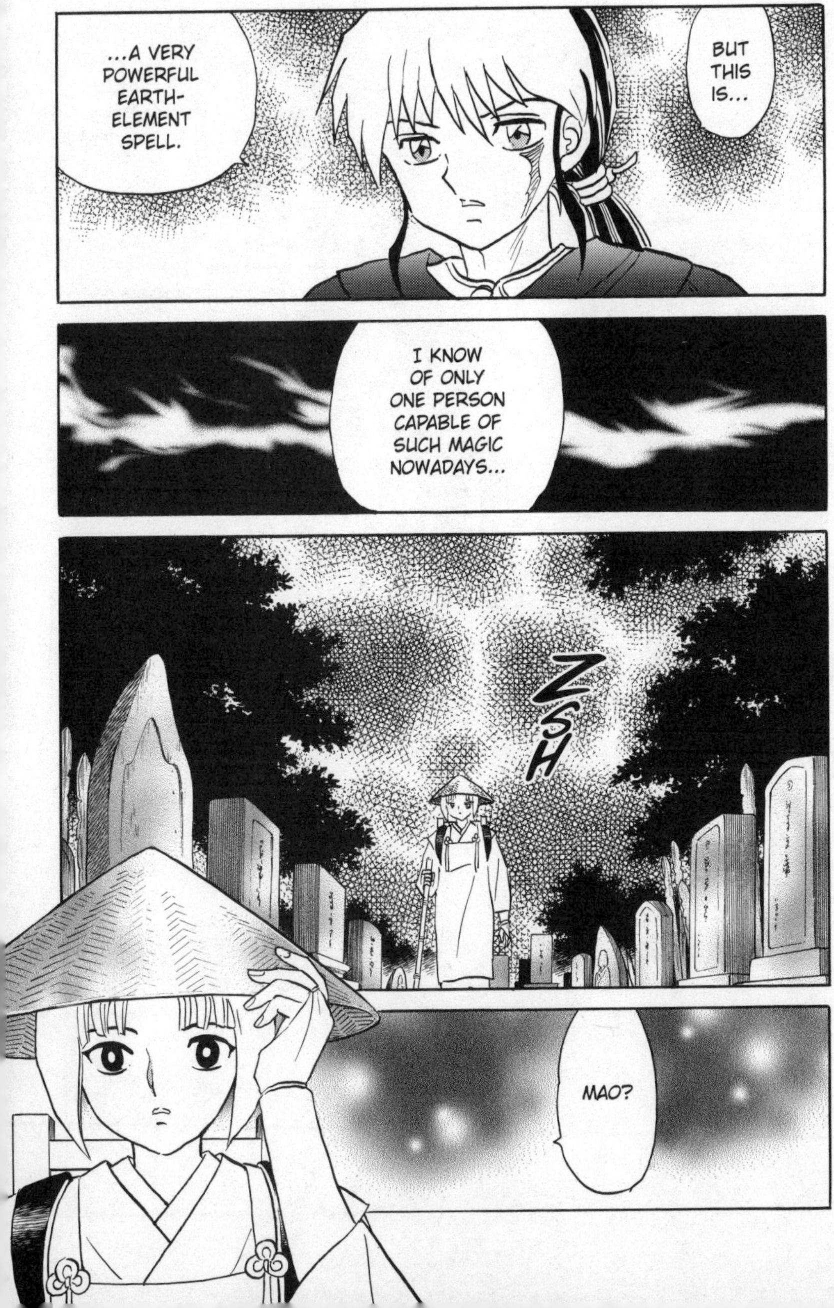
BUT THIS IS...
...A VERY POWERFUL EARTH-ELEMENT SPELL.
I KNOW OF ONLY ONE PERSON CAPABLE OF SUCH MAGIC NOWADAYS...
ZSH
MAO?

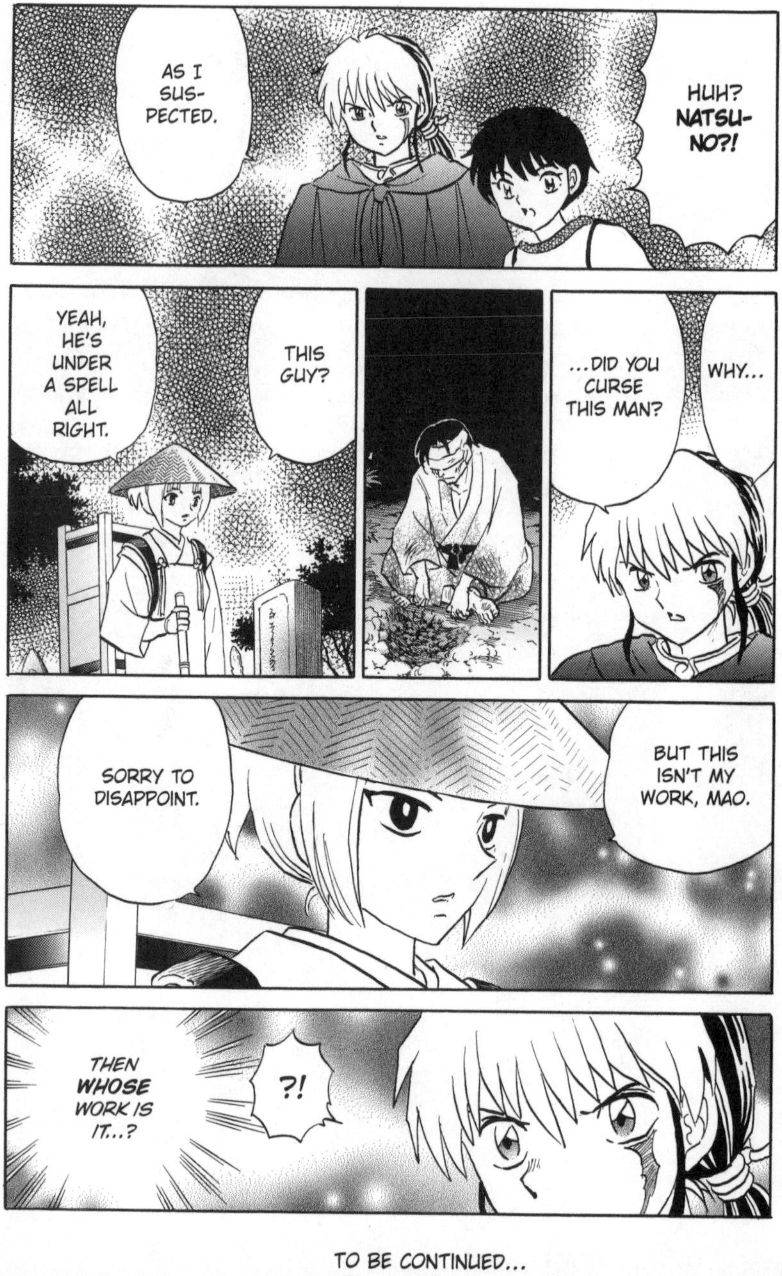
HUH? **NATSUNO?!**
AS I SUSPECTED.
WHY...
...DID YOU CURSE THIS MAN?
THIS GUY?
YEAH, HE'S UNDER A SPELL ALL RIGHT.
BUT THIS ISN'T MY WORK, MAO.
SORRY TO DISAPPOINT.
?!
*THEN **WHOSE** WORK IS IT...?*

TO BE CONTINUED...

Rumiko Takahashi

The spotlight on Rumiko Takahashi's career began in 1978 when she won an honorable mention in Shogakukan's prestigious New Comic Artist Contest for *Those Selfish Aliens*. Later that same year, her boy-meets-alien comedy series, *Urusei Yatsura*, was serialized in *Weekly Shonen Sunday*. This phenomenally successful manga series was adapted into anime format and spawned a TV series and half a dozen theatrical-release movies, all incredibly popular in their own right. Takahashi followed up the success of her debut series with one blockbuster hit after another—*Maison Ikkoku* ran from 1980 to 1987, *Ranma ½* from 1987 to 1996, and *Inuyasha* from 1996 to 2008. Other notable works include *Mermaid Saga*, *Rumic Theater*, and *One-Pound Gospel*.

Takahashi was inducted into the Will Eisner Comic Awards Hall of Fame in 2018. She won the prestigious Shogakukan Manga Award twice in her career, once for *Urusei Yatsura* in 1981 and the second time for *Inuyasha* in 2002. A majority of the Takahashi canon has been adapted into other media such as anime, live-action TV series, and film. Takahashi's manga, as well as the other formats her work has been adapted into, have continued to delight generations of fans around the world. Distinguished by her wonderfully endearing characters, Takahashi's work adeptly incorporates a wide variety of elements such as comedy, romance, fantasy, and martial arts. While her series are difficult to pin down into one simple genre, the signature style she has created has come to be known as the "Rumic World." Rumiko Takahashi is an artist who truly represents the very best from the world of manga.

MAO
VOLUME 8
Shonen Sunday Edition

STORY AND ART BY
RUMIKO TAKAHASHI

MAO Vol. 8
by Rumiko TAKAHASHI

Original Japanese edition published by SHOGAKUKAN.
English translation rights in the United States of America, Canada, the United Kingdom, Ireland, Australia, and New Zealand arranged with SHOGAKUKAN.

Original Cover Design: Chie SATO + Bay Bridge Studio

Translation/Junko Goda
English Adaptation/Shaenon K. Garrity
Touch-Up Art & Lettering/James Gaubatz
Cover & Interior Design/Ian Miller
Editor/Annette Roman

Printed in the U.S.A.

Published by VIZ Media, LLC
P.O. Box 77010
San Francisco, CA 94107

10 9 8 7 6 5 4 3 2 1
First printing, November 2022

ratings.viz.com RATED T+ OLDER TEEN

PARENTAL ADVISORY
MAO is rated T+ for Older Teen and is recommended for ages 16 and up. This volume contains fantasy violence.

VIZ MEDIA
viz.com

SHONEN SUNDAY
shonensunday.com

Coming Next Volume...

Natsuno is compelled by a mysterious force to collect one grotesque item after another. Will she find what she seeks at a performance by a mysterious yokai theater troupe? Then, Yurako recalls how her family, the Goko clan, exploited her powers for profit. Plus, Mao and Nanoka investigate a group of teens whose dabbling in the occult leads to disastrous results.

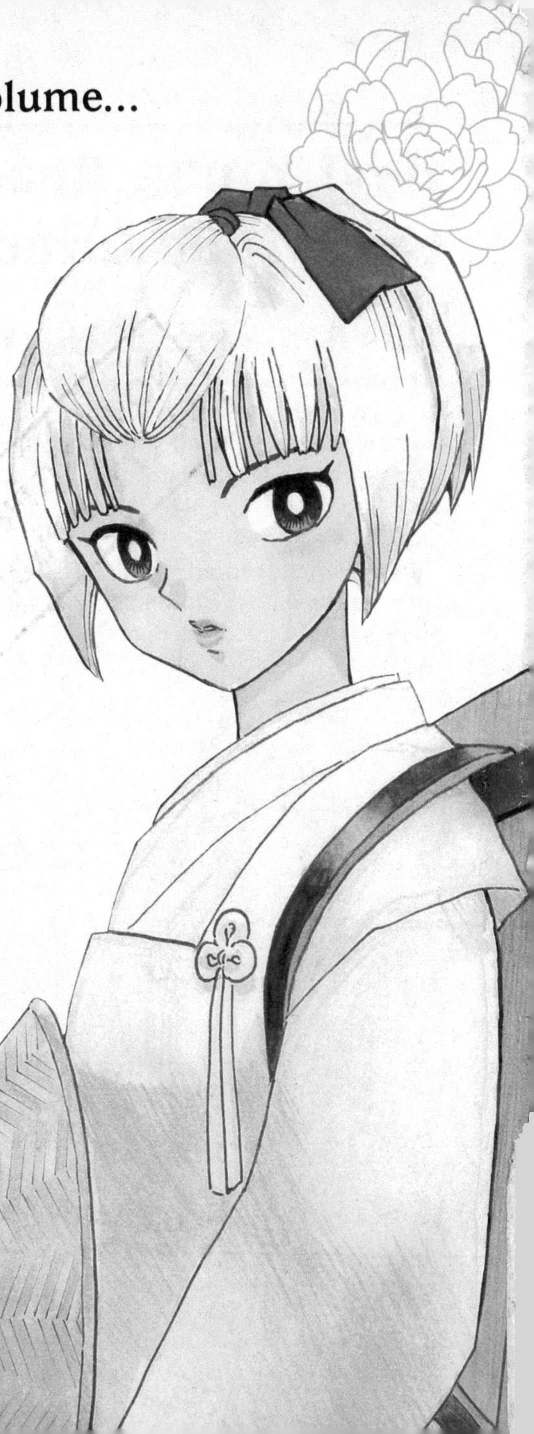

Hey! You're Reading in the Wrong Direction!

This is the end of this graphic novel!

To properly enjoy this VIZ graphic novel, please turn it around and begin reading from right to left. Unlike English, Japanese is read right to left, so Japanese comics are read in reverse order from the way English comics are typically read.

This book has been printed in the original Japanese format in order to preserve the orientation of the original artwork. Have fun with it!

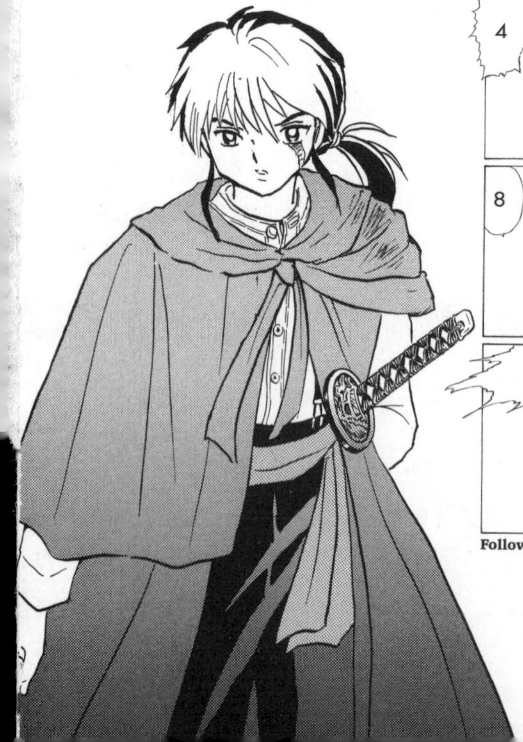

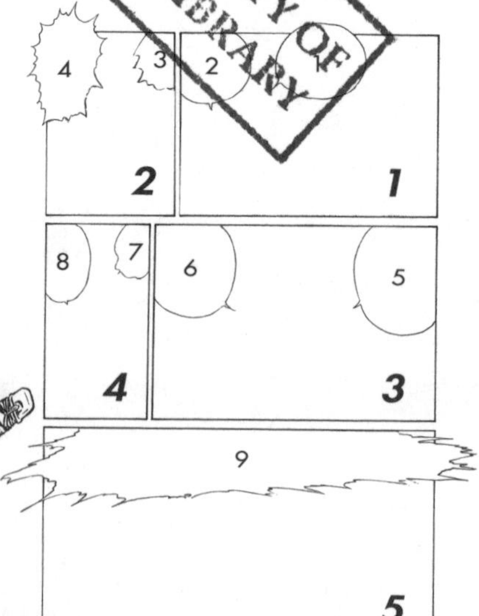
1
2
1
3
4
2
5
6
3
7
8
4
9
5

Follow the action this way